The Outer Banks

of North Carolina

1584-1958

THE
Outer Banks
OF
North Carolina
1584-1958

By DAVID STICK
Illustrated by Frank Stick

Chapel Hill
THE UNIVERSITY OF NORTH CAROLINA PRESS

To my father
FRANK STICK
whose love for the Outer Banks
is contagious

Foreword

Serious research for this book was begun more than ten years ago, but it soon became apparent that so much interesting material was available on the subject of Outer Banks shipwrecks that the book was threatened at the outset with being overloaded with accounts of ship sinkings. Consequently, I digressed from the main subject long enough to devote a full volume to shipwrecks, and this was published under the title *Graveyard of the Atlantic*.

For several years the research was continued on a part-time basis. Then a project was instituted by the National Park Service to compile basic information on the Outer Banks and the Cape Hatteras National Seashore Area. A grant was made to the Coastal Studies Institute of Louisiana State University for studies on the geological formation, geographical history, archaeology, and natural history of the Banks. At approximately the same time, a grant was offered me by the Old Dominion Foundation, through the Eastern National Park and Monument Association, to enable me to continue with my historical research, and I should like at this time to gratefully acknowledge this financial assistance which made it possible for me to work full time on the project in 1955 and 1956. One direct result of this was a close working agreement with the Coastal Studies Institute personnel, particularly Gary S. Dunbar who prepared the geographical history of the Banks. In one important area, the study of census returns, I have relied entirely on his research; and his many constructive criticisms are deeply appreciated.

Because of limited research facilities in the Banks area, it has been necessary for me to acquire my own library of books, pamphlets, periodicals, maps, photostats, and microfilm copies of manuscript material concerning the area, and I wish to make a special acknowledgment of the invaluable assistance of the many antiquarian booksellers who have located Banks material for me. Without my library I could never have written this book, and without the cooperation of the antiquarian booksellers, I could never have put together the library.

I am indebted, equally, to a large number of librarians, writers, researchers, and friends who have known that I was attempting to learn everything I could about the Outer Banks and who have let me know whenever they came across pertinent material. Their unselfishness and thoughtfulness have more than compensated for the frustrations, distractions, and disappointments with which research is periodically marked.

I doubt that my wife Phyllis has paused long enough from her household chores these past few years to realize how important it is to a writer to have a wife who herds the children into the other end of the house on rainy days, keeps visitors away from my study when I am trying to write, serves my meals at whatever odd hours I may call for them, and is always on the alert to sense my mood and offer encouragement when it is needed.

In the chapter references at the end of the book I have mentioned many of the individuals who have contributed specific information, though the continued encouragement and help of Huntington Cairns, Aycock Brown, and my mother, Maud Hayes Stick, should be acknowledged separately.

The first draft of the manuscript was written while I was living on the beach at Kill Devil Hills, with a view of the ocean from my study, and this final rewriting has been done on Colington Island, with Roanoke Sound just below my window. Yesterday, at dawn, the broad expanse of that sound was calm and peaceful, its surface mirroring many-hued reflections from the rising sun; last night a soft breeze ruffled the water and the three wild ducks which have stayed on here this spring took refuge in our cove. This morning I understand why, for the wind is blowing at gale force and the waves are breaking like ocean seas, submerging our little dock each time one rolls in to shore. Already my old skiff is sunk at the landing, and a branch from our big live oak has fallen across the swing, which means there will be work other than writing to be done tomorrow. But that's the way it is here on the Banks—and, anyway, the story is now written.

DAVID STICK
Colington, N. C.
April 6, 1958

Contents

Maps

The Outer Banks
of North Carolina
1584-1958

Sands, Sounds, and Inlets

STRETCHING ALONG the North Carolina coast for more than 175 miles, from the Virginia line to below Cape Lookout, is a string of low, narrow, sandy islands known as the Outer Banks. They are separated from the mainland by broad, shallow sounds, sometimes as much as thirty miles in breadth, and are breached periodically by narrow inlets which are forever opening and closing.

In the center, at Cape Hatteras, the Banks jut out so far into the Atlantic that the Gulf Stream currents caress the shoals, warming the atmosphere and making it possible for tropical fruits and plants to thrive, and for pelicans to fish along the shore. Here the northbound Gulf Stream swerves out to sea as it encounters the cold waters coming down from the Labrador Current, and at the junction of the two is Diamond Shoals, the Graveyard of the Atlantic, a point of constant turbulence and of countless shipwrecks.

Above Cape Hatteras, on the North Banks, is Kill Devil Hills, scene of the Wright brothers' first flights in a heavier-than-air machine. Opposite, on Roanoke Island, is Fort Raleigh, site of the attempts at English colonization in America under Sir Walter Raleigh in the 1580's and of the lost colony of 1587. Between the North Banks and Cape Hatteras are Bodie Island, Oregon Inlet, and Chicamacomico

Banks, long stretches of open beach and surf, teeming with fish, dotted with the broken remnants of wrecked vessels.

Below Cape Hatteras the Banks turn sharply toward the west—to Ocracoke, where the pirate Blackbeard was killed, and on to Portsmouth, Core Banks, Cape Lookout, and beyond to Shackleford Banks and Beaufort Inlet.

Since the early colonial days these Outer Banks have formed a barrier blocking the passage of large ocean-going vessels and retarding the commerce and prosperity of northern Carolina. At the same time, however, they have served as a natural breakwater, protecting the mainland areas against the ravages of sea and storm. Were it otherwise the coast would be far inland along the plain, and the small towns on the shores of Pamlico and Albemarle sounds, and along the Neuse and Pamlico rivers, might be major port cities—if they were there at all.

Actually, the Outer Banks are a series of undersea sand bars claiming kinship to the Newfoundland Banks, the Bahama Banks, and many others with similar names all over the oceanic portions of the world. They differ from the rest in the way they were formed, in that they are above water instead of beneath it, and in being populated by human beings and fish, instead of by fish alone.

If it seems difficult for the layman to get a clear understanding of how and when the Banks were formed, consider that the geologists and other scientists continue to come up with conflicting views among themselves, usually stating their theories categorically, with never a "probably," "possibly," or "maybe" by way of qualification.

Today they give little credence to the notion of a hundred years or so ago that the Banks were formed by silt, coming down from the rivers to the sea, forming a submerged delta in the sound areas, with an outer fringe along the Banks. Instead the modern geologists recite a succession of changes—first the lowering of the level of the sea as water was withdrawn to form the ice-age glaciers; then, as the icecap melted, the return of the sea to a higher level, in the process of which the sediment brought down from the rivers was worked over, and the coarse sands were deposited in reefs. These sand reefs were then gradually rolled landward and became the Banks, building up above the surface through the action of the regular currents such as the Gulf Stream and of storm waves and winds, just as dry shoals periodically appear off the capes and inlets and in the sounds today.

There seems to be agreement on all sides that vegetation has stabilized the Banks and made them suitable for human residency. The raw beach sands pushed up by the sea contain ample mineral matter to grow a great variety of things, but the salt content must be removed first. This is accomplished only when there is sufficient rainfall both to cleanse the sand near the surface and to push the underlying salt-water table downward and to the sides so that a large pocket of fresh water is formed beneath the Banks. Such a pocket resembles a large buoyant ball placed on the surface of the ocean, its underside displacing the salt water and forming a concave depression on the surface as it floats. As a result you can drive a shallow well almost anywhere on the Banks, even within a few feet of the ocean, and draw fresh water. But since all surface water on the Banks is accumulated in this manner from rainfall alone, it is possible in periods of drought—or in areas where too many pumps are drawing away the fresh water—to exhaust the supply until more rain replenishes it.

Once the salinity is removed from the sand and ample fresh water has accumulated, vegetation begins to take hold. Seeds, carried in the air, or transported by gulls or shore birds, begin to sprout, and the grasses grow and anchor the sand. Then bushes and trees take root, until finally, as was the case when white men first viewed the Banks, a lush growth of cedar, pine, and live oak, mingled with dense grape vines, covers much of what was once a bare sand beach—and before that, even, an underwater reef.

In the known history of the Outer Banks, this is when man moved in with his sharp blade, his hungry livestock, and his fire. He began chopping away at the trees—building homes and boats, burning firewood, shipping the great cedar and oak logs inland for ship construction. Then he turned the stock loose on the areas thus far denuded, and the stock in turn kept the grass cropped down, never pausing long enough in their grazing to let the bushes and little trees get started again. On the North Banks in the winter months, when the strong northeasters blew in from across the open sea, the winds picked up the loose sand, blew it horizontally across the Banks until an obstruction was encountered—most frequently a stand of the trees still remaining—and deposited it there, piling it up again, until the sand pile itself became enough of an obstruction to stop the sand blown across the beach by the next northeaster.

Thus the sand waves formed and moved across the Banks, driven by winds from far out at sea, blowing up the gently sloping northeast sides of the first small dunes to their crests, then dropping off on the other side. They grew on and up, higher than the trees that had stopped the first blown grains, until they were mountains of sand, covering hundreds of acres, towering seventy, eighty, ninety feet, or more, above the bare Banks behind them.

Then, when they could go no higher the sands which had accumulated at the very first blew on again, piling over the crest to the southwest; and so the dunes moved, covering live forests in their path, uncovering dead ones left behind. Today, all up and down the Banks, you can see the stumps of cedar and oak, left there by the sand waves in their steady march.

For centuries this was a one-way process of destruction and erosion. On the North Banks, at Pennys Hill, Corolla, Poyners Hill, and Duck, the great dunes are still there, covering much of the landscape; at Nags Head and Kill Devil Hills they are even larger and more numerous, and you can stand on top of Run Hill just south of the Wright Memorial, or Jockeys Ridge at Nags Head, and watch the tiny grains of sand slide down on the still-living trees beyond as the dunes move toward the sound.

At Chicamacomico the older folks remember vast numbers of stumps, dead limbs, and tree trunks east of the communities, and their ancestors, who were "older folks" when these were just youngsters, remembered the dunes that were once there; still earlier men witnessed the formation of those dunes and the gradual destruction of the forests. Yet today the dunes have disappeared, and only occasional tree remnants are found as reminders of the great forests of earlier times. Further south at Kinnakeet, the last great sand wave moved across the beach and the forest in the 1880's and 1890's, and today the beach there is flat and unwooded.

In addition to these continual changes on the face of the Banks, the geologists tell of a more gradual but no less certain change: of the entire Banks moving slowly to the westward, a few feet this year, inches the next, so that at some time in the far distant future they expect the Banks and mainland to join. If this is true, then Pamlico Sound, a shallow inland sea more than three times the size of Puget Sound in the state of Washington, will have to be filled up first.

Pamlico Sound extends from Roanoke Island to below Ocracoke Inlet and is the hub of an intricate network of sounds, bays, rivers, creeks, runs, lakes, and ponds which submerge the greater part of northeastern North Carolina.

To the map maker, Pamlico Sound might resemble the palm of a monstrous right hand, stretched out for begging, with Cape Hatteras at the wrist. The thumb is a series of smaller sounds extending to the north; the little finger is another series of small and narrow sounds running along the Banks to the south and west; the fingers between are three long bays, with major river systems leading off from each toward the Piedmont and the mountains of North Carolina and Virginia.

The thumb is formed by Croatan and Roanoke sounds (really a single body of water, with Roanoke Island in the middle) and Currituck Sound; the little finger is formed by Core Sound and Back Sound. From Back Bay in Virginia, at the north end of Currituck Sound where the Banks and the mainland join, to the southern junction of Banks and mainland below Beaufort, the meandering coastline measures more than 200 miles.

Of the three great bays, the northernmost is Albemarle Sound, known to the early settlers as Bay of Albemarle or Albemarle River, into which are emptied the waters of the Chowan and Roanoke rivers, as well as numerous creeks and smaller rivers. The middle bay is the mouth of the Pamlico-Tar river system, whose wide shallow waters extend westward from Pamlico Sound almost to the town of Washington, a distance of about thirty-five miles. The southernmost of the three bays is the mouth of the Neuse and Trent river system reaching up as far as the town of New Bern, again almost thirty-five miles from Pamlico Sound.

Into these three great bays, according to figures on water discharge supplied by Robert E. Fish, Assistant District Engineer of the U.S. Geological Survey in Raleigh, flows an average of approximately fifteen billion gallons * of water each day, the bulk of which continues on into Pamlico Sound and from there through openings in the Banks

* The daily flow, of course, is not constant, and this is simply an average. Mr. Fish says: "It is estimated that the average annual streamflow into Albemarle and Pamlico Sounds would total 5,600,000,000,000 gallons." The rough figure is based on "stream-flow measurement stations operated in those drainage basins and from previous studies in the area."

to the sea. In any given year the amount of water passing from the rivers and creeks to the bays, and then through Pamlico Sound in the search for an outlet to the Atlantic Ocean, is roughly the same as in any other year, which means that nature must maintain, through the Banks, sufficient openings to carry off approximately the same amount of water from one year to the next. There have been times when there were as many as eleven small inlets between the Virginia line and Cape Lookout and other times when there were as few as three comparatively large ones. From generation to generation, however, the aggregate size of the inlets seems to have remained about the same; the three large ones, for example, were able to carry off approximately the same amount of water as the eleven small ones.

This vast amount of fresh water coursing down from the mountains and plains to the sounds, and not the strong ocean tides, the currents, or great ocean waves, caused most of the openings through the Banks. Literally, therefore, they are outlets from Pamlico Sound to the ocean, not inlets, as they are invariably called. And taken as a group they are about as restless and unpredictable as bodies of water can ever be, for they are subjected to constant turbulence as the fresh inland waters and the salt sea waters collide, so that the inlets themselves are forever changing shape, size, and depth, sometimes opening wider, at other times shoaling up and closing altogether, yet throughout it all maintaining a leisurely but steady movement down the Banks.

Most of the southern movement, and most of the filling action, comes from the ocean, where the littoral drift along this coast from north to south causes sand to deposit in shoals and reefs on the northern sides of the inlets. Without the countering action of the fresh water flowing out of the inlets on the ebb tides, cutting away the shores on the southern sides when the southbound ocean currents are encountered, it is possible that all inlets along the Banks could close up entirely.

The inlets do close from time to time, and when they open again, or when other inlets cut through to take their place, it is almost invariably the action of sound waters which forces them open. Autumn is the time for inlet opening on the Banks, and most generally it occurs in September, as the result of a peculiar series of actions which take place in the sounds when hurricanes pass over.

Almost anyone on the Banks can tell when a hurricane of great intensity begins building up in the Caribbean, for tremendous ground swells roll in from the open sea and pound against the shore. In succeeding days, as the hurricane gets closer, the swells grow even larger, pushing sea water higher and higher up on the beach; and though the skies may be clear, the temperature balmy, and the winds only soft breezes, the weathered Banker begins then to batten down for a blow.

As the great funnel of counter-clockwise moving air that is the hurricane moves in toward the Carolina Banks, the skies begin to cloud over and the winds pick up in intensity. When gale and hurricane-force winds north of the hurricane eye reach out over the Banks, they blow from the eastern half of the compass, forcing great quantities of ocean water through the inlets and pushing this and the water in the shallow sounds far up the bays and estuaries along their western shores. At such times men who choose to can walk half a mile or better into Pamlico Sound from the Banks without getting their ankles wet.

Meanwhile, the ocean waters, built up into giant rollers across many hundred miles of open sea and driven by those same easterly gale and hurricane winds, are not only forced through the inlets, but if the tide is high just as the hurricane approaches, they are likely to roll across low parts of the Banks as well, cutting away all semblance of protective dunes in the low spots along the back of the beach.

As the hurricane eye passes over or near the Banks, the wind dies down—to a still calm, even, in the very center of the eye—and then as it moves northward it picks up power and force again, until hurricane intensity is once more reached, but this time the wind comes from the opposite direction, from the western half of the compass. (This change can be demonstrated by thinking of an automobile driver, turning his steering wheel for a left hand turn. The steering column in the center is the eye. At the top the wheel is turning to the left; at the bottom it is turning to the right. The hurricane winds, above the eye, are moving to the left, or west; below the eye they are moving to the right, or east.)

When this change in hurricane wind direction occurs on the Banks, it has a tendency to break down the giant ocean rollers as they pound in on the shore, thus halting much of the erosive action along the beach. The same westerly winds, however, now move in behind the waters that have been blown up the bays and estuaries and push them back across the shallow sounds against the Banks, much as a person can blow coffee from one side to another of a shallow saucer. The result, more than once, has been the equivalent of a giant tidal wave sweeping across the marshes and the beach, and where protective dunes had been cut away by the force of the ocean waves, or by the more gradual action of the easterly winds, old inlets reopened or new ones formed.

There are, of course, other factors which have caused inlets to open or close or change their course, particularly in the areas opposite the smaller sounds which are not fed by major river systems as is Pamlico Sound. Old Hatteras Inlet is reported to have been closed when a large English vessel sank in the channel and shoals built up around the wreck; and New Inlet, above Chicamacomico, was once opened artificially, though it closed right up again in short order. The changes and movements have occurred so frequently, however, that there is hardly a section of the entire Banks which has not, at one time or another, been cut through by an inlet.

Between the Virginia line and Cape Lookout there have been twenty-five different inlets which remained open long enough to acquire names and appear on printed maps, and there have been dozens of others which were only temporary cuts. Of these only one, Ocracoke Inlet, has been continuously open throughout the known history of the Outer Banks.

To confuse the matter further there have been instances when a single inlet had two or more names at approximately the same time, an example being Normans Inlet or Hunting Quarter Inlet on Core Banks in the 1730's. In addition, there have been several names which were so popular that they were applied on the Banks to different inlets at entirely different times. There have been four separate New Inlets, on the North Banks, at Nags Head, at Chicamacomico Banks, and at Core Banks; there have been two different Drum Inlets across Core Banks. There was a Hatorask Inlet below Bodie Island in 1585; a Hatteras Inlet across the center of what is now Ocracoke Island from the middle of the seventeenth century until the 1750's or 1760's; and finally another Hatteras Inlet, approximately seven miles east of the other, which today divides Ocracoke Island and Hatteras Banks.

Beaufort Inlet, beyond Cape Lookout, has been a primary port of entry since the early colonial period. Two others, Oregon Inlet and

Hatteras Inlet, were created during a severe hurricane in September, 1846, and have remained more or less as major inlets to the present time. The only others open today—Barden Inlet at Cape Lookout and Drum Inlet and Swash Inlet in the Core Banks area—are minor cuts of comparatively recent origin.

PRINCIPAL OUTER BANKS INLETS

COMMON NAME	OTHER NAMES	LOCATION	OPENED	CLOSED
Old Currituck	Currituck	Va.-N.C. boundary	pre-1657	1730's
Musketo	—	Just S. of boundary	pre-1657	1670's
New Currituck	New Currituck	Just S. of boundary	1730's	1828
Crow	—	Crow Island	1790's	1790's
Caffeys	Providence Carthy's Caffee's	N. of Duck	1790's	early 1800's
Trinity Harbor	—	S. of Duck	pre-1585	pre-1657
Roanoke	Old Inlet New Inlet View Passage	S. of Nags Head	pre-1657	1780 to 1810
Gunt	Gun Gant	Bodie Island	pre-1733	1770's
Port Lane	—	Bodie Island	pre-1585	pre-1657
Hatorask	Port Fernando Hatoras Hatorasck	Bodie Island	pre-1585	pre-1657
Oregon	—	S. of Bodie Island	1846	still open
New	Chickina- commock Chick	S. of Pea Island	1730's	1930's (periodic)
Loggerhead	—	N. of Rodanthe	pre-1851	late 1870's
Chacandepeco	—	N. of Cape Hatteras	pre-1585	pre-1657
Hatteras	—	W. of Hatteras	1846	still open
Wells Creek	West	Ocracoke Island	1840's	1850's
Old Hatteras	Hattaras Passage de Hattarxis	Ocracoke Island	pre-1657	1750's to 1760's
Ocracoke	Wokokon Wosoton Woccock Okok Ocacock Ocracock	W. of Ocracoke Island	pre-1585	still open
Whalebone	—	Portsmouth Island	1860's	early 1900's
Swash	—	Portsmouth Island	1930's	still open
Drum	—	Core Banks	1930's	still open
Cedar	Porters	Core Banks	1808	1830's
Normans	Hunting Quarter	Core Banks	1730's	1730's
Old Drum	—	Core Banks	1730's	late 1700's

The accompanying chart shows the location of Outer Banks inlets at various times from 1585 to 1956, and make clear the great extent to which Outer Banks history has been affected by geographical changes. Such changes are continuing to this day, for an even dozen new cuts were formed across Portsmouth Island and Core Banks in the storms of 1954 and 1955, and the majority have remained deep enough to pass an outboard motorboat at low water. Even more recently, in the spring of 1956, severe northeasters so eroded sections of the North Banks that five summer cottages were washed out to sea, while in other areas the beach built out a hundred feet or better. All of which demonstrates that the Banks, the sounds, and the inlets are changing still and can be expected to continue changing in the years and centuries to come.

Exploration

U NTIL THE establishment of permanent English colonies
along the eastern seaboard beginning with the one at Jamestown in
1607, England had lagged far behind Spain and France in exploring,
exploiting, and settling the new world.

During the sixteenth century Spanish fleets and Spanish armies
overran much of Mexico, Central America, and the Caribbean;
Spanish vessels transported great quantities of rich loot back to Europe
over an established sailing route which passed close to Cape Hatteras;
and Spanish adventurers and settlers built forts and towns throughout
the conquered area, the northernmost being St. Augustine, Florida,
which was founded in 1565.

Meanwhile, the French were concentrating most of their efforts
on the mainland of North America, making one futile attempt to
establish a colony in Canada in 1541, and following this with a settlement in South Carolina in 1562, which was abandoned, and another
in the same vicinity in 1565, which was wiped out by the Spaniards.

Thus, long before the English expeditions of Hawkins, Drake, and
Gilbert, and the English attempts at colonization under Sir Walter
Raleigh, practically all of the eastern coast of what is now the United
States and southern Canada had been explored by Spanish and French
mariners. In the course of these exploratory voyages it was customary
to make frequent landings on the shore and to prepare charts and

written descriptions of the lands which were visited and of the natives encountered, partly at least to establish later claims to the land involved.

Among the earliest explorers to visit the coast of North Carolina were those under command of Lucas Vásquez de Ayllón, a Spaniard who had received a charter from the Spanish king which gave him the right to explore and colonize much of the eastern seaboard. In 1521 Ayllón sent one of his captains, Gordillo, in charge of an expedition which landed at River John The Baptist, thought to have been the Cape Fear, and others of Ayllón's explorers spent considerable time at a place called Chicora, in that same vicinity.

Though Ayllón seems never to have gotten as far north as the Outer Banks, other Spanish mariners of that era certainly did, for they had long since learned that they could save considerable time and trouble on the voyage from the West Indies and Central America to Europe by taking advantage of the trade winds and the Gulf Stream currents and by passing close by the Outer Banks at Cape Hatteras.

However, it was an Italian, Giovanni da Verrazzano, a navigator in the employ of the French, and using French ships, who left the first written record of explorations of what is thought to have been the Outer Banks. In a report to the King of France, Verrazzano stated that he landed on the coast in 1524 and sent exploring parties ashore "in the latitude of 34 degrees," which would have placed him on the present North Carolina coast just above Cape Fear. Proceeding along the shore he came to anchor again at a place which at least one historian, Justin Winsor, thought was Raleigh's Bay, a name used in times past to designate the area between Cape Lookout and Cape Hatteras.

"While at anchor on this coast," Verrazzano said, "there being no harbor to enter, we sent the boat on shore with twenty-five men, to obtain water; but it was not possible to land without endangering the boat, on account of the immense high surf thrown up by the sea."

As this boat lay off the shore a large number of native people came down to the beach, indicating by various signs that they were friendly and that the explorers would be treated with kindness if they went ashore. The twenty-five men in the boat then decided to let one man swim to the beach with some knick-knacks for the natives, including some little bells and looking glasses.

This man succeeded in swimming in through the breakers, and when the natives approached him he tossed the gifts toward them, turned, and attempted to swim back through the surf to the boat. As swimmers have discovered on innumerable occasions since then, it proved much more difficult to swim out through the heavy surf than it had been to effect a landing, and after being buffeted about and knocked to the bottom by wave after wave, he finally crawled part way up on the beach and fell to the sand, where he lay as if dead. Verrazzano continued:

When these people saw him in this situation, they ran and took him by the head, legs, and arms, and carried him to a distance from the surf. The young man, finding himself borne off in this way, uttered very loud shrieks in fear and dismay, while they answered as they could in their own language, showing him that he had no cause for fear.

Afterwards they laid him down at the foot of a little hill, when they took off his shirt and trousers and examined him, expressing the greatest astonishment at the whiteness of his skin.

Our sailors in the boat, seeing a great fire made up and their companion placed very near it,—full of fear, as is usual in all cases of novelty,— imagined that the natives were about to roast him for food. But as soon as he had recovered his strength, after a short stay with them, showing by signs that he wished to return aboard, they hugged him with great affection, and accompanied him to the shore, then leaving him that he might feel more secure, they withdrew to a little hill, from which they watched him until he was safe in the boat.

To Verrazzano in 1524 the Banks looked like an isthmus, and the sounds back of them seemed to be an endless sea. He named the Banks "Verrazzano Isthmus" and reported to the French king that the sounds must certainly be the "oriental sea ... which is the one without doubt which goes about the extremity of India, China, and Cathay." This misconception by Verrazzano, that the Atlantic and Pacific oceans were separated at this point only by the narrow strip of land we know as the Outer Banks, was accepted not only by the French king, but by other Europeans for more than 150 years, and many a fruitless search was made in that time for what was known as Verrazzano's Sea.

About thirty-five years after Verrazzano's visit, according to stories told later by the Roanoke Indians, a ship was wrecked on Ocracoke

Island, and some of the sailors managed to reach shore. These survivors became restless, however, and "with the helpe of some of the dwellers of Sequotan, fastened two boates of the Countrey together, and made mastes unto them, and sailes of their shirtes, and having taken into them such victuals as the Countrey yeelded, they departed after they had remained in this Island three weekes." Soon afterwards, however, the Indians found the improvised vessels cast away on an adjoining Banks island and assumed that all of the occupants had been drowned.

The Indians told of still another wreck, this one about 1564, "which happened upon their coast of some Christian shippe, being beaten that way by some storme, and outragious weather, whereof none of the people were saved, but onely the shippe, or some part of her, being cast upon the sande, out of whose sides they drew the nailes, and spikes, and with those made their best instruments."

Twenty years later—on July 4, 1584, to be exact—two English barks approached the Outer Banks, probably in the vicinity of Core Banks, then started beating up the coast in search of a navigable inlet. These were the vessels, under command of captains Philip Amadas and Arthur Barlowe, sent out by Sir Walter Raleigh to explore the American coast and locate a suitable site for an English settlement.

They found an entrance through the Banks above Cape Hatteras, probably at the present-day Jeanguite Creek north of Kitty Hawk, and "cast anker about three harquebushot within the havens mouth." Then they gave thanks to God "for our safe arrival thither" and went ashore on the south side of the inlet "to take possession of the same, in the right of the Queenes most excellent Majestie."

Let Captain Arthur Barlowe describe the North Banks as he first saw them in that summer of 1584:

Wee viewed the lande about us, being . . . very sandie, and lowe towards the water side, but so full of grapes, as the very beating, and surge of the Sea overflowed them, of which we founde such plentie . . . that I thinke in all the world the like aboundance is not to be founde.

We passed from the Sea side towardes the toppes of those hils next adioyning, being but of meane heigth, and from thence wee behelde the Sea on both sides to the North, and to the South, finding no ende any of both waies. This lande laye stretching it selfe to the West, which after wee founde to be but an Island of twentie leagues long, and not above sixe miles broade. Under the banke or hill, whereon we stoode, we behelde the vallies replenished with goodly Cedar trees, and having discharged our harquebushot, such a flocke of Cranes (the most part white) arose under us, with such a crye redoubled by many Ecchoes, as if an armie of men had showted all together.

This Island had many goodly woods, full of Deere, Conies, Hares, and Fowle, even in the middest of Summer, in incredible aboundance ... [and] the highest, and reddest Cedars of the world.

It was three days before they saw any "people of the Countrey." Then an Indian man came to the ships in his canoe, and after accepting presents from them, fell to fishing near the boats, and he soon filled his canoe "as deepe, as it could swimme," dividing his catch, half for each boat. The next day he returned with a number of other Indians, whom Barlowe described as "very handsome, and goodly people, and in their behaviour as mannerly, and civill, as any of Europe. ... They are of colour yellowish, and their haire blacke for the most, and yet we sawe children that had very fine aburne, and chestnut colour haire."

The wife of Granganimeo, brother of the chief werowance or king of this Roanoke tribe, was "very well favored, ... and very bashfull. She had on her backe a long cloke of leather, with the furre side next to her bodie, and before her a peece of the same: about her forehead she had a broad bande of white Corrall, and ... in her eares she had bracelets of pearles, hanging downe to her middle."

The men wore cloaks similar to those of the women, and Granganimeo "had upon his head a broad plate of golde, or copper." Their hairdress was similar, too, "onely the women weare their haire long on both sides, and the men but on one."

Later, Barlowe and his fellow explorers visited at the house of Granganimeo, in the Indian village on the north end of Roanoke Island, and described it as "having five roomes." There was a great fire in the main room of the house, before which the Englishmen's damp clothes were dried. Later, Granganimeo's wife "brought us into the inner roome, where shee set on the boord standing along the house" various types of food, including a kind of wheat cereal, roasted venison, boiled and roasted fish, melons, roots, and different kinds of fruit, both raw and cooked.

Barlowe said that the English explorers were "entertained with all love, and kindnes" and that he "found the people most gentle, loving, and faithful, void of all guile, and treason, and such as lived after the manner of the golden age."

Barlowe's glowing description of the Banks and the native Indians may have been colored in an effort to impress Raleigh with his findings, and if that was the case he succeeded admirably. For during the three years which followed his discovery no less than forty English vessels visited the Outer Banks; a force of more than a hundred Englishmen lived for almost a year on Roanoke Island; the first accurate English descriptions of North America were put down on paper, in the writings of Thomas Hariot and the drawings of John White; and Great Britain gained a foothold on this continent, one result being that most of us living here today speak English instead of Spanish.

It should be clearly understood that this was no fly-by-night affair, no get-rich-quick scheme on the part of a few individuals. Rather, it was an important and considered effort to expand British rule and at the same time to wrest control of the new world from Spain. It was not the first such effort, since already Hawkins and Drake had established an English claim to much of North America, and Raleigh himself had participated in the unsuccessful colonizing effort of his half-brother, Sir Humphrey Gilbert. Certainly it was not the last, for it was followed in 1607 by the Jamestown settlement in Virginia and the Sagadahoc settlement in Maine, and thereafter British colonies began spreading along the Atlantic seaboard with the rapidity of a contagious disease.

The people who helped Raleigh finance the effort—including London merchants, sea captains, and even Queen Elizabeth—hoped to receive a profit on their investments and generally succeeded in doing so. There is little doubt, also, that some of the individuals who participated in the ventures were concerned primarily with the prospect of finding treasure comparable to that discovered in South and Central America by the Spaniards, while others seem to have been genuinely interested in developing agriculture and other natural resources for a basis of trade with the mother country. In the broad aspect, however, the purpose was to expand British rule and influence; and David B. Quinn, probably the leading authority on the subject, is now convinced that the primary reason for establishing a colony at this particular place and at that particular time was to provide a base for English privateering operations against the Spaniards.

For four years Raleigh's ships maintained a steady traffic between England and the Outer Banks. In the spring of 1584, and in 1585, 1586, and 1587 they left the homeland at about the same time of year, followed the same general route to the Canary Islands and across the Atlantic, usually stopped at the same place in the West Indies— Tallaboa Bay, Puerto Rico—and reached the Outer Banks at about the same time in early summer. A Spaniard concerned over these activities —and the Spaniards were concerned—could almost have set his calendar by the goings and comings of these vessels carrying colonists and supplies to the land the English called Virginia, in honor of their virgin queen.

The formal beginning of these colonization attempts was the granting of Letters Patent to Raleigh by Queen Elizabeth under date of March 25, 1584,* giving him the right to explore and take possession of any "remote, heathen and barbarous landes, Contries and territories not actually possessed of any Christian Prynce nor inhabited by Christian people."

Amadas and Barlowe departed for the new world the following month, and their report was so encouraging that Raleigh prepared a second expedition, this one consisting of seven vessels and something like 600 men, which left England the following spring, April 9, 1585, with the express intent of establishing an English base on the lands Amadas and Barlowe had discovered.

This was a force well calculated to accomplish such a purpose, for approximately half of the 600 men were soldiers, and the expedition was under command of an experienced and respected leader, Sir Richard Grenville. After reaching the Outer Banks at Ocracoke, Grenville explored the country to the south and west, then moved up the Banks to Roanoke Island, selecting a site on the north end of the island for the fort and settlement.

If it had been Grenville's intention to take personal charge of the establishment of this base, and to remain there throughout the winter with his 300 soldiers, he must have changed his mind after inspecting the country. For he not only did not remain, but when he departed

* Dates used in this chapter are old style.

for England in late August he took the bulk of his soldiers with him, leaving only 107 men on Roanoke Island under the command of Ralph Lane.

Lane, an experienced soldier, constructed a fort on the north end of the island, explored Albemarle Sound and the Chowan and Roanoke rivers, and almost certainly sent a party as far north as Chesapeake Bay. Two Indians, Manteo and Wanchese, had been taken to England by Amadas and Barlowe in 1584, and they returned to Roanoke Island with Grenville and Lane in 1585. Despite this, Lane's relations with the Indians steadily deteriorated, the bad feeling culminating in an English attack on the main village of the Roanoke tribe, under the guise of a friendly visit, and the murder of the Indian chief, Wingina.

Lane's men hunted and fished on the Banks, and sometimes kept a lookout there to warn them of the approach of Spanish ships. Soon after the attack on the Indian village a large fleet of English vessels was sighted, the fleet of Sir Francis Drake, returning from successful raids on Spanish settlements in the Caribbean and Florida. Drake was prepared to supply Lane with whatever he might need—shipping, food, equipment, even manpower—to strengthen his colony, but even as arrangements were being made a severe storm struck the Banks area, scattering Drake's fleet. The specific vessel offered Lane was driven far out to sea and did not return, and despite Drake's further offer of assistance Lane decided to abandon the settlement. On June 19 he and his colonists boarded Drake's ships and departed for England.

Within a few days a relief vessel fitted out by Raleigh, "a ship of 100 tunnes, fraighted with all maner of things" for relief of the colony, reached the Banks, found Lane's fort deserted, and "returned with all the aforesayd provision into England." Meanwhile Grenville had gotten together a fleet of three vessels, and making a direct and more rapid crossing of the Atlantic by way of Bermuda, arrived on the Banks just two weeks later. Unable to account for the disappearance of Lane and his colony, but being "unwilling to loose the possession of the Countrie, which Englishmen had so long helde," Grenville left fifteen men at the fort on Roanoke Island.

There was still hope for the Raleigh colonies that fall of 1586 as, one after the other, Drake's fleet, Raleigh's relief vessel, and the three ships under command of Grenville returned to England. There remained on Roanoke Island the fort Lane had built, manned by the fifteen men Grenville had left there. At home Thomas Hariot, a member of the Lane expedition, was putting the finishing touches on *A Briefe and True Report of the New Found Land of Virginia* (which constituted the first English book drafted in America), and John White was no doubt working on his drawings (which remain today among the best and most detailed pictures of North American scenes and people during the period of early exploration and colonization). Both were to be published shortly by Theodore de Bry, and these were expected to—and in fact did—generate a tremendous amount of interest in the prospect of permanent settlements on the coast of North America.

Further, there were plans to be made for still another expedition to Virginia, this one under the direct command of the artist John White and twelve assistants, to whom Raleigh granted an appreciable interest in the venture.

For the fourth successive spring, there on the coast of England in 1587, ships owned and outfitted by Raleigh and his associates made ready for the voyage across the Atlantic to the newly-found land of Virginia. And for the first time women and children were included among the colonists.

John White's three ships departed from England in early May, reached Puerto Rico in late June, arrived at Hatorask, on the Banks opposite Roanoke Island, on July 22, 1587. There had been serious talk of moving north along the coast (to Chesapeake Bay) after stopping at Roanoke Island to pick up the fifteen men left by Grenville. White claimed later that the pilot, Simon Fernándo (or Fernández, Ferdinándo), refused to transport the colonists further, and ordered them to leave the vessels at Hatorask. Whether or not this is true, they did disembark there, went in small boats to Roanoke Island, found the fort demolished but the houses "standing unhurt," and the fifteen men gone. Later, the still friendly Croatoan Indians, Manteo's people, told them the Roanoke tribe had attacked the men left by Grenville.

White's colonists repaired the buildings, started new ones for the "Cittie of Ralegh," and began making plans for a permanent stay. The prospect must have been brightest of all on August 18, for on that day a child was born, Virginia, daughter of Elenor (or Elenora, Elyoner) and Ananias Dare, granddaughter of Governor John White.

Earlier, Manteo, the Indian, had been baptized; the following Sunday, Virginia Dare, the first child born of English parents in America, was baptized also.

When it was time for the vessels to return to England the colonists asked White to return with them to handle the securing of needed supplies and the recruiting of additional colonists. He refused at first, then finally agreed, and on August 27, 1587, White departed for England, leaving behind on Roanoke Island his daughter and granddaughter and 110 other colonists.

In Spain, meanwhile, the mighty Spanish Armada was being readied for an all-out attack on England. When White was ready to return to his colony the following spring he was permitted to have only two small ships—a 30-ton bark and a 25-ton pinnace, neither of which was as large as the lifeboats on the average modern ocean liner—which were soon captured by a large Spanish ship. White was one of the few survivors fortunate enough to escape and return to England, and it was not until 1590 that he was able to sail again for America. This time he was little more than a passenger in the three-vessel fleet of John Watts, and though the ships left England on March 20, so much time was spent in Spaniard-hunting throughout the West Indies that they did not arrive on the Outer Banks until mid-August. When at last White led a party through the inlet at Hatorask and up the sound to Roanoke Island the houses had been "taken downe," his own chests had been dug up and broken into, and his daughter and granddaughter and their fellow colonists had disappeared—to be known to this day as the lost colony.

What happened to the lost colony of Roanoke? Theories, theories, theories, a dozen different ones at least, each backed by shreds of evidence or purported logic. Did they move inland, as the Jamestown colonists suspected, or try to reach England in one of the small vessels left them? Some are certain they were killed there on Roanoke Island by the Indians though White found no bodies. Others are certain that the Spanish attacked, but David B. Quinn has convincingly refuted this just recently. In his brief visit to the shambles of the Cittie of Ralegh, John White found, carved on a tree by the sound, the letters "CRO," and on another near the fort, "CROATOAN." He interpreted this to mean that the colonists had joined the friendly Indians at Croatoan, now Hatteras Island. Concrete evidence to substantiate

any of these stories has not been found, and the fate of the lost colonists remains as much a mystery today as it was when John White
departed from the Banks in late August of 1590.

When the English next attempted a settlement in America, they
went farther north to Chesapeake Bay and established their base on
Jamestown Island, leaving Roanoke Island and the Outer Banks in the
undisputed possession of the native Indians for another seventy-five
years.

Permanent & Settlement

THE FIRST LAND grant issued by the Lords Proprietors of Carolina following the receipt of their royal charter in 1663 was to Sir John Colleton, one of the Proprietors, for "the island heretofore called Carlyle now Colleton Island," the present-day Colington.

The grant was dated September 8, 1663, and by the winter of 1664-65 Colleton's agent, Captain John Whittie, had established a "plantation" on Colington Island. Houses and other buildings were constructed, corn was planted, and a number of cattle turned loose to graze. So far as can be determined this was the beginning of the permanent settlement in the Banks area.

In succeeding years, with Peter Carteret in charge of the plantation, an effort was made to grow tobacco, to cultivate grapes and start a winery, and to raise hogs both at Colington and nearby Powells Point. But the only appreciable profit shown on Carteret's accounts was from the sale of oil extracted from dead whales which washed up on the Banks.

This was an organized business venture, financed by Colleton, Peter Carteret, and two others of the Lords Proprietors. As the Carolina colony grew there were other instances when men of means secured grants for large tracts of Banks land which they probably never saw and which were managed by their agents or caretakers. A much larger percentage of the early Banks residents, however, were individuals of modest circumstances, who either squatted on the large holdings or secured grants for small tracts of their own.

Because the Banks islands provided excellent natural grazing lands without requiring fencing, it was not long before the raising of cattle, horses, hogs, and sheep was an important occupation on the Banks, though most of the stock seems to have been owned by the larger, non-resident property owners. When Sir William Berkeley sold a half interest in Roanoke Island to Joshua Lamb of Massachusetts in 1676, for example, it was specifically provided that Lamb should receive half of "all the Cattle, hoggs and other stock . . . thereon," and the first attempt to survey the boundary between Virginia and Carolina in 1692 was begun at "a place called Cowpenpoint on the North side of Corotuck River, or Inlett."

There were other factors, equally important, in the early settlement of the Banks. For one thing many of the islands were almost inaccessible, with the ever-dangerous surf pounding ashore on one side and shallow underwater shoals on the other, so that they provided excellent hideaways for persons attempting to escape the law. In 1696 Edward Randolph, Surveyor General of British Customs in the American colonies, complained to the home government with regard to the Outer Banks that "Pyrats & runaway Servants resort to this place from Virginia."

In 1699 it was reported that "one Grand at ye sand-banks had entertained some persons suspected of being runaways," and the next year Randolph filed articles of high crimes and misdemeanors against the governors of several provinces, specifically citing the laxity of acting Governor Henderson Walker of "That part of the Province of Carolina that Lies North and East of Cape Fear," in a case of suspected piracy on Currituck Banks.

Much of this agitation probably stemmed from the case of *H.M.S. Hady*, a swift frigate which was driven ashore on the North Banks between Roanoke Inlet and Currituck Inlet in 1696 and was robbed by the Bankers, who "got some of her guns ashore and shot into her sides and disabled her from getting off."

As shown earlier in the accounts of the Colington plantation, the sea was producing still another commodity which was providing income for those first residents of the Banks. This of course was the whales which drifted ashore and from which the Bankers extracted oil, bone, and sometimes ambergris. To make certain that the Lords Proprietors would receive a percentage of all such profits they had appointed Robert Houlden in 1678 to receive "all wrecks, ambergrice or other ejections of the sea."

Special permits were issued to certain individuals giving them the right to take possession of any whales they could find washed up on the beach, and in 1694 a North Banks resident named Mathias Towler was hailed into court for alleged abuses of his permit. It seems that Timothy Pead and Charles Thomas had found a dead whale on the beach and had made arrangements to cut it up, boil the blubber for oil, and extract the bone. They employed a woman named Anne Ros and "some of her owne family" to assist in the work, and after ten days of cutting, boiling, and scraping Anne Ros and her family had produced three barrels of oil.

At that point Mathias Towler appeared on the scene, produced his "Lycence from the Honble Governour for whaling," and proceeded to take possession of what was left of the whale. He moved in on the operation with little preparation, however, for he was forced to bargain with Anne Ros to buy eight empty barrels which she and her family had brought to the scene when they were employed by Pead and Thomas. This development was too much for Pead and Thomas, and they tried to repossess the carcass.

The result of all this was that practically everybody involved in the fracas swore out a warrant against someone else, and when court convened in September there were no less than four separate cases on the docket. Towler ended up in possession of the whale and oil, but the court ordered him to pay Timothy Pead two shillings and six pence, Charles Thomas ten shillings, and Anne Ros a fair price for her barrels and labor.

An indication of the extent of this business came soon after the Towler case when John Lawson reported that the recovery of dead whales was the occupation of certain people "that inhabit the Banks and Sea-Side, where they dwell for that Intent, and for the Benefit of Wrecks, which sometimes fall in upon the Shoar."

Before 1700 most of the residents of the Banks were stockmen, runaways, whalers, or simply small landowners trying to gain a foothold in the new colony. Their habitations were almost invariably situated in the wooded hammocks on the sound side, where they could find building sites in close proximity to the sloughs and creeks in which their boats were kept and where they were protected from the strong winds on the back of the beach and the high tides which periodically flooded the marshes.

As in later times, it is probable that most of them had small gardens for home consumption, did a little fishing to provide seafood for the table, hunted game and wildfowl in the winter, and took a walk on the beach after a storm to see if anything of value had come ashore. Consequently, in addition to whatever he considered his main occupation, each of them was at the same time a farmer, a fisherman, a hunter, and a wrecker.

Vessels bound for Carolina during those early days of settlement entered the colony through Roanoke Inlet, opposite Roanoke Island, or Currituck Inlet, at the Virginia boundary, and before 1700 the bulk of the Banks settlement was scattered between those two.

There were no towns in the Banks area, though as early as 1676 the Lords Proprietors had ordered their representatives in Carolina to establish three port towns, of which "the Chiefe towne and the place where the Councell Assemble should meete," was to have been located on Roanoke Island. This choice was dictated by the proximity to Roanoke Inlet, the desirability of having pilots stationed there, and of having customs officers and other government officials near the point where vessels were entering the colony. Nothing was done about this, however, and when the first two ports were established— with the names "Port Roanoke" and "Port Currituck"—the collector for the first was located at Edenton and the second wherever that individual happened to be at a given time.

There were continued efforts to make it easier for vessels to enter the colony through Roanoke Inlet. In 1715 George Tompson was appointed pilot for Roanoke Inlet, having "fitted himselfe with a good Boat and Two able young men to attend ye said business." That same year an act was passed for establishing "a Town on Roanoke Island for the Encouragement of Trade from Foreign Parts," but the project failed. In 1723 still another attempt was made to establish a town there, and this time it was given a name, Town of Carteret, but this effort was not successful either.

This failure to establish a port town on Roanoke Island was influenced by two developments then taking place. The first was that the settlement in the interior was spreading out below Albemarle Sound, while more and more habitations were appearing on Chicamacomico Banks, Kinnakeet Banks, and Hatteras Banks, so that Roanoke Inlet was no longer centrally located. The second was that Roanoke Inlet, which was said to have had a depth of between eleven and fifteen feet in 1665 and ten feet in 1700, was shoaling up and gradually closing. Both from the standpoint of convenience and safety, more and more vessels were finding it expedient to enter the colony through Ocracoke Inlet instead of Roanoke or Currituck.

Actually, the ascendancy of Ocracoke Inlet to the position where it was the most important port in northern Carolina had begun in 1715, for in that year it was made an official port of entry—though it was called Port Bath and vessels were required to go all the way up to Bath Town for clearance. In that year also, an act was passed for "settling and maintaining pilots" there as well as at Roanoke Inlet. From then on the maritime traffic through Ocracoke Inlet increased tremendously and more and more pilots located there, forming the nucleus of what was soon to become the largest community on the Banks.

Meanwhile the Indians who had inhabited the Banks area before the arrival of the first settlers were having a difficult time. The only Indians living permanently on the Banks were those referred to by the Raleigh colonists as Croatoans, later known as the Hatteras Indians, whose villages were located in the wooded area west of Cape Hatteras. As Croatoans these Indians had befriended the Raleigh colonists, and as Hatteras Indians they claimed descent from the lost colonists and remained friendly to the white settlers.

Other Indian tribes, residents of the islands in the sounds and of the nearby mainland, spent considerable time on the Banks. These included the Corees, who lived on Core Sound and frequented the Cape Lookout section of the Banks (and possibly the Woccons and Neuse); the Machapungas, sometimes called Mattamuskeets, who lived on the mainland between Albemarle Sound and the Pamlico River (and may have been the same tribe the Raleigh colonists found living in that area and on Roanoke Island and were called Roanoaks by them); and the Poteskeets, whose base was on the mainland near North River, opposite Currituck Banks.

The Corees, also called Caranine, Connamox, Coramine, and Cora-nine, apparently resided on Harkers Island and were described as "a bloody and barbarous people," and as later events proved, the Macha-pungas or Mattamuskeets were of the same ilk.

John Lawson told of the occasion when the Machapungas were invited to a feast on the "Sand-Banks" by the Corees, the two tribes having "been a long time at War together, and had lately concluded a peace."

Thereupon the Machapunga Indians took the Advantage of coming to the Coranines Feast, which was to avoid all Suspicion, and their King, who, of a Savage, is a great Politician and very stout, order'd all his Men to carry their Tamahauks along with them, hidden under their Match-Coats, which they did; and being acquainted when to fall on, by the Word given, they all (upon his Design) set forward for the Feast, and came to the Coranine Town, where they had gotten Victuals, Fruit, and such things as make an Indian Entertainment, all ready to make these new Friends welcome, which they did; and after Dinner, towards the Evening, (as it is customary amongst them) they went to Dancing, all together; so when the Machapunga King saw the best Opportunity offer, he gave the Word, and his Men pull'd their Tamahauks or Hatchets from under their Match-Coats, and kill'd several, and took the rest Prisoners, except some few that were not present, and about four or five that escap'd. The Prisoners they sold Slaves to the English.

Both of these tribes joined the Tuscarora confederacy in 1711, and in 1713 the fighting men in the Machapunga and Coree tribes, num-bering between fifty and sixty, made a concerted attack on the white settlements at Roanoke Island and on the mainland west of Croatan Sound. More than forty white people were killed or carried off by the Indians in those first surprise attacks, but in the months that fol-lowed the settlers practically wiped out the Corees and Machapungas.

The Hatteras Indians, who did not participate in this massacre, were in turn attacked by the warring Indians the following year. Under the date May 28, 1714, the North Carolina Council was in-formed that "ye Hatteras Indyans have lately made their Escape from ye Enemy Indians" and they were supplied with corn "for their Sub-sistance untill they can return to their owne habitations againe." A year later the Council learned that the Hatteras Indians were "reduced to great poverty" and an additional sixteen bushels of corn was provided them.

At the same time the Poteskeet Indians complained that "the Inhabitants of Corratuck Banks have and doe hinder ye Said Indyans from hunting there and threaten them to breake their guns, and that they Cannot subsist without the liberty of hunting on those their usuall grounds." Consequently the Council issued an order that the Bankers were not to interfere with the Poteskeets thereafter.

By that time, however, with the Corees and the Machapungas all but wiped out, with the Hatteras Indians reduced to poverty, and the Poteskeets having difficulty finding a place to hunt, these native peoples who had been described by Captain Arthur Barlowe in 1584 as "most gentle, loving, and faithful, void of all guile and treason, and such as lived after the manner of the golden age" were an impotent factor on the Banks.

Still another "golden age" was at hand, however—the golden age of piracy, which had begun with the signing of the Peace of Utrecht in 1713 and the turning loose of large numbers of privateers who, without official commissions or letters of marque, had ceased being privateers and were now pirates. The point most often overlooked is that this so-called golden age of piracy lasted for only five years and seriously affected Carolina and the Outer Banks for less than twelve months.

A number of the more notorious pirates operated off the Carolina coast between 1713 and 1718, including Captain Pain, Christopher Moody, John Cole, Robert Deal, Charles Vane, Richard Worley, "Calico Jack" Rackam, Anne Bonny, and Francis Farrington, and some no doubt rendezvoused on the Banks. But it remained for the most feared and infamous of the lot, the pirate Blackbeard, to make the Banks his headquarters while terrorizing coastal shipping and corrupting the highest officials of the colony.

Apparently Blackbeard did not turn to piracy until 1716, but his success and rise were meteoric. By the spring of 1718, when he moved in on the Carolina Banks, Blackbeard had acquired a fleet of four vessels manned by something like 400 pirates, and had captured at least twenty-five ships with much valuable cargo. At that point, however, he had begun "to think of breaking up the Company, and securing the Money and the best of the Effects for himself," and at Beaufort

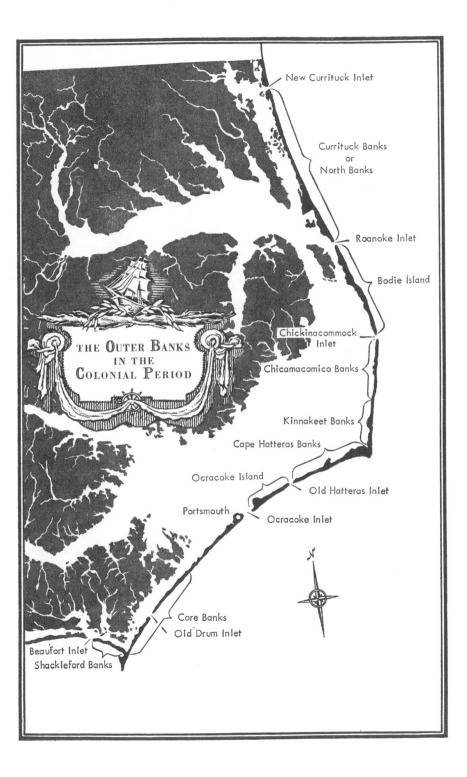

THE OUTER BANKS
IN THE
COLONIAL PERIOD

New Currituck Inlet

Currituck Banks
or
North Banks

Roanoke Inlet

Bodie Island

Chickinacommock
Inlet

Chicamacomico Banks

Kinnakeet Banks

Cape Hatteras Banks

Ocracoke Island

Old Hatteras Inlet

Portsmouth

Ocracoke Inlet

Core Banks
Old Drum Inlet

Beaufort Inlet
Shackleford Banks

Inlet—on the pretext of cleaning the ships—he and his cohorts sank two of the four vessels, marooned seventeen of the most troublesome pirates on an uninhabited Banks Island, and transferred the bulk of the booty to a small sloop. Then Blackbeard sailed up the coast to Ocracoke Inlet and on to Bath, where he received the royal pardon from Governor Eden.

For several months in the summer and early fall of 1718 Blackbeard —known also as Captain Drummond, Edward Teach, or Thatch— sailed out of Bath and Ocracoke in his *Adventure* sloop on "trading voyages." In early September, when he arrived off Ocracoke Bar with a French ship laden with sugar and cocoa he explained that he had discovered her at sea, a wreck, abandoned by her crew, and pro- ceeded to divide the cargo with Governor Eden and Government Secretary Tobias Knight. This was bad enough, but when he began raiding small trading vessels in the sounds some, at least, of the Caro- linians decided it was time to do something, and realizing that they could expect no help from their own Governor Eden, they turned to Governor Alexander Spotswood of Virginia for assistance.

In late November two small sloops, fitted out by Governor Spots- wood, manned by crewmen from the British warships *H.M.S. Pearl* and *H.M.S. Lime,* and under command of Lieutenant Robert May- nard, left the James River for Ocracoke. The smaller of the two sloops, the *Ranger,* had a picked crew of twenty-two men, with a Mr. Hyde in charge; the larger, under the personal command of Maynard, carried thirty-two men. The two vessels reached Ocracoke in the late evening of November 21, and Maynard decided to wait until dawn to attack.

An observer, sitting on one of the small dunes near Ocracoke Inlet at dawn the next morning, or half-hidden in the tall tree growth toward Cockle Creek, would have seen the two sloops move off slowly in the direction of the *Adventure.* Then the booming noise of the guns, as Blackbeard opened fire, and almost simultaneously, aboard the sloops, the King's colors hoisted to each masthead.

Even at this early juncture the observer, mariner or landsman, could not have failed to see that the pirate, outnumbered two to one in vessels and almost that much again in manpower, had one factor in his favor equally as important as the other two combined. For he had eight guns in working order and trained gunners to go with them, while the two attacking sloops had none, so that Blackbeard's guns were drawing only small arms fire in return.

Across the still water, echoing up to the dune-covered shoreline and woods beyond, came a shout from the pirate vessel: "Damn you for villains. Who are you?"

And a reply from Maynard: "You can see by our colours we are not pirates."

In answer the *Adventure* fired a broadside, raking the attackers standing in the waists of the two craft. The *Ranger*, with several of her crewmen hit and Mr. Hyde killed, was disabled by the blast. On the nearer sloop, Maynard's, twenty men were down, killed or wounded. But the Lieutenant's marksmen had shot away the *Adventure*'s jibstay and fore-halliards, and like the attacking vessels she was now unmanageable. Then the pirate vessel struck a shoal and held fast, while Maynard ordered his men below decks for fear of another broadside, and only Maynard and the helmsman remained topside as the sloop drifted down toward Blackbeard's vessel.

The pirates, experienced fighters, waited until the very moment when the two vessels came together, then threw in "grenadoes"—case bottles filled with powder, shot, and slugs of iron, with a quickmatch in the mouth—and as these exploded they swarmed aboard, anxious to complete the kill. Fifteen pirates gained the deck, were met first by Maynard and the helmsman, then were confronted by ten more of Maynard's crewmen storming up from the holds.

The two leaders faced each other and hardly had time to aim their pistols as both fired. Blackbeard was hit but drew his sword and closed in for the struggle. It lasted but a moment, for Maynard's sword broke, and as he stepped back to cock a pistol the pirate charged him. One of Maynard's crewmen close by turned suddenly, slashed down with his own sword at the lunging pirate, and cut deep into Blackbeard's neck. Another man might have fallen then, but the pirate chief fought on. All over the deck of the small craft the others were engaged, stepping over and around and even on the bodies of the dead and wounded who had fallen under the earlier broadside, fighting on until the sea around was tinctured red by human blood running down the scuppers.

Blackbeard himself, blood gushing from the neck wound and from Maynard's early pistol shot, was struck again and then again, five times in all. He was hacked and slit and cut by sword thrusts until his body was covered with gashes, yet he still stood his ground and his men with him. He stepped back to cock a pistol, half raised it, then slumped forward and crumpled to the deck. The remaining pirates, observing the death of their leader, jumped overboard into the shallow water, then quickly surrendered.

In the lull following the battle at Ocracoke that morning an observer, adding up the score, might have counted the following: for the pirates, nine killed, including Blackbeard, the remaining fifteen captured; for Maynard's forces: eight killed, eighteen wounded.

Later, Maynard sailed up the Pamlico River to Bath, Blackbeard's head, severed from the body, hanging from the bowsprit. The prisoners were taken to Williamsburg where they were tried in the admiralty court and all but one hanged.

Back at Ocracoke, in the sloop *Adventure* and ashore where the pirates had their storehouses, only sugar and cocoa from the French ship was found. Where, then, was Blackbeard's treasure? One man thought he knew, for when someone had asked Blackbeard whether his wife knew where it was hidden, this man claimed to have heard him reply that "nobody but himself and the Devil knew where it was, and the longest Liver should take it all."

The death of Blackbeard at Ocracoke Inlet on November 22, 1718, marked the end of large-scale piracy on the Banks—the end, in fact, of the so-called golden age of piracy throughout the Western hemisphere. It paved the way also for the settlement of the remainder of the lower Banks.

As early as 1711 a man named Patrick Mackuen was reported living on Hatteras Banks, and in that same year William Reed had secured a grant for 502 acres near Cape Hatteras and another for 480 acres at "Keneckid Inlet." This was soon followed by other grants on Hatteras Island, one to William Russel for 431 acres in 1714, and to John Oneall for 440 acres and Henry Gibbs for 540 acres in 1716. Meanwhile, all of the present-day Core Banks and Shackleford Banks, an estimated 7,000 acres, had been acquired by John Porter in 1713.

Soon after Blackbeard's death, probably in 1719, John Lovick was granted Ocracoke Island, consisting at that time of 2,110 acres; and in 1722 Matthew Midget secured a grant for Bodie Island, 1900 acres.

Since Sir John Colleton had been granted Colington Island in 1663,

Governor Samuel Stephens had acquired title to Roanoke Island at least by 1669, and people had been settling all along the North Banks before 1700, the only Banks lands not in private hands by 1722 were scattered parcels north of Bodie Island and others between there and Hatteras Inlet.

This acquisition of so much of the Banks by individuals had little relationship at the tim to actual settlement. William Reed, for example, did not live on his Hatteras property. John Porter sold his 7,000-acre holding to Enoch Ward and John Shackleford, and they in turn divided it in 1723, with Ward getting the Core Banks section and Shackleford the western part, which came to bear his name. But Porter, Ward, and Shackleford were all non-resident property owners, and apparently it was not until after John Shackleford's death in 1734 that his heirs and Ward began selling off smaller parcels of the land.

This same thing applied on Ocracoke Island, which was acquired from John Lovick by Richard Sanderson, who still owned the entire island, with a large "Stock of Horses, Cattle, Sheep & hoggs" at the time of his death in 1733.

The record of early land ownership on the Banks has been traced as fully as possible in existing grants and deeds, but it is something else again to try to determine who was actually living on a certain part of the Banks at any given time before 1750.*

One thing which can be traced quite accurately, however, is a change in occupational activities on the Banks in the thirty years or so following Blackbeard's death.

Stock raising continued in importance, and whaling took on a new aspect as the result of instructions from the Lords Proprietors as early as 1715 to attempt to induce some of the New England whalers to settle in the province. In 1726 a New Englander named Samuel Chad-

---

* For example, there was a George Booth living on Knotts Island before 1730; Matthew Midget and his family were living on Bodie Island at the time of his death in 1734; John Mann was located "near ye Sea Coast" in 1736; a man named "Old Will" was living near the Fresh Ponds before 1738; Valentine Wallis had built a house on the "north side of cutting sedge marsh" on Hatteras Banks before 1740; Thomas Wallis was living 6½ miles south of Chickmacomack Inlet in 1744; Thomas Oliver was living at a "plantation called Oyster Shell Banks" on Hatteras when he died in 1745; and Richard Etheridge willed the "plantation whereon I live, commonly known as Whale House" when he died in 1750 at "Bay of Kitty Hawk." But these are only scattered references which just begin to tell the story of early Banks settlement.

wick was issued a permit to use three boats "to fish for whale or other Royall fish on the Seay Coast" of North Carolina, and he apparently was joined by Ephraim Chadwick, Ebenezer Chadwick, and John Burnap. The next year a man named Josiah Doty, "Master of a Sloop or Ship with a great Company of men and Severall Boats with Tackle & stores under his care," spent a successful season in the Cape Lookout area, taking "a great number of whales" from which he realized 300 barrels of oil and "one thousand weight of whalebone" without making any division with the governing authorities. At about this time Cape Lookout became the headquarters, not only for the New England whaling vessels, but for shore-based whalers as well, and numerous old deeds, grants, and maps in that area have references to "whalers hut" and "whalers camp."

In all probability the first windmills were erected on the Banks during this period, for it was not long before reference was being made in deeds to such landmarks as "mill point" and "windmill point." An interesting type of windmill evolved, which was peculiarly adapted to conditions on the Banks. The sails or vanes could be set to take advantage of current wind conditions, and the mill itself was mounted on a sort of vertical axle so that it could be moved around to face the wind. These windmills were used primarily for grinding corn, which the Bankers secured from the mainland in exchange for fresh and salted fish and oysters. They varied in size and capacity, and at one time or another there seems to have been at least one in each Banks community. They became so numerous, in fact, that at a later date Charles F. Johnson said of the Banks windmills: "There are a greater number than I supposed were in existence in the whole country."

The really important occupational change, however, occurred in the vicinity of Ocracoke Inlet. In 1731 Governor George Burrington reported that "Curratuck Inlett is shut up and Roanock is so dangerous that few people care to use it but go around to Ocacock." By that time four-fifths of the inhabitants of North Carolina were settled in the area served by Ocracoke Inlet, and Burrington suggested that the unwieldy port system then in force—with the collectors located at the larger towns far up the sounds and rivers—be changed and that a central customs house be established at Ocracoke Inlet.

At Ocracoke, he said, "there is a good harbour and water sufficient for a ship that carrys 300 tunns. From this place the goods brought in may by small vessels be carried within Land to all places in this Country that doe not depend on Cape Fear River for their trade, and be a port for the three districts of Roanoke, Currituck and Bath Town."

Though Burrington's suggestion was ignored, from that point on the bulk of the ships bound to or from North Carolina were forced to use Ocracoke Inlet, and it was necessary for pilots to be stationed there permanently to take the vessels safely through. One of the first formal requests for appointment as a pilot was that of Captain Miles Gale, dated November 9, 1734. Included among the other early Ocracoke Inlet pilots were James Bun, David Wallace, John Dixon, Francis Jackson, George Howard, and Lorable Gaskins.

Locating pilots at the inlet was only part of the answer, however, as was shown by a petition from Robert Hewan and others in 1739 complaining "that the navigation from Ocacock Inlet to the several Ports and Rivers in this Province is very dangerous." They asked that "the most dangerous places from the said Inlet to the several rivers may be buoyed and beaconed" and an act was passed which provided for the payment of duty by all vessels entering Ocracoke Inlet, the proceeds to be used for improving the navigation. But in February, 1740, "several Masters, Owners of Vessels and others" filed another petition with the colonial assembly, stating that they had been paying the duty but that "the sd Navigation is no ways made better or Easier." Similar efforts to improve navigation continued for many years, but the complaints always seemed to outnumber the accomplishments.

Not long after this, however, the perils of navigation assumed a comparatively minor status in view of a much more threatening development. During Queen Anne's War, between 1702 and 1713, French and Spanish warships had attacked the North Carolina coast, but except for the brief period of pirate menace in 1718, the Banks had been comparatively free from armed attacks ever since. Then in the spring of 1741, with England and Spain once more at war—the War of Jenkins' Ear, to be followed by King George's War—two Spanish privateers, one of them a large "high stern black sloop, with about one hundred men on board," appeared off the Banks, and in a ten-day period in late April and early May they captured a total of six vessels, including two registered at Edenton. They operated close to shore near the mouths of the inlets, with no apparent fear of re-prisal; they were so bold, in fact, that a Pasquotank ship owner, James George, "had the mortification to see his vessel and cargo taken before his face, as he stood on shore."

By the end of June it began to appear that the Spaniards liked the Banks and intended to stay for a while. They had moved ashore on Ocracoke Island where they erected a tent town and established a base of operations from which they were able to control ship move-ments through the inlet and at the same time harass vessels sailing along the coast. In addition they had "burnt several houses, and de-stroyed great numbers of cattle" on the coast and had fitted out some smaller vessels for operations in the sound.

Captain Thomas Hadley, commanding a sloop bound for the West Indies, encountered the Spaniards one calm Sunday morning in early July about thirty miles up the sound from Ocracoke Inlet. The priva-teers, using a long boat, had little difficulty boarding the becalmed sloop and capturing the crew, but Hadley managed to get away from them at Ocracoke and made his way down the coast to the Cape Fear River, where his report caused great concern. The merchants and ship owners fitted out the letter-of-marque ship *William* and a small schooner, and they recruited a hundred hands for the larger vessel and fifty for the smaller.

Meanwhile, every vessel arriving on the coast seemed to bring re-ports of new depredations by the invaders, and every craft overdue on a return voyage was presumed a victim of the large black sloop. At this point, however, Captain Peacock arrived at Cape Fear with the first heartening report that had been received in months. He had seen, Captain Peacock said, "a fine clean ship with a sloop on one side and a schooner on the other, lying at anchor off the bar of Ocacock Inlet," and being short of provisions, he had tried to approach them. When he was within a few miles of the three vessels he spotted fires on shore and saw that the tent town on Ocracoke Island had been set afire. Even as the tents burned men could be seen hurrying from shore to the three vessels off the bar, one of which was a large black sloop; and as soon as these men were on board the three craft weighed anchor and bore away before the wind, leaving Captain Peacock very much confused, and as short of provisions as before.

Thus the Spanish privateers abandoned their base on Ocracoke

Island; but the resulting respite was brief, for other ships of Spain appeared, and the attacks continued. On August 5 the *William* captured a Spanish schooner which had been deserted by her crew at Hatteras Inlet. In its issue of January 9, 1742, the *South Carolina Gazette* reported that "a Spanish Privateer has again lately been on that coast, and taken two Vessels off Okerecock" and in June it printed a confirmation "of Capt. Bladwell's engaging a Spanish Brigantine Privateer off Okerecock, on the 26th of May last."

After this there were only fragmentary reports of continued Spanish attacks for several years. Then, in the summer of 1747 "several small Sloops & Barcalonjos came creeping along the shore from St. Augustine, full of armed men, mostly Mulattoes & Negroes." In these shallow-draft vessels the privateers were able to elude the single large British warship then in the area and made landings all along the coast, including Ocracoke and Beaufort. They especially enraged the residents of the Outer Banks, Governor Johnston reported, for they "landed in several different places among these very Bankers, and killed all their Cattle and Hogs, and done a great deal of mischief." At Beaufort, where it was necessary on at least three different occasions between June and September to call out volunteers for the militia regiment under command of Colonel Thomas Lovick and Major Enoch Ward, the Spaniards took several vessels in the harbor and actually invaded the town.

Again, in the summer of 1748, the Spaniards returned, all but destroying the town of Brunswick on the Cape Fear. This was too much for the coastal folk to take, and they descended on Governor Johnston with demands for protection. They wanted strong forts and declared that there was no safety without them, and when the Governor was reluctant to approve such expenditures because of a shortage of money, the Assembly passed a special bill providing for the issuance of new currency to take care of the expense.

The plan, as originally outlined, called for the construction of four forts, large ones at Ocracoke and Cape Fear, smaller ones at Beaufort Inlet and Bear Inlet. A poll tax of one shilling per taxable was levied to raise the money, and 6,000 pounds was appropriated for the forts—2,000 each for those at Ocracoke and Cape Fear, 1,500 pounds for the one at Beaufort Inlet, and 500 pounds for the fort at Bear Inlet.

To supervise the construction of the fort at Ocracoke the Assembly named Benjamin Peyton, Samuel Sinclaire, Francis Stringer, James Macklewean, John Haywood, and Peter Payne; for the one at Beaufort Inlet, Thomas Lovick, Arthur Mabson, John Clitherell, and Joseph Bell. This was the first appreciable expenditure authorized for the Banks area, but the funds remained in the treasury, unspent, for five more years.

Ironically, the Bankers got a good measure of revenge against the Spaniards in quite a different way. In mid-August, 1750, five Spanish ships, laden with a rich cargo of "cocoa, balsom and cochineal" and carrying valuable specie and plate, picked up the Gulf Stream off Florida and headed north on the first leg of the circuitous passage home to Cadiz. As they moved up the coast the skies became overcast, the seas roughened, the winds steadily increased in intensity. By the time they reached Cape Hatteras on August 18 the five Spanish vessels were in the midst of a terrible tempest. One after another those sails which had been left standing were ripped off by the hurricane-force winds; then other rigging was torn loose, and spars; and finally even the giant masts snapped under the terrific strain.

One of the smaller vessels went ashore near Drum Inlet and her crew managed to salvage most of her cargo; the second was lost near Cape Hatteras; the third and fourth were stove to pieces, with only a few crewmen surviving. Meanwhile the fifth and largest, *Nuestra Señora de Guadalupe*, without masts or rudder, was drifting off the Banks. Commanded by Don Juan Manuel de Bonilla, she was a 500-ton frigate, carrying a cargo valued at one million pieces of eight, and an additional 400,000 pieces of eight in specie. In this "most shattered and dangerous condition" she was maneuvered in close to shore by Commander Bonilla, and on the third of September she was taken through Ocracoke Inlet and came to anchor in the protected harbor there.

On September 25, Governor Gabriel Johnston assembled his Council in special session to present the latest report from the coast. Although no message or requests for assistance had been received from Don Juan Manuel de Bonilla at Ocracoke, he suggested that since England and Spain were at peace the government of North Carolina should make every effort to help protect the vessel and its cargo and treasure.

One of the members of the Council, Colonel Innes, who was experienced in dealing with Spaniards and knew the language, was dispatched to Ocracoke for a first-hand investigation of affairs there. Enroute to the coast Colonel Innes received information that the Bankers—"a set of people who live on certain sandy Islands lying between the Sound and the Ocean, and who are very Wild and ungovernable, so that it is seldom possible to Execute any Civil or Criminal Writs among them"—were plotting to attack and pillage the *Nuestra Señora de Guadalupe* in force. When this information was transmitted back to Governor Johnston, he sent a rush message to South Carolina requesting that the British warship *H.M.S. Scorpion* be transferred to Ocracoke.

The Bankers, meanwhile, were finding their way to revenge blocked by others in addition to Governor Johnston and the North Carolina Council. A man named Tom Wright had come up from Charleston, was mingling with the Spaniards incognito, and was advising them to ignore the government of North Carolina and ship their valuable cargo to Charleston instead.

At the same time the customs officers were maintaining that the Spaniards had unlawfully "broke Bulk and twice unladen and as often reladen the said ship," and when Governor Johnston refused to authorize their seizure of the vessel on those grounds, they went straight to the Surveyor General of the customs for the American colonies—who happened to be in Virginia at the time—and were instructed by him to seize it anyway. Governor Johnston thwarted this, however, by having her seized himself—for her own protection, he claimed.

While the residents of the area were sitting by watching this tug of war between the Governor of North Carolina and the customs officers, Don Juan Manuel de Bonilla was having other troubles. His crew had become mutinous and ungovernable, and they forced Bonilla to transfer some of the most valuable cargo—a hundred chests of plate and thirty bags of cochineal—to two northern sloops which had appeared at Ocracoke. When the transfer was completed, however, both boats cut their cables and headed for the open sea, leaving both Bonilla and his mutinous crewmen behind.

By the time *H.M.S. Scorpion* arrived from Charleston, Bonilla was so concerned over his mutinous crew, the disappearance of the treasure laden sloops, and the prospect of bad weather that he petitioned

Governor Johnston to direct the *Scorpion* to transport the balance of the cargo to Europe. Governor Johnston agreed to this, but at the same time he presented Bonilla with a claim for salvage and promptly commandeered something over 16,000 dollars for his trouble, though the British government forced him to give it back some time later.

So Captain Bonilla finally left the Banks and returned to Cadiz, but with less than half of the cargo and specie which had been aboard the vessel when she entered Ocracoke Inlet. And the residents of the Banks, having been hemmed in from all sides as these various intrigues were in progress, probably were as glad to be rid of this group of Spaniards as they were when the crew of the "large black sloop" had departed nine years earlier, after burning the tents on Ocracoke.

Not long after this, concrete steps were taken to protect Ocracoke Inlet and at the same time to provide suitable facilities for the hundreds of vessels using it as a port of entry.

In 1753 an act was passed by the North Carolina Assembly for "laying out a Town on Core Banks, near Ocacock Inlet, in Carteret County, and for appointing Commissioners for completing the Fort at or near the same place."

Under the terms of this act Joseph Bell of Carteret County, John Williams and Joseph Leech of Newbern, Michael Coutanch of Bath Town, and John Campbell of Edenton were named commissioners "with full power and authority to lay out fifty acres of land on Core Banks, most convenient to the said harbour, adjoining the said Banks, for a town, by the name of Portsmouth, into lots of half an acre each, with convenient streets, as they may think requisite."

Further, because "the said Town will be a Maratime Town, far distant from the Bulk of the Inhabitants of this Province, and liable to the Depredations of an Enemy in Time of War, and Insults from Pirates and other rude People in Time of Peace," the 2,000 pounds previously authorized for a fort to guard Ocracoke Inlet was to be turned over to the new commissioners for the construction of a fortification to be known as Fort Granville.

Two years later, when newly-arrived Governor Arthur Dobbs set out for a tour of the coast, reaching Ocracoke Inlet May 9, 1755, he found that the town of Portsmouth and Fort Granville existed in name only. But within twenty-four hours he had not only fixed a site for Fort Granville on Core Banks but had designed the structure, describing it later as "a fascine Battery, secured by piles, with 2 faces; one to Secure the passage in coming down a Narrow Channel to this Harbour, and the other to play across the Channel where it is not above 300 yards wide."

He then hurried off to the town of Beaufort, found that the original commissioners had selected a fort site within 200 or 300 yards of town, decided this would not do, and picked out his own site on the southwest point of the inlet within half a mile of the main channel.*

Having laid the groundwork for the construction of Fort Granville at Ocracoke Inlet and Fort Dobbs at Beaufort Inlet, the new Governor then moved on for a first-hand look at Cape Lookout Bay, which had been described to him in glowing terms by a surveyor named Daniel Dunbibben. Judging by his later writings Dobbs was almost overcome with the perfection of the harbor and of the fortifications he envisioned there at the Cape, but his efforts to get the government in London to finance the project failed.

Work was begun shortly on forts Granville and Dobbs, and when the Governor inspected them in June of 1756 he found Fort Dobbs almost finished—though it was later said to have been "built in so slight a manner, and having no guns, powder and ball" that it was considered "in no condition of defence" and was not garrisoned. Fort Granville, on the other hand, was "almost piled and filled, and the house ready to be framed," and even the town of Portsmouth was finally taking shape, for the commissioners had completed their survey and had already sold the first lots.

By late 1757 Fort Granville was sufficiently well along to be put in active use, and Charles McNair was appointed captain of the company to be stationed there. In 1758 the Assembly passed an act providing for a garrison of fifty-three officers and men, though from then on the strength of the Fort Granville complement varied yearly according to the exigencies of war, the state of the colony's finances, and the whims of the Assembly. There were twenty-five troops in

* Governor Dobbs's judgment in his selection of a site on Bogue Banks at the southwest side of Beaufort Inlet has been sustained by succeeding generations of military engineers. For one or another fort has been located there almost continually from his day until ours, all within a few hundred feet of the site he selected in 1755. The fort he designed was named Fort Dobbs (another Fort Dobbs was built in the western part of North Carolina at about the same time); it was replaced in 1808 by Fort Hampton, and it in turn was replaced in 1834 by Fort Macon, which remains today as a state park.

1762, only five in 1763, and with the signing of the Treaty of Paris ending the French and Indian War in 1764 the garrison was discontinued, and the barracks were ordered rented in order to provide funds for taking care of the guns.

Though there is no record that a gun was ever fired from Fort Granville and today no vestige of it remains, the fact that troops were stationed there for a time did serve as an impetus in the development of the town of Portsmouth. One of the chief beneficiaries of this was a man named Valentine Wade, who bought lot number 21 in Portsmouth March 19, 1757, at a time when work was well along on Fort Granville. Valentine Wade apparently saw an opportunity for an enterprising businessman to get a good start in the new town, and he began construction of a tavern—so far as is known, the first on the Outer Banks. He got along well enough to be named a justice of the peace, but by 1759 there was dissatisfaction in the town with the way in which Wade's tavern was being operated, and in August of that year the feeling had reached such a pitch that John Bragg, an Ocracoke Inlet pilot, and Joseph Ryall, a soldier at Fort Granville, swore out a complaint warrant against him.

The two presented their formal complaint to the Council of the colony, in session at Wilmington, September 1, 1759, charging that "Valentine Wade, one of his Majestys Justices of the Peace for the county of Carteret, and who keeps a Tavern in the Town of Portsmouth in said County, Permits, suffers and encourages disorderly persons to dance and play at cards and dice in his house upon the Lords Day."

The Council ordered Wade to appear at the next term of court to defend himself, but when he failed to show up he was "struck out of the Commission of the Peace."

The action of pilot Bragg and soldier Ryall was one of the first public expressions of moral or religious concern on the Banks. Though a minister named James Adams had served in Currituck County as early as 1708, there is nothing to indicate that any minister actually visited the Banks until October 7, 1766, when the Reverend Alexander Stewart went to Portsmouth "for the bathing in the salt water" and reported that he "baptized twenty seven children from the different islands round me." There is no record of Stewart's ever returning, but in 1772 the Reverend Mr. Reed, in a letter to the secretary of the

Society for the Propagation of the Gospel in Foreign Parts, said: "As part of this parish lies along the Sea Coast, I expected some Benefit from the Sea air, but finding the people sickly, & poor accommodations, I soon returned."

By that time the two largest communities on the Outer Banks were located at Ocracoke Inlet, the town of Portsmouth on the south side, and Pilot Town or Ocracoke village on the north. A beacon had been placed on one of the small islands inside the inlet and a favorite name for this unofficial port of Ocracoke Inlet was Beacon Island Roads. Among the people attracted to this busy port of Beacon Island Roads were a number of Negroes, some of whom were slaves brought down by their owners, the others freemen of color, and by 1773 they were seriously affecting the business of the pilots. In February of that year eight Ocracoke Inlet pilots—John Williams, George Bell, John Bragg, William Bragg, Adam Gaskins, Richard Wade, William Styerin, and Simon Hall—complained by way of a petition to Governor Josiah Martin and the General Assembly that these Negroes were piloting vessels from Ocracoke Bar to the inland towns at "Great prejudice and Injury" to the regular pilots who had "settled at Oacock Bar in order to attend and carry on the Business of their Calling, at Great Costs and Expence."

Thus on the eve of the Revolutionary War and at the end of the period of initial settlement on the Outer Banks, the business of piloting at the port of Beacon Island Roads had become so competitive that the government had to be petitioned to restrain it. A long call, that, from the period only forty years or so before when the first pilot was finally induced to locate at Ocracoke Inlet.

The Revolution

By THE TIME the American Revolution had progressed from the tea party to the shooting stage, the Outer Banks had assumed an important status in the struggle for independence. For the same string of sandy islands which had served to obstruct the trade and retard the growth of the colony now proved to be an effective outer defense line for North Carolina.

As far as the British were concerned, they had been trained and equipped for a different type of warfare. With their fleets of large and powerful vessels they were able to blockade or occupy practically every Central Atlantic and New England port boasting a deep-water harbor and an adjacent city or town; they successfully bottled up Hampton Roads and with it the far-flung waters of Chesapeake Bay; and even on the Cape Fear River, they could pretty well come and go as they pleased.

But the Outer Banks were something else again. Even if they could count on favorable weather and could enlist the services of experienced pilots, the British just could not get through the narrow inlets and shallow sounds with their large warships. Though it might seem, on paper, a fairly simple matter to station vessels outside the inlets and intercept all the smaller craft going in and out, in practice it was a dangerous, frustrating, and often impossible proposition.

For this reason the so-called "ports" of northeastern North Carolina remained more or less open throughout the war. Most of the trade of the state, and a good part of Virginia's, was funneled through the inlets, particularly Ocracoke. When Washington's bedraggled troops were burrowed down in those frightful winter quarters at Valley Forge, one of the main hopes of getting supplies to them was by a route from Ocracoke Inlet, through the sounds and rivers to South Quay in Virginia, and then overland and by lesser water courses to Valley Forge.

The British engaged in continued efforts to put a stop to this damaging trade. Their privateers and warships captured numerous merchant craft off the Carolina coast, and again and again they attempted to block the inlets, invade the sounds, and land foraging parties on the Banks. With each successive British attack, however, the Carolinians in rebellion responded with defensive and retaliatory measures of their own. Independent companies of troops were stationed at strategic points along the Banks; a fort was constructed at Cape Lookout with the help of a boatload of Frenchmen; armed galleys were built in Virginia to guard Ocracoke Inlet; and Carolina-owned privateers and Carolina-built warships gave the enemy as good as they received on the open sea.

Open warfare came to the Outer Banks on April 14, 1776, almost a year after the upland armies had taken to the field. At four o'clock that afternoon the small armed sloop *Lilly* came in over Ocracoke Bar and approached the schooner *Polly*, a merchant vessel awaiting favorable winds and tides for her outward passage.

The *Polly*, owned by James Buchanan and Archibald Campbell of Edenton, was loaded with Indian corn, staves, and heading, and she was bound for the islands of Madeira. On board, in addition to her master, Silas Henry, and her regular crew, was James Buchanan, one of the owners; for he and his partner Campbell were fully aware of the potential dangers from British privateers and cruisers on the high seas. It seems probable, however, that they had not anticipated trouble while still anchored in the calm harbor inside Ocracoke Inlet.

The *Lilly*, it developed, was commanded by Captain John Goodrich, a resident of Portsmouth, Virginia, who was familiar with the waters on the North Carolina coast and was well known to the pilots at Ocracoke and to many of the merchants, mariners, and other residents of the inland towns. What some of them may not have known, however, was that their friend John Goodrich, owner of considerable property in Virginia, had decided that the best way to safeguard his holdings was to cast his lot with the powerful forces of Great Britain instead of with the American rebels. Already he had served as "superintending pilot on board the *Otter Man of War*, when she sailed up Chesapeak Bay for the purpose of burning the vessels at Baltimore, and if resisted, the Town of Baltimore" itself. Since then he had been enlisted in the services of Britain's Lord Dunmore, "for the avowed purpose of annoying the sea coasts and seizing the ships bound to and from America." He and his sloop *Lilly* had been assigned to service as tender to the armed sloop *Fincastle*, commanded by Lieutenant John Wright of the British Navy, but when Goodrich entered Ocracoke Inlet on the afternoon of April 14, the *Fincastle* was still at sea, several hours sail behind him, headed for the Ocracoke rendezvous.

As the *Lilly* came up beside the Edenton merchantman, Captain Goodrich appeared on deck, hailed Captain Henry and ordered him to come on board the sloop and bring his ship's papers with him. There was no recourse for Henry other than to comply, but half-owner James Buchanan insisted on accompanying him; and when they were at last on board the *Lilly*, Captain Goodrich took possession of the *Polly*'s papers, examined them carefully, then informed Buchanan that his craft was a lawful prize. There seems to have been a gentlemanly agreement between the two that Buchanan and Captain Henry and their crew could remain on board the *Polly* while both vessels awaited favorable conditions for the outward passage.

At dusk that same evening the *Fincastle* passed through the inlet, apparently unaware of Goodrich's success, and at eight o'clock sent a party to board the *Polly*, "plundered the said schooner of all the live stock, disarmed the men, and left a prize master and four armed men on board."

Thus the *Polly* was captured twice, and throughout April 15 and 16 the wind and tide were such that the heavily-laden merchantman could not pass through the inlet, and the three vessels remained there at anchor within sight of the pilots ashore on Ocracoke. Captain Goodrich and his superior officer, Lieutenant Wright, apparently straightened out their signals during this uneasy respite, for the pilots, keeping a close watch, saw a boatload of men from the *Lilly* relieve the prize crew from the *Fincastle* and then watched as the British warship weighed anchor and crossed over the bar to the open sea. That was exactly what the pilots had been waiting for.

In the darkness before sunrise the next morning five small boats put out from the landing at Ocracoke, rowed out into the harbor, and slipped up beside the anchored *Lilly*. With the bulk of his crewmen on board the prize schooner, Captain Goodrich was left with only three or four Negroes on the *Lilly*, but he kept a close watch and was one of the first to hear the noise of the oars as the pilots approached in the darkness. He immediately shouted to his Negro crewmen to fire on the boarding party, but even as he gave this command one of the Ocracokers confronted him, with gun drawn; and without a shot being fired Goodrich and his crewmen were taken prisoner.

The small boats moved on then to the *Polly*, caught her prize crew by surprise, and took them prisoners too. By the time the first rays of the rising sun lighted the harbor there at Ocracoke, the armed British sloop *Lilly*, her Edenton merchantman prize schooner *Polly*, and Captain John Goodrich and his entire crew were captives of the alert Ocracoke pilots.

The captured vessels and prisoners were transferred to Edenton, where a special court of vice admiralty was convened with Richard Cogdell as judge. Both vessels were ordered sold, two-thirds of the proceeds from the *Polly* and her cargo being awarded to her owners, Buchanan and Campbell, and the balance going to the pilots for their efforts.

The pilots, back at Ocracoke a few days later and still flushed with success, watched another small British cruiser come in through the inlet in search of easy prizes. Again they took matters into their own hands, as reported in a letter from Thomas Jones to James Iredell, dated April 28, 1776, in which Jones said: "Since Goodrich was taken, the pilots and others at the bar have taken another tender by boarding, having on board 1,000 pounds of gunpowder and sixteen men."

Though the news of these exploits of the Ocracoke pilots must have cheered the members of the North Carolina Provincial Congress, then in session at Halifax, it also pointed up the fact that Ocracoke was vulnerable to attack by any small British vessels which chanced that way.

Just five days after Captain Goodrich had entered the inlet and taken possession of the *Polly*, a special committee appointed to investigate the situation on the Banks made the following report: "The sea coast from the Virginia line to Occacock Inlet, as also the coast from Occacock to Bogue Inlet, and from that inlet to the South Carolina line, is totally defenceless, and all the sea banks covered with cattle, sheep and hogs, and the few inhabitants living on the banks are chiefly persons whose estates consist in live stock, and exposed to the ravages of the small armed vessels and tenders."

It was the opinion of the committee, however, that "if the armed vessels and tenders are prevented from getting supplies of fresh provisions from the sea coast, it will be impossible for the war to be of long continuance in this Province, as the seamen and soldiers will be afflicted with the scurvy and other diseases, arising from the constant use of salt provisions, and therefore be under the necessity of quitting the coast, and by that means save to the back inhabitants of this Province the very great trouble and heavy expense of frequently coming down to the assistance of their brethren on the sea board."

The solution, so far as this committee could determine, was to raise a new regiment of troops and station independent companies along the Banks. Ten days later the North Carolina Provincial Congress approved just such a procedure, calling for five independent companies, one to be stationed between Currituck and Roanoke inlets, a second at Ocracoke, a third in the Core Sound area between Ocracoke and Swansboro, and two more on the lower coast of North Carolina. Each company was to consist of a captain, two lieutenants, an ensign, four sergeants, four corporals, two drummers, one fifer, and sixty-eight rank and file, all to receive the same pay as troops in the continental army.

The following officers were named to take charge of the companies on the Banks:

For the company between Currituck Inlet and Roanoke Inlet— Dennis Dauge, Captain; John Jarvis, First Lieutenant; Legrand Whitehall, Second Lieutenant; and Butler Cowall, Ensign.

For the Ocracoke Company—James Anderson, Captain; Benjamin Bonner, First Lieutenant; James Wahob, Second Lieutenant; and John Brag, Ensign.

For the Core Sound Company—Enoch Ward, Captain; Reuben

Benthel, First Lieutenant; Benjamin Chainey, Second Lieutenant; and Charles Dennis, Ensign.

The Captains of each of these companies were specifically "encouraged to exert themselves in taking armed vessels" of the enemy, and provisions were made that they should receive prize money from any such captured craft other than those belonging to Americans or friendly powers. Each Captain was authorized, also, to "purchase at the expence of the public three good suitable boats," providing the cost did not exceed ten pounds each; and the captains were given the responsibility of recruiting their own companies.

In less than a month and a half Captain James Anderson wrote the Council of Safety: "I have the happiness to Inform you that I have fully made up my Company at Ocracock. . . . I hope to be Capable of guarding against all Enemies who may offer to oppose us here." Captain Anderson hoped to be able to do with his paid troops what the Ocracoke pilots had been doing all along without cost to the government, and it was almost inevitable that his arrival at Ocracoke would cause dissension. That it did is attested by the fact that the North Carolina Provincial Congress appointed a committee later in the year "to inquire into the conduct of Capt. Anderson, stationed at Ocracock Bar, and the complaint of the pilots there," but details of the controversy have not come to light.

Meanwhile, Captain Ward at Beaufort was having other troubles, for he reported in August that "the man whose House we have occupied as barracks grows uneasy for fear he should gett no pay, and talks of takeing the House, which if he should the soldiers would be destitute of a place to shelter themselves in."

At least one soldier in Captain Ward's company ceased to be concerned over these housing difficulties. This was David Wade, who had enlisted with Ward for a period of six months beginning June 1, 1776, but claimed that he was neither properly sworn in by the Captain nor asked to sign the articles. As a result, when the six-month period was up he applied for a discharge, but was refused, so he left the company anyway, moved over to the Banks, and "entered with Capt. Pinkum to go a whaling." Captain Ward then "sent a file of men and took him in custody and put him under guard" and from his place of confinement Wade managed to get off a petition to the

Council of State. After due consideration the Council ordered Captain Ward to give him a formal discharge.

The presence of these armed companies on the Banks was a deterring factor, but it did not put a complete stop to the raids of enemy cruisers on shipping, nor did it prohibit foraging parties from coming ashore to steal cattle and other provisions. More important, these land forces were totally unable to deal with the activities of the cruisers at sea, even at the very mouths of the inlets. Warships were needed for this assignment, and the North Carolina Council had moved in late 1775 to provide the proper craft. At that time, "taking into consideration the necessity of fitting out Armed Vessels for the protection of the trade of this Province," the Council had appointed commissioners to secure three such vessels, one each at Edenton, New Bern, and Cape Fear. By the summer of 1776 the commissioners at Edenton were well along toward fitting out and manning the brig *King Tammany* for this purpose, at Newbern the *Pennsylvania Farmer* was about ready for duty, and on the Cape Fear work was progressing on the *General Washington*.

These vessels still were not the final answer to the problem at the inlets, however, for they were designed for deep-water service. What was needed was shallow-draft craft, equipped with oars as well as with sails so they could operate in the sounds and go through the inlets without dependence on the unpredictable winds.

Since a large part of Virginia's commerce was passing through Ocracoke Inlet and Pamlico Sound, a delegation was sent to Virginia in the spring of 1776 to discuss the possibility of joint action. This resulted in an agreement whereby Virginia was to build, at South Quay near Suffolk, two large row galleys specifically designed for the purpose of guarding Ocracoke Inlet and the surrounding waters.

Thus, by the early fall of 1776, the business of providing adequate protection for the Banks seemed well advanced. Independent companies of armed troops were stationed on Currituck Banks, at Ocracoke Inlet, and at Core Sound; the armed brigs *Pennsylvania Farmer*, *General Washington*, and *King Tammany* were being readied for duty; and the row galleys *Caswell* and *Washington* were taking shape on the Virginia ways.

On October 1, 1776, the North Carolina Council issued orders for the *Pennsylvania Farmer* to put to sea for a four-week cruise toward the south in hopes of intercepting part of the British merchant fleet scheduled to sail from Jamaica to England, while the *King Tammany* was ordered to "proceed to Occacock Bar and there lay for the protection of the Trade until the return of the *Pennsylvania Farmer* from her intended cruize."

Not long after these orders were issued the Council received a most disquieting letter from New Bern. It was written by James Davis, who had set up the first printing press in North Carolina in 1749 and had printed the bulk of the early laws and journals of the colony.

"The Provincial armed vessel *Pennsylvania Farmer* sailed from this Town a few days since," Davis wrote, "after lying here with 110 men on board at the Expence of near Forty Pounds per day, upwards of six months, in the most inglorious, inactive, and dissolute state that perhaps was ever suffered in any Country." James Davis was a writer, as well as a printer, and he wasted few words in getting to the point. "One Hundred and ten pints of Rum poured out to them every morning, kept them continually drunk and ready for any mischief, especially as they consist of men of all nations and conditions, English, Irish, Scotch, Indians... and the most abandoned sett of wretches ever collected together." The officers on the *Pennsylvania Farmer*, he said, were not properly qualified to command such a vessel, and two of them "with a number of the men went off with the Boat with Intent to join Lord Dunmore's Fleet, and actually reached Currituck County." The crew had "wasted near 100 pounds of powder in wantonly firing at and bringing too all Boats, Canoes and Vessels of every sort," and "even Passengers in the Ferry Boat have been insulted." The result, Davis said, was that "this crew of Banditti" had caused New Bern to be "a continued scene of Riot, Outrage and Robbery."

The truth of these charges seems never to have been determined, but on October 18, 1776, the Commissioners at Edenton wrote the Council that they had been informed the *Pennsylvania Farmer* was undergoing repairs and "will not be ready for some considerable time to proceed on her intended cruize." They suggested that the orders be reversed, and on October 21 the Council dispatched the *King Tammany* on a four-week cruise to attempt to intercept the Jamaican fleet and ordered "the Armed Brig, the *General Washington*, now lying at Washington" to "proceed with all possible dispatch to Occacock Bar and to remain within the said Bar in Order to protect the Trading Vessels which may be coming into or going out of that port, until one of the aforesaid Armed Vessels shall return there."

During the winter of 1776-77 the *General Washington* and *King Tammany*, and possibly the *Pennsylvania Farmer*, took turns guarding the Ocracoke station. With Captain Anderson's independent company ashore at Ocracoke and Captain Ward's company at Core Sound, the enemy privateers caused little trouble.

By the spring of 1777, however, the three armed brigs, not having been particularly successful in their cruises against enemy shipping, were dispatched to the West Indies for salt and other commodities, leaving Ocracoke exposed again. In September, 1777, a year and a half after the capture of Captain John Goodrich by the pilots, the enemy privateers and cruisers moved in toward the Banks once more.

This time three vessels, the large brig *Lord Howe*, a smaller ten-gun brig, and a sloop, appeared at Ocracoke and for several weeks cruised back and forth between Cape Lookout and Cape Hatteras. They were so successful in blockading Ocracoke Inlet that a large number of merchant vessels were stranded there waiting to pass out through the inlet, and when the enemy finally slipped in across the bar several of them were captured, including "a large French brig." The rest escaped up the rivers.

The English vessels also made raids on other parts of the Banks, and the *North Carolina Gazette* of New Bern, in its issue of September 19, 1777, stated that "The utmost Dispatch is making here to drive these Sheep stealers from whence they came, for 'tis supposed the fat Mutton on the Banks has been the chief temptation to this desperate Manoeuvre."

Among the measures to which the paper referred was an order from Governor Caswell to Captain John Nelson of the Craven Militia to "March with the greatest expedition and most Secret Manner to Core Banks, there to repel, or do your best endeavour to repel, the enemy at or near that place, and by all means to remove the Stocks of Cattle & Sheep so as at every event to prevent their falling into the enemies hands." Caswell also issued a call for ten of the Ocracoke pilots, those "on whose Fidelity you can depend," to go up to New Bern to serve on board armed vessels being made ready there. After almost a year and a half people began thinking again about the two row galleys, the *Caswell* and the *Washington*, which were supposed to be under construction at South Quay in Virginia. It developed, however, that these were far from completed, though Governor Patrick Henry and his associates in Virginia promised to do everything in their power to put them in readiness at the earliest possible time.

One heartening note in all this confusion was the following, which appeared in the *North Carolina Gazette* of October 24, 1777:

Since our last, Capt. Ward, of the Independent Company stationed on Core Banks, has taken a Prize Schooner called the *Liverpool*, commanded by Capt. Mayes, from Providence to New York, loaded with Fruit and Turtle for Lord Howe. This vessel put into Cape Lookout Bay, under the Sanction of a Pretended Friend, but Capt. Ward's Vigilance soon discovered her to be an Enemy, and in the night boarded her with some of his Company, and took her. She is about 30 tons, has been fitted as a Privateer, and now mounts several Swivels, and is reported a very fast Sailer.

This was the last reported incident concerning British privateers in 1777, and just as well too, for in the ensuing months all defensive units were removed from the Banks. In early November the brig *King Tammany* was chartered to merchants in Edenton; at about the same time the Independent companies at Currituck Banks, Ocracoke, and Beaufort were disbanded, and John Easton at Beaufort was ordered to "take and keep in his possession until directed all guns, ammunitions and other arms" and to "sell all the public boats" belonging to the Ocracoke and Beaufort companies. In December the *General Washington* was offered for sale, while her sister ship, the *Pennsylvania Farmer*, was reported to be idle and in poor condition.

Not only were there no defensive units on the Banks, for some reason were no raids by the British either, and for a while it seemed almost like peacetime again. In December, Captain John Sheppard, master of the scow *Diamond*, complained to the Assembly that he had "been defrauded of greatest part of the cargo of said vessel by some of the inhabitants at or near Ocracock." Under the date of January 16, 1778, a proclamation signed by Governor Caswell appeared in the *North Carolina Gazette* offering a reward of fifty pounds to any "white freeman who will, on oath, inform the Attorney General of this State, of the names and places of abode of all or any" of the persons who "have unlawfully possessed themselves of a large quantity of goods, the property of said Sheppard." In January, 1778, the sloop *Success,* bound from Bermuda to North Carolina with a cargo of salt, was wrecked at Cape Hatteras. The loss could have been no more serious if the cargo had been gunpowder or pieces of eight, for the acute shortage of salt in North Carolina had caused great concern since the very outbreak of the war.

As early as September, 1775, the Provincial Congress had offered a bounty of 750 pounds "to any Person who shall erect and build proper works for Manufacturing common Salt on the sea shore," and two such works were started in the Beaufort area the next summer. One, operated by Robert Williams and located at Gallants Point, which is now in the town proper, was designed to produce salt by flooding specially constructed beds with salt water, but just when production seemed certain to Williams "there fell a heavy rain and blasted all my hopes for this fall." The other, about three miles from Beaufort on the Newport River, was operated by Richard Blackledge who concentrated at the outset on producing salt crystals by boiling salt water in large vats or pans. He was drowned while attempting to cross the sound in an open boat, however, so that no appreciable amount of salt was produced.

At this point the North Carolina Council wrote to the delegates to the Congress in Philadelphia: "It is impossible for us to describe the distressed Situation of this State for the want of Salt. The Inhabitants in general say only let them have that article and they will fight so long as they have Existence, in support of the just rights of their Country. Without it, themselves, Families and Stocks must perish."

The delegates to Congress then enlisted the aid of Benjamin Franklin, at whose suggestion they secured pamphlets on "making Salt by Sun Evaporation or by Culinary fire." When these had been distributed in North Carolina it was reported from the coast that "The Humour of Salt boiling seems to be taking place here.... Every Old Wife is now scouring her pint pot for the necessary operation."

Though the residents of the Banks were by this means able to provide their own salt, it became necessary to dispatch special vessels to the West Indies for sufficient supplies to take care of the inland residents and the troops. On February 15, 1778, Governor Caswell wrote to General George Washington at his winter quarters at Valley Forge that "a considerable quantity of salt and salted provisions," as well as blankets and shoes, had been secured and were being sent on to the troops. Because of the effective British blockade of the northern ports it was necessary to use Ocracoke Inlet as the point of entry for these needed supplies, shipping them from there to South Quay on small vessels, then overland the sixteen miles to Suffolk, and from there by barge, canal boat, wagon, or even horseback across Virginia and Maryland to Pennsylvania and Valley Forge.

While the British backs were turned on Ocracoke other needed supplies were brought in there that winter, but at least one other vessel, a French ship, was "cast on Occacock bar" and "all her valuable cargo of sugar, coffee, rum, &c." was lost.

The winter lull came to an end in April of 1778 when a small sloop "came up with Occacock Bar and anchored" and signaled for a pilot. She was a familiar craft which had sailed from Ocracoke not too long before, and without hesitation the pilots boarded her. Too late they discovered that she had been captured by the British after leaving Ocracoke and was now a privateer, manned by a crew of about thirty men and equipped with four small guns. Her captain informed the pilots that he was after "the Frenchmen, and if they did not immediately carry him over the bar into the road where lay a French ship and a brig, with a considerable quantity of tobacco on board, he would instantly put them to death. The pilots accordingly carried the sloop in," and the privateers captured both French ships and a Bermudan sloop loaded with salt as well.

"Thus," the *North Carolina Gazette* editorialized in its issue of April 10, 1778, "has a small sloop with 4 guns and 30 men robbed this state of two fine vessels with more than 100 hogsheads of tobacco and a considerable quantity of salt. This surely shews the necessity of keeping some force on Occacock Island, otherwise our trade will be annihilated."

Just about the time this was appearing it happened that the row galley *Caswell*, built by the state of Virginia at South Quay, was being turned over to North Carolina, and five days later Governor Caswell reported to the Assembly that he had heartening news from Willis Wilson, who had been appointed captain of the galley. "I think it necessary to acquaint you," the Governor said, "that Captain Wilson informed me he had one hundred and forty five men on board the said ship, and that the ship was properly fitted to proceed to Ocracock Bar."

By early May the *Caswell* had taken up her station at Ocracoke, and for the first time since the outbreak of hostilities, that important point of ingress and egress was properly guarded. Ironically, an old acquaintance chose this particular time to return to the Banks.

Captain John Goodrich, by parole or other means, was back in the service of Great Britain once again, this time in command of a 10-gun sloop, and he seems to have been bent on getting even with the pilots who had captured him at Ocracoke two years earlier.

The presence of the *Caswell* galley at Ocracoke Inlet may have caused him some brief trepidation, but Captain John Goodrich was not a man to be turned easily from his charted course. He passed by Ocracoke and followed the coast down past Cape Lookout until he came to Beaufort Inlet, figuring no doubt that the pilots on duty there were of the same breed, if not the exact same individuals, as those who had so humiliated him earlier at Ocracoke.

A brief note, in the May 15, 1778, issue of the *North Carolina Gazette*, tells the story of the resulting encounter quite succinctly. "A few days ago," the paper reported, "Captain Goodrich decoyed the pilots at Old Topsail Inlet, came in and took a brig, a prize sent in by the continental frigate *Rauleigh*, and a vessel just arrived from Charlestown with a valuable cargo and a large sum of money on board. He endeavoured to carry off the brig, but not being able to get her out, set her on fire and left her."

Captain John Goodrich thus evened the score with his former pilot friends, and in succeeding months he was slated to bring the balance still further over on his side.

With the arrival of the *Caswell* galley to guard Ocracoke Inlet and the return of Captain John Goodrich to the Outer Banks, there is small wonder that little notice was taken at this time over the appearance, at Cape Lookout, of a large French frigate which seemed bent on establishing a permanent base there.

This was the frigate *Ferdinand*, owned by a Captain de Cottineau who had come here for the express purpose of offering his services to General Washington and the American cause. He was accompanied by Monsieur le Chevalier de Cambray, an artillery captain with similar intent, and it was fortunate for North Carolina that they chanced to touch at Cape Lookout instead of at a more distant port. For De Cottineau and De Cambray found, as had others before them, that Cape Lookout Bay was an excellent harbor, protected from almost all of the heavy winds, and a suitable anchorage for a small fleet of vessels. They found, also, that the place was without fortifications of any kind, and since certain repairs were necessary which would detain the *Ferdinand* there for some time, the Frenchmen resolved to correct this American oversight by building at least enough fortifications to protect their own vessel in event of attack.

Captain de Cambray proceeded to make a detailed survey of Cape Lookout Harbor and the neighboring Banks, and he and De Cottineau then selected a suitable location for the fortifications. By the time De Cambray had finished drawing the plans for the fort, however, the two seem to have decided that while they were at it the sensible thing would be to build a permanent fort which could be manned by North Carolina troops. As De Cottineau later said, it "could assure a retreat to all the Continental vessels as well as to a great quantity of strangers . . . a good shelter against the Winds and the Enemies . . . being the only safe harbour from Cape Henry to Cape Fear, where strangers may go in without danger."

To this end the two Frenchmen made contact with the government officials of North Carolina, going to New Bern for that purpose. They found that a fort at Cape Lookout had been contemplated since early in the war; that a surveyor named Christopher Neale had been ordered by the Council in the fall of 1776 to "proceed to Cape Lookout Bay and make a full and compleat survey thereof, in the most secret manner"; that this survey had been transmitted to the Continental Congress in May of 1777 with a request that a fort be built there "on the Continental Establishment." But the Continental Congress had failed to provide funds for such a structure, and the state officials had neglected to further the project on their own.

De Cottineau then made a specific proposal, offering "to furnish 80 men and his boats to build a fort at his own expences, and . . . even to put some of the frigate guns upon it untill the Assembly should send some." The Assembly session for the spring of 1778 had not yet begun, but the officials to whom the Frenchmen made this offer, including Governor Caswell, not only accepted the proposal but raised something like 1200 pounds in a private subscription among themselves to enable De Cottineau to hire local craftsmen and slave labor to speed up the job.

In addition, Governor Caswell instructed the Beaufort militia to assist the Frenchmen in defense against possible enemy raids on the proposed installations, and Thomas Chadwick wrote Caswell from Beaufort on April 11 that he had met with De Cottineau "and have with him fixed on a proper place for a Guard to be placed at, about half way between the Bay and the Inlet, it being the most convenient to alarm the Country from."

In late April, as the Carteret militia stood in readiness to assist in the defense of Cape Lookout, and as the French captains De Cottineau and De Cambray guided the crew of the *Ferdinand* and a handful of local laborers on the actual construction job at the fort, the North Carolina Assembly met in New Bern and took official cognizance of these efforts.

The Assembly passed a resolution expressing "a most grateful sense of the important Services" rendered by De Cottineau and De Cambray in "planning and erecting a Fort at Cape Lookout." Since the work was not yet done, the Assembly passed "An Act for fortifying Cape Lookout Bay," in which Christopher Neale, John Easton, and William Thompson were named commissioners "for erecting a Battery and Fortification at the said Bay and Harbour of Cape Lookout." A sum not exceeding 5,000 pounds was appropriated, and they were instructed, also, to receive "such Aid and Assistance as Captain Cottineau, Commander of the French Frigate *Ferdinand*, now lying in the Bay of Cape Lookout aforesaid, shall offer and freely contribute."

By the time this bill was passed and commissioners Neale, Easton, and Thompson were notified and had an opportunity to look into the matter, De Cottineau was reporting to Governor Caswell that, despite a delay in getting timbers, enough of the fort was completed to withstand any ordinary attack. In addition, he said, "the house for Garrison is ready, also the powder house and the well." Since he and De Cambray were anxious to head north and join the Continental Army, he offered to send ten of his own gunners ashore, under command of a chief gunner named James Martin who "had been employed 6 years in the artillery," and at the same time leave six guns from the *Ferdinand* for the defense of the fort. Further, he had paid practically all of the expenses out of his own pocket, including "one pound of tobacco that I allowed per day to every one of my crew," so that he did not think that "the 1200 pounds are yet over."

In this state, De Cottineau said, the fort was "sufficient for some time," and all that was needed for it "to be perfectioned in its capacity" was "15 days work with about 60 men." After this the Frenchmen departed from North Carolina, taking with them letters of introduction to General Washington and leaving behind at Cape Lookout a nearly completed fort, together with guns, ammunition, barracks, powder house and well. When it came time to select a name for the new fort one might almost assume that Fort de Cottineau, Fort de Cambray, French Fort, or Fort Ferdinand would have seemed appropriate. Instead, however, the officials decided—probably because the land seems to have been owned by a man named Enoch Hancock—that the installation should be known as Fort Hancock.

The Revolution was a long war for America, longer than World War I and World War II combined and almost twice as long as the Civil War. Further, it was undertaken on this side by thirteen newly formed and independent states, under the direction of governors and generals who had to formulate policies, organize governments, and build armies without precedent or experience to guide them—men who could never be quite certain whether the men sitting beside them at council tables or the troops lined up behind them on the field of battle were on their side or the enemy's.

Mistakes were made, costly ones in terms of lives and property and time lost, but the wonder was that thirteen effective state governments could be organized, that a union of these states could be formed, and that effective military operations, both defensive and offensive, could be carried on. In accomplishing all this many steps were taken as temporary expedients which were replaced by later and more permanent action.

On the Outer Banks the temporary expedients were the formation of independent armed companies to serve there and the fitting out of armed vessels. Neither of these measures was undertaken until the spring of 1776, when the British began seriously to threaten the trade through the inlets; both had been abandoned by the fall of 1777. They were replaced during the spring of 1778 by more permanent facilities, Fort Hancock at Cape Lookout and the *Caswell* galley at Ocracoke, but even these were not the final answer to the problem.

The *Caswell* galley took her station at Ocracoke Inlet in May of 1778. She was supplied with a tender, which Captain Willis Wilson described as being "in a most wretched condition," and a company of Marines was added to bring her complement to 170 men. The matter of supplying her crew with adequate provisions was never worked out satisfactorily, however, and Captain Wilson complained to Governor Caswell soon after his arrival at Ocracoke that he was "in a fine hobble" as a result of the peculiar arrangement whereby both Virginia and North Carolina were sponsoring his vessel. At the time he was recruiting men for the ship, the Virginia Navy Board had allowed him to pay a bounty of twenty dollars per man for signing, with pay at the rate of half a dollar a day, but because "the merchants give such exhorbitant pay for seamen," it was "entirely out of my power to procure them at the price above mentioned." When apprised of this situation, Governor Caswell authorized Wilson to promise each man "twenty dollars a month, exclusive of the Virginia pay," but the North Carolina Assembly was reluctant to approve the additional sum. Even when the matter was cleared by the Assembly, payments were invariably late, at one time being seven full months in arrears.

The *Caswell* galley effectively guarded the trade at Ocracoke throughout the late spring, summer, and fall of 1778. On June 26 Wilson reported that "the enemy (one ship, two sloops and a brig) take a peep at us every now and then, but are not disposed to venture in," and for almost a year after that the British stayed away from Ocracoke.

Meanwhile, there was considerable correspondence between Virginia and North Carolina regarding the *Caswell*. In late November, Governor Patrick Henry of Virginia wrote Governor Caswell of North Carolina that the Congress wanted Virginia to furnish galleys to attack East Florida, and he expressed the hope that "the *Caswell* might be sent with them on this expedition, for I suppose from the particular construction of that vessel, and the nature of the service, that she would be of great use on this occasion." Governor Henry offered to "order one of our best to her station" to replace the *Caswell*, and a week after this letter was written the North Carolina Council agreed to the trade.

It seems doubtful, however, that the *Caswell* was ever dispatched on this Florida expedition or that a replacement was sent to Ocracoke. On February 6, 1779, Patrick Henry wrote Governor Caswell suggesting that North Carolina had not lived up to her part of the bargain when Virginia agreed to build the *Caswell* and *Washington* galleys, and he wondered whether "Virginia ought not to be reimbursed, in some considerable degree, the great expenditures incurred by the adoption of the plan recommended from your Legislature, for protecting the trade of Ocracoke?"

Henry's successor, Governor Thomas Jefferson, wrote Caswell on June 22, 1779, with a new proposal. "The *Washington* and *Caswell* gallies belonging to this Commonwealth," he said, "originally built for the protection of Ocracock Inlet, in conjunction with others proposed to be built by your State, being so much out of repair as to render it necessary to incur a considerable expense to refit them for service, their condition and future station were submitted to the consideration of our General Assembly." It was their opinion, Jefferson said, that if North Carolina could make use of the vessels, Virginia was prepared "to offer them to you at such fair estimation as may be agreed on between us."

The end to all this was reported by Thomas Jefferson in a postscript to the above letter, dated June 30, 1779. "Since writing the within," he said, "I learn that the *Caswell* Galley is sunk at her Station, that her bottom is eaten out, and her original Form such that she could not be hove down to be refitted." It had taken almost two years to build the *Caswell*, and she had served on active duty for not much more than half that time. Even the "permanent" measures were not permanent.

Fort Hancock, the other "permanent" facility, lasted longer than the *Caswell*, but not long enough to see out the war. In charge of Fort Hancock were: John Tillman, Captain; Zepheniah Pinkham, First Lieutenant; and George Robertson, Second Lieutenant, though Robertson later resigned and was replaced by John Denny. The complement of the fort was completed with the enlistment of "Two Serjeants, One Drummer, and Fifty Privates," who received the same pay as soldiers in the continental service and were enlisted for a period of one year.

Actual work on Fort Hancock had been begun by the Frenchmen

at about the time the *Caswell* galley was delivered to North Carolina authorities at South Quay; so rapidly was the construction work carried on that the fort was manned within only a few weeks of the time the *Caswell* arrived at Ocracoke. A small boat was purchased for the fort, guns were moved over from Ocracoke to complete her armament, and cannon balls from the old *Pennsylvania Farmer*, which had been sold, were provided by the commissary at Beaufort.

For two years Captain Tillman's company remained on duty at the fort, and not once during this period was there any contact with the enemy, insofar as known records show. Finally, in May of 1780, the North Carolina Assembly passed a resolution "That on the first day of June next the Garrison of Fort Hancock be disbanded & discharged, and that John Easton, Esqr., of Carteret County, be impowered to take into his Care all the military and other stores of the said Garrison belonging to this State, to be disposed of as His Excellency the Governor, or the General Assembly, may hereafter direct." *

---

* The construction and manning of Fort Hancock is a phase of Revolutionary War history which seems to have been overlooked by historians. So far as can be determined it was the only real fort built in North Carolina during the Revolution, yet there appear to be no references to it in works of history except for the index to the Colonial and State Records, where the name is listed five times and is overlooked at least a dozen other times.

One reason, undoubtedly, is that the name was not selected until after the fort was ready for occupancy. In searching the record, this writer found numerous indications that a fort was built at Cape Lookout before any reference to the name "Fort Hancock" was discovered. Another was that the letters of De Cottineau and De Cambray are very hard to understand; or, as is noted in a comment following one of the letters in the State Records, the phraseology was "Bad English and worse French."

When additional contemporary references were pieced together to provide satisfactory proof that a fort was built at Cape Lookout by the Frenchmen, that it was named Fort Hancock, and that it was manned by a company under Captain John Tillman for approximately two years beginning in the spring of 1778, efforts were made to locate some visible remains of the fort at the actual site. Maps and charts failed to show anything. A careful study of blown-up aerial photographs of the Cape Lookout area proved equally unproductive. Finally, a personal aerial reconnaissance in a light plane chartered specifically for that purpose was undertaken, and several landings were made on the beach to inspect formations which, from the plane, seemed possible sites. This, too, failed to produce results.

Similar failures resulted from numerous interviews with persons familiar with the Cape and others who had studied Outer Banks or Revolutionary War history. Then, in an interview with Jimmy Guthrie, seventy-five-year-old resident of Harkers Island who was born at Diamond City near the Cape, the usual question was asked: "Have you ever heard of Fort Hancock?" The answer was "No!" But several minutes later Mr. Guthrie suddenly turned to his wife, who had been brought up at Diamond City also, and asked: "Could that have been the Old Ruins?"

The two of them then told of playing, as children, around the ruins of an old

Though neither was in service in the closing years of the war, both Fort Hancock and the *Caswell* galley seem to have been effective safeguards against British raids on the lower Banks, for while they were active the attention of the enemy was diverted elsewhere.

The *North Carolina Gazette* had reported in May, 1778, that "there are now cruising on this coast, three privateers, Capt. McFarling in a 16 gun brig, and Captains Neale and Goodrich, in 10 gun sloops." Later that month Francis Brice of Wilmington wrote Governor Caswell that he had shipped some of the government's pork on a small sloop to the north but "Goodrich has laid hands on her."

It was on the upper Banks, above Cape Hatteras, that enemy activity seems to have been concentrated during this period, and though Captain John Goodrich participated in the raids there, another captain appears to have inflicted at least as much damage.

"The cruizers are yet very troublesome on our coast, having lately cut several vessels and small craft out of Roanoke and Currituck inlets," the *North Carolina Gazette* reported, July 17, 1778. "Besides Capt. Goodrich, there is a Capt. McLean, a little Scotchman, well known here, cruizing off our inlets; he has taken several of our vessels, and thus, exultingly, with Scotch gratitude, returns the many and singular favours and polite treatment lately received here."

The man to whom they referred was Captain John McLean, and one of the vessels mentioned was a small schooner owned by a Mr. Etheridge of Currituck County, which McLean had captured at Currituck Inlet. Soon after this he took a French snow, bound from North Carolina, and a second schooner, and though there is no indication of the disposition of the two latter vessels, it is known that he transferred part of his own crew and four of the captured Frenchmen to Etheridge's schooner, then fitted her out with two three-pound guns and two swivel guns, and proceeded to make a privateer of her.

Like a criminal drawn back to the scene of his crime, McLean then dispatched the new privateer on an expedition to the very area in which she had been captured from Etheridge; but this time the

fortification at Cape Lookout, of the remains of breastworks which were still there in 1899, and of finding pieces of old brick, scraps of metal, and coins at the site. The location, they said, was northwest of the present lighthouse and quite near where The Drain has since cut through.

Little is to be found there today resembling a fort, however, and it can only be hoped that someone will yet come forward with additional information.

people of Currituck were prepared, and they managed not only to retake the Etheridge schooner but to capture the six English crewmen and the four Frenchmen as well.

Not long after this a severe storm struck the North Carolina coast, New Bern was inundated by heavy rains, crops and fodder were "every where blown down and the blades stripped off," and people in the inland towns waited anxiously for word from Ocracoke where a number of vessels had been lying at anchor.

When word finally did come, however, it was of an entirely different nature than that expected, and it came from Hatteras rather than from Ocracoke. The *North Carolina Gazette*, August 21, 1778, reported it as follows: "There is a great probability of the loss of Capt. Goodrich, in a 10 gun sloop, that has lately done so much mischief on this coast. The sloop was seen off Hatteras by the pilots the day before the late gale of wind, and the day after there came ashore the roundhouse of a vessel, several gun-carriages, swabbs, and other things belonging to guns, a square sail boom, and other spars, which indicates the loss of some vessel; and as that sloop has not been seen since, it is likely to be her."

If John Goodrich's sloop was the wrecked vessel, then the captain himself must have escaped, for he was back in action soon after. In Congress at Philadelphia a short while later the Virginia delegates were making what Cornelius Harnett, one of our own delegates, described as "a very great noise... relative to a Captain Harper, driven into Currituck by Goutrage." These second-hand reports indicated that Goutrage (Goodrich) had chased the Harper vessel into Currituck Inlet, where once again the residents of Currituck came to the defense. This time, however, it was charged by the Virginia delegates that after chasing off Goodrich the Currituckers took possession of the Harper craft and kept it for themselves instead of returning it to Harper or turning it over to the proper authorities.

Conditions on the North Banks as the result of these continued raids were pointed up shortly after this when the government proposed to draft the Bankers for an expedition to South Carolina and Georgia.

From "Currituck Liberty Plains," under date of November 16, 1778, Samuel Jarvis, long-time representative from Currituck County, wrote to Governor Caswell: "The coast is much infested at this time with the enemy which are constantly landing men and plundering, being short of provisions will hazard their lives to gain. Yesterday Goodrich in his Sloop came in Currituck Inlet and burnt two outward bound vessels with good cargoes on board; also killed several cattle before the Inhabitants could get to their relief, it being five or six miles distance from the mainland. Those who live on the Banks, as well as on the Island of Roanoke, are near and has often kept off Boats when coming to plunder. If those people are taken away, their families certainly will suffer, both from the enemy and want of Bread, as they all get it in small boats at this season of the year."

Jarvis forwarded a "petition from the Inhabitants of the Banks," undoubtedly the same one which was considered by the North Carolina Council on December 1. It was described as a "petition of Samuel Midgett, Caleb Brickhouse, Enoch Daniel, and others, inhabitants of Roanoke Island, North and Hatteras Banks, in Currituck county, praying to be exempt from serving on the expedition to South Carolina and Georgia, on account of their distressed situation in being exposed to the daily ravages of the enemy in plundering said island and banks."

The Council advised Governor Caswell to grant the request of the petitioners, and in the ensuing months the ravages of the enemy continued. There was brief consideration of a plan to erect a battery at Currituck Inlet, and a bill for this purpose was introduced in the Assembly on February 1, 1779, but it got no further.

At about this same time the British ship *Tartar*, with a crew of seventy officers and men, was stranded on the North Banks. Residents of the area and the alert Currituck militia under command of Colonel Jarvis confronted the stranded British sailors, captured them, and took possession of the vessel. Under the terms of the capitulation Colonel Jarvis guaranteed the prisoners safe conduct to New York, and for some time thereafter the Virginia authorities were quite concerned over the appearance, in their midst, of seventy Britishers with no more credentials than whatever Colonel Jarvis had been able to supply.

Patrick Henry complained that "they lay me under great embarrassment, as I wish to observe the capitulation," but he said the procedure followed by Colonel Jarvis was all wrong and "to have him lose such a number of people, without a guard, in our State, is a dangerous thing." Henry may have gotten to the crux of the matter when he added that "the prisoners say that the Vessel, &c., is of vast value, and that Col. Jarvis has got it, and that therefore they expect to be maintained here and to have all the rights of prisoners and the stipulations executed."

In late May or early June of 1779, when the enemy brigantine *Surprise* came ashore near Currituck Inlet, the Bankers and Colonel Jarvis' militia made certain that there would be no duplication of the *Tartar* controversy. This time they captured Captain Beaton of the *Surprise* and his thirty crewmen, and they sent the lot of them under guard to a suitable prison in this state.

Not long after this Adam Gaskins, a pilot at Ocracoke, sent word to New Bern that the privateers had gathered there again, three of them, that one had crossed the bar, and that a small schooner "which we all judge to be a privateer" was headed for New Bern. There were feverish activities in that town for the reception of the vessel, but Gaskins' warning in this instance was a false alarm.

On Hatteras Island, meanwhile, the residents were reported by W. Russell, commander of the Hyde militia, as being apprehensive "from the encroachments of the enemies' privateers, tenders, &c." That this apprehension was well founded was demonstrated within a few days when two brigs, a schooner, a sloop, and a small boat "came to anchor a little to the Northward of Cape Hatteras," and "seeing a gang of cattle near the shore," they proceeded to send three boats in to the beach with a raiding party.

Unknown to the Britishers, a group of Bankers, anticipating this move, "were concealed amongst the Hills" and when the raiders left their boats and started up toward the cattle, the Bankers ran out from behind the sand hills, "rushed down upon them, killed five and took their muskets and several other articles they left behind." According to a letter written shortly afterwards by Thomas Bonner of Beaufort County, the five vessels anchored offshore kept up a constant firing which enabled the remainder of the party to escape. Even then, the Bankers succeeded not only in protecting the livestock and killing five of the enemy, but the equipment which the fleeing raiders left behind was of such value that it was "sold amongst themselves for eight or nine hundred Dollars."

Following this raid Samuel Jarvis got off another petition to the Governor from "Liberty Plains," this one requesting relief in combatting the enemy's depredations on the coast. Down at Ocracoke, totally unprotected now that the *Caswell* galley was out of service,

Captain Adam Gaskel of the Ocracoke militia forwarded his own petition, "setting forth the necessity of his Company remaining on the Banks to be in Readiness on any alarm to prevent the Privateers from cutting out Vessels and committing other depredations" and "praying to be exempt from the military duty." The Council refused to exempt these men from the draft but did provide that after they were drafted they should "remain on duty in said Comp'y on the Banks, & for the Protection of Ocracock Inlet; they having Lately behaved with singular bravery in attacking and taking a number of armed boats with their Crews, Persons that were attempting to cut out some Vessels then laying in the River."

This action was made official in November, 1779, when the Assembly formally established the Ocracoke Militia Company, "consisting of not more than twenty-five men, to be composed and Officered of the Inhabitants of said Island, and to be stationed there for its Protection and Defence." The men in the company were given the same pay and rations as the garrison of Fort Johnston on the Cape Fear, and "four pieces of Cannon, Eighteen and twenty-four pounders, imported into this State by Capt. Borrits, from Spain," were ordered delivered to the Ocracoke Militia Company.

After four years of war, after experiments with independent companies of armed troops, with armed brigs, with specially designed row galleys, and with the fort at Cape Lookout, the officials of the new state had finally found out what the Ocracoke pilots could have told them at the outset: given decent pay, provisions, arms, and equipment, the Bankers themselves could handle the enemy about as well as anyone else.

The war was far from over, but on the Banks folks had become accustomed to the privateers, the cruisers, and the raids on their cattle and sheep. With their militia companies they were ready for the enemy, and except for a couple of isolated instances, they pretty well handled the situation.

In October, 1780, "two large Gallies with sliding Gunter mast, with, as was judged, about 60 men in each, came over Roanoke Bar and went through the marshes," but they slipped out again without doing appreciable damage. Meanwhile, the British were attacking Hampton Roads and taking possession of Portsmouth, Virginia, an operation which Joseph Hewes said was participated in by privateers and "a number of Tories, among whom old Goodrich is the principal, and who, it is said, has lent the British Government 200,000 [pounds] to forward the expedition."

This caused apprehension at Beaufort, where a number of prominent citizens met on November 6 and drew up what they described as "The humble petition of the few remaining inhabitants of . . . Carteret County." They pointed out that "nearly all the young and able-bodied men belonging to the said County have gone to Sea, and the remainder being either aged or infirm, when absence from their families would be their total ruin." Further, they claimed to have information of the enemy "fitting out against the town and vicinity of Beaufort," and they requested that their "present Quota of Men" should be retained there.

That more extensive operations against the Banks, the sounds, and the towns of northeastern North Carolina had been given serious consideration was revealed later in a letter written by the infamous Brigadier General Benedict Arnold, in command at Portsmouth, Virginia. In the letter dated February 13, 1781, and written to Sir Henry Clinton, Arnold said: "I intend . . . to send some Boats with four or five hundred Troops thro' Curratucks Inlet, to Sweep the Albemarle Sound as high as Edington, & to go to New Bern and destroy their Shipping, Stores, &c." While this was being done he planned, also, to have "a few armed Vessels take Post at Ocracoke Bar" while "a Frigate Cruises without. This movement I am convinced will have a good effect, first, by destroying the Navigation of North Carolina, and thereby distressing the Inhabitants, and secondly by taking off their attention from my Lord Cornwallis and General Leslie."

Benedict Arnold's plans were never carried out, probably because the necessary shipping was not made available to him. Throughout 1781 British vessels continued to enter the inlets and raid the Banks, particularly along the northern coast, for tidewater Virginia was in the firm control of the enemy at that time, and one British military force pushed down almost to the Virginia–North Carolina line.

During this period it was sometimes difficult to determine which lands in the vicinity of the Virginia border were still held by General Isaac Gregory's North Carolina militia and which had been captured by the British. It was equally hard, on occasion, to distinguish friend from foe, as witness the strange affair of the *Fortune* galley.

The *Fortune*, apparently owned by persons active in the fight for American independence, was surprised at night and captured by a disorganized band of Loyalists, who promptly elected an old man named Robinson as their captain and then sailed off in search of a British outpost.

Captain Robinson and his crew obviously were under the impression that the British had penetrated much further south than was the actual case, for while still in a part of Currituck firmly held by Gregory's militia, they landed to inquire the route to the nearest British installation. The particular place where this landing was made was known as Morse's Point; the specific individuals from whom they sought directions were Captains Weeks and Killam of General Gregory's command.

Weeks and Killam, no doubt sensing an opportunity to effect a bloodless capture of the vessel, informed Robinson "that they were British officers, and that they would conduct him to Camp." Captain Robinson accepted this offer, the two officers boarded the *Fortune*, and after enlisting the aid of a man named Munden as pilot, they started up Northwest River toward Gregory's headquarters. Before reaching there, however, Weeks and Killam induced Robinson to proceed with them by a shorter overland route, while Munden was left to bring the galley around by water.

Just about the time Weeks and Killam were entering General Gregory's camp with their unsuspecting captive, however, the remaining Loyalists on board the *Fortune* were hailing a passing oyster boat to inquire who commanded at the base toward which Munden was taking them. Learning from the oysterman that they were headed for General Gregory's headquarters and realizing at last that their new captain had been duped by Weeks and Killam, the Loyalists quickly overpowered Munden, put him in chains, turned the *Fortune* around, and made for open water.

For some reason, instead of heading for British-held Virginia, they went down Currituck Sound, past Roanoke Island, and finally abandoned the *Fortune* galley near Lake Mattamuskeet, where she was found adrift some time later.

As for old Captain Robinson, it was reported by General Gregory later that even after his arrival at camp he "seemed to be in high spirits to think he had so perfected his purpose, not doubting but he was really in a British Camp until the evening." Robinson and his associates, General Gregory concluded, "were as grand a set of Tories as men can be."

Not long after this episode another British galley entered Currituck Inlet, "burnt a small sloop," passed into Albemarle Sound, and took another. Then she raided the town of Edenton and was headed back down the sound again when she was overtaken and captured "by the towns men" of Edenton. When the captives were taken to the Edenton jail, it was discovered that one of them was a man named Michael Quinn, a former officer in the Continental Army who had turned traitor. Later, as the prisoners were being transported overland to Halifax, Quinn "was murdered by the Guard by order of Colo. William Linton," which resulted in Linton's arrest and created a great stir over a period of several years.

Lord Cornwallis surrendered at Yorktown on October 19, 1781, but the final articles of peace which ended the war were not agreed upon until 1783. This was a period of half-hearted war, with almost everyone apparently believing that the fighting was nearly over—with the exception of some of the fighting men. Not long before, there had been a plan in the North Carolina Assembly to secure new armed vessels to protect Ocracoke and the sounds, as well as a request for Virginia to assist in the project. It seemed almost like 1776 all over again, except that this was 1781, Cornwallis had been beaten at Yorktown, and there was no need really to worry about further defenses for the Banks. Or was there?

In early April, 1782, more than five months after the battle of Yorktown, Brigadier General Jethro Sumner received a communication from General Nathanael Greene. It was dated March 30, and included in the packet was an unsigned note in Greene's handwriting as follows: "A force consisting of four vessels, mounting in the whole to 40 guns and man'd with two hundred and fifty seamen are preparing in Charlestown & will sail in a few days. Their object is to plunder and destroy the town of Beaufort in North Carolina in which they are informed is a large quantity of public and private stores; should they be repulsed there they will proceed to Ocracoke with the same view."

When the above information was transmitted to Governor Burke of North Carolina, he ordered a force of 500 men raised in the New

Bern area and 500 more in Edenton district, but when he transmitted this information to the newly convened General Assembly on April 17, they suggested "the impropriety of embodying the Militia . . . as the Enemy have embarked and put to sea."

Governor Burke was required, therefore, to dispatch hurried instructions to New Bern and Edenton countermanding his earlier orders, and to all appearances the war on the Outer Banks was over. Except for the remains of Fort Hancock at Cape Lookout, the carcasses of numerous cattle and sheep killed by British raiding parties, and the hulks of vessels wrecked or destroyed, there was little physical evidence to show that the Banks had been involved in the Revolution at all.

Statehood

Bᴜ ᴛʜᴇ ᴇɴᴅ of the Revolution in 1783 the pattern of settlement on the Outer Banks was well established. Approximately 1,000 people were living on the Banks proper and on the nearby islands, many in fairly extensive communities in the wooded hammocks on the sound side where most of the present-day villages are located.

In the more than a hundred years since the first settlers had located on the Banks, the occupational pattern had seen only minor changes. At Ocracoke and Portsmouth, the two largest communities, piloting vessels through the inlet was the basic source of income. In fact Jonathan Price said of the approximately thirty heads of families at Ocracoke in 1795, "They are all pilots." At Roanoke Island, on the other hand, practically every man who signed a deed or other legal document before 1800 styled himself "planter" or "farmer"; the people living in the small and scattered settlements southwest of Portsmouth on Core and Shackleford banks were engaged to a large extent in raising stock and in catching whales and porpoises from the beach; while in the Kitty Hawk area they were primarily farmers and stockmen; and on Hatteras Banks there was a fairly even distribution of mariners, stockmen, and farmers.

These occupational designations were those adopted by the individuals themselves, however, and were misleading, for with the exception of the Ocracoke Inlet pilots, the Roanoke Island farmers, and the Core Banks whalers, the activities of the Bankers in one area were quite similar to those in any other and similar to the activities of their ancestors a century earlier. They raised garden stuff for the table, owned stock which grazed on the open Banks range, caught their own fish, dug their own oysters and clams, put up their own houses, built and sailed their own boats; and of course, when a vessel was wrecked in the vicinity of a particular community, practically everyone who could walk turned beachcomber. Commercial fishing had not yet assumed importance.

The family names of the residents in the various localities were essentially the same as today.* These Bankers were primarily English —of 220 family names on the Banks before 1860, at least 157 were of English derivation—but there were some who could claim Italian, Danish, Greek, French, and possibly even Arabic ancestry. The Hatteras Indians had practically disappeared, the last known reference to them being in a deed in 1788 from "Mary Elks, Inden, of Hatteras Banks" to Nathan Midyett for a tract of land which included the site of the old Indian town. Slave ownership was not widespread, mostly limited to one or two in a family, and there were only a few free Negroes.

The great majority of the Banks' settlers had come down from tidewater Virginia or from the nearby Carolina mainland, but because of the isolation of the Banks and the continued traffic through the inlets by vessels from New England and the West Indies, the average Bankers' ties with those distant points were as close as with the nearby mainland.

---

* Family names, prominent in the late 1700's, included:

Ocracoke	—Bragg, Dixon, Gaskins, Howard, Jackson, O'Neal, Stiron, Wade, Wahab, and Williams;
Portsmouth	—Bragg, Bun, Casa, Dixon, Gaskill, Gaskins, Stiron, Tolson, Wade, and Wallis;
Cape Hatteras Area	—Austin, Ballance, Basnet, Burrous, Clark, Farrow, Gray, Jennett, Oliver, O'Neal, Quidley, Rollinson, Scarbrough, Stow, Wallis, Whidbee, and Williams;
Kinnakeet	—Farrow, Hooper, Meekins, Miller, Price, Scarbrough, and Williams;
Chicamacomico	—Flower, Meekins, Midgett, O'Neel, Pugh, and Wallis;
Kitty Hawk	—Best, Etheridge, Luark, Perry, Tillit, Tolar, and Twiford;
Roanoke Island	—Baum, Beasley, Daniel, Dough, Etheridge, Midgett, and Wescot.

It is probable that even at that time the house style was developing which was to become dominant on the Banks in later years, the two-story house, one room deep, usually with a one-story appendage on the rear containing the kitchen. Sailboats and skiffs provided the basic mode of transportation—and even today many Bankers would pole their skiffs half a mile down the shore in preference to walking—though a distinctive high wheeled cart, with wide tires or bearing surfaces and drawn by beach ponies or oxen, was evolving.

The Banks islands were areas of striking topographic contrast, even as they are today. There were the densely wooded sections, sometimes with the forest growth extending most of the way across the beach toward the sea, and scattered among these were the low and barren stretches of "bald beach" which usually marked the sites of former inlets. There were the high, wind-blown sand hills, forever changing shape; the smaller sand waves, moving steadily across the beach and engulfing forests in their way; and elsewhere, the sand hills and sand waves of earlier centuries, their progress retarded, covered now with thick vegetation.

Immediately following the Revolution there was a brisk trade in Outer Banks real estate and many of the larger holdings, particularly within the confines of previously established communities, were divided into small parcels. Of sixty-two deeds and grants recorded for North Banks property in the Currituck Courthouse between 1783 and 1789, for example, at least forty were in the Kitty Hawk area—fifteen at Kitty Hawk Bay, nine on Colington, and sixteen at Jeanguite Creek, all of them within five miles of the present-day Kitty Hawk Post Office. Instead of indicating a large increase in population, however, this could simply have been a reaction to independence from Great Britain and a concerted effort to acquire good title to the family homestead from the new and sovereign state of North Carolina.

Certainly the state of North Carolina, in the six years between the end of the Revolution in 1783 and the adoption of the United States constitution in 1789, was more conscious of the peculiar needs of the Banks than had been the officials sent out from England during the colonial period; for efforts were made to establish the first lighthouses on the coast and to provide better means of water communication between the inlets and the inland ports. The first North Carolina lighthouse was authorized for Bald Head at Cape Fear in 1783, and a second for Ocracoke in 1789. A site for the Ocracoke lighthouse, not to exceed one acre, was deeded to the state by William Williams, John Williams, Joseph Williams, Henry Garrish, and William Howard, Jr., September 13, 1790, but it was not long after this that the federal government assumed responsibility for lighthouse construction, and the Ocracoke project was abandoned.

Meanwhile, there had been a plan in 1783 to construct a canal from Clubfoot Creek to Harlowe's Creek, connecting Pamlico Sound with Beaufort Inlet, and another in 1786 to connect Currituck Sound with North River—neither of which materialized at that time.* A third canal was planned through the Dismal Swamp to make possible inland water communication between Chesapeake Bay and the North Carolina sounds.

Roanoke Inlet was still open but not navigable, and to replace it an even more ambitious project was proposed in 1787. The North Carolina General Assembly incorporated "The Raleigh Canal Company, for improving the navigation of Albemarle Sound" and authorized seven prominent residents of eastern North Carolina to solicit subscriptions and undertake the construction of an inlet, to be known as Raleigh Canal, from Roanoke Sound to the ocean in the vicinity of Nags Head. There was considerable interest in this project over a period of two years, and for a while Governor Samuel Johnston was active chairman of the Raleigh Canal Board of Commissioners, but the project did not materialize.

That the Bankers were being subjected to the usual run of storms and attendant shipwrecks was indicated by the publication in the *State Gazette* of Edenton, April 23, 1789, of excerpts from a letter written April 16 by John Wescot of Roanoke Island:

On the 10th inst. we had a very violent gale of wind, with an amazing rise of tide, supposed to be about 9 feet above common high water mark. The following vessels had suffered, viz. Schooner *Dolphin*, Baum, from Edenton for Baltimore—stranded—crew and cargo saved, but the vessel much damaged:—Schooner *Fanny*, E. Bosman, from Murfreesborough for

---

* Two North rivers flow into the sounds, one near Beaufort in Carteret County, the other on the north side of Albemarle Sound in Currituck County. This, of course, was the North River in Currituck County, and the modern inland waterway now follows the same general route proposed in 1786. Also, the Clubfoot Creek–Harlowe's Creek Canal was built at a later date and has since been replaced by the paralleling Adams Creek Canal which is a part of the inland waterway.

Norfolk, C. Bee supercargo—stranded on the north point of New-Inlet—the vessel, with her rigging, and part of her cargo, may be saved—the master and men all lost—The names of the master and supercargo were found among the papers saved:—A small schooner, lighter to the *Dolphin*, George Pugh—entirely lost, crew and vessel.—

Any person interested in the above vessels, may have more particular information by applying to Mr. John Gallop, who has in his possession the articles saved.

So many vessels were being wrecked on the Banks, and so many valuable cargoes salvaged by the alert Bankers, that it had become necessary to divide the entire coast into wreck districts. Each had specially designated "Vendue Masters" whose job it was to take possession of any vessels, cargo, or wreckage which came ashore and, after proper advertisement, to conduct an auction or vendue of the materials. A typical vendue announcement was the following which appeared in the *State Gazette* for May 2, 1794:

On Thursday the 8th instant, will be sold by the subscriber, on Captain Samuel Butler's wharf, Sails, rigging, anchors, cables, blocks, &c, &c. also the hull of the schooner *Success*, as she lies on Gull shore, within five miles of Chickamacomick, for the benefit of the owners and under writers. At the same time will be sold a quantity of mens shoes; also a few elegant saddles, which were on board the said schooner when cast away; all for ready money.

ROBERT EGAN, Vendue Master.

Sometimes, as in the above case, the vendues were held in the port towns, but more frequently they were conducted at the scene of the wreck. In an act setting up wreck districts in 1801, the vendue master or wreck commissioner was further charged with the responsibility for rounding up the Bankers to help him assist any vessel which grounded on the coast.

Frequently, however, by the time the vendue master learned of a wreck and was able to take charge, the more valuable cargo had been picked up by wreckers, in which case the owners of the wrecked vessel could present their case to the vice admiralty court. The difficulty, of course, was in proving who had taken the salvaged goods, but occasionally such cargo was so extensive or of such an unusual nature that detection was impossible. When the Spanish brigantine *El*

San Pedro was wrecked on the coast in August, 1796, the owners claimed that several residents "took possession of her the said brig, and her cargo, consisting of a number of pipes of rum and boxes of sugar, under a pretence of saving and preserving . . . the said brig and cargo, and wasted and made away with a considerable part thereof." The Spaniards offered to pay "a reasonable salvage" but refused to meet the price set by the salvors, and the case finally ended up in the vice admiralty court.

In 1794 the federal government finally got around to authorizing construction of two lighthouses on the Banks, the first "on the headland of Cape Hatteras" and the other "on an island in the harbor of Ocracoke, called Shell Castle." The natural sandstone lighthouse at Cape Hatteras, first of three which have been located there, was not completed until 1802,* though work progressed much faster on the smaller, wooden structure at Shell Castle.

The government lighthouse was not the only structure going up on Shell Castle at that time, however, for two individuals, one a resident of the little town of Portsmouth on Core Banks and the other a prominent merchant and ship owner of the town of Washington on the Pamlico River, were building a virtual trading city there.

These two, John Wallace of Portsmouth and John Gray Blount of Washington, had secured state grants in November of 1789 for five islands just inside Ocracoke Inlet. The largest of these was a fifty-acre "island" of sand known as Dry Sand Shoal; another was "an island of marsh" containing twenty acres and called "Bacon Island" or "Beacon Island"; the other three were "oister rocks," huge piles of oyster shells varying in size from forty-acre Long Dry Rock to twenty-five acre Old Rock and fifteen-acre Remus's Rock.

Wallace and Blount had promptly changed the name of "Old Rock" to "Shell Castle" and made preparations for converting it into a major shipping and trading center. Here vessels from the open sea could tie up at Wallace and Blount docks, unload their cargoes, take

---

* To correct an erroneous statement which has appeared frequently in features about Cape Hatteras, this was not the first lighthouse authorized by the federal government, the neighboring Cape Henry Lighthouse in Virginia having that distinction; nor was it even the first in North Carolina, for funds had been appropriated more than two years earlier to complete the lighthouse on Bald Head Island at Cape Fear.—See Acts of Congress dated March 27, 1790, for Cape Henry and April 2, 1792, for Bald Head.

on supplies, undergo repairs, and then load their outbound cargoes, without ever having to cross the Ocracoke Swash, enter Pamlico Sound, or venture close to the old port towns up the rivers.

The two seem to have been well suited for the business venture they were planning. John Wallace was a resident of the Banks who had accumulated considerable land in the area and was fully acquainted with the peculiar navigation problems at Ocracoke Inlet. John Gray Blount was a former member of the Council of State, a representative to the General Assembly, partner in the prosperous firm of John Gray and Thomas Blount, Merchants, owner of extensive land holdings in the vicinity of Washington, and operator of a small fleet of vessels trading to the West Indies and Europe.

Blount, long concerned over the difficulty in shipping his cargoes to and from the Pamlico River, was interested primarily in having a facility at Ocracoke where his own vessels could exchange cargo—with his small scows, flats, and lighters operating between there and Washington in the sounds and rivers, while his larger vessels used Ocracoke as a base for ocean voyages. To a great extent, therefore, Blount was the silent partner, with Wallace residing on Shell Castle and taking active charge of the business.

They started out, probably as early as 1790, with the construction of wharves, a warehouse, a grist mill and windmill, and one or more residences. They soon added a small store and began branching out in all directions, operating a fishery, pretty well controlling pilotage in the inlet, and providing small boats as lighters for those vessels which had to cross over the swash to the sound.

Soon after the business was started, John Wallace acquired the unofficial title of "Governor of Shell Castle," and at times he conducted himself like a feudal prince of old. In 1792 one of the clerks wrote to Blount complaining that Wallace was bungling up the business for fair. Every time he relieved the clerk in the store, he not only failed to make notations about the sales but would pocket all of the money he took in and drink up most of the rum besides.

At about the same time another friend of Blount's, whose vessel was detained at the Castle for several days, stated in a letter: "I could not have formed any Idea of the Business to be done with advantage at your Castle, had I not been an Eye-witness of the Same." He suggested that the proprietors should acquire another lighter as soon as possible and urged them to establish a ship chandlery there. But Wallace and Blount were concerned, and justifiably so, as to what would happen to their trading center if a severe hurricane were to strike Ocracoke Inlet. Shell Castle was described by a contemporary as "a rock of oyster shells, half a mile in length and about sixty feet in width, dry at low water," * the inference being that it was not dry at high water.

The test came in August of 1795 when a severe hurricane struck that part of the coast. Wallace and Blount were elated when the storm "did hardly any damage" to their plant, and thereafter the Shell Castle facilities were expanded regularly. Additional warehouses and a lumber yard were added; new wharves were built; a large store and ship chandlery was completed in 1797, and so were extensive cisterns. A porpoise fishery was added, more lighters and other types of boats were bought, the residences were remodeled, and by 1800, when a tavern was constructed, the main building at Shell Castle was 300 feet long.

The Shell Castle Lighthouse was completed and lighted in 1798, and the following year Blount and Wallace sold the government nearby Beacon Island, and arrangements were made to build a fort there. In its issue of May 23, 1800, *The Newbern Gazette* printed government specifications for the Beacon Island structures, which included a one-and-a-half-story dwelling house, 38 feet long and 26 feet wide; "two other houses, each 26 feet by 12" and a "barracks, 60 feet long by 16 feet," also a story and a half in height. All the lumber was to be pure heart, free from sap, and judging from the specifications the buildings were designed to withstand a real bombardment, for the sills were to be 10 x 12 inches in diameter (roughly five times as big as the average house sills today), corner posts were 6 x 10, joists 9 x 4, and rafters 6 x 4. In addition contractors were asked to bid on the delivery to "The Port of Beacon Island" of "from one to three thousand bushels of good clean sifted flaked lime; and from one to six thousand bushels of good oyster shells" for the fort. There has long been a question as to whether this Beacon Island Fort was

* Viewing Shell Castle Island from the air 172 years after Jonathan Price wrote that passage, it would be difficult to describe it more accurately. Today there is no sign of the extensive Wallace-Blount installations.

actually constructed, but recent research has uncovered several maps of that period which show a fort there.

The Wallace–Blount business at Shell Castle continued to prosper, and by 1800 the census showed a total of twenty-five people living there, including five white males and fifteen slaves owned by Wallace. In addition to the lighthouse, an official United States port of entry was established at Shell Castle, and in early May, 1806, when William Tatham arrived at Ocracoke Inlet to begin an accurate survey of the coast between Cape Hatteras and Cape Lookout, "Governor Wallace" provided him and his associates with "a couple of private rooms" as office space. By that time Shell Castle was an important and established ingredient in North Carolina's growing maritime trade, for of all the canals proposed in the decade following the Revolution only the Dismal Swamp Canal had been constructed, and Ocracoke Inlet was still the main port of entry for a large part of North Carolina.

William Tatham, a close friend of Thomas Jefferson, James Madison, and other political leaders, was an inventor, surveyor, and scientist. He was widely travelled, well read, and the owner of what has been described as the largest collection of American maps then in existence. For four months in the summer and early fall of 1806 this inquisitive man examined the North Carolina coast, mainly from a whaleboat, and almost every place he looked he found something to interest him.

After sailing along the coast near Cape Lookout, for example, and taking bearings by several of the largest sand hills, he found on landing at the Cape that he was unable to distinguish the hills he had already picked out. He therefore put up signals along the shore—a barrel in vertical position on top of a pole at one point, a white pipe at a second point, colored flags at others—and then showed the Beaufort pilots how they could follow an exact course through the inlet by lining up these various markers.

He discovered that "European hydrographers have copied all the Inlets &c into the modern configurations although many of them do not now exist at all, or from their reported shiftings are not in the place where they originally existed."

On examining the inside of the Banks, Tatham observed that the sites of the former inlets were "generally demarked with what is commonly called a bald-bank without, and a slough within" and determined "from the position of many wrecks which I have examined, that it is not unusual for vessels coming in shore in a gale to seek a harbour by their Charts, and, as these bald beaches have still the appearance of inlets when at Sea, it is not to be wondered that a great many vessels run directly upon them."

He was impressed with the "two story houses, and comfortable living" he found in the wooded areas near Cape Hatteras. On examining Cedar Inlet, which had cut through Core Banks not many years before, he found "seven large fishing Canoes, and several seine employed" at a place where there had been "a high bank with Cedars growing on it." There were fisheries also at Cape Lookout, where the catch consisted primarily of porpoise and in the preceding year had produced 200 barrels of oil. This was carried on for the most part by the residents of Beaufort and Core Sound, for he reported that there were only four small houses at the Cape, "4 poor families, 2 very old men, 2 middle aged men & one Boy, who all subsist on the Fish they can catch." One of the Cape Lookout residents was a man named Samuel Guttery, who provided Tatham with considerable information and was described as being seventy-one years old "and remarkably active." In fact, Tatham stated that "the general appearance of the people on this coast bespeaks health & long life; and the existing instances of longevity are very frequent in comparison with the state of population."

William Tatham completed his survey of the coast in late September, 1806. "On Sunday, the 28th of September," he said, "—an ill fated day, ever to be remembered,—I put my baggage, instruments, &c. with my whole Summer's work, on board the *Governor Williams* Cutter, laying at anchor at Portsmouth, to be conveyed to Newbern for completing the service there," and "after breakfasting on board, I concluded to preceed the cutter to Newbern in the Whale Boat, in order to save time by preparing for her arrival." Tatham never saw his baggage, charts, instruments, and notes again, for a hurricane struck the Banks, the cutter was sunk, and when he rushed back to Ocracoke Inlet on October 3, "such was the scene of distress when I arrived, that we lay on our oars & counted thirty one wrecks in one single view around us."

One of the few things Tatham did not comment on at length was stock raising on the Banks, but this subject was adequately covered by another visitor to Portsmouth four years later, who said that "the Banks are justly valued for their advantages in raising stock; Horses, Cattle, Sheep, Goats &c. are raised in considerable numbers without the least expense or trouble to the proprietors more than that of marketing; The food in the Summer Season is mostly of a kind of Wyre grass & young Rushes that grow most luxuriantly—In the winter the rushes retain in a Considerable degree their verdue, & shelter from the inclemency of the weather a tender under growth, which together yield a subsistance for the stock."

This unidentified reporter found that a resident of Portsmouth, seven years earlier, had "of his own mark, Sheared 700 head of Sheep, had between two hundred & fifty, & three hundred head of cattle & near as many Horses." He reported that "the flesh of the beef & mutton is acknowledged by Epicures, to be vastly superior in point of sweetness to that raised on the Main"; that in his opinion Portsmouth Island, which he described as being twenty-five miles long, was overstocked; and that "much benefit would result from a diminution of one third the present number." This same visitor reported also that the soil on Portsmouth Island was not used for agricultural purposes other than "in Gardens & the raising of a few sweet potatoes, for the growth of which article, it appears to be peculiarly well adapted."

Formal religion and education, both relatively overlooked on the Banks during the colonial era, were subjects for thought and planning following the Revolution, and as early as 1783 a man described as "James Gamewell, Minister of the Gospel" was listed as purchasing a homesite in the Kitty Hawk section.

As for formal education, the 1806 survey of "Ocracock Bar" by Thomas Coles and Jonathan Price includes a drawing of a rather extensive two-story building on Portsmouth, surrounded by cedar trees, which is identified as "Academy"; and in a deed dated February 4, 1808, William Howard, Sr., of Ocracoke sold to "the subscribers of the school house on Ocracock," for ten dollars, a piece of land "lying where the school house now stans," with "a privilidge of geting wood for the benefit of sd school house . . . of any Kind Except live Oak & Cedar."

Those particular woods, live oak and cedar,* which Howard did not want cut for firewood, were used extensively in the Banks communities for boat construction. Large quantities were shipped across the sound for the same purpose, particularly to Beaufort, where in 1806 William Tatham described a family named Pigot, "several ingenious brothers, excellent ship-wrights," and said that five vessels were on the stocks when he was there. As early as 1810, however, it was reported that the supply of live oak and cedar on nearby Shackleford Banks was "by no means so abundant as it has been."

The census of 1810 showed forty people residing on Shell Castle, of which ten were white males, but the following year "Governor" John Wallace died, and soon afterwards John Mayo, an associate at Shell Castle who was named administrator of his estate, sold all his perishable property and hired out several of his slaves. The death of Wallace, combined with earlier storm damage, caused the decline of Shell Castle, and it is probable that its end as an important trading center came during the War of 1812 when the channel which served it began to shoal up.

When war broke out between the United States and Great Britain, the Banks once again provided protection against British raids on the mainland, as well as a base of operations for American privateers. One of the most successful of the privateer captains was Otway Burns, a native of Swansboro, who fitted out a fast Baltimore clipper which he named *Snap-Dragon*, armed with four 12-pound guns and a pivot gun. A fort—named Fort Hampton—had been constructed near the site of old Fort Dobbs on Bogue Banks just west of Beaufort Inlet in 1808, and Burns used that port as his main base, though he sometimes put in at Ocracoke. Ranging from Newfoundland to the Caribbean, the *Snap-Dragon* took a staggering toll of British shipping, in the first seven months alone capturing ten vessels, 250 prisoners, and cargo valued at approximately one million dollars.†

---

* This was red cedar, once virtually extinct on the Banks but now making a comeback. White cedar, or juniper, is sometimes found in swampy areas, and the live oak still thrives.

† Following the war Burns settled in Beaufort, represented Carteret County in the General Assembly for twelve years, and operated a shipbuilding business there. In 1842, his business no longer prospering, he moved to Portsmouth, where he lived until his death in 1850, serving part of that time as keeper of the Brant Island Shoals Lightboat in Pamlico Sound.

Though a British attack on the coast had been expected since the outbreak of hostilities, it did not materialize until the summer of 1813. At daybreak, July 12, the residents of Portsmouth, Ocracoke, and Shell Castle awoke to find a formidable British fleet anchored just off the Bar, including nine large war vessels. Barges soon put off from the ships—one observer counted nineteen barges, each carrying forty men —and when they entered the inlet they attacked two American privateers, the *Anaconda* and *Atlas*, and a revenue cutter, capturing the privateers and forcing the cutter to retreat up the sounds. Then the British troops landed at Portsmouth and Ocracoke, collected hundreds of cattle and sheep, and after five days on the Banks weighed anchor and sailed away, announcing before their departure that the entire coast of North Carolina was under blockade.

While all this was going on, the cutter reached New Bern and word spread quickly along the mainland that the Banks were in the hands of the British. In each town it was expected that the enemy would attack there next. Mrs. Thomas Blount, writing from the town of Washington to Mrs. Dorothy Payne Todd Madison, wife of the President, said: "We are in hourly expectation of the British coming up here. . . . I am so frightened that I scarce can write, the men flying to armes and the drums beating."

The British did not return, however, and when the war was over attention was once more turned to the subject of navigation aids along the coast. A lighthouse, long planned, was at last completed at Cape Lookout, and because the Ocracoke Inlet channel had moved, it was found necessary to provide a small light vessel in place of the Shell Castle Lighthouse. This was put in service in 1820 but was soon found inadequate, and in 1822 a permanent lighthouse was authorized for Ocracoke Island. The Ocracoke Lighthouse was completed in 1823, and except for minor alterations is the same structure in service there today.

In 1822 an appropriation was also made for placing buoys on the shoals off Cape Hatteras, but these were washed away in one of the first storms. In 1823 Congress appropriated $25,000 for "a light-vessel, not to be under two hundred and fifty tons" to guard Diamond Shoals off Cape Hatteras. This lightship was placed in service in the spring of 1825, drifted off her station that fall, was returned to the shoals the next year, and in August, 1827, broke loose in a hurricane and was wrecked near Ocracoke Inlet.*

Meanwhile, great public interest had been shown in the use of steamboats on inland water routes, and steamboat companies seemed to be springing up everywhere. One was formed by a group of North Carolinians who purchased the newly launched steamboat *Norfolk* and in 1818 put her in service between Elizabeth City and New Bern, but the operation was a failure and in 1820 the vessel was sold at auction. Other North Carolinians were greatly concerned over the failure of the state government to provide "internal improvements" which would make possible safe and reliable water transportation throughout the eastern part of North Carolina. The champion of this drive for internal improvements was Archibald D. Murphey, who envisioned an all-weather inland waterway from Chesapeake Bay through eastern North Carolina to Charleston, in addition to deep channels in all of the major rivers and stabilized inlets connecting with the Atlantic Ocean.

One of Murphey's specific projects was a survey to determine if navigation could be improved at Ocracoke by deepening the swash within the bar, and he emphasized the importance of this by mentioning that it had even been suggested that camels be used to take vessels across the swash. Above all, however, he was anxious to find out whether the leading engineers would consider feasible a plan he had devised for opening and stabilizing an outlet through the Banks to provide access from Albemarle Sound to the sea. Such an outlet had been considered in 1788 when there was talk of digging the "Raleigh Canal" near Nags Head, but Murphey's plan involved much more than just the digging of a canal.

Murphey had studied old maps and other documents and had learned not only that there had been an inlet opposite Roanoke Island in the early days of settlement, through which most of the Albemarle shipping had passed, but that the closing of old Roanoke Inlet had been accompanied by a widening and deepening of Croatan Sound, a connecting link between Albemarle Sound and Pamlico Sound. He reasoned, therefore, that Roanoke Inlet had been kept open by the

* Details of the harrowing experience of the captain, his wife, three daughters, and crewmen are recounted in David Stick, *Graveyard of the Atlantic* (Chapel Hill: The University of North Carolina Press, 1952), pp. 14-16.

force of the water coming down the Chowan and Roanoke rivers and Albemarle Sound to the sea but that this flow of water was somehow diverted to Croatan Sound, thus causing Roanoke Inlet to close. His conclusion was that if Croatan Sound could be blocked off and a canal dug near the site of old Roanoke Inlet, the waters from Albemarle Sound would once again pass out to sea through Roanoke Inlet and keep it open.

In 1820 an English engineer named Hamilton Fulton, hired by the Board of Internal Improvement at a salary almost double that of the governor of North Carolina, made a detailed survey which took him from May until September to complete, and his conclusion was that Murphey's plan would succeed.

"In order to open a communication between Albemarle sound and the sea near Nag's Head, and keep that communication permanently navigable," he said, "it will be necessary to cut off all connexion between Albemarle sound and Pamplico, by embankments across Croatan and Roanoke sounds." These embankments were to be built of stone. The one across Croatan Sound was to be three and one-quarter miles in length, extending from Pork Point, on the west side of Roanoke Island just below the present airport, to Fleetwoods Fishery, below Manns Harbor on the mainland. The one across Roanoke Sound was to be in almost the exact location of the present-day Roanoke Sound bridge, crossing one and one-quarter miles of open water and two small marsh islands. Both were to extend five feet above the normal height of the water and were to be fifteen feet wide at the top, with gently sloping sides.

As for the inlet itself, Fulton proposed locating it approximately a mile above the Roanoke Sound embankment and said "the sides of the new inlet must be protected by a facing of rough stone, from the bottom to 5 feet above high water, and not less than 10 feet thick. There must be, likewise, a facing of stone extend from each side of the inner end of the inlet for a quarter of a mile, in opposite directions along the shore of Roanoke Sound."

Practically everybody who read Fulton's plan over a period of the next twenty years or so seemed to approve of it, but his estimate of the cost was approximately two and one-third million dollars. Neither North Carolina nor the federal government was in a position to spend that much on it. Nonetheless, the public clamor for this outlet from

Albemarle Sound to the ocean at Nags Head was so persistent that at least six different surveys were authorized by one or the other of the governments in the years that followed, each ending with approval of the Murphey–Fulton plan but usually presenting possible alternatives, including one for a tidal lock, another for a canal through Roanoke Island, and a third for half-mile jetties into the ocean.

Meanwhile, at its session of 1827-28 the North Carolina General Assembly authorized the formation of the Ocracoke Navigation Company, with the right to improve the channels and then charge tolls to vessels passing through, but this never got beyond the authorization stage. Finally, in August, 1830, a special dredging machine designed by Lieutenant George Dutton of the U.S. Engineers was put to work there dredging out the channels.

Detailed drawings of Dutton's dredging machine, preserved in the National Archives, show it to have been approximately sixty-five feet long and propelled by steam-driven paddle wheels. The digging was done by means of buckets or scoops attached to a continuous conveyor belt that ran down through a special shaft in the hull of the vessel, the mechanism closely resembling the ditch-digging machines in use today. With this machine Dutton was able to dig a channel eight and one-half feet deep (below the water line), depositing the excavated sand on scows from which it was dumped on shoals half a mile or so away. After seven years of work, Flounder Slue, the main channel, was still filling up about as fast as the dredge could dig it, and the work was suspended. This project cost the government $133,732.40.

To make matters worse, Currituck Inlet had closed up once and for all in 1828, leaving Ocracoke as the only navigable inlet through the Banks above Beaufort, and maritime traffic was reaching new peaks. The census of 1840 listed 531 people at Ocracoke and 400 at Portsmouth, and that fall federal post offices—the first on the Banks—were established in both communities. Before that time a person with a letter to be delivered had to entrust it to a friend or to the captain of some ship going in the right general direction, and this applied even after the public mails had been established, for the early routes extended no closer to the Banks than Edenton and New Bern.

In 1842 the Committee on Commerce of the U.S. House of Representatives issued an interesting report. "Ocracoke Inlet," the report stated, "is the outlet for all the commerce of the State of North Carolina, from the ports of Newbern, Washington, Plymouth, Edenton, and Elizabeth City, and the whole extent of country for many miles around them;... more than two thirds of the exports of the State of North Carolina pass out to sea at this point." Figures kept for a full year showed that "one thousand four hundred sail of loaded vessels pass through the aforesaid inlet in the space of twelve months, bound to various ports," and because vessels were frequently detained at the inlet by adverse winds or tides, it was "not uncommon to see from thirty to sixty sail of vessels anchor in the roads at a time."

In such a vast accumulation of shipping there was inevitably a certain amount of sickness, and the question of what to do with sick seamen at Ocracoke Inlet was a matter of great concern for many years. At first the government entered into a contract with an individual to care for them at the rate of $1,500 annually, but later it became the responsibility of the port collector to secure room, board, and medical attention for any sick seamen in his district. For this he was authorized to pay "$3 a week for board, 25 cents per day for attendance... and apothecary rates for medicine."

In 1841 the Ocracoke Inlet collector, a man named S. Brown, wrote to Congressman William H. Worthington outlining the difficulties encountered under this system. He complained that masters of vessels, finding sick seamen on board and "fearing to take them to sea lest they should be quarantined at their ports of destination, will land them here regardless of consequences." Because most of the houses at Ocracoke and Portsmouth were small, "with but two rooms, and one story high (with very few exceptions,) and not any ways calculated to accommodate sick persons," Brown frequently had difficulty securing a place for the men to stay. "I have, on one occasion," he said, "having 17 sick seamen on my hands, been compelled to fit up a common boat-house as well as I could, and put part of them in that —a situation not at all calculated for a person in the best of health, much less to one laboring under severe bilious fever or some other dangerous disease. At another time I was under the necessity of procuring an old house built on a shell rock, two miles or more from any inhabitants, to accommodate several seamen thrown out here having small-pox; the inhabitants would not suffer them to be landed on either Ocracoke or Portsmouth Island."

Congressman Worthington promptly took up this cause and pushed through Congress legislation for a hospital at Ocracoke Inlet to accommodate all sick seamen in northeastern North Carolina, and in 1846 the hospital was built.

That same year, however, a September hurricane opened two new inlets through the Banks, the first located midway between Old Hatteras Inlet and the village of Hatteras, the second on Bodie Island. Both inlets continued to enlarge and were given names—Hatteras Inlet for the first, Oregon Inlet for the second—and much of the water which had been passing out through Ocracoke Inlet was diverted by the new cuts.

As early as 1837 plans had been made for constructing a lighthouse at Pea Island, north of Chicamacomico, but there was so much agitation to have the site moved further north to Bodie Island that nothing was done until 1848. In that year, however, the first of three Bodie Island lighthouses was built a short distance south of the newly-opened Oregon Inlet.

Though the first federal census had been taken in 1790, it was not until 1850 that the records were kept in a manner that would make possible a division of population in the various Banks communities, except at Ocracoke and Portsmouth. The figures for those two Banks islands show the following changes:

POPULATION

	1800	1810	1820	1830	1840	1850
Ocracoke	137	209	344	490	531	536
Portsmouth	246	387	382	411	400	505

FAMILIES

	1800	1810	1820	1830	1840	1850
Ocracoke	21	37	45	68	74	79
Portsmouth	27	47	38	51	53	71

The figures for all of the Banks and Roanoke Island as shown in the 1850 census are:

	RESIDENTS	SLAVES	TOTAL	FAMILIES
Portsmouth and Core Banks	388	117	505	71
Ocracoke Island	432	104	536	79
Buxton to Cape Hatteras	577	84	661	103
Kinnakeet	318		318	65
Chicamacomico	206		206	37
North Banks	546	30	576	102
Roanoke Island	442	168	610	88
TOTAL	2909	503	3412	545

The scarcity of accurate records, and even more so of miscellaneous private correspondence and other papers concerning the Banks, leads to the conclusion that the bulk of the residents have never bothered much with putting things down on paper or that the same elements of nature which had opened inlets, destroyed houses, sunk boats, and even uncovered graveyards have obliterated most of the documentary material too. Consequently it is difficult to find factual information on many phases of early Banks history, as the records of religious activity, social and recreational pursuits, and individual living conditions are exceptionally meagre.

Fortunately, however, some of the people who visited the Banks were so impressed with the unusual topography and the isolation of the residents that they have put down their observations for preservation. One of these was Edmund Ruffin, famous as an authority on agriculture and as an editor (and usually credited with firing the first shot in the Civil War, in the defense of Fort Sumter in 1861) whose *Sketches of Lower North Carolina*, published in 1861, contained a wealth of detail on Outer Banks conditions between 1856 and 1860.

Twice a year on Core Banks, in May and again in July, Ruffin said, the stock owners held a "horse-penning," at which time all of the horses on the island were corralled and the colts branded. Ruffin described the Core Banks horses as "of the dwarfish native breed" and said they were wild. A man could approach them within gunshot, "but he could not get much nearer, without alarming the herd, and causing them to flee for safety to the marshes, or across water, to which they take very freely, or to more remote distance on the sands." He attended one of the pennings and left the following description:

The "horse-pennings" are much attended, and are very interesting festivals for all the residents of the neighboring main-land. There are few adults, residing within a day's sailing of the horse-pen, that have not attended one or more of these exciting scenes. A strong enclosure, called the horse-pen, is made at a narrow part of the reef, and suitable in other respects for the purpose—with a connected strong fence, stretching quite across the reef. All of the many proprietors of the horses, and with many assistants, drive (in deer-hunters' phrase) from the remote extremities of the reef, and easily bring, and then encircle, all the horses to the fence and near to the pen.

There the drivers are reinforced by hundreds of volunteers from among the visitors and amateurs, and the circle is narrowed until all the horses are forced into the pen, where any of them may be caught and confined. Then the young colts, distinguished by being with their mothers, are marked by their owner's brand. All of the many persons who came to buy horses, and the proprietors who wish to capture and remove any for use, or subsequent sale, then make their selections. After the price is fixed, each selected animal is caught and haltered, and immediately subjected to a rider. This is not generally very difficult—or the difficulties and the consequent accidents and mishaps to the riders are only sufficient to increase the interest and fun of the scene, and the pleasure and triumph of the actors.

After the captured horse has been thrown, and sufficiently choked by the halter, he is suffered to rise, mounted by some bold and experienced rider and breaker, and forced into a neighboring creek, with a bottom of mud, stiff and deep enough to fatigue the horse, and to render him incapable of making more use of his feet than to struggle to avoid sinking too deep into the mire. Under these circumstances, he soon yields to his rider—and rarely afterwards does one resist.*

Ruffin said that "all of the horses in use on the reef, and on many of the nearest farms on the main-land, are of these previously wild 'banks ponies.'" He described them as "all of small size, with rough and shaggy coats, and long manes. They are generally ugly. Their hoofs, in many cases, grow to unusual lengths. They are capable of great endurance of labor and hardship, and live so roughly, that any others from abroad seldom live a year on such food and under such great exposure." By the same token, he said, when the Banks ponies were removed to the mainland, "away from the salt marshes, many die before learning to eat grain, or other strange provender" while "others injure, and some kill themselves, in struggling, and in vain efforts to break through the stables or enclosures in which they are subsequently confined." The horses fed "entirely on the coarse salt grasses of the marshes" and "supply their want of fresh water by pawing away the sand deep enough to reach the fresh water, which oozes

* Seasonal pennings continued to be events of primary importance on all parts of the Banks until state laws were passed forcing removal of the stock, beginning with the North Banks in the 1930's. As a boy, the author participated in the last all-day pennings on the open range on Bodie Island and has not been able to sit a horse comfortably since then.

into the excavation, and which reservoir serves for this use while it remains open."

Ruffin admitted that he was not an experienced hunter, but from residents of upper Currituck Sound he secured a detailed account of commercial hunting there and in nearby Virginia waters. This occupation was so extensively followed in the North Banks area that he described it as "a branch of industry of considerable importance for its amount of profit."

There are ducks of various kinds, of which the canvas-back is the most esteemed. There are also wild geese, and swans. Altogether they congregate in numbers exceeding all conception of any person who had not been informed. The shooting season continues through the winter. From description, I cannot imagine any other sport, of field or flood, that can be more likely to gratify a hardy sportsman—unless the certain and great success is such as, by the certainty, to take away much of the pleasure of such amusements. The returns in game killed and secured, through any certain time, to a skilled and patient and enduring gunner, are as sure as the profits of any ordinary labor of agriculture or trade, and far larger for the capital and labor employed.

Decoy ducks and geese are used to attract the flying flocks of wild ones. In most cases, the decoys are made of wood, painted to resemble the designed originals. In cases the decoys are living geese and ducks, or wild kinds tamed or confined; and these are tied by one foot so as to swim at the place where it is designed that the flocks shall settle on the water. The wooden decoys are of course anchored, so as to float in natural positions. A small and natural-looking "blind" or screen, made of a few bushes, with rushes, dry water-grass, &c., is constructed within gun-shot distance of the place where the decoys swim. Behind the "blind" the gunner hides himself, and remains perfectly silent and still, to await the arrival of the "raft" of wild ducks. They are often so numerous as entirely to cover acres of the surface of the water, so that the observer from the beach would see only ducks, and no water between them. These great collections are termed "rafts."

The gunner places his decoys, and takes his position, sometimes hours before daylight. It often happens that he waits, in the coldest weather, for hours before he gets his first shot. The flocks of birds, very frequently flying high over the position, are attracted to join any others they may see swimming, and so are apt to come over to the wooden decoys. But the living decoys seem to understand and enjoy the sport, and to join in it heartily. The decoy ducks loudly and frequently quack in full chorus, so as the more strongly to invite the unsuspecting victims of their treachery. The living decoy ducks are arranged in two rows, on the right and left of the gunner, and tied by lines long enough to allow each duck to swim to some distance on every side from its place of anchorage. It is said, that when the wild ducks are drawn to the place, and alight among and surround the decoys, the latter will speedily swim apart on either side, as far as their confining lines permit, from the central space, which is swept by deadly shot.

The most effective shots are made after the ducks are alarmed (designedly) and just as the whole raft takes wind. They then are far more exposed, and are killed, or crippled, in great numbers even by a single discharge. In some cases, the wild fowls continue to come so fast, that the gunners do not leave their blinds until near sunset, when they go to pick up and save the dead birds that have not floated off, too far, and are lost. As there is no tide, or current, there is not usually so much loss by this delay as might be supposed.

Ruffin talked with one man, the owner of extensive property on the sound shore, of whom he said:

The shooting (as a business) on his shores is done only by gunners hired by himself, and for his own profit, and who are paid a fixed price for every fowl delivered to him according to its kind, from the smallest or least prized species of ducks, to the rare and highly valued swan. Mr. B. has employed thirty gunners through a winter. He provides and charges for the ammunition they require, which they pay out of their wages. In this manner he is obliged to know accurately how much ammunition he gives out; and it may be presumed that the gunners do not waste it unnecessarily, at their own expense. Mr. B. in this manner, and for his own gunners and his own premises only, in one winter, used more than a ton of gunpowder, and shot in proportion, which was more than four tons, and forty-six thousand percussion caps.

A final observation by Ruffin, in which he quite accurately foretold a later development, was that the occupation of all of the residents of Portsmouth was connected with the vessels passing through the inlets. "Pilots, and sailors, or owners of vessels, make up the greater number of the heads of families and adult males—and the remainder are the few, who as shopkeepers, &c., are necessary to minister to the wants of the others. If Ocracoke Inlet should be closed by sand, (which is no improbable event,) the village of Portsmouth would disappear—or, (like Nagshead) remain only for its other use, as a summer retreat for transient visitors, sought for health and sea-bathing."

Even as this was written the newly-opened Hatteras Inlet was taking the trade away from Ocracoke Inlet, and in 1859, according to records kept by John W. Rolinson of Hatteras, fifty-six schooners from the West Indies, bound for Edenton, Elizabeth City, New Bern, Washington, and Plymouth, entered through Hatteras Inlet. Two years later, when the Civil War came to the Outer Banks, Hatteras had far surpassed Ocracoke as the most important inlet on the coast.

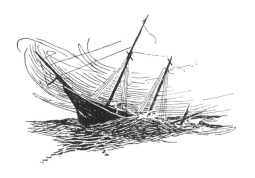

Watering Places

THE BELIEF was prevalent throughout eastern North Carolina in years gone by that the swamps and marshes covering so much of the low land west of the sounds gave off a poisonous vapor, known as miasma, which caused a fever that often proved fatal. The leading physicians concluded that miasma came from the vast quantities of decomposing animal and vegetable matter in the swamps and marshes, literally filling the air with the poisonous vapors during the hot summer months, particularly at night. Laymen called the resulting illness "chills and fevers"; the physician's name for it was "malaria."

Hundreds of slaves died of this fever each summer and many of their masters with them, and all the poor physicians could do was to dose the patients with ineffective medicine or draw out a bit of the polluted blood, and then suggest that it would be a good idea to leave the swamp country during the next miasma season.

Even when these outbreaks of malaria across the sounds were reaching epidemic proportions, however, the residents of the Banks were relatively free of it, and it was reasoned that immunity was brought on by regular breathing of the salt air and regular bathing in the salt water, just as other ailments were said to be cured by mineral baths. It was this, more than anything else, which resulted in the establishment of a popular "watering place" on the Banks opposite Roanoke Island, known as Nags Head.*

Long before Nags Head became popular—long before it got its peculiar name, in fact—outlanders had started taking advantage of the vacation opportunities on the Banks. There are recorded visits to Portsmouth and Ocracoke for the sea bathing as early as the 1750's and 1760's, and it seems probable that people started going to Beaufort for vacations about the same time. In 1795 Jonathan Price said of Ocracoke that "this healthy spot is in autumn the resort of many of the inhabitants of the main," and in 1810 a Beaufort resident named Jacob Henry, describing his home town in a letter to a friend, said the climate there was "highly favorable to health & Longevity & much benefit is experienced by those who make occasional excursions hither to obviate the debility." In addition, Henry said: "The Town is in every point of view a desirable situation for a summer residence. It is strictly a marine Village & those who are fond of the amusement connected with the water may here receive full gratification; whilst bathing in the Surf and walking on the beach are likely to recover the Valetudinarian."

Probably because Beaufort was already an established shipbuilding and commercial fishing center the resort business there was of only secondary importance. Nags Head, on the other hand, was specifically selected as a likely site for summer vacationing, and from the first has been predominantly a resort community. In the early 1830's a planter of Perquimans County is reported to have explored the various sections of the Banks with the view of finding a suitable place to build a summer residence where he and his family could escape the poisonous miasma vapors and the attendant fevers.

From a distance he was attracted to the veritable mountains of yellowish sand rising up from the low beach above old Roanoke Inlet, and when he sailed closer he saw smaller hills beside them, covered with a lush growth of live oak, cedar, and pine. He went ashore there, hiked through the woods, and found the houses of a few Banker fishermen, wreckers, and stockmen in the woods above the

* For many years the apostrophe was retained in the name "Nag's Head," though it has long since been dropped.

sand hills. He explored the beach and the sound shore and picked his house site overlooking the latter, near the tallest of the sand hills. But when he finally located the owner of the land and offered to buy a few acres, he was told that he would have to buy 200 acres, or nothing. So the Perquimans planter bought the 200 acres, paying the Banker fifty cents an acre for it, and later built his summer house there. When it was finished his neighbors came to visit in miasma season, and soon they, too, got the sand between their toes, breathed in the salt smell of the air, and decided that this was the place for them to escape the summer fevers. Within twelve or fifteen years, it was reported, the original Perquimans planter had "sold to others, who have followed his track, some seven hundred dollars worth, and has now a much larger portion of his possessions unoccupied."

The resort community grew so rapidly along the sound shore at Nags Head that by 1838 there was a definite need for some sort of a public house in which visitors could secure board and a place to sleep and where entertainment could be provided at night for the summer residents. According to a contemporary report a hotel site was selected by a carpenter in a valley between two of the larger dunes, midway between sound and ocean. He drew up plans for the structure and "induced a number of gentlemen to subscribe one hundred dollars each, to build the house." When completed this first Nags Head hotel was said to have had accommodations for 200 guests, including the original subscribers, each of whom was assigned a special room, with his name painted over the door.

From the outset, however, "the Hotel was indifferently kept," and as a result the stockholders soon sold out. During the 1840's the property changed hands several times. In 1849 an Elizabeth City man named Thomas White was the proprietor, and when a Norfolk man arrived from Elizabeth City one afternoon—"having accomplished the distance of 52 miles in just five hours . . . on board the fine, fast sailing packet schr. *Lizzie G. Russell*" (fare, $1.00 plus 25 cents for meals)— he found Mr. White in the Hotel tavern, which was "crowded to overflowing," and was informed that all rooms were taken.

This gentleman was fortunate enough to meet a friend who put him up at his own cottage, and that night at about 9 o'clock he was escorted to the ball room of the hotel for a dance. "There was in the room as fine a company as you have seen for many a day," he said,

"A company that would have done credit to any of the popular watering places in the country. I venture nothing in saying that the ladies were as pretty, and as tastefully dressed, as if they had just returned from the venders of fashion in Paris." He was impressed too, with the ability of the dancers—"Indeed we never saw a dance conducted with more regularity and ease"—and was "particularly delighted to see how perfectly familiar the little children (who have a night apart for them occasionally) are with the figures and time." During the evening he heard one old gentleman remark: "I'll be dog on'd if they can't dance before they are large enough to crack corn."

At about this same time a man named George Higby Throop spent two months at Nags Head as tutor to the children of a Bertie planter, and in 1850 his observations were published in a book called *Nag's Head, or Two Months among the "Bankers."* * Throop reported that one of the features distinguishing Nags Head from other summer resorts was that "a very large proportion of the visitors are actual residents in private dwellings" while "the majority of those who take up their quarters in the hotel are unmarried." He said that most of the summer cottages—the one in which he stayed had five apartments—were owned by "planters, merchants and professional men" who each summer transport their families to Nags Head "with the plainer and more common articles of household furniture, one or more horses, a cow, and such vehicles as are fitted for use on the sandy roads; a buggy sometimes, but oftener a cart. . . . One, two, three, sometimes half a dozen servants accompany the family. Indeed, I know one gentleman who has some sixty negroes (children and invalids for the most part) living here, not far from his own residence. It costs but little, if any more, to keep them here than it would to leave them at home."

Throop said that a number of families from a given area—Elizabeth City, Hertford, Edenton, or the Salmon River section, for example—would get together and charter a packet schooner to make regular trips "and for a stipulated sum carry them back and forth, and convey horses, furniture, provisions, and other freight during 'the season.' "

He mentioned a lovely little chapel, "a wooden structure, of small pretensions to architectural beauty," located "about a stone's throw

* The book was published under the pseudonym "Gregory Seaworthy." Richard S. Walser has done an outstanding job of identifying the author as Throop, his findings appearing in the *North Carolina Historical Review* for January, 1956.

from the hotel . . . in the centre of a diminutive forest of live-oaks."
This was approached "from several directions along paths shaded and
overhung by the evergreen foliage, and it is not until you are within
a very few yards of it that you are conscious of its existence."

As for amusements, Throop reported:

Gentlemen who are fond of fox hunting bring their horses and hounds,
and go galloping over the treacherous sands, much to the hazard of both
horse and rider. The disciples of Walton . . . can fish here without the aid
of the "Complete Angler," and catch an abundant supply. Then there
are excursions to the Fresh Ponds, to Roanoke Island, Kill Devil Hills,
and the New Inlet. Bathing occupies, too, and right pleasantly, many an
hour that might else hang heavily upon one's hands. Then there is the
drive on the beach, or if you prefer it, the walk; alone, in the
        "Society where none intrudes,
        By the deep sea,"
                        or with one or more companions
of your own choosing. Besides these, there is a bowling-alley, where the
boarders from the hotel and the residents from the hills meet at nine or
ten in the forenoon, and remain until the dinner hour. . . . Sometimes as
early as eight o'clock, but oftener at nine, or a later hour, the musician
makes his appearance [at the hotel]. The twang of the strings, even, as he
tunes it, is enough to call the little folks around him; and it is not long
before the ladies make their appearance; the sets are formed, and the long
drawn *Balance-All* gives the glow of pleasure to every face.

Of the few Bankers living in the woods north of the summer colony,
Throop knew "but little of their character and habits," but a doctor
friend told him that "many of them are miserably poor, and . . . have
singular prejudices concerning medicine." One day he asked a Negro
servant, Old Jack, what he thought of the Bankers.

"What do I think?" Jack replied. "I isn't got but one 'pinion 'bout
dat, Maussa Gregory; and dat is, dey is the triflin'est, laziest, most
unaccommodatin'——"

"Not *all* of them!" Gregory interrupted.

"No, Maussa," Jack replied. "Not exactly all on 'em; but when
you takes away all of de bad sort, de isn't any left."

Old Jack, whose duties included the purchasing of crabs and fish
from the Bankers, admittedly found them hard bargainers, and his
opinion may have been influenced by his business dealings. Certainly

there was little social intercourse in those days between the Bankers who were the permanent residents of Nags Head and the comparatively wealthy outlander planters who constituted the bulk of the summer colony. This seems to have been as much from the Bankers' choosing as from any aloofness on the part of the visitors, for Throop reported "they look jealously, I am told, upon strangers; but are clannish, and therefore honest and social among themselves."

From the very first "one of the features of Nags Head which a stranger would be most likely to remember," was "the gradual entombing of whole acres of live-oaks and pines by the gradual drifting of the restless sands across the beach." Much of the 200 acres bought by the original Perquimans planter in the early 1830's had, by 1849, been claimed by the drifting sand, and the sites of the three original resort houses were by then reduced to bare hills. Already, people were complaining that the resort was changing and that it was not like the old Nags Head. They longed for the days when Nags Head was "but another name for happiness; lovers walked on the sea-shore; Doctors practiced without fees," and it was "respectable to be seen in homespun."

In one way, however, Nags Head had not changed during those first twenty years or so, for in the late 1840's the packet schooners were still forced to anchor half a mile out in the sound because of the shallow water, and passengers and freight were transported to shore on scows, flats, and other small craft. Occasionally, some venturesome soul would take his high-wheeled cart a quarter of a mile or so into the sound in order to shorten the lighterage distance, but landing or embarking at Nags Head was, any way you looked at it, a laborious problem.

Though all of the early houses were built nearer the sound than the ocean, the summer visitors spent a good deal of time on the beach. J. W. Page of Merry Hill in Bertie County found a bottle on the beach September 22, 1849, which had been released at sea in order to chart currents off the coast. Page returned this to the Coast Survey, stating: "It was picked up opposite the residences of the summer visitors at that place, whose notice it could not long have escaped, as of the five or six hundred visitors a greater or less number are on the beach or bathing at all hours of the day."

In the winter of 1849-50 the Nags Head Hotel once again changed ownership, being purchased this time by A. J. Bateman of Edenton, who assured the residents of eastern North Carolina that "the Establishment will undergo not only a change of Manager, but also an entire alteration in the mode in which it will be conducted." Bateman planned to do extensive remodeling on the interior of the hotel, was "preparing to add a Piazza to the Sea-side of the building, which will materially enhance its comfort," and was stocking the tavern with "a great abundance of Ice" and "none but the best article" when it came to brandy, gin, and wines. Rates for the 1850 season were $20.00 a month for room and board ($18.00 for board alone), or $7.00 per week, or $1.50 per day, with "children under twelve years and servants half price."

After one season of operating the hotel Bateman finally discovered some of the reasons why his predecessors had failed to make a go of the business. "The chief objection heretofore to visiting Nags Head has been the difficulty of reaching it," he and his new partner, A. Riddick, announced in an advertisement in the *American Beacon* of Norfolk, March 29, 1851. Previously it had been necessary, as a visitor had discovered two years earlier, to make the trip from Norfolk by land, a route which proved to be "a very tedious and unpleasant one" as the larger part of the ride was along the beach, or by packet schooner from Elizabeth City. Bateman and Riddick now made arrangements for the steamer *A. H. Schultz* to make regular trips every Saturday from Franklin Station, Virginia, to Nags Head, returning Sunday night to make scheduled connections with the railroad cars enroute to Norfolk. This route took the Nags Head bound vacationist down the meandering Blackwater River in Virginia to the Chowan, thence to Albemarle Sound, and finally across Roanoke Sound to the destination. For this trip the fare was $2.50 plus meals.

Bateman and Riddick had other ideas. They had discovered that "the long and fatiguing walk through the sand to reach the beach for bathing or other purposes was also a source of much inconvenience," so they announced in July that they had begun the construction of a railroad, approximately one mile long, "from the Hotel to the Ocean, that persons preferring a ride to walking may be accommodated." The railroad was to be "provided with cars drawn by horses, which will be always in readiness for the use of visitors and a pleasant ride will be substituted for a fatiguing walk." In addition, they announced that "the hotel is being enlarged by the addition of 40 rooms," and "a good Band of Music" had been engaged to play nightly throughout the season.

These improvements to the facilities, coupled with an intensified advertising campaign by Bateman and Riddick, brought many new faces to Nags Head. In one five-day period in July the packet schooners *A. Riddick, Lizzie G. Russel, Mary Skinner, Wave, Mariah,* and *Sarah Porter* arrived at Nags Head with freight and passengers. In fact the *Riddick* and the *Russel* managed three round trips each to Elizabeth City during that time. In mid-August J. Parker, Jr., C. C. Robinson, and W. I. Hunter conducted a three-day excursion from Norfolk to Nags Head, via the Seaboard and Roanoke Railroad to Blackwater and the steamer *A. H. Schultz* from there to Nags Head, with the band of the *U.S.S. Pennsylvania* hired for the occasion. Among the large number of people listed as arriving at Nags Head on August 15 and 16 were residents of most of the communities in the Albemarle Sound area, a number from eastern Virginia, and others from Arkansas, Indiana, Alabama, Louisiana, and Maryland.

During that same month six Norfolk editors spent a week at Nags Head, and in the issue of August 25, 1851, the editor of the *American Beacon* devoted four full columns to his report on the visit. He was surprised to find so many "picturesque dwellings on the hills occupied by the intelligent and wealthy Carolinians, who for twenty years have regularly congregated at Nag's Head about the first of July, to pass in refined social intercourse, surrounded by the health reviving breezes of old Ocean, the season of the year that would expose them to sickness on their plantations." He found that many of the houses were "of considerable size, and are built in the fashion of regular homesteads with spacious porches and balconies and convenient out houses as if for permanent occupancy. They are generally situated on high hills with beautiful wooded sides commanding a magnificent prospect of the ocean and sound, and separated in many instances by most romantic vallies thickly covered with stunted pine and oak and luxuriant grape vines."

He was impressed, too, with "the most celebrated and remarkable ridge of sand called 'Jockey Ridge' of very great elevation, sharp and thickly wooded two thirds of its length and extending near to the ocean shore." He heard of Jockey Ridge "that the lady who may accompany you to its summit if not already a wife will shortly become yours" and was told the story of the disconsolate lover who had climbed to the top of the hill, intent on self destruction:

> But when he came near
> Beholding how steep
> The sides did appear
> And the bottom how deep;
> Though his suit was rejected
> He sadly reflected
> That a lover forsaken
> A new love may get;
> But a neck that's been broken
> Can never be set.

The editor reported that the hotel was "a spacious, comfortable, and highly respectable edifice with a Piazza extending all around and upper balconies on the front and rear. There are several comfortable adjuncts in the fashion of detached cabins, and the present liberal proprietors intend to increase the number. The Hotel contains a gallant little parlor which has already been dedicated to music and the graces by the lovliest of womankind—and quite a spacious ball room." He concluded these observations by stating that "the dining hall, although in the wrong place, is certainly the right place to find all that the lovers of good eating can desire, especially in the fish and crab line."

In 1852 the hotel owners, Bateman and Riddick, announced even more extensive improvements. "The Rail Road from the Hotel to the Ocean, a distance of 800 yards, is completed; a substantial Wharf has been built from the landing on the Sound shore, to an anchorage, a distance of half a mile. Plank Walks have been laid from the Sound to the Hotel, and from the Hotel to the Ocean. The rooms have been improved and several new ones added." The store connected with the hotel was to be operated under the personal supervision of Mr. Riddick, who had paid particular attention to the selection of "Family Groceries," while the bar had been rented to two "efficient Gentlemen."

Thus, in the early 1850's, with a hotel larger than any of those situated on the modern Nags Head beach area a hundred years later, with a railroad and boardwalks from the hotel to the ocean, and a new wharf extending half a mile out in the sound to deep water, Nags Head was "the place where the good farmers and others in the several Albemarle Sound counties seem to have agreed to meet by common consent, after their summer toil and the harvest is ended, to have a short season of family intercourse; for they meet as a large family."

Meanwhile, down at the lower end of the Banks near Beaufort, plans were being made for starting another community which was destined to rival Nags Head as a favorite vacation spot for North Carolinians. Extensive land holdings at Sheppards Point, on the mainland across the Newport River from Beaufort, had been purchased by former Governor John Motley Morehead and his associates, and in 1853 they announced plans for construction of the Atlantic and North Carolina Railroad from Goldsboro to that point and plans for the establishment there of "a great commercial city" which they called Morehead City.

By the spring of 1856 the *Newbern News* reported that a crew of 600 men with 130 horses was already employed in construction of the railroad. The first lots in the new city were offered for sale at public auction in November, 1857. Morehead expressed his confidence that "the interior communication by water and land must make this a great commercial city," and the people responded, buying $30,000 worth of lots at an average price of more than $200 each. Many of the lots were in Morehead City proper and the balance in another part of the development on Bogue Sound designated as "Carolina City." The railroad was completed in early 1858, and the official opening celebration was held for three days beginning April 29. More than 10,000 people visited the new city during this three-day period and within a month it was reported that every lot in Morehead City had been sold.

Early that fall a writer for the *Greensboro Patriot* rode over the Atlantic and North Carolina Railroad to Morehead City, inspected the facilities there, and made the following report to his readers:

Ever since our school-boy days we had heard of Beaufort Harbor, having learned from our geography that there was such a place away down on the sea-coast, many hundred miles distant, where the people lived on fish, and used oyster-shells as cups, with which to drink water out of old pine stumps; but we had never had an opportunity to visit that section of the country, and see for ourselves, whether or not the men of that region—as had been reported and believed in the interior by many—were scaly, had broad tails and thorny fins growing from their backs, the result of living on fish and diving after crabs. Well, we went, we saw, and we have returned. We saw not only the mighty ocean, the deepest inlet and the finest harbor on the Atlantic coast, south of Norfolk; but we found the waters covered over with vessels of various sizes and descriptions, freighted with produce of every section of the state, transporting it from our shores to distant parts of the world, and bringing in return whatever was most pleasant and desirable. We found there, also, an active, good looking, thriving and intelligent population, men of character and stability, who were putting forth all their energies to avail themselves of the many advantages and the great market facilities with which nature has so bountifully blessed them.

After that Morehead City continued to grow, and it became through the years not the great port city that Morehead had envisioned but a famous resort and watering place.

Meanwhile, at Nags Head, the hotel was sold at auction in 1856 to Dr. O. B. Savage of Gatesville, for $5,000, but there was no diminution in the popularity of the resort.

In 1859, when a writer-artist for *Harper's New Monthly Magazine* visited Nags Head he found the summer houses "all of the same model, scattered over the sand-hills." The railroad had been extended by then to the end of the wharf on which oxen pulled cars loaded with baggage. The hotel was not visible from the landing, he said, but it "came forward piecemeal as we mounted the shore. First a row of attic windows, then the second, and then the first story of a long, low building that threw out its arms, right and left, as if to welcome the wayfarer."

Wind-blown sand had piled up on all sides of the hotel, concealing it "till you come within a few yards," and to the *Harper's* correspondent "the elements obviously grudge it the narrow resting place it occupies." There were between 200 and 300 people when the correspondent arrived, and that night he found "the celebrated band in full squeak."

Even as this report appeared in print the threat of civil war was looming over the land, though a Nags Head visitor in 1860 said that "the denizens upon this sand bank know but little of the excitements and troubles in the busy world without." The Bankers were soon to learn, however, for in the fall of 1861 there was fighting at Hatteras Inlet and later at Chicamacomico. By January of 1862 the Confederate States Army had moved in on Nags Head, taking over the hotel as the command post of General Henry A. Wise who was in charge of the defenses of Roanoke Island. When the island fell, Wise and his staff were forced to retreat up the Banks, but before abandoning the post they set fire to the hotel so it could not be used by the enemy. Thirty years after the Perquimans planter had settled on Nags Head as the best possible summer retreat in which to escape the poisonous vapors of miasma, the place was once more deserted except for the small group of Bankers living up in the woods.*

* As soon as the war ended, however, the summer residents returned, and in August, 1867, the *Norfolk Journal* reported that Nags Head "has never been patronized more than during the past season." Soon after this a new hotel was constructed, some of the summer residents moved their cottages over to the ocean side, and from that day until this Nags Head has remained a popular resort.

Storms and Shipwrecks

Bʏ ᴛʜᴇ ᴛɪᴍᴇ the first outlanders began spending their summers at Nags Head in the 1830's, the sea lanes off the Outer Banks were in such constant use that it was not uncommon for the vacationists to see, from the top of Jockeys Ridge, as many as half a dozen vessels off the shore. On an average day dozens of ships would pass by, ships of all rigs and shapes and sizes, carrying cargo and passengers to and from most of the leading ports of the world. There were coastwise schooners and tiny sloops bound north with raw materials or returning south with merchandise; there were brigs loaded with coffee from South America or sugar and molasses from the West Indies; there were lumbering barques from Europe and the Gulf, fast sailing packets, great full-rigged ships, and naval craft of just about every conceivable type. For the sea lanes were the highways of the world, and route number one passed in close to shore along the Carolina Banks.

This, too, was the heyday of the new steam-packet; and these slim side-wheelers, luxuriously furnished and equipped with auxiliary sails, were breaking all records on the passenger runs in their attempt to take the trade away from the stage routes and newly-built railroads. Regular steam-packet schedules were maintained between most of the east coast ports, and so great was the competition that the traveller, bound north from Charleston for example, could take his pick of half a dozen packets in the course of a given week.

In clear weather, when the sea was calm and the wind was light, there was pleasant sailing off the Banks, with only the choppy waters beyond Cape Hatteras to contend with; but when the sky clouded over and the storms blew up, any vessel unfortunate enough to be caught there was in for the battle of her life.

Year after year as the coastwise traffic increased, the toll of wrecked vessels mounted, until the entire coast from the Virginia line to Beaufort Inlet was strewn with the remnants of lost vessels. Some conception of the extent of physical loss, of the suffering and drama and personal sacrifice, can be gained by studying the record of any of the severe storms which struck the Banks during that period. In late September, 1837, for example, a particularly violent hurricane known as "Racer's Storm" had blown up south of Jamaica, crossed Yucatán, struck the Gulf coast of Texas, curved to the east to move over Louisiana, Mississippi, Alabama, Georgia, and South Carolina, and arrived off the North Carolina coast on October 9.

Even before the heart of Racer's Storm had reached the Banks, it had caused the loss of one ship, the schooner *Cumberland*, which had struck on Core Banks on October 8 with the loss of her entire cargo of coffee, hides, and cigars being transported from Curaçao to New York.

Before the hurricane had passed, however, it was credited with sinking two more ships, seriously endangering a third, and taking something like ninety lives in one of the worst maritime disasters in Outer Banks history.

First of the three vessels to encounter the wrath of Racer's Storm was the brig *Enterprise*, of Warren, Rhode Island, which was within twenty miles of the Virginia Capes on a passage from Wilmington to Georgetown, D.C., when she was beaten back by the storm of October 8.

"I hauled offshore while the gale continued increasing," said Captain William Brayton. "On the 9th hove to under close reefed main topsail [and] at 8 P.M. a heavy sea boarded her and started the deck load. Sounded the pumps and found 3 feet of water in the hold; set both pumps to work and commenced heaving over deck load."

From then on Captain Brayton and his crew worked feverishly, cutting away the masts, hand bailing, and attempting to get up a small sail on the stump of one mast. The following morning, according to Captain Brayton, the *Enterprise* "got into the breakers running mast-head high and the wind blowing tremendously swept everything by the board, the vessel striking heavily in going through the breakers." Soon after she hit, the waves were washing over her to such an extent that the crew members were obliged to jump overboard and try to gain the shore through the breakers. In this attempt one seaman was lost, but the others reached the beach on Bodie Island.

At the same time the *Enterprise* was first encountering difficulty off the North Banks, two larger vessels, elegant steam-packets, were proceeding along the same coast in the face of the hurricane winds.

The steam-packet *Charleston*, with a full crew and passenger list, was enroute from Philadelphia to her home port in South Carolina; half a day's sail behind was the steam-packet *Home*, bound from New York to Charleston, the same run on which she had just recently broken all speed records.

The *Charleston* ran into the winds of Racer's Storm off the North Banks on Sunday afternoon, October 8. A passenger wrote in his diary: "The wind and swell of the sea have increased considerably.... The waves tower above the upper deck, while the gulf which yawns below seems as though it would swallow us up."

That night the vessel rounded Cape Hatteras, keeping well offshore, but the intensity of the winds increased, the waves seemed to grow even larger, and the passenger noted that "the boat rolls so that I have to hold on with one hand, while I write with the other."

At 2 A.M. the next day "a sea broke over the stern of the boat like an avalanche; the concussion was so great as to break in the bulk heads, and shatter the glass in some of the windows, far from where it struck. It broke the sky-lights in the after cabin, and pouring into it in torrents, made a clear sweep over the after deck, as deep as the bulwarks, nearly four feet. The violence of the sea lifted the deck fore and aft of the wheel house, making an opening about one inch wide the whole length of the boat, through which the water poured into her sponsons every time she shipped a sea, and she rolled like a log in the water."

The situation at that time was so acute that the Captain called on passengers and crewmen alike to bail for their lives. "Buckets were procured, and we commenced as fast as we could," the passenger's diary stated, "but every sea we shipped brought in vastly more than all of us could bail out, and the water soon became so deep as to run into the top of my boots." It became evident then that some other means had to be resorted to.

We took our mattresses and pillows and stuffed them into the lights, but the returning waves washed them out. We then barricaded them with settees, stationed men to hold them in; this succeeded in part, but no sooner was this accomplished, than a tremendous sea struck us on the other side, and opened a way for the water in there, and into the ladies' cabin.

The boat rolled and pitched so dreadfully that we could scarcely stand even when holding on, and she had shipped so much water that she leaned on the side towards the sea, exposing her to its full action. I stood bailing and handing water from the time it first broke into the cabin, until eight o'clock in the morning, wet to the skin, and nearly ready to sink with fatigue. As the day dawned, the storm raged more furiously, the billows rose as high as our smoke-pipe, and as they curled and broke, fell on us with amazing power. About 10 o'clock the engineer told us he thought the engine could not hold out much longer, she was so disarranged and injured by the heavy shocks of the sea. We knew that, as far as regarded outward means, this was our only hope of safety, and this intelligence was appalling. Our captain was collected and energetic, but the winds and waves laughed at the puny power of man, and defied all his efforts.

At half past ten, A.M., a sea of immense volume and force, struck our forward hatch, towered over the upper deck, and swept off all that was on it. It broke the iron bolts that supported the smoke pipe, stove in the bulwarks, tore up the iron sheathings of the engine, and made almost a wreck of the upper works. . . . It engulfed the fire under the boiler of the engine on that side, and lifted the machinery so as to permit the escape of a volume of steam and smoke, that nearly suffocated us, and so shifted the main shaft of the engine that it no longer worked true, but tore away the wood work, and almost destroyed its further usefulness. It swept all the rooms on both sides, and threw them open to every succeeding wave. The crash was awful, the boat trembled and quivered as though she was wrecked, and the big bell tolled with the shock, as though sounding the funeral knell of all on board. . . .

I never had an adequate idea of a storm before. The whole sea was white with foam, and the wind blew up the water in such quantities that the atmosphere was thick with it. Every sea stove in some new place;

windows and doors gave way with awful crashes, and several times the fires were nearly extinguished. The captain, who had stood at his post near the helm, now came down from the upper deck and told us the fury of the storm was such that he feared he could not save the vessel, that her upper works were fast becoming a wreck, and as soon as they went she would fill and sink; therefore, if it met with the approbation of the passengers, he would endeavor to run her ashore, in the hope of saving our lives.... He told us to continue working at the pumps and buckets, and in handing wood for the engines, as long as we could possibly stand; and to avoid giving way to improper excitement; that when the vessel should strike, we must make for the bow after the first sea had swept her decks. ... He then ordered the carpenter to be ready with the axe to cut away the mast the moment she should strike, and having made these arrangements, resumed his station at the helm. The boat now rolled more than ever, shipped nearly every sea that struck against her, and swung round from the shock, so as not to obey the helm. An almost constant stream of water swept the decks, and at every stroke of the sea the boat groaned, and the bell rung with a sound that seemed peculiarly awful.

We all procured ropes and fastened them around our bodies, for the purpose of lashing ourselves to the wreck, and having embraced each other, prepared to take our part in the work, and to meet the awful impending catastrophe.... As we were then 25 or 30 miles from shore, the captain's anxiety was, to put the boat in as soon as possible, before she became unmanageable, or began to sink. He steered for Cape Lookout, ... though he could not tell certainly where he was, but concluded it must be the nearest land, and that it would be as good a place to be wrecked on as any.

This was in the late afternoon of Monday, October 9, as the *Charleston*, half filled with water, most of her superstructure washed away, her engines laboring ineffectively, headed almost directly into the northerly winds in the attempt to reach shore before she sank.

Less than fifty miles to the eastward, meanwhile, almost exactly the same condition existed on the *Home*. An hour after leaving her New York berth at the start of the voyage, the *Home* had stranded on Romer Shoals and remained aground for five hours. Early the following morning, off the Virginia coast, a boiler pipe had broken, and Captain Carleton White of the *Home* had headed his vessel toward the safe harbor in Chesapeake Bay. The ship's engineers had repaired the broken pipe, and the mouth of Chesapeake Bay had been left far behind when, at about 9:00 A.M. Monday, the pipe had broken loose again, the engines had been stopped, and the *Home* had begun drifting toward a lea shore on the North Banks. Captain White had decided then to beach his vessel on the Banks, but just in time the pipe had been repaired again and the engines had been started. As she pulled offshore again, passing almost directly over Wimble Shoals off Chicamacomico, a giant wave struck her broadside, washing away much of the superstructure, and exposing all of the cabins on one side.

As had been the case on the *Charleston*, the passengers of the *Home* formed a bucket brigade, attempted to keep the water from gaining in her holds, and labored unceasingly as she rounded Cape Hatteras and turned on a more westerly course. The water at last reached such a depth that the fires in the boilers were extinguished, the engines stopped for good, and under sail alone by late afternoon on Monday, the captain of the *Home*, like the captain of the *Charleston*, was doing his best to beach his vessel on the Banks before she sank.

By 8:00 P.M. on Monday, had there been any way to compare the progress of the two vessels, it would have been obvious that, of the two, the *Home* had the better chance of reaching shore. Though she was proceeding under sail power alone, she had passed Cape Hatteras much closer to shore than had the *Charleston* and was at this time within only a few miles of the beach, while the *Charleston* was still a considerable distance at sea. Still, the crew and passengers on the *Charleston* worked desperately to reach the shore. "We all went to handing wood for the engine," the passenger wrote in his diary, "but so much had been washed over that we had hardly enough for three hours; the sea had broken down the doors and windows, &c., on deck, and we carefully collected these and put them in to keep up the fire. But with all the steam we could raise, we could not steer for shore, the wind and current carrying us down along shore, but not in towards it."

The situation on the *Charleston* seemed hopeless. Then "about 9 o'clock at night the sea began to be more calm, though the fury of the storm was not lessened, by which the captain was induced to believe that we had doubled the cape and were coming under its lee. By incessant exertions we now nearly cleared the hold and cabin of water, and as the boat shortly came into comparatively smooth water, the captain thought he would try to weather the night at anchor, thinking the storm might abate by morning. Some protested against this and insisted upon running on shore at once, but the captain would not ... and after running two hours, dropped two anchors."

On the *Home*, meanwhile, the efforts to reach shore were at almost that exact same time rewarded, for, as Captain White reported later, he was informed by the mate, Mr. Mathews, that the boats were all in readiness for launching, and then "we made the breakers on the starboard bow and ahead. Mr. Mathews was standing forward, and said, 'Off the starboard bow it looks like a good place.' ... I ordered Trost, the man at the helm, to port his helm; ... I then said to Trost, 'Mind yourself, stand clear of that wheel when she strikes, or she will be breaking your bones;' He answered, 'Yes, sir, I'll keep clear.' The boat immediately struck on the outer reef, slewed her head to the northward, the square sail caught aback, she heeled off shore, exposing the deck and upper houses to the full force of the sea. The squaresail halyards were let go, but the sail would not come down, as it was hard aback against the mast and rigging; it had previously been split, and was now blown to ribbons."

Aground at last, the thankful passengers rushed forward, huddled on the inshore side of the boat, seeking protection from the breaking sea. One of the boats had been smashed when the *Home* struck; a second was launched with several people on board, capsized when she hit the water, dumped her living cargo into the pounding surf; the third was launched too, landed right side up, pulled away from the wreck, then she too capsized. A survivor reported later that it was his opinion "not one of the individuals" in the lifeboats ever reached shore.

As well as could be determined the *Home* had struck at 10:00 P.M. The reef on which she grounded was approximately a quarter of a mile offshore, seven miles east of the village of Ocracoke and just about where old Hatteras Inlet had closed up a number of years before.

When the *Home* struck there were something like 135 persons on board, 90 passengers, and 45 crewmen. The *Home* was a new vessel, sleek and narrow, her cabins and furnishings designed with pride and care to provide every convenience for the passengers. This was only her third run, but the two previous trips had been completed in record time, and on the day before the departure from New York on this third voyage an editorial in the *New York Daily Express* had congratulated the owner, James P. Allaire, on the construction of such a fast and elegant vessel and had expressed the hope that he would make a fortune from its operation. In all the planning for the *Home*, however, Mr. Allaire had provided, in addition to the three lifeboats, only two life preservers, and these at the time of the stranding were taken over by two able-bodied men, leaving the large number of women and children with no protection of any kind.

Within minutes of the grounding, most of the people gathered on the land side had been washed overboard; then the forecastle deck broke loose and floated in toward shore, and less than an hour after the breakers had first been sighted, the *Home* had gone to pieces with only her boiler still standing above the water.

The wind had abated somewhat just before the vessel struck, but the hurricane-driven waves pounded with great force across the bar and churned in toward the beach, carrying with them pieces of wreckage, some with human beings lashed to them, and the lifeless bodies of others who had been washed from the wreck with nothing to hold to.

"The scene the next morning was too horrid to describe," one of the survivors said later. "The shore was lined with bodies constantly coming up. All hands were engaged in collecting them together. The survivors in groups, were nearly naked, and famished and exhausted. The few inhabitants appeared friendly, but many of the trunks that came on shore were empty."

One of the survivors, an elderly lady, had been washed up on the beach lashed to a settee; another, tied to a spar, had been pulled from the surf unconscious. Six or seven others, including Captain White, had drifted ashore on the forward part of the boat, which had broken loose soon after stranding. A count that morning showed that of the 135 persons on board the *Home* when she struck, approximately 90 had lost their lives.

The question which comes to mind immediately is this: if ninety lives were lost on the vessel which managed to reach shore, what was the fate of those on the *Charleston* who had been thwarted in a similar attempt? A Beaufort Inlet pilot could have provided the answer, for he went out that morning after the storm in response to the signal of a battered steam-packet laying just off the inlet. He found her to be the *Charleston* and learned that she had ridden out the storm the night before at anchor in the lee of Cape Lookout. Casualties? There were none; all passengers and crewmen had survived the ordeal.

On Ocracoke Island the survivors of the *Home* were provided shelter and clothing by the residents of the village, and as soon as possible they arranged passage to the mainland and from there to Charleston or their homes. Captain White remained on the island for three weeks, supervised the interment of the dead, and was present for a vendue of the few items which had been salvaged. Later, at Charleston, there were charges that Captain White had been drunk on the passage, that a passenger, Captain Salter, had been forced to take command in the last trying hours. For years after the grounding of the ship Captain White secured affidavits and statements in an attempt to prove that the charges were false, that a friend of Salter, a Captain Hill, had been mistaken for White by some of the passengers. Though the evidence he produced seemed conclusive, still the damage had been done, and some people chose always to believe the original unsubstantiated charges rather than the carefully documented refutation.

In New York, meanwhile, according to the Charleston *Southern Patriot*, October 23, "The intelligence of the loss of this boat . . . excited extraordinary sensation. The Bulletin rooms of the Newspaper offices were crowded by thousands of persons, and it was with difficulty that the demand for the details of the disaster could be met." The *New York Express* reported: "The loss of the *Home* with nearly a hundred passengers, has cast a gloom over Wall-street, as well as the whole city" and "has entered more closely into the business concerns of the city, than any similar loss ever experienced. There has almost been a pause in money, as well as other operations."

There were other results, more beneficial and far-reaching. Almost immediately after news of the wreck of the *Home* had been received, the owners of other steam-packets voluntarily equipped their vessels with large numbers of life preservers, and the following year Congress passed the so-called "Steamboat Act," which made it mandatory to provide life preservers for all passengers.

As so often happens following such a disaster, numerous suits were filed in the courts, and one of them—the Croom case—was not decided finally for thirty years. The Croom case resulted from the fact that a wealthy North Carolinian named Hardy Bryan Croom, his wife, two daughters, and young son had all perished in the wreck of the *Home*. Croom's brother tried to prove that the wife and children had died first; the mother of Mrs. Croom, on the other hand, attempted to prove that the young son was the last to die. If this were so, he had, technically, inherited his father's estate, and when the son died a few minutes later everything should have passed to his nearest relative, his maternal grandmother. The final decision of the case was to assume that all members of the family died simultaneously, since it was not proven conclusively that any one lived longer than the others. The Croom case has been recognized, according to D. H. Redfearn of Miami, Florida, who has made a detailed study of it, as "the outstanding case in the United States on the question of survivorship in a common calamity."

In all the contemporary reports and observations concerning the *Home*—including numerous newspaper articles and editorials, pamphlets, and court records—there seems to have been no inference that the disaster might have been prevented if Captain White, instead of trying to run for the beach, had remained at sea in an effort to ride out the storm. The direct comparison between the fate of the *Home*, on the one hand, and the *Charleston*, on the other, apparently was not mentioned at all.

Racer's Storm was just one of many hurricanes which have swept up the Atlantic coast leaving wrecked ships in its wake. Not typical, because there is no such thing as a typical storm or a typical shipwreck; but it is representative, at least, of what the mariners of old encountered, year after year, in the troubled waters off the Banks.*

* For detailed and authentic accounts of many other shipwrecks along the entire North Carolina coast, and information on more than 650 vessels totally lost there, see David Stick, *Graveyard of the Atlantic* (Chapel Hill: The University of North Carolina Press, 1952).

The Civil War

THE CONFEDERATE STATES OF AMERICA was formed in early February, 1861, and for the next three and one-half months North Carolina walked the tight-rope of neutrality, still a member of the United States of America, yet bound by tradition, geographical location, and economic necessity to the new confederation. In January, 1861, independent militia units had taken possession of Forts Johnston and Caswell on the Cape Fear River, but the state officials ordered them returned to the United States and the legislature censured the seizure. In late February the people of North Carolina went to the polls, voted down a proposal to call a special convention to consider secession, and reaffirmed their desire to remain in the Union. Meanwhile, Governor Ellis, a secessionist, began acquiring military supplies for the eventual use of the Confederacy if war actually came, and in this manner "he got in so many stores, that it was observed at the beginning of the war that North Carolina troops were the best armed, and best clothed men that passed through Richmond."

North Carolina did not formally secede until May 20, a month after Lincoln's call for troops "to suppress the rebellion," but before that time she had begun raising troops and acquiring a navy. This "North Carolina Navy," at the time it was turned over to the Confederate States, consisted of four vessels: the *Winslow*, a side-wheel steamer;

and the *Ellis*, the *Raleigh*, and the *Beaufort*, all small river boats, propeller-driven, and originally designed for canal use.

The *Winslow*, armed with a single 32-pound gun, was sent to Hatteras Inlet to attempt to capture enemy shipping moving along the coast. Under the command of Thomas M. Crossan, formerly of the United States Navy, she was remarkably successful in this operation, reportedly capturing and bringing into the inlet as prizes at least sixteen vessels, including the brigs *Hannah Butley*, *Gilvery*, and *Itasca*, all loaded with molasses; the bark *Lenwood*, with 6,000 bags of coffee; and the schooners *Lydia French*, *Gordon*, *Priscilla*, *Henry Nut*, and *Sea Witch*, carrying such diversified cargoes as fruit, mahogany, and salt.

While the *Winslow* was conducting these raids out of Hatteras Inlet, the three other vessels in the fleet—sometimes called "The Mosquito Fleet"—were confined to operations in the sounds and rivers. They were smaller than the *Winslow* and were all of similar design and size. Captain William H. Parker, who took over command of the *Beaufort* in the early fall of 1861, described her as being ninety-four feet long and seventeen feet wide, and carrying thirty-five officers and men. She was equipped with one 32-pound gun in her bow, her iron hull was a quarter of an inch thick, and Parker complained that "her magazine was just forward of the boiler, and both magazine and boiler were above the water line and exposed to shot."

It soon became obvious to the officials of the state and the Confederacy that these small vessels were not capable of preventing the enemy from taking over control of the inlets, and since loss of the inlets would render useless the basic supply route to much of the state, plans were made for defending them with shore fortifications.

Already there was one formidable work, Fort Macon, on the eastern point of Bogue Banks at Beaufort Inlet, and two others, Fort Johnston and Fort Caswell, were located near the mouth of the Cape Fear. All of these had been occupied by North Carolina troops immediately following secession. This still left the entire Outer Banks area unprotected, so plans were made immediately for the construction of forts at each of the inlets. A small one, Fort Oregon, was constructed on the south side of Oregon Inlet;* a second, Fort Ocracoke or Fort

---

* Since that time Oregon Inlet has moved to the south, and the site of Fort Oregon has long since eroded.

Morgan, was built on Beacon Island, just inside Ocracoke Inlet; * and two more, Fort Hatteras and Fort Clark, were begun on the east side of Hatteras Inlet.†

Since Hatteras Inlet was at that time the only inlet on the Outer Banks which could admit large ocean-going vessels, the fortifications there were of primary importance. Fort Hatteras, the principal fort, was located one-eighth of a mile from the inlet and commanded the channel. It was roughly square, approximately 250 feet wide, constructed of sand, and the outside was sheathed by two-inch planks driven into the ground, covered over with turfs of marsh grass which had been hauled in from the other side of Hatteras village. Fort Hatteras was armed with twelve smooth-bore 32-pound guns, suitable for controlling the channel in the nearby inlet but with comparatively short range. Four more of these were secured from Norfolk but were not mounted. A large ten-inch rifled gun, newly-made in Richmond, reached the fort in late August and was mounted, but the authorities had failed to provide ammunition for her.

Fort Clark, some three-quarters of a mile east of Fort Hatteras and nearer the ocean, was considerably smaller, mounting five of the 32-pounders and two smaller guns, one of them a hundred-year-old brass field piece. It was so located to provide a cross fire against the channel in the inlet.

Work on these fortifications was started in the early summer of 1861, at which time, according to Doctor Edward Warren who was temporarily stationed at Hatteras Inlet while the work was in progress, "the mosquitoes held possession of it by day and night. . . . While one laborer worked upon the fortifications another had to stand by him with a handful of brush to keep him from being devoured by them. The poor mules looked as if they had been drawn through key-holes and then attacked with eruptions of small-pox."

Despite the mosquitoes and the difficulty in securing proper guns and other equipment, by early fall all four of the forts were near enough completion to be manned. Small detachments of North Carolina troops were sent to Oregon Inlet and Ocracoke Inlet, and a larger

* Beacon Island, today, is little more than a dry shoal with no visible sign of the fort.
† Though Hatteras Inlet now is in approximately the same location as in 1861, the east point is flooded regularly, and the fort sites have washed away.

force—approximately 580 men, including eight companies of the Seventeenth North Carolina Regiment, under Colonel W. F. Martin, and some detachments of the Tenth North Carolina Artillery—was stationed at Hatteras Inlet.

As early as June, when work on the forts was just beginning, Union General Benjamin F. Butler "sent to the War Department a memorandum stating that there were works being built at Hatteras, and that it was being made a depot for the rebel privateers." He "suggested that something should be done to break it up" and was of the opinion that "a small expedition might achieve that purpose."

Though the Union Army command seems to have paid no attention to Butler's suggestion, it was not long before the Navy saw the wisdom of such an operation, and in the early fall began preparations for a movement against Hatteras Inlet. It evolved into a joint Army-Navy campaign, with Commodore Silas H. Stringham in charge of the naval forces and Butler commanding the troops. The object was to put a stop to the privateering raids being made so successfully from the inlet by the *Winslow* and other vessels which sometimes used it as a base and, at the same time, to cut off the important Confederate supply route from the sounds to the interior, the key of which was Hatteras Inlet. Specific orders to Stringham and Butler, therefore, called for them to capture the forts and then block up the inlet. "Certain schooners loaded with stone" were towed to the scene of the battle for the latter purpose.

The naval force assembled for this expedition consisted of only seven warships, but they included some of the finest in the service and altogether mounted a total of 143 guns. In addition to the flagship, the *Minnesota*, the vessels were the *Wabash, Susquehanna, Pawnee, Monticello, Harriet Lane* and *Cumberland*. The troops, 880 men from the Ninth and Twentieth New York Volunteers and detachments from the Union Coast Guard and the Second U.S. Artillery, were transported on the chartered steamers *Adelaide* and *George Peabody* and on the tug *Fanny*.

The fleet departed from Hampton Roads in midday, August 26, rounded Cape Hatteras the next morning, and arrived off Hatteras Inlet in the late afternoon. It developed that Daniel Campbell of Maine, who had been shipwrecked near the inlet in the spring and detained there as a prisoner, had effected his release and immediately reported to Admiral Stringham at Fort Monroe, providing considerable detailed information on the location and strength of the Hatteras Inlet defenses. When the fleet reached the inlet that evening, Stringham ordered the *Monticello* "to make a reconnoissance of the point, with a view to ascertain whether any important changes had taken place, and to look out a proper location for landing." She reported that the situation was essentially as represented previously by Campbell, and arrangements were made to begin the attack early the next morning as planned.

The plan of attack, worked out in detail before the departure from Fort Monroe, was a simple one. The vessels of the fleet were to open fire on Fort Clark while the troops effected a landing some three miles up the coast to the east at a point almost directly opposite the village of Hatteras. When the bombardment of Fort Clark had rendered her guns ineffective, the fire of the fleet was to be transferred to Fort Hatteras, and the troops were then to advance along the shore and take possession of Fort Clark. If Fort Hatteras still resisted, the troops were to join in the bombardment from the land side, using field pieces to be landed for that purpose and whatever guns could be made operative in the captured Fort Clark.

In actual operation the plan did not work out quite that way. Long before dawn that morning of August 28 the men were roused from their bunks and pallets, the sailors and marines on board the warships and the soldiers on the transports, and at sunrise there was a scene of almost frantic activity throughout the fleet. Four landing craft—two of them wooden flat-bottom fishing boats, the other two iron-hulled surfboats—were drawn up beside the transports and rapidly filled with troops and equipment, including two heavy field pieces. On the *Minnesota* a detachment of forty-five marines and twenty sailors who were picked gunners prepared to join the landing force. On the other warships the gun crews were making last minute inspections, checking fuses and ammunition, giving their guns a final and affectionate wipe-down with rags and swabs.

At 8:45 A.M. the *Wabash* and the *Cumberland* headed in toward Fort Clark, the *Minnesota* following; at the same time the transports stood in toward the wreck of the bark *Linwood* on the beach opposite the village, while the *Monticello, Pawnee,* and *Harriet Lane* prepared to cover the landing.

Promptly at 10 A.M. the *Wabash* and *Cumberland* opened fire on Fort Clark from long range, and the defenders responded, though the first fire of their smaller guns reached only half way to the attacking craft. Ten minutes later the *Minnesota* passed inside the other two, delivered her fire, then moved out to sea again, and shortly after that the *Susquehanna* joined in. From then on the bombardment continued steadily, each of the four vessels in turn passing inside the others to deliver a broadside, then moving out again, firing on the run, presenting an elusive target for the shore batteries even when they were within range and forcing the Confederate gunners to try to hit them "on the wing." This was a new maneuver in American naval warfare, this constant movement of attacking vessels, and it proved so effective that it was destined to be copied in numerous other battles to follow.

In contrast, the landing of troops through the surf, begun at 11:30 A.M., was encountering the greatest difficulties. A strong southerly wind was blowing in toward Hatteras that morning, and the surf was running high. One after another of the large landing craft came in through the surf, were caught in the breakers, and thrown up against the beach. The two wooden boats broke up as they landed, literally went to pieces in the surf, and the iron-hulled ones filled with water and sank. Even so a total of 319 soldiers, sailors, and marines managed to reach shore safely, without a single loss of life or serious injury; and more remarkable, the sailors somehow got the two heavy field pieces and the ammunition up on the beach. But that was the extent of it, for the men were soaked through, most of their powder was wet, and they were without adequate food, water, or supplies. The wind grew even stronger, the surf higher, and the transports moved out to sea with the remaining troops to wait for the blow to pass.

On the warships there was great concern for the safety of the troops. On the beach in front of Fort Clark a detachment of horse was suddenly seen, twenty or thirty of them, charging up the shore at top speed toward the landed troops, scattering a herd of cattle in their way. Quickly the gunners on the nearest warships directed their fire toward this unexpected threat, landed their shot instead in the very midst of the herd of cattle, and watched the horses veer off and scatter. Only then did they discover that this was no charge of Rebel

THE CIVIL WAR
ON THE
OUTER BANKS

South Mills

Winton

Elizabeth City

Albemarle Sound

Roanoke Island

Plymouth

Croatan Sound

Fort Oregon

Bodie Island Lighthouse

Washington

Live Oak Camp

Chicamacomico

Cape Hatteras Lighthouse

Pamlico Sound

Fort Hatteras

Fort Clarke

Newbern

Fort Morgan

Ocracoke Lighthouse

Morehead City   Beaufort

Fort Macon

Bogue Sound

Ocheltree '58

cavalry but the stampeding of a herd of terrified Hatteras beach ponies seeking safety from the bombardment.

The troops formed on the beach, put their field pieces in order, and attempted to dry out their clothes and ammunition. In the early afternoon a detachment of Confederates was seen leaving Fort Clark and heading up the beach toward the landing place; then they stopped, turned about, and returned to the fort again.

The relentless bombardment by the naval vessels continued, the return fire from Fort Clark growing more and more feeble, until it stopped altogether. Then, unexpectedly, in both forts, the Confederate flags were lowered, and men were seen running away from Fort Clark, across the narrow marsh causeway to Fort Hatteras, and to the sound shore beyond where several Confederate vessels were waiting. Immediately, Colonel Max Weber, in charge of the troops which had landed, ordered a detachment to take possession of Fort Clark. When the small group moved in, they found the fort deserted and raised the United States flag over the captured installation.

To all outward appearances the battle was over, and all that remained was for the Federal forces to take formal possession of Fort Hatteras. The *Cumberland,* no longer needed, was released by Commodore Stringham and headed out to sea. Meanwhile the *Monticello* entered the inlet, moving slowly to avoid the shoals, passed over the bar and into the channel, and was almost within hailing distance of Fort Hatteras when she was greeted by a broadside from the fort's guns. One shell ripped through her topsail, another tore away the davit holding her port waist boat, and others struck her hull, leaving gaping holes in her side. The *Monticello* returned the fire and was joined by the other warships as she tried to slip out of the trap. A *Boston Journal* correspondent aboard the flagship viewed this unexpected turn of events with alarm and reported that "for fifteen minutes a brisk fire was kept up, which it seemed probable would sink the vessel." But somehow she got turned around in the inlet without grounding or taking a fatal shot from the shore battery, passed quickly over the bar, and was soon safely out of range of the Fort Hatteras guns. In the confusion the fire from the other ships had not been aimed carefully, and many of the shells landed on Fort Clark, already held by a small detachment of Federal troops and with the United States flag flying over the parapets. So intense was this misguided fire that one man was seriously wounded, and the others—only twenty of them had gained access to the fort—were forced to abandon the installation, leaving their flag still flying.

The tides had changed there at Hatteras Inlet when darkness came, the tides of water and of battle. The wind had shifted, blowing even harder than before, and Commodore Stringham was forced to withdraw his vessels for fear of wrecking them on the dangerous coast. Meanwhile, the *Winslow*, the *Ellis*, and other Confederate vessels had come down the sound with reinforcements, including most of the garrison from Fort Morgan and Commodore Samuel Barron who was in charge of all Confederate naval defenses in Virginia and North Carolina. Commodore Barron was an experienced officer who had served for more than forty years in the United States Navy, and only six months earlier he had been in command of one of the very ships participating in the attack, the *Wabash*. Since the guns mounted on Fort Hatteras were for the most part former naval guns, Commodore Barron was asked to assume command of the fort for the remainder of the battle, and he immediately took personal charge. Most of the defenders, including the officers, were entirely without prior military experience. Captain Thomas Sparrow, who arrived that afternoon with the reinforcements from Ocracoke, said: "I had never before seen a shell explode. It was sometime before I got to understand the thing. I saw from time to time beautiful little puffs of white, silvery smoke hanging over the fort without at first being able to account for them. I soon learned to know that it was where a shell had burst in the air, leaving the smoke or gas behind it, while the fragments had descended on their mission of destruction."

Men were detailed first to repair damage to the fort and to the guns; then Barron called for troops to make a raid on Fort Clark, recapture that work, and move up the beach to annihilate the Federal troops still stranded there. It developed later that these were exactly the maneuvers which had been anticipated, both by the stranded troops and by the commanding officers on the fleet, and it was assumed by both that morning would find Fort Clark back in the hands of the Confederates, and the 319 soldiers, sailors, and marines under Colonel Weber either dead or captured. However, Commodore Barron could not convince the officers at Fort Hatteras of the importance of this movement,* so he finally called it off entirely and concentrated instead in preparing for the defense of Fort Hatteras.

By daybreak on August 29 the storm had abated and the vessels of the Federal fleet once more moved into position. They found the flag still flying over Fort Clark and the troops still safe on the beach. In addition, when they opened fire on Fort Hatteras, they were joined by the two field guns, operated by the naval gunners behind a temporary emplacement on shore, and even one of the guns from Fort Clark.

The calmer sea made it possible for Stringham's vessels to anchor just out of range of the Confederate guns. At first the fire fell short, then the gunners got the range, and as Major W. S. G. Andrews of the defending force said later, "For three hours and twenty minutes Fort Hatteras resisted a storm of shells perhaps more terrible than ever fell upon any other works." Soon after the bombardment began "the men of the channel battery were ordered to leave their guns and protect themselves as well as possible." During the height of the attack "the shower of shell . . . became literally tremendous, as we had falling into and immediately around the works not less, on an average, than ten each minute, and, the sea being smooth, the firing was remarkably accurate." Suddenly a shell scored a direct hit on the ventilator of the bombproof, starting a blazing fire in the room adjoining the magazine. Word immediately spread through the fort that the magazine was on fire, and Commodore Barron hastily called a council of officers "at which it was unanimously agreed that holding out longer could only result in greater loss of life, without the ability to damage our adversaries." He therefore "ordered a white flag to be shown."

Once more, Federal ships moved in toward Hatteras Inlet, the little tug *Fanny* in advance carrying the Union commander General Butler; then the transport *Adelaide* with all of the remaining troops on board, more than 500 of them; finally, the warship *Harriet Lane*.

As the *Fanny* came in to shore a messenger appeared with a brief note from Commodore Barron to General Butler: "Flag Officer Samuel Barron, C.S. Navy, offers to surrender Fort Hatteras, with all

---

* One of the defending officers said later: "Much of the disaster which occurred on Thursday may be attributed to the fact that we did not possess ourselves of Fort Clark by the bayonet that night. But wiser and older heads than mine thought otherwise."

the arms and munitions of war. The officers allowed to go out with side arms, and the men without arms to retire."

To this Butler promptly replied: "Benjamin F. Butler, Major-General United States Army, commanding, in reply to the communication of Samuel Barron, commanding forces at Fort Hatteras, cannot admit the terms proposed. The terms offered are these: Full capitulation, the officers and men to be treated as prisoners of war. No other terms admissible. Commanding officers to meet on board flagship *Minnesota*, to arrange details."

Despite the confident and demanding tone of this note, General Butler was greatly concerned. "This, to me, was a moment of the greatest anxiety," he said later. "The *Adelaide*, in carrying in the troops, at the moment that my terms of capitulation were under consideration by the enemy, had grounded upon the bar.... At the same time, the *Harriet Lane*, in attempting to enter the bar, had grounded, and remained fast; * both were under the guns of the fort.... By these accidents, a valuable ship of war and a transport steamer, with a large portion of my troops, were within the power of the enemy. I had demanded the strongest terms, which he was considering. He might refuse, and seeing our disadvantage, renew the action. But I determined to abate not a tittle of what I believed to be due to the dignity of the Government; not even to give an official title to the officer in command of the rebels."

There was a period of anxious waiting, and it was three quarters of an hour before a boat put off from shore. In the boat was Commodore Barron, accompanied by the two ranking Confederate Army officers, Colonel W. F. Martin and Major Andrews. They had agreed to Butler's terms and were taken in the *Fanny* to the *Minnesota*, where the formal articles of capitulation were signed.

According to the correspondent of the *New York Herald*, the Confederate officers were amazed, on reaching the *Minnesota*, to learn that Butler had complete information regarding their defenses "and inquired anxiously how he knew what they were doing the day before, and who was the person among them to whom signals had been made from the fleet." To this "the General simply replied that he possessed means of accurate information." He failed to inform them that his

* The *Harriet Lane*, given up for lost, was finally floated some days later.

aide, Lieutenant Fiske, had that morning gone through the surf to the beach and "returned in a similar manner to the fleet, bearing with him, in a package strapped on his shoulders, the official documents, letters and books of the commanding officers, which he had found in Fort Clark."

Losses in the two-day battle had been surprisingly light on both sides. No deaths had been reported to the Federal force, and the only serious injury was that received by the soldier who had been hit in the course of the misguided fire on Fort Clark. There were conflicting reports concerning Confederate losses, varying from four to fourteen killed and from twenty to forty-five wounded. A few of the Confederates had escaped on the *Winslow* and *Ellis*, but the majority of the defenders, more than 700 of them including Commodore Barron, were taken prisoner. "The rebels taken in these forts," it was later reported, "were carried to New York, and made to serve as a buncombe advertisement of the prowess and superiority of the North; for being a peculiarly small-sized, squalid and sickly looking lot, they were paraded from Annapolis to New York, in charge of a guard composed of the largest and most soldierly looking men that could be picked out."

Throughout the North, when news of the victory had been received, there was great rejoicing. "This was our first naval victory, indeed our first victory of any kind, and should not be forgotten," Admiral David D. Porter said later. "The Union cause was then in a depressed condition, owing to the reverses it had experienced. The moral effect of this affair was very great, as it gave us a foothold on Southern soil and possession of the Sounds of North Carolina . . . and ultimately proved one of the most important events of the war."

With Hatteras Inlet in his possession, General Butler took another quick look at the orders which had been given him by the War Department. As he admitted later, "My orders were distinctly to sink vessels there and abandon the place." Yet it appeared to General Butler that this was "a very important situation to be held for our own purposes. It was the opening to a great inland sea, running up 90 miles to Newbern, and so giving water communication up to Norfolk. It seemed to me that if we ever intended to operate in North Carolina and southern Virginia, we should operate by way of that inland sea." Accordingly, he consulted with Commodore Stringham and "determined to leave the troops and hold the fort." Since this was in direct violation of "express and written orders," he then proceeded to Washington "to be court-martialed, or to make such representations as I could to have my actions and doings sanctioned."

General Butler "reached the capital by way of Fortress Monroe and a special train from Annapolis, a little after midnight on the morning of Sunday the 1st of September, and immediately communicated the intelligence to members of the Cabinet. The news was then quickly spread by telegraph over the country." And in the days that followed, Butler's presumptuous action was upheld.

As for the Confederates, even as Commodore Barron was surrendering to the Union forces, a large body of reinforcements had been enroute to Hatteras Inlet. This was the Third Georgia Regiment, which had left Norfolk, August 27, the officers on the small steam tug *Junaluska* and the bulk of the troops on canal boats which were towed behind. This flotilla was intercepted in the sound on August 30 by a schooner carrying some of the officers who had escaped from Fort Hatteras, and the regiment was landed instead on Roanoke Island. "Here," according to Georgia Colonel Claiborne Snead, "these Georgians, just one day after the fall of Fort Hatteras, solitary and unaided, planted the Confederate flag... and from that day ... were continuously at work... building entrenchments and batteries... for the protection of the inland coast of North Carolina."

Meanwhile, the gunboat *Winslow*, having withstood the secondary fire of the Federal fleet at Hatteras Inlet for two days, had evacuated a number of the wounded from Fort Hatteras and proceeded with them to New Bern, while the gunboat *Ellis* escaped down the coast to Ocracoke Inlet. The North Carolina troops holding Fort Morgan on Beacon Island immediately spiked their guns on the arrival of the *Ellis* and set fire to the gun platforms in an attempt to destroy them. The *Ellis* then took on board the garrison of the fort, moved into the villages of Ocracoke and Portsmouth to pick up "the sad and weeping wives" of the officers who had been captured at Fort Hatteras, and headed up the Pamlico River to Washington.

Shortly after this the *Junaluska*, which had brought the Third Georgia Regiment from Norfolk to Roanoke Island, was ordered to Oregon Inlet "which was still held by its garrison." When the steamer arrived "a council was held and it was resolved to evacuate the place and remove the guns, &c. to Roanoke Island."

Thus, with the capture of Fort Hatteras, the Union forces had gained control of all three of the inlets which cut through the Banks, and the Confederates were forced to reorganize and form a secondary line of defense on Roanoke Island.

The force which General Butler had decided to leave to hold the Banks was approximately the same size as the Confederate garrison captured in Fort Hatteras. It consisted of detachments of the Ninth and Twentieth New York Volunteers and the Union Coast Guard, under command of Colonel Rush C. Hawkins, the warships *Pawnee* and *Monticello*, and the shallow-draft tug, *Fanny*.

No sooner had the decision been made to hold the forts, and the occupation force sent ashore, than difficulties were encountered. "Just before the squadron sailed," Colonel Hawkins said, "General Butler sent word on shore that the three schooners left by the enemy inside the inlet were loaded with provisions that could be used by the troops. An examination proved that the only food-materials were fruits from the West Indies, which were fast decaying.* For the next ten days the diet of the stranded soldiers consisted of black coffee, fresh fish, and a 'sheet-iron pancake' made of flour and salt-water. This diet was neither luxurious nor nutritious, and it produced unpleasant scorbutic results."

Within two weeks, however, an adequate supply line had been established between Newport News and Hatteras Inlet, and Hawkins' troops went about the business of repairing the forts and putting them in a better condition for defense. A detachment was sent to Ocracoke Inlet to make certain the fort there could not be reoccupied by the Confederates, and it was reported that several vessels—hulks loaded with stone—were sunk in the channel. The southwest face of Fort Hatteras was pushed outward in a point, thus commanding both the bar and the channel of Hatteras Inlet, and preparations were made for the installation of larger guns, 96-pound and 100-pound rifles and a 10-inch gun in place of the old 32-pounders. In mid-September reinforcements arrived (the remainder of the Twentieth Indiana Volunteers Regiment, under command of Colonel W. L. Brown, the seven other companies of Hawkins' Ninth New York Regiment, and

---

* In his official report, General Butler had made special mention of "the valuable aid of Capt. Haggerty, who was employed in visiting the prizes in the harbor while we were agreeing on the terms of capitulation."

a company of the First U.S. Artillery) practically doubling the strength of the garrison. In addition, the small Union gunboats *Putnam* and *Ceres* were assigned to temporary duty at the inlet.

At this point rumors began filtering through to Colonel Hawkins that the Confederates on Roanoke Island were planning to make an attack on Fort Hatteras. "In the latter days of September," Hawkins said, "information of the intended movement from Roanoke Island made immediate action necessary," and he dispatched Colonel Brown's Twentieth Indiana Regiment, some 600 men strong, to the north end of Hatteras Island with the intention of establishing a base at Chicamacomico. The troops embarked on the *Putnam* and *Ceres* and left Hatteras Inlet on September 29, reaching the destination without incident, and set up a field camp at Chicamacomico which they called Live Oak Camp. Two days later Hawkins dispatched the tug *Fanny* to Chicamacomico with supplies for the regiment, including "250 Sawyer's shells, 75,000 canister shot, 1,000 overcoats, 1,000 dress coats, 1,000 pairs of pantaloons, and 1,000 pairs of shoes."

Somewhere between Roanoke Island and Hatteras Inlet, it now developed, somebody was giving out false information to one or the other, and possibly to both, of the military commanders in the North Carolina sounds. Just two days after Colonel Hawkins had sent half of his garrison north to Chicamacomico to forestall a supposed Confederate attack on Hatteras Island, the senior Confederate officer on Roanoke Island, Colonel A. R. Wright, having learned that a Federal gunboat was in the Chicamacomico area, "determined at once to intercept and capture her, and if possible to learn the intentions of the enemy, who were evidently meditating some hostile movement upon his position."

Neither Hawkins, the Union commander at Hatteras Inlet, nor Wright, the Confederate commander at Roanoke Island, it was discovered later, had any intention at that time of making any movements against the enemy. But both were so concerned about their defenses that they converged on Chicamacomico, each to thwart the "offensive moves" of the other, and the result was about as confused an engagement as can be imagined.

It began with Colonel Wright and the Confederate naval commander, Commodore W. F. Lynch, preparing a fleet to attack the gunboats. The *Winslow* and the *Ellis* had not yet reported to Roanoke

Island, the *Beaufort* was undergoing repairs at New Bern, and the vessels of the "Mosquito Fleet" in Commodore Lynch's command included only one, the *Raleigh*, with any sort of armament. Consequently, "a long navy thirty-two pounder which had been recently rifled and reinforced with heavy steel rings in the navy yard at Portsmouth," and just lately mounted on one of the partially finished fortifications on Roanoke Island, was transferred to the *Curlew*, described as "a large side-wheel steamer, formerly used as a passenger boat on the Albemarle Sound." The gun was mounted temporarily on a pivot on the bow of the *Curlew*, and since Lynch had neither sailors nor gunners to man his fleet, crews were picked from the ranks of the Third Georgia Infantry regiment. The gunners selected had "practiced for a few days with the guns in the fort," but their practicing had never reached the firing stage; in fact, none of them "had ever seen a cannon discharged, and . . . few of them had ever been on shipboard."

Thus staffed and armed, Commodore Lynch went forth to battle with the *Junaluska* and *Raleigh* supporting his new warship, the *Curlew*. In the sound off Chicamacomico they encountered the *Fanny*, armed with two rifled guns, and "a brisk fire was opened which was promptly responded to." The battle lasted for approximately fifteen minutes, at which time "one shell exploded on the deck of the *Fanny*" (Confederate version) or "The *Fanny* got aground" (Federal version), and she was captured, together with forty-three soldiers and her crew, plus the valuable cargo listed as being worth approximately $150,000.

Historians have since determined that this was "the first capture of an armed vessel during the war," and insofar as the great bulk of the Confederates were concerned "it dispelled the gloom of recent disasters." But when the Confederate commanders on Roanoke Island interrogated the prisoners they had taken on the *Fanny* and learned that a large Federal force already was encamped at Chicamacomico, some of the old gloom returned.

"The situation of the Confederates was alarming," Colonel Snead said later. "It was evident that the new position taken by the enemy was intended as a base of operations . . . from which to assail Roanoke Island and capture the small garrison thereon."

As so often happened there had been exaggerated reports of the size of the Federal force in the vicinity—it was generally assumed by the

Confederates to be five times larger than it actually was—so that the commanding officer, Colonel Wright, "seeing that a crisis was near at hand, and fully appreciating the danger of being isolated and attacked at a disadvantage, determined at once to move forward and strike the first blow."

The plan, as worked out by Colonel Wright and Commodore Lynch, was for the "Mosquito Fleet" to transport all of the available troops to Chicamacomico, where the Third Georgia Regiment would land on the Banks above Brown's Indianans, and Colonel Shaw's North Carolina Regiment would land below them, thus cutting off all avenues of escape. Once the Indiana regiment was disposed of, part of the land forces would proceed down the Banks to destroy the Federal lighthouse at Cape Hatteras, while the remainder, with the vessels of the fleet, would attack and attempt to recapture forts Hatteras and Clark.

It took the Confederates four days to unload the *Fanny* and to prepare the vessels and troops at Roanoke Island for the expedition to Chicamacomico. "At one o'clock on the morning of the 5th of October," Colonel Snead reported, the two regiments "were embarked on the steamers *Curlew, Raleigh, Junaluska, Fanny, Empire,* and *Cotton Plant.* Passing through Croatan Sound into and down Pamlico Sound, the little fleet arrived off Chicamacomico, and about three miles therefrom, just after sunrise. All the vessels were of too deep a draft to get nearer this point of the island, except the *Cotton Plant,* which was enabled to advance a mile further on."

Out there in the shallow sound two miles from Chicamacomico that morning, three companies of Georgia infantry and one of artillery, with two six-pound boat howitzers, slipped overboard from the *Cotton Plant* and "proceeded towards the shore, the officers and men wading in water up to their middles for three fourths of a mile, and opening a rapid fire upon the enemy, who stood in line of battle on the beach."

The Federal defenders would seem to have had a decided advantage at that point, able to pick off the Confederates one by one as they waded in toward shore, but by then other vessels of the "Mosquito Fleet" had moved off toward the south in an obvious attempt at an encircling movement. For this reason the Indiana troops abandoned their position and "began a retreat, moving hastily and in great disorder towards Fort Hatteras" some thirty-five miles down the Banks.

As soon as they reached shore the Georgia troops took out after the fleeing Indiana regiment and were soon joined by reinforcements who landed in scows and small boats. This was the beginning of what was aptly referred to later as the "Chicamacomico Races." *

The chase down the Banks was begun about 9:00 A.M. and was described as "a march I shall never forget" by one of the fleeing Indiana soldiers.

The sun was shining on the white sand of the beach, heating the air as if it were a furnace. The first ten miles was terrible. No water, the men unused to long marches, the sand heavy, their feet sinking into it at every step. As the regiment pushed along, man after man would stagger from the ranks and fall upon the hot sand. Looking back, I saw our Colonel trudging along with his men, having given up his horse to a sick soldier. But the most sorrowful sight of all was the Islanders leaving their homes from fear of the enemy. They could be seen in groups, sometimes with a little cart carrying their provisions, but mostly with nothing, fleeing for dear life; mothers carrying their babes, fathers leading along the boys, grandfathers and grandmothers straggling along from homes they had left behind. Relying on our protection, they had been our friends, but in an evil hour we had been compelled to leave them.

Throughout the morning and into the afternoon the Federal troops toiled on, followed closely by the Georgians. "Hunger was nothing in comparison with thirst," the Indiana soldier said. "It was maddening. The sea rolling at our feet and nothing to drink. I started to take a scout to watch the movements of the enemy's vessels. I skirted the Sound for some ten miles. In every clump of bushes I would find men utterly exhausted. The enemy's vessels were now nearly opposite, steaming down the Sound to cut off our retreat. I would tell them this, but they would say, 'they did not care, they would die there,' so utterly hopeless did they seem."

By late afternoon the Confederate fleet, having passed well to the south of the retreating Federal troops, attempted to move in and land the North Carolina regiment, but the vessels grounded far out in the sound, and the troops were unable to reach the shore. While they

---

* The land forces were almost evenly matched in numbers, the Confederates having between 500 and 700 men, the Federals about 600. The commanders of each force claimed, however, that the enemy outnumbered them more than two to one.

were in this condition the fleeing soldiers moved over to the ocean side and "silently stole along, the roar of the surf drowning the footsteps of the men and the commands of the officers, yet every little while we would watch, expecting to see the flash of the enemy's cannon, or hear the report of the bursting shell in our little band."

Finally, at midnight, the Federal troops reached the Cape Hatteras lighthouse. "Here," the Indiana soldier said, "we found water, and using the lighthouse as a fort, we encamped for the night, and woke up next morning feeling like sand-crabs, and ready, like them, to go into our holes, could we find them."

Meanwhile, the men of the Third Georgia Regiment, confident that the escape would soon be blocked by the projected landing of Colonel Shaw's North Carolinians, had pursued the fleeing Federals throughout the day, hauling the two heavy howitzers with them through the deep sand. Occasionally stragglers were encountered, and several who offered resistance were killed or wounded, while about forty others were taken prisoner.

The Georgians halted for the night on the beach between Kinnakeet and the lighthouse, and the next morning, "learning that Col. Shaw had not effected a landing at the point where he was expected to intercept the enemy, orders were given to countermarch back to Chicamacomico."

At about this same time the Ninth New York Regiment, hurrying up from Fort Hatteras to reinforce the Federal force, joined the Indiana troops at the lighthouse, then took out after the now retreating Confederates. Colonel Snead, who was commanding the Confederate Light Guards, described the retreat in these words: "At about one o'clock, just after the Third Georgia regiment had emerged from the grove of Kinakeet upon a long, barren sand beach, . . . the U.S. steamer *Monticello* hove in sight on the southeast, hugging the shore closely, which she could safely do in the waters of this particular locality. When within range she opened with round shot, following the fire up with shell, grapeshot and canister, moving in close proximity and at an even pace with the Confederates, and keeping up a furious cannonade till the shades of evening closed the scene. Fortunately a rough sea, causing her to career alternately from side to side, prevented precision in the aim of her guns; and every man who started in the pursuit from Chicamacomico returned in safety, except a member of the Governor Guards, who died from exhaustion." *

Thus the Chicamacomico Races ended, with the Confederate troops embarking on their gunboats and returning to Roanoke Island, while the Indiana and New York regiments abandoned their temporary base at Chicamacomico and returned again to Fort Hatteras. Undoubtedly both sides were convinced that they had successfully foiled a major offensive movement of the enemy.

With most of the Banks and the lower sounds in the firm possession of the United States forces, and with Roanoke Island and the upper sounds held by the Confederacy, it became more and more apparent as the fall of 1861 wore on that a major battle for the control of northeastern Carolina would almost inevitably result. There also seemed little question that the scene of this battle would be the Confederate stronghold of Roanoke Island.

Roanoke Island, then as now, was high on the north end and low and marshy toward the south. The basic change in the geographic situation of the island since the Civil War is that the extensive string of low islands in Croatan Sound, stretching from the lower end of Roanoke to the mainland and known as "Roanoke Marshes," have for the most part washed away.

In 1861 a Federal lighthouse, built on pilings, was situated on one of the larger marsh islands near the middle of the sound. A good but narrow channel—one observer said it was only 200 yards wide—cut through the marshes to the west connecting Croatan and Roanoke sounds.†

When the Confederates began to reinforce Roanoke Island after the fall of Hatteras Inlet, they had to decide on one of two entirely different means of defense. The first was to attempt to control the narrow channel through the marshes by building forts or batteries on the low terrain on the south end of the island and on the mainland

* The Federal report on the results of the *Monticello*'s fire, on the other hand, claimed that "several officers were killed, and the shore for a distance of four miles was strewn with killed and wounded."

† There is a recurrent story on Roanoke Island that Croatan Sound is of recent formation and that the grandparents of people living there today were able to walk across the marshes from Roanoke Island to the mainland simply by placing a fence post across the channel. If so, it must have been a mighty long fence post, for Croatan Sound is shown as a large body of water on all of the early survey charts, and large sailing vessels have been passing through that channel from early colonial times.

opposite, possibly even on the marsh islands themselves. The second, obviously presenting less of a construction problem, was to let the enemy ships pass through the marshes and then try to stop them on the broad northern reaches of Croatan Sound. The Confederate engineers chose the easier course.

Having decided not to take advantage of the narrow natural channel through the marshes, however, they devised a plan for the creation of a similar but artificial bottleneck at the northern end of the sound. For this purpose they drove a line of heavy pilings across the sound, at intervals sank old vessels filled with sand, and left only a narrow opening through which ships could pass. At the western end of this obstruction, Redstone Point on the mainland, they sank an old canal boat in the mud and mounted eight guns on her deck to form a battery which they called Fort Forrest. At the eastern end, on Roanoke Island, they built three forts: a 12-gun emplacement named Fort Huger, north of the line of pilings and sunken vessels, at Weir Point (the eastern terminus of the new Croatan Sound Bridge); a small four-gun battery named Fort Blanchard about half a mile to the south; and an eight-gun fort on Pork Point just below the line of obstructions, named Fort Bartow, which could not be seen from the water. In addition, just in case the Union commander decided to send some small boats up Roanoke Sound to attack the island from the other side, they erected a two-gun battery at a place called Midgett's Hammock, just below Ballast Point on the south side of Shallowbag Bay.

All avenues of attack were therefore effectively blocked, except for the possibility of an approach by land forces from the south end of the island. In the middle of Roanoke Island, however, there was a vast morass with marshes along the shore and deep cypress swamps between, and only a single narrow causeway cut through this morass to connect the north end with the south. Though there seemed to be little chance that an enemy would attack from that direction the defenders took no chances, constructing a fortification completely across the causeway, a three-gun emplacement which they named Fort Russell.

Meanwhile, in early October, Colonel Ambrose Burnside of the United States Army casually mentioned to one of his superiors a plan he had been thinking of for some time. Within a few days he "was summoned to go to Washington, where in the presence of the President, Secretary Seward, General McClellan and Commodore Goldsborough" he outlined his plan for the organization of "a division of from 12,000 to 15,000 men, mainly from States bordering on the Northern sea-coast, many of whom would be familiar with the coasting trade ... and to fit out a fleet of light-draught steamers, sailing vessels, and barges ... with a view to establishing lodgments on the Southern coast."

By October 23 this plan had been formally approved, Colonel Burnside had been promoted to the rank of General, headquarters for the new division had been established at Annapolis, Maryland, and Burnside himself was scouring the seacoast areas of New England for the men and vessels he needed.

The formation of an expedition of this kind practically at the back door to the national capital naturally caused a great amount of speculation, but the utmost secrecy was maintained as to the destination of the force. In early January, after the division had been formed and was in the process of departing from Annapolis, a prominent "public man" approached President Lincoln and "almost demanded that the President should tell him" where Burnside's force was going. Finally Lincoln said to him:

"I will tell you in great confidence where they are going, if you will promise not to speak of it to anyone."

The promise was quickly given, and Lincoln said:

"Well, now, my friend, the expedition is going to sea."

It was not long after this that the expedition did go to sea, leaving Annapolis on January 9, 1862, making a brief stop at Fort Monroe, and finally setting sail from there on the night of January 11. Even the captains of the ships did not know where they were bound until late that night when the sealed orders were opened off Cape Henry. The immediate destination, they learned, was Hatteras Inlet; after that, Roanoke Island.

Many people who saw this Burnside expedition at Annapolis or as it passed down the Potomac River and Chesapeake Bay, not having the slightest idea where it was bound, nonetheless expressed the opinion that it would never get there. Even General Burnside admitted that it was "a motley fleet," but he seemed to take pleasure in describing how it had been formed.

"North River barges and propellers," he said, "had been strengthened from deck to keelson by heavy oak planks, and water-tight compartments had been built in them; they were so arranged that parapets of sand-bags or bales of hay could be built upon their decks, and each one carried from four to six guns. Sailing vessels, formerly belonging to the coasting trade, had been fitted up in the same manner. Several large passenger steamers, which were guaranteed to draw less than eight feet of water, together with tug and ferry boats, served to make up the fleet." In addition, "light-draught sailing vessels were also added" to transport rafts, scows and extra stores, and "coal and water vessels were chartered in Baltimore."

General Burnside, aware of "the great criticism which had been made as to the unseaworthiness of the vessels of the fleet," took for his headquarters ship the smallest vessel in the entire fleet, the little propeller-driven tug *Picket*.

In all, there were more than eighty vessels in the flotilla which left Newport News the night of January 11, and despite a very rough passage around Cape Hatteras, no losses had been reported when they reached Hatteras Inlet on January 13, though a number of the ships, especially the schooners, were scattered by the storm.

Most of the vessels had little difficulty passing over the outer bar at Hatteras Inlet, but getting across the shallow swash and into Pamlico Sound was something else again. One storm after another struck the area, battering the ships near the bar and stranding many of those which had managed to cross the swash. One of the first vessels to attempt to pass through was "the splendid and commodious steamer *City of New York*" which struck the beach and within twenty minutes was "lashed to pieces by the angry breakers." Others which stranded or were lost included the *Grapeshot, Zouave, Louisiana*, and *Pocahontas*.

"Of all forlorn stations to which the folly and wickedness of the Rebellion condemned our officers," one of the men wrote later, "Hatteras was the most forlorn." It was a thirsty place, too, for the storms had driven all of the water vessels out to sea, and water was doled out in such small quantities on some of the troopships that the men broke open casks of vinegar and drank all they could get. General Burnside admitted later that on one occasion, when "a flag of distress was hoisted on many of the vessels in consequence of the want of water . . . I for a time gave up all hope, and walked to the bow of the vessel that I might be alone. Soon after, a small black cloud appeared in the angry gray sky . . . and in a few moments a most copious fall of rain came to our relief."

Neither was the food situation anything for the General to be pleased about. According to one report "the meat ration consisted entirely of pork, which had been boiled and put in barrels before leaving Annapolis, and had now become sour and mouldy." There did not seem to be enough food, either, and the sutlers on the troopships did a good business in dispensing extras. On the *Cossack*, for example, "Cheese was sold by the lump of two and a half to three pounds for $3, while at home the best was selling for fifteen cents per lb," and "peaches put up in bottles, in indifferently bad whiskey" also sold for three dollars. "Indifferently bad" in this instance meant that it was very weak, and a party of three persons on the *Cossack* "spent $21 in trying to get up a 'good feeling,' but had to give it up in disgust, for want of funds."

Strong winds and weak whiskey, poor food and no water, were not the only problems facing the 11,500 troops there at the inlet. Soon after the arrival several men died of typhoid fever, though the threatened epidemic did not materialize. Some of the vessels were infested with "graybacks" or body lice, and one soldier described seeing, on a sunny day, the decks covered with naked men "with clothes turned wrong side out, and each one busily skirmishing with the marauders." Boredom, often the soldier's greatest enemy, played a part too, and the men who could find them turned to cards and checkers for relief, while "any scruples as to the use of them disappeared under the mental famine."

On January 26 the storms finally ended and the vessels began to move over the swash. By January 28 a total of thirty-three had crossed over; the next day the figure was forty-one; and on the night of January 31 a total of sixty-two could be counted in the sound. The last vessel crossed the swash February 4, and the next day Burnside's eighty-vessel fleet set sail for Roanoke Island.

During the long period that the Burnside expedition was detained at Hatteras Inlet, the Confederate defenders of Roanoke Island were having troubles of their own. In early January, Brigadier General Henry A. Wise, a former governor of Virginia, was ordered to take command of the defense of the island. In Richmond, Wise was told by the War Department that twelve batteries had been constructed on Roanoke Island, and he was authorized to increase the size of the "Wise Legion" to 10,000 men through volunteer enlistments. He soon found, however, that volunteers were not to be had, and when he requested that some of the troops in the Richmond area be assigned to him, he was turned down.

In the meantime, Wise had sent an engineer officer to Roanoke Island to inspect the defenses, and shortly before the Legion left Richmond this officer returned. He reported that "The island is in anything but a satisfactory state of defence; the works had been constructed with such an utter want of care and skill that they will scarcely be of any service. Of the twelve batteries which are put down upon the list furnished by the Secretary of War, there is only one that can be regarded as serviceable; all the others are totally useless."

When this report was transmitted to Secretary of War Benjamin, the General was ordered to proceed at once to Roanoke Island and put the works in proper condition for defense.

The disappointment of General Wise over these developments seems to have permeated his troops at the time of the departure from Richmond. "The men," one of his colonels reported, "were laboring under an impression that they were being sent on a desperate service, in which, cut off from all communication with the rest of the army, they would, in all probability, fall a prey to the enemy." At Petersburg, on the march from Richmond, "a mutinous feeling became evident amongst the troops" and two soldiers were ordered shot as an example to the others. At Portsmouth, Virginia, where Wise had understood he would receive horses for his artillery, there were none, and the artillery was rendered practically useless. At Roanoke Island, when Wise finally arrived there with his small Legion, he immediately put the troops to work and established his own headquarters in the Nags Head Hotel.

At this time General Wise had at his disposal approximately 5,000 troops and Commodore Lynch's "Mosquito Fleet," consisting of the *Seabird*, *Appomattox*, *Curlew*, *Ellis*, *Beaufort*, *Raleigh*, *Forrest*, the captured gunboat *Fanny*, and the schooner *Black Warrior*. Each of these vessels was armed with a 32-pound gun, and for the most part they were manned by foreigners who had been taken from the vessels captured earlier by the privateer *Winslow.**

When it became obvious that the Burnside expedition, with more than eighty vessels and a very large land force, was making final preparations for an attack on Roanoke Island, General Wise hurried off to Richmond and made a last minute appeal to Secretary of War Benjamin and President Davis for additional troops. Again he was refused, though he pointed out that there was a force of 20,000 Confederate soldiers on occupation duty in the Norfolk area at the time.

On his return to Roanoke Island in early February, General Wise was stricken with pneumonia, and when the Federal fleet moved in for the attack on the morning of February 7, he was confined to his bed in the Nags Head Hotel. Command of the defensive forces had been turned over to Colonel H. M. Shaw of the Eighth North Carolina Battalion.

At approximately 10:00 A.M. on February 7, the first of the Federal gunboats began passing through the Roanoke Marshes channel, followed by the naval vessels and transports. "The mainland of North Carolina lay on our left," a correspondent for the *Illustrated London News* reported, "and this we had to hug closely for two miles or so, the deep water running there. Every moment I expected to see a puff of white smoke followed by a whiz come from among the tall brakes on the bank, but for some reason or other the Confederates had neglected placing a battery here, which appears to me the more astonishing from the fact that at any time during this two miles I could have almost thrown a biscuit on shore."

As the fleet moved up Croatan Sound, the seven Confederate gunboats were drawn up in battle formation behind the line of sunken ships and pilings, and at 10:30 a signal shot was fired. Shortly afterwards the first of the gunboats came up opposite the shore batteries and opened fire, and by noon the vessels were all in position, some concentrating their fire on the Mosquito Fleet, the remainder trading shots with the shore batteries.

---

*Captain W. H. Parker, commander of the *Beaufort*, said: "I made up a crew principally of men who had been in the prizes captured by the *Winslow*. I had but one American in the crew—a green hand who shipped as a coal heaver....The crew was composed of Englishmen (two of whom were splendid specimens of man-of-war's men) Danes and Swedes. I never sailed with a better one, and I never knew them to fail in their duty."

The naval battle lasted throughout the afternoon. On two occasions the Confederate vessels passed through the line of obstructions, then turned about and headed north again, trying to lure the Federals through that narrow unmarked channel and into the direct fire of the two more northern forts. But Admiral Goldsborough would not be tempted, and his vessels remained concentrated just south of the line of obstructions, maintaining a constant fire.

On shore the barracks building at Fort Bartow was set afire, and burned intermittently throughout the afternoon. The attack was being pressed at such close range that the vessels of both fleets were receiving frequent direct hits. Several of the larger Federal craft grounded, were pulled off by small tugs assigned that specific duty, but continued their fire throughout. In mid-afternoon one of the 100-pound shells from the Parrott gun on the Federal flagship *Southfield* "struck the hurricane deck of the *Curlew* in its descent, and went through her decks and bottom as though they had been made of paper," and her captain, Commander Thomas T. Hunter, headed for the mainland with the intention of grounding her. He ran the vessel ashore "immediately in front of Fort Forrest, completely masking its guns." The *Curlew* could not be set afire for fear of burning the floating battery, and Fort Forrest could no longer participate in the attack because the *Curlew* obstructed her line of fire. Commander Hunter, an excitable individual, admitted later "that during the fight this day he found to his surprise that he had no trousers on."

The *Forrest* was hit also and was forced to retire, but the remaining Confederate vessels continued in the action until late afternoon when their ammunition was exhausted and they were forced to retreat up Albemarle Sound. Still the vast fleet of Federal warships had not silenced the shore batteries on Roanoke Island, and at dusk they were still trading shots with the defenders, their position no more advanced than when the naval battle had begun that morning.

Meanwhile, the passage of the Federal transports through the narrow channel of Roanoke Marshes had been a slow process, and it was not until mid-afternoon that the last of them—excepting one which stranded and remained aground throughout the night—came to anchor out of range of the Confederate fire, down the sound from the scene of battle.

In anticipation of their arrival, General Burnside had determined a site for the landing of his troops which was some three miles below Fort Bartow and in that middle section of the island on which the Confederates had neglected to place major defensive works. Shortly after noon he had ordered Lieutenant Andrews, a topographical engineer, to take a party of ten soldiers in a small boat to inspect the shoreline of the island. Lieutenant Andrews had with him at this time a Negro boy named Thomas R. Robinson, "who escaped to Hatteras about a week before, belonging to Joseph M. Daniel of Roanoke Island."

These two, the New York topographical engineer and the escaped Roanoke Island slave boy, would seem in retrospect to have been the true Federal heroes of the battle of Roanoke Island. At the very height of the naval battle they landed in their small boat at a place called Ashby's Harbor (later the village of Skyco) which young Robinson, who was described by a reporter for the *New York Commercial* as "unusually intelligent, although illiterate," had pointed out as the best harbor along the western shore of the island.*

Having taken careful soundings in the harbor before landing, Andrews then inspected the shoreline which was dominated by a large house, the residence of Captain Ashby. Soon he saw the glitter of bayonets nearby, and on a point near the landing there were indica-tions of a defensive battery. "He returned to the boat and shoved off," the *New York Commercial* reporter said, "when about thirty men sprang up from the tall grass, and discharged their muskets at the boat." One of the bullets almost struck the Lieutenant; another hit one of the soldiers in the jaw, inflicting a painful injury. But Lieutenant Andrews, his ten soldiers, and young Robinson managed to return to General Burnside's flagship with accurate information on the size and depth of Ashby's Harbor and on the shore defenses which con-trolled it.

Three gunboats were immediately ordered to rake the defensive position with shrapnel, and soon the Confederates were seen abandon-ing their temporary battery, and the bayonet-armed troops moved inland. Even as the gunboats fired, the general order was given for

---

* That the slave boy was correct is attested by the fact that this very spot was chosen in the latter part of the century for the docks of the Old Dominion Steamboat Company, operating large passenger and freight vessels between Norfolk and New Bern.

the troops to disembark, and throughout the fleet of transports, men could be seen hurrying down the rope ladders hung against the hulls of the vessels and rapidly filling the small boats alongside. As the landing craft pulled away from the transports, they were joined together in long files, one behind the other, twenty or thirty in a line, and towed in toward shore by the light-draft steamers.

The first Federal troops landed at Ashby's Harbor shortly after 4:00 P.M., and so expert had the training been for this particular operation that by 5:00 an estimated 4,000 men had reached shore. As darkness came on, rain came with it, and the landing proceeded more slowly. The Fifty-First Regiment of Pennsylvania Volunteers, one of the last to reach the shore, "landed on the island a few minutes before eight o'clock, in a most disagreeable swamp and a heavy rain.... The point of landing was ... full of muskrat holes, and the night being one of dense darkness, many a leg unceremoniously entered the apertures, pitching its possessor headlong into the mire."

Long before midnight a force of 7,500 Federal troops was bivouacked there at Ashby's Harbor, and by dawn the next morning the troops were ready for the full-scale attack against the defensive positions.

The Confederates, of course, had expected the landing to be made further north, in the vicinity of their forts Bartow, Blanchard, and Huger. But when the troopships had anchored in the lower part of the sound and it had become evident that Burnside was considering a landing on the southern part of the island, Colonel Shaw had made a last-minute attempt to oppose such a landing. He had at his disposal only three movable guns, a 6-pound and an 18-pound field gun and a 24-pound navy howitzer, which were intended for the defense of the three-gun battery straddling the causeway which connected the north and south parts of the island. Colonel Shaw had ordered these removed from the three-gun battery and transported to the suspected landing sites. The two larger field pieces had been taken to the south end of the island to a place called Pugh's Landing, in the vicinity of the present-day Wanchese; and the small one, the six-pounder, had been set up on a point near Ashby's Harbor.

When Burnside by-passed Pugh's Landing and his gunboats began shelling the Ashby's Harbor area preparatory to the landing there, all three of these Confederate field pieces had been hurriedly withdrawn.

On the morning of February 8 they were once more mounted in their regular positions in the three-gun battery astride the causeway, and the infantry force not engaged in or attached to any of the batteries, about 1,050 men, had been deployed by Colonel Shaw as reserves along the causeway in the rear of the battery.

On the surface this might seem a meagre force to attempt to repel the 7,500 troops approaching up that causeway, supported by six 12-pound howitzers which had also been landed at Ashby's Harbor, but the Confederates were banking even more heavily on the terrain than on guns and men. "Every engineer and every scouting party who had examined the ground had pronounced the deep and heavily wooded marshes to the right and left of the Confederate position to be impassable," it was reported, thus leaving only the narrow causeway for a Federal advance. The three guns of the battery not only controlled the causeway, they also covered an area on either side which had been cleared for a distance of several hundred yards toward Ashby's Harbor, the trees left where they had fallen, their branches sharpened above and below the waters of the swamp.

Quite obviously, General Burnside had not learned that the swamps on either side of the causeway were impenetrable. For when his force reached the cleared space in front of the battery he deployed his troops in three divisions—the first, consisting of five regiments under command of Brigadier General John G. Foster, was ordered to advance along the exposed causeway, supported by the six field howitzers from the rear; the second, four regiments under Brigadier General Jesse L. Reno, was to attempt a flanking movement through the impenetrable swamp to the left of the causeway; the third, four regiments under Brigadier General John G. Parke, was to attempt a similar flanking movement through the impenetrable swamp to the right of the causeway.

For two hours on that narrow causeway and in the swampy stump-filled muck beside it, the troops under General Foster tried to advance on the Confederate battery. It was slow, tortuous going, with no place to duck when the guns of the battery opened fire and no place to hide from the musket shot of the defenders. At the end of the two hours the howitzers seemed to have made no progress toward knocking out the three guns in the Confederate battery, and certainly the troops had made little forward movement. At this point "Major Kimball, of

Hawkins' Zouaves [Ninth New York Regiment] offered to lead the charge, and storm the battery with the bayonet." *

Throughout the battle the two flanking columns had been attempting to pass through the impenetrable swamps to right and left. An officer described the troops as "edging through briers and underbrush, the officers slashing with swords, the men breaking and treading upon the brush for a footing; sometimes clinging to clumps of brush to buoy them up, and others so deep in mire as to need assistance to extricate themselves." To the left of the causeway, the Twenty-Seventh Massachusetts Regiment at last passed through the swamp, only to discover that a "sheet of water fifty yards wide lay between us and the fort; but the order was, 'Forward!' and, with muskets and cartridge-boxes raised above our heads, we plunged into the land-locked waters."

At almost the exact time that General Foster was ordering the Hawkins' Zouaves to make a frontal charge on the battery and the Twenty-Seventh Massachusetts Regiment was emerging from the swamp and pond and charging in from the left, other troops, part of the force under General Parke, had likewise penetrated the swamp and were charging from the right. It was too much for the Confederate defenders to withstand, and "they broke into a precipitate retreat."

From that point on it was simply a matter of when and where the defenders would surrender. They moved rapidly up the causeway toward the north end of the island with the Federals following closely. There was one brief encounter, when some of the Confederates took up temporary positions beside the causeway, fired on the advancing Union men, and downed three; then the retreat was resumed. By this time Colonel Shaw was aware that by sheer force of numbers the enemy must inevitably conquer his troops, and he sent forward a flag of truce to ask for terms. He was informed that the terms were unconditional surrender and, after brief consultation with his officers, surrendered Roanoke Island to the Federals.

In the aftermath, some of the troops attempted to escape in small boats to Nags Head and were intercepted by Burnside's forces. A Confederate relief detachment, landing on the north end of the island in the morning, got there just in time to be captured. And when the prisoners, an estimated 2,675 officers and men, were lined up and

* General Foster is supposed to have shouted above the din: "You are the man, the 9th, the regiment, and this the moment! Zouaves, storm the battery! Forward!"

divested of their equipment, many were found to be carrying only squirrel rifles, fowling pieces, and carving knives. Others, however, had fancy "Yankee Killer" knives which had been hastily discarded in the retreat, and thereafter many a New England home proudly displayed one of these, retrieved after the surrender, as a memento of the battle of Roanoke Island.

The next day Hawkins' Zouaves were sent to Nags Head to capture General Wise and the troops who had managed to escape by that route, but the sick general and his supporters had long since departed up the Banks.

The Federal troops captured, in addition to the three forts and the batteries, "two large encampments, commenced ... by the Third Georgia regiment, and completed by the rebels now our prisoners." These were "composed of wooden quarters for from four to five thousand men" and were described as "about twenty-four long gabled buildings, with chimneys and out-houses." They were of sufficient size to accommodate almost all of the conquering troops.

Union losses (including naval losses of 3 killed and 11 wounded) were listed at 40 killed, 225 wounded, and 13 missing.

Confederate losses were put at only 23 killed, 58 wounded, and 62 missing, with 2,675 captured.

Immediately following the surrender of Roanoke Island, units of Commodore Goldsborough's fleet pursued the Confederate "Mosquito Fleet" to Elizabeth City, where most of the vessels were destroyed and the town was captured.

Burnside's army remained on Roanoke Island for approximately a month, and during this time the towns of Edenton and Winton were also attacked and taken. In early March the bulk of the troops embarked, returned to Hatteras Inlet to pick up a reserve force left there, and moved on to New Bern. Here another major engagement was won by the Federals, while the following month a spirited fight preceded the capture of other Confederate works at South Mills in Camden County.

There remained, then, only one entrance through the Banks which was not in Federal hands. This was Beaufort Inlet, commanded by the strong fortification on the Bogue Banks side known as Fort Macon. This fort had been built in 1834 on approximately the same site as the earlier Fort Hampton and the still earlier Fort Dobbs, and it had been occupied by North Carolina troops when the state seceded and joined the Confederacy.

As a preliminary to the attack on Fort Macon, a Federal force passed by land from New Bern to Beaufort, capturing Havelock Station (March 18), Carolina City (March 21), Morehead City (March 22), and finally Beaufort (March 23).

"Thus," Colonel Rush C. Hawkins summarized later, "all the important positions around or in the vicinity of Fort Macon had fallen into the possession of the Union forces without contest or the loss of a man. General Parke, who had established his headquarters at Carolina City, demanded a surrender of the fort, which was refused. The evidence of preparations completed and in hand left no doubt upon the mind of General Parke that Colonel White intended to make a desperate defense. It was therefore decided to besiege the fort, and as soon as possible to make a combined land and sea attack."

In attempting to accomplish this, however, General Parke ran into unexpected difficulties at the very outset. General Burnside reported later that "there were no vessels or boats at Morehead City or Beaufort, and Core Sound was guarded by the batteries of the enemy," while "the fort also protected the entrance to the harbor."

Two or three days after his arrival at Morehead City, Parke "discovered a small sailing vessel coming up Bogue sound, and at once sent out a launch (which we succeeded in carrying over the country on a hand car) with some armed men and captured her. On it we found a mail of the enemy and some corn for the fort, of all of which we took possession. With this vessel General Parke succeeded in throwing across, during the forepart of the night, some 200 men who held their position on that bank until they were re-inforced the next night; and finding some scows on the opposite bank, they were brought over, and he succeeded within a week in getting his whole command of 3,500 men on to the banks. The channel across there," Burnside added, "was very intricate and shallow, and the transportation of the troops was attended with very great difficulties."

Once he had located his force on Bogue Banks, General Parke began the construction of batteries with which to attack the fort. "The configuration of the sand-hills was singularly well adapted to facilitate the operations of the Union forces," Colonel Hawkins said later. "These ridges or hills intervened between the working parties and the fort to such an extent in height as to permit the erection of besieging works to go on by day as well as by night, without any serious inconvenience from the enemy's fire."

Even so, it took almost a month for the completion of the entrenchments, during which period vessels of Goldsborough's fleet successfully blockaded the inlet. General Burnside said that "the hardships and difficulties which the troops had to undergo in the transportation of the guns, mortars, ammunition, and provisions, through the intricate channels and over the sand hills, exceeded anything that I have ever known in the way of land service."

The object of all this preparation, Fort Macon, was described by Colonel Hawkins as "an old-style, strong, stone, casemated work, mounting 67 guns, garrisoned by above 500 men, commanded by Colonel Moses J. White." * The defenders were North Carolinians, principally from the Tenth and Fortieth artillery regiments, and at least a third of them had been recruited in the Morehead City–Beaufort area.

For the attack on this formidable defensive position which was well supplied with ammunition and provisions, the Federals had erected three siege batteries, one armed with three rifled 30-pound guns; the second with four 8-inch mortars; the third with four 10-inch mortars. These had been erected less than a mile from the fort, the closest being only 1,250 yards distant. In addition, three blockading steamers, the *Daylight, State of Georgia* and *Chippewa,* and a bark, the *Gemsbok,* were prepared to assist in the siege, and two barges, or "floating batteries," with a total of five guns had been towed down Bogue Sound to provide fire from still a third direction. There had been a plan to erect yet another battery on the western point of Shackleford Banks, but this had been abandoned.

On Thursday, April 24, the news was broadcast in the town of Beaufort that the attack was scheduled for that day, "but owing to some delay or misunderstanding, not a gun was fired." At dawn the next morning "along the river-front of Beaufort, a score of glasses were kept pointed at the banks, where, through the grey mist, the

* There are, however, conflicting reports as to the number of guns and size of the defending force. Though Hawkins said there were 64 guns, General Burnside listed it as 54, and another source gave the figure as 44. As to the number of men, Colonel White said later that his morning report showed only "263 men for duty."

embrasures . . . just unmasked, could be made out. At half-past five o'clock there came from the ten-inch mortar-battery a huge puff of white smoke, and in another minute the smoky balloon of the bursting shell was seen high in the air, and far beyond the ramparts of the Fort." In short order the other Federal guns joined in, most of the early shots landing in the inlet or along the shore, and then the guns of the fort responded. The four attacking vessels moved into position, the two floating batteries opened fire, and the siege was on.

Officers of the recently formed United States Signal Corps had been stationed at Beaufort, Morehead City, and Carolina City to observe the effect of the fire from the siege batteries, and "at half-past ten the following message was flagged over from Morehead:

" 'The Parrotts go too high, and the heavy shells burst too far beyond the fort.' "

Adjustments were made immediately, "the guns of the one were depressed, and the fuses of the other shortened; and after that for several hours two shots out of three must have struck the work." One after another the guns of Fort Macon were rendered useless as direct hits were scored from the nearby batteries. But the fire of the Confederate defenders was effective too, one eight-inch shot striking the deck of the gunboat *Daylight* and passing through a number of bulkheads to lodge in the machinery in the engine room, another hitting the wheel of one of the gun carriages in a battery, splintering it.

"A private in the Third artillery, whose duty it was to watch the Fort and warn his comrades of coming shot and shell, was driving an alignment-stake about this time, when a gun was fired by the enemy," an observer for the *New York Tribune* wrote. "He saw the puff and cried out as usual, 'Down!', but failing to get shelter in time, the ball—a twenty-four pounder—struck him in the chest and tore him to pieces. His breast-bone and ribs were split off as if they had been the lid of a box, his heart fell out, and a bruised mass of flesh and blood was hurled in Lieut. Flagler's face and over his person. Dabs of flesh and clots of blood were splashed over the walls and platforms of the battery, and the quivering remains of the poor fellow were pitched headlong into the sand."

Inside the fort there were scenes of even greater destruction. A single shell had struck one gun, "killed the gunner, and displaced the piece; then passing to the ten-inch gun, it dismounted it, killed two men, and wounded three more; then striking the brick revetment, it glanced to the next gun, which it disabled, and wounded Capt. Pool's son, who was acting as captain of the gun, after which it fell into the ditch. The concussion prostrated every man at all three guns."

Though rough seas had forced the naval vessels to retire comparatively early in the engagement, by late afternoon the bombardment had so shattered the defensive works within the fort—it was determined later that 560 direct hits had been scored on the fort, and many of the guns were out of commission—Colonel White "finding that our loss had been very great, and from the fatigue of our men being unable to keep up the fire with but two guns, a proposition was made to General Parke for the surrender of Fort Macon." As a result a truce was called that night, and early the next morning, on board one of the blockading vessels, the articles of capitulation were agreed to and signed.

Union losses in the battle were listed as only one killed and two wounded; the Confederates as eight killed and twenty wounded.

With the capture of this fort, Burnside's control of the Banks and the sounds was complete. He now had "what he has so long needed, a port of entry and a good harbor for heavy-draft vessels. The transports, gunboats, and store-ships will no longer need to run the gauntlet of Hatteras Inlet and the Swash; for at Beaufort they tie up at the railroad-wharf in three fathoms water within half an hour after crossing the bar."

Soon after this Burnside was relieved of duty and transferred to command of the Army of the Potomac, taking the bulk of his troops with him. The forces left in North Carolina proceeded to gain control of other Confederate-held points further inland, and the gunboats which were being built on the rivers were for the most part captured or destroyed before they could damage the Federal cause. Small bands of Confederate troops did return to the Banks upon occasion, usually in attempts to blow up lighthouses. In this way Bodie Island Lighthouse and the old Cape Lookout Lighthouse were destroyed by the Confederates, the newer Cape Lookout Lighthouse was badly damaged, and minor damage was inflicted on the others.

For all practical purposes, however, the capture of Hatteras Inlet, Roanoke Island, and Fort Macon had brought an end to organized

Confederate resistance on the Banks and in the sounds. It had done more than that, even, for with Federal forces in firm command of these inlets and sounds, they had effectively blocked off the basic maritime supply route to the rest of northeastern Carolina and had tightly shut the back door to Norfolk and Chesapeake Bay.

Federal
Occupation

AT THE TIME of the capture of Hatteras Inlet and Chicamacomico by the Federal troops, there were approximately 1200 persons
living on Hatteras Island,* including nearly a hundred slaves. Settlements were located about where the villages are today, but the names
were almost entirely different. The present-day villages of Rodanthe
and Waves were known as Chicamacomico; Salvo was Clarks; just
north of the modern Avon were the small communities of Scarborotown (Scabbertown) and Little Kinnakeet; Avon itself was known
as Big Kinnakeet; Buxton was The Cape; Frisco was Trent; and of
them all only the village of Hatteras had its modern name.

Approximately half of these 1200 or so people, including almost
all of the slaves, were located in Cape Hatteras district, west of the
lighthouse; and the only post office on the island, at the village of
Hatteras, had been established less than two years before.

"The islanders mingle but little with the world," a Confederate

* In the census of 1860 Banks and mainland districts were combined. However, the
1850 census gave the figure as 1,185, including 4 free Negroes and 84 slaves; and the
census of 1870 gave it as 1,302, including 30 Negroes. There were 205 dwellings on the
island in 1850 and 256 in 1870.

officer said of them. "Apparently indifferent to this outside sphere, they constitute a world within themselves."

Another observer wrote: "Queer folks in this region! Several hundred are scattered along the bar, who get their living by fishing, gathering oysters, wrecking and piloting. Most of them were born here, never saw any other locality and all are happy. There are women here who never wore shoes. The people seldom see money, indeed they have no use for it."

When he took over command of the newly captured forts at the inlet in early September, 1861, Colonel Rush C. Hawkins set out to cultivate friendly relations with the Bankers. "As they were mostly of a seafaring race," he said, "I concluded they could not have much sympathy with the revolt against a government which had been their constant friend."

In this he was right, for as soon as the battle of Hatteras Inlet was over and the forts secured by the Federal troops, residents of the nearby communities appeared, expressed their happiness at the results, and offered to take the oath of allegiance to the United States and assist the Federal forces. "Within ten days after the landing," Hawkins said, "nearly all of the male adults had taken the oath of allegiance."

From the Confederates, meanwhile, there were claims that the Bankers were not truly on the side of the Union; rather, they were opportunists whose "neutrality was evinced by raising white flags to the house-tops on the approach of either Confederates or Federals." To a certain extent this may well have been true, but certainly when the die was cast and it was necessary to choose sides, the bulk of the Bankers chose the northern side.

One of the reasons cited by Colonel Hawkins for sending a force to Chicamacomico was "for the purpose of protecting the natives who had taken the oath." When Confederate troops landed there and pursued the Federals down the Banks toward Hatteras in the "Chicamacomico Races," the Reverend T. W. Conway, chaplain of the Federal troops, described the reaction of the residents as follows:

There was one thing that convinced the members of the Twentieth Indiana Regiment that those people were loyal and true to the Union. When the regiment was retreating, the people of Chicamacomico left their homes, without shoes and hats, and almost in rags, mothers carrying their infants in their arms, old men on their crutches, the strong men carrying the sick and the lame on their backs—the whole population put themselves in mass in front of the retreating regiment, and marched through the burning sand until many of them fell from exhaustion by the road-side, and were left to fall into the hands of the rebels. The rebels, finding that the entire community had retreated, took it as a living evidence that they were friends of the Union and enemies to the rebellion. So they went into their houses, stripped them of everything valuable [that] they could take away, and destroyed what they could of the rest. There were at least 500 of these fugitives. They went down to the next neighborhood, who were just as poor as themselves. Some of them returned again to their devastated homes; others remained with their neighbors.

Soon after his arrival at Hatteras Inlet, the Reverend Mr. Conway had been invited to conduct church services for the Bankers. "Accordingly," he said, "on the first Sabbath I entered the pulpit of the nearest church to the point occupied by the regiment of which I was chaplain, and when looking at my congregation, what did I see? Half the congregation was made up of National soldiers, and the other half of natives of North Carolina. . . . I was invited to preach in other places; I went up twelve miles, and visited three different congregations. My experience was the same. They were all glad to see me, and to extend to me their hospitality."

Further doubts as to the sympathies of the Bankers would seem to have been dispelled in early October. For, on the twelfth of that month "a Convention of one hundred and eleven delegates of the citizens of Hyde County, of which Hatteras is a part, assembled at a church near the inlet, and adopted a 'Statement of Grievances and a Declaration of Independence,' in which they loudly proclaimed their loyalty to the United States, and expressed in the most decided manner their abhorrence of the spurious government designating itself 'The Confederate States of America.'"

A select committee of three, composed of Caleb B. Stowe, William O'Neil, and the Reverend Marble Nash Taylor, was named to draw up the Declaration, and their names were signed to it. In outspoken language the leaders of the state government were charged with treason. "They have arrogated the authority, through a Convention summoned with indecent haste, and acting in flagrant defiance of the wishes of the people, to perform an act legally impossible, and therefore without effect or force, in decreeing the secession of this Commonwealth from the Federal Union," the document stated. Further, "the ordinances of this Convention have never been submitted to the people for their ratification or rejection; they have commissioned ten men as Representatives of the State in a body called the Confederate Congress, unknown to and unauthorized by the laws, and occupying an attitude of open hostility to that Constitution which North Carolina has formally and definitely ratified and accepted as the supreme law of the land," and "they have withheld from the electors the poor privilege of designating such Representatives."

In addition to adopting this resolution, the Bankers set up the machinery for the formation of a provisional government of the state, called on loyal North Carolinians in every county to express their dissatisfaction with the secession move, and set Monday, November 18, as the date for a second convention at Hatteras, this one to establish the new government and name temporary officers.

On that date, it was reported, "a provisional or temporary Government for this Commonwealth was instituted at Hatteras, Hyde County, by a Convention of the people, in which more than half the counties of the State were represented by delegates and authorized proxies." Ordinances were adopted, "declaring vacant all State offices, the incumbents whereof have disqualified themselves to hold them by violating their official oaths to support the Constitution of the United States, . . . pronouncing void and of no effect the Ordinance of Secession from the Federal Union, . . . continuing in full force the Constitution and laws of the State, . . . and appointing a Provisional Governor, and empowering him to fill such official vacancies, and to do such acts as in his judgement might be required for the safety and good order of the State."

The Convention named the Reverend Marble Nash Taylor, Methodist minister assigned to Hatteras by the North Carolina Conference, as Provisional Governor. Two days later he issued a proclamation calling upon "all the good people of this Commonwealth to return to their allegiance to the United States, and to rally around the standard of State loyalty, which we have reerected and placed side by side with the glorious flag of the Republic." In this proclamation, Taylor said: "I adjure you as North Carolinians, mindful of the inspiring traditions of your history, and keeping in view your true interests and welfare as a people, to rise and assert your independence of the wicked tyrants who are seeking to enslave you."

Governor Taylor called for an election in the Second Congressional District, "at which Mr. Charles Henry Foster was elected a member of the National House of Representatives," and when the United States Congress assembled at Washington at noon, December 2, "The case of Mr. Foster, represented to have been elected from the Hatteras District of North Carolina, was referred to the committee on elections." When the case came up for consideration, however, Foster was denied his seat in the House, and the *New York Times* correspondent expressed what seems to have been the general feeling around Washington with regard to the new provisional government.

"The actual de facto jurisdiction of this Government is confined to the sand-bar recently captured by the United States Navy at Hatteras. The portion of this bar protected by the United States flag may be fifteen or twenty miles long, by about one mile wide. Would it not be a hazardous experiment to reconstruct the political edifices on such a foundation?"

Hardly anything further was heard from "Congressman Charles Henry Foster," who seems to have been a perennial congressional candidate, or from "Governor Marble Nash Taylor," apparently a Yankee on temporary duty in the South, or even from the "Provisional Government of North Carolina." But the condition which spawned them continued to exist, and even on Roanoke Island, when the Confederates were preparing their defenses there, Commander Thomas T. Hunter stated that he regarded "the maintenance of Roanoke Island possible only so long as it is defended by troops from another State, or from a more loyal part of North Carolina."

Possibly the correspondent of the *Illustrated London News* summed up the feeling of the residents of Roanoke Island most clearly when he said, after the fall of the island to the Union forces:

With regard to the sentiment of the people on the island, it appears to me to be quite as much one way as the other. I think all they want is to be let alone by both parties. The following were more especially the sentiments of a Mr. Jarvis, farmer and fisherman, whose house had been taken possession of by the Zouaves: he was a perfectly bewildered individual. His family was in one of the negro shanties, and he was outside, mourning over the events of the day. He had "nothing agin the North," and had sold a great many shad to go there. But the troops had killed one of his pigs, and his wife had lost her temper and her flat irons. "Do you own any negroes, Mr. Jarvis?" queried I, "Well, I *did*, but three of 'em went to Hatteras last week, two more have run away, I don't know where, and there's one in the kitchen I'll give away if anybody wants him!"

Whether the Union sentiment, especially on Hatteras Island, was of the genuine, inbred type or simply an expedient to make the best of changing conditions, the fact is that many of the Bankers did side with the North. As a result their association with other North Carolinians on the mainland was to a large extent terminated, their market for fish and other seafoods was cut off, and they no longer had the buying power—or more accurately, the trading power—to secure corn and other foodstuffs across the sound. In fact, within two months of the capture of Hatteras Inlet by Federal forces theirs was a pitiful condition, for supplies of salt, flour, and other foods were exhausted and there seemed no way to replenish them.

Word of the condition of the Bankers reached New York, however, and several of the leading citizens, including historian George Bancroft and poet William Cullen Bryant, decided to do something about it. Accordingly, they called a special meeting to be held at Cooper Institute the night of Thursday, November 7, 1861, to hear a report on the condition of the residents of Hatteras Island from two eye-witnesses—the Reverend T. W. Conway and the Reverend M. N. Taylor, who had come north for the express purpose of trying to secure supplies for the loyal residents of the Banks.

The report on this meeting, at which time "Cooper Institute was filled to overflowing ... with a very intelligent audience," occupied almost a full page in the November 8 edition of the *New York Times*.

The speakers were impassioned in their call for aid to the loyal North Carolinians at Hatteras; the audience was enthusiastically responsive. William Cullen Bryant said:

It requires infinitely more courage to be a friend to the Union in North Carolina than here. Here one may be a friend of the Union, and yet be a coward and a sneak. There he must be a martyr and a hero.... These loyal men of the sand beaches of North Carolina cannot take a step in the mainland without incurring danger of the jail and the gibbet. They have risked everything; they have risked starvation; they have risked exile from their homes; they have risked the loss of liberty, the loss of life, by the noble stand they have taken. Shall we abandon these worthy men and their helpless families? Shall we, twenty millions of us, with our fertile fields, with our busy work shops, with our well-stored warehouses, with our teeming mines, with our vast commerce visiting every sea—shall we leave these three thousand people * to the fate which the rebels design for them?

The filled house at Cooper Institute that night unanimously adopted a resolution offering "our kind sympathy and fraternal affection to those loyal inhabitants of North Carolina, who, deprived of their usual means of support by rebel forces, are reduced to great distress and suffering" and pledging "to send them at once such necessary assistance in food and clothing as they may need."

To accomplish this purpose a "Committee of Relief" was appointed to "collect from the City, and elsewhere, such funds as may be necessary for the purchase of food and supplies, and to forward and distribute the same in the most judicious manner." The committee consisted of nineteen prominent individuals, including Theodore Roosevelt, John J. Astor, and Samuel Colgate.† The treasurer of the committee, to whom contributions were to be sent, was J. M. Morrison, Treasurer of the Manhattan Bank, and the secretary was W. E. Dodge, Jr.

By November 13, less than a week later, the *New York Times* reported that $1,707 had been donated to the committee; by November 20 the amount was $6,000; and in its issue of November 26 the *New York Times* published the following: "Schooner *E. Sheddon*, Capt. White, lying at the foot of Beeker Street, East River, will sail for Hatteras Inlet in a few days. She will commence immediately to take in a full cargo of provisions for the union men in North Carolina. These provisions are furnished by private donations. Chas. H. Marshall and other influential citizens contributed a liberal share. The *E. Shed-*

---

* At the time, the population of the island was variously and incorrectly reported at between 3,000 and 4,000 people.

† The members were: J. M. Morrison, W. M. Vermilye, Charles H. Marshall, W. J. Hoppin, Robert Lennox Kennedy, John J. Astor, R. M. Minturn, Jr., Charles H. Trask, C. A. Davidson, William Oothout, Theodore Roosevelt, Cornelius K. Sutton, George B. Satterlee, William E. Dodge, Jr., Howard Potter, Charles Dennis, Edward G. Bogert, Franklin M. Ketchum, and Samuel Colgate.

don is about 200 tons register, and will carry a freight of nearly 250 tons."

The issue of November 29 reported that contributions amounted to $8,238.56 plus dry-goods and food and said that the schooner *E. Sheddon* had started taking in her cargo of "flour, pork, beef, molasses, boots, shoes," and other donations.

When fully loaded the *E. Sheddon* proceeded to Hatteras Inlet with its valuable cargo. "By the time they reached there, however, a profitable employment had been afforded to the natives by the soldiers, which relieved the wants of the people, so that a considerable portion of the produce sent for charity was sold and the money returned to the New York Committee."

There remained other problems, however, insofar as the residents of North Carolina were concerned. "Soon after the capture of the forts," Colonel Hawkins said later, "the 'intelligent contraband' began to arrive, often bringing news of important military activity in several directions." These were the Negroes, former slaves, who had escaped from their owners and fled to the protection of the Union banner. Not until the capture of Roanoke Island, however, was there a marked influx in these "contrabands." Then they began to arrive in large numbers, and General Burnside appointed a New York artist, Vincent Colyer, to be "Superintendent of the Poor" in the North Carolina Department.

"I commenced my work with the freed people of color, in North Carolina, at Roanoke Island, soon after the battle of the 8th of February, 1862," he reported. "A party of fifteen or twenty of these loyal blacks, men, women and children, arrived on a 'Dingy' in front of the General's Head Quarters, where my tent was located. They came from up the Chowan River, and as they were passing they had been shot at by their rebel masters from the banks of the river, but escaped uninjured."

Immediately upon their arrival on the island the able-bodied Negro men were offered eight dollars a month and "one ration of clothes" to work on the construction of a new fort, known as Fort Burnside and located on the north end of the island, and to work on docks nearby. By late spring of 1862 there were approximately 1,000 contrabands in the area.

In the absence of a church, the contrabands on Roanoke Island "had constructed a spacious bower, cutting down long, straight, pine trees and placing them parallel lengthwise for seats, with space enough between for their knees ... constructing a rude pulpit out of the discarded Quartermaster's boxes, and over-arching the whole with a thick covering of pine branches," Colyer reported.

After the capture of New Bern, Superintendent Colyer was transferred there, and Sergeant Thompson was placed in charge of the Negroes on Roanoke Island. For almost a year the work on fortifications and docks was continued, but by early 1863 both were nearly completed, and many more contrabands had joined those already on the island, including a very large number of women, children, and old men. In May of 1863 the situation had become so acute—the island filled with Negroes with nothing to do and no means of support—that General Foster, then in charge of the Department, appointed the Reverend Horace James to the "Superintendency of the Blacks in North Carolina" and ordered him "to establish a colony of negroes upon Roanoke Island." The plan, as outlined later by James, was "to settle colored people on the unoccupied lands, and give them agricultural implements and mechanical tools to begin with, and to train and educate them for a free and independent community."

Roanoke Island was selected for this experimental community, James said, because "our forces held no other suitable or safe place in the State. Not a square mile of territory (excepting Hatteras Banks) lying outside of the interior fortifications of New Berne, Beaufort, and Morehead, but has been repeatedly overrun by rebels and guerillas."

General Foster's specific orders were "to take possession of, and assign to the negroes, the unoccupied and unimproved lands of the island, laying them out in suitable lots for families." Sergeant George O. Sanderson, formerly of the Forty-Third Massachusetts Regiment, was named assistant superintendent and began the preliminary surveys. James described the colony as follows:

With compass, chart, and chain, and a gang of choppers, the old groves of pine, gum, holly, and cypress were penetrated, crossed and recrossed, and the upper, or northern, end of the island was laid out in acre lots, and at once assigned to the families. Broad, straight avenues were laid out, 1,200 feet apart, up and down the island, nearly parallel with its shores and parallel with one another, which were named "Roanoke Avenue", "Lincoln Avenue", "Burnside Avenue", &c. At right angles with these were the streets, somewhat narrower than the avenues, and 400 feet apart, numbered "First Street", "Second Street", &c., in one direction from a certain point, and "A Street", "B Street", &c., in the other direction.

This arrangement divided the land into ... sections, containing each twelve one acre lots, square in form, every one having a street frontage. Along these the houses were disposed, being placed in line, and all at the same distance from the street. The lots were neatly enclosed, and speedily improved by the freedmen, soon making "the wilderness and the solitary place glad" at their coming. Wives and children with alacrity united with the men in performing the work of the carpenter, the mason, and the gardener. So zealous were they in this work, as to spend, in many cases, much of the night in prosecuting it, giving no sleep to their eyes until they could close them sweetly, under their own dear roof-trees.

As soon as the work of surveying was started in early June, 1863, James went north "to procure materials and implements with which to furnish the projected colony with an outfit, and in a few weeks raised in New England and New York between eight and nine thousand dollars," a large part of which was spent for a steam mill and sawmill, with a 70-horsepower engine, "carrying several circular saws, a turning lathe, and a grist mill." By the time he returned to Roanoke Island, the military forces had begun enlisting colored soldiers, the first Negro recruits being signed up on June 19, 1863. In a short time more than a hundred had joined the service, and by the end of July this company—"The first company of colored troops raised in North Carolina, and so far as I know, the first in the country," James said— was transferred to active duty in South Carolina.

"This removal of the vigorous young men, who would have worked upon the soil, and fished in the Sounds for the support of the colony, necessarily changed the character of the enterprise," James commented, and it was converted "into an asylum for the wives and children of soldiers, and also for the aged and infirm, where the children might be educated, and all, both young and old, be trained for freedom and its responsibilities, after the war."

Even so, the contrabands remaining on the island seem to have been enthusiastic about the prospects of acquiring their own homes. Before the sawmill was set up many of them went in small boats to Nags Head and Bodie Island and brought back lumber which had drifted up on the beach. Others used logs and boards, "split by hand," and made chimneys of sticks and clay.*

In the winter of 1863-64 the population of the contraband town had almost doubled, and in a census taken January 1, 1864, there were found to be 2,712 Negroes there. By spring, however, the mill was in operation, "near the military headquarters of the island," and "the officers of the Government, the troops, the attaches of the army, the white natives, and the negroes" were reported by James to be "sharing alike in the benefits of this Northern institution."

Meanwhile, the first teacher had arrived in the community on October 19, 1863—"Miss Elizabeth James, a lady sent out by the American Missionary Association"—and "for more than three months she "labored alone and unattended, living in one log cabin, and teaching in another." She was joined in January, 1864, by S. S. Nickerson, a little later by Miss Mary Burnap, and by the fall of 1864 there were seven teachers on duty there. "The only abandoned house on the island was fitted up for a teacher's home," and construction of schools was begun with new lumber turned out in the community mill.

Among the contrabands who settled in the colony were some who "manufactured spinning wheels for sale, doing it without the use of a lathe"; many women, who could "card, spin and weave"; others who were supplied with shoemaker's tools and with cooper's tools, both of which they knew how to use. "It is common to find colored men acquainted with splitting and shaving shingles, and not a few are constantly engaged in this business, selling them at from $3.00 to $7.00 per thousand," James said. Approximately a hundred of the most active men on the island were employed by the Quartermaster and Commissary departments of the army, and others were kept busy repairing the fortifications. There were some boat builders among them and a number of fishermen, but "the shad season in 1864 was much less productive than usual, the nets being broken and destroyed by ice and storms in the early spring." Some of the women, of course, secured employment with the garrison, as laundresses, cooks, and servants.

By January 1, 1865, James reported that a total of 591 houses had

* The only extensive clay deposit this writer has seen in the Banks area is located on Roanoke Island approximately where the contraband town was laid out. Recently, much of the clay has been removed for road construction.

been built in the colony, and he valued them at an average of $75.00 each. "One of them," he said, "was recently sold for $150." There were by then 3,091 contrabands in the colony, including 1,297 children, and only 217 males between the ages of eighteen and forty-five, "and the larger portion of these, even, are exempts on account of physical disability."

The reaction of the approximately 500* permanent residents of Roanoke Island, whose total number of dwellings in 1860 had been only eighty-seven, was varied. Some cooperated willingly, let their lands be used for the experimental colony; others attempted in every possible way to block the experiment. Land prices zoomed—to four or five times the previous value. "The average value of the wood and waste lands, on which the colony has been settled," James said, "was only two dollars an acre before the war." The worth of the lots and buildings in the colony itself, on the other hand, was estimated by the end of 1864 at more than $44,000, "a sum large enough to have purchased the whole island three years ago, with all the improvements of two hundred years, under the rule and culture of its white inhabitants."

The Reverend Horace James, was, of course, a biased reporter, and his glowing statements on the accomplishments of this experimental colony were tempered later in the reports of the Freedman's Bureau which was established the following year. Even so, the colony might have continued to prosper and the descendants of those contrabands might be living still on their homesteads but for an order, issued in 1865, which "necessitated the restoration to original owners who had received pardon, of all abandoned property to which they could prove title."

Under this new policy, Major General John C. Robinson, Assistant Commission for Freedmen's Affairs for North Carolina, reported as follows under date of November 8, 1866:

Every effort has been made to break up the colony of freedmen on Roanoke Island, but there are still seventeen hundred colored persons remaining there, living upon lands seized by the government and divided into one acre lots. The place is barren, and there is every appearance of great destitution during the coming winter. To remedy this the superintendent of the eastern district and the assistant superintendent on the island

* The 1860 Census listed the population of Roanoke Island as 419.

recommend that the land be restored to the original owners, so as to compel the freedmen to remove to other points, where they can procure employment. I have made arrangements for the transportation of these people from the island, and have reason to believe that great numbers of them will be induced to leave during this month.

Thus was ended the experiment, instituted soon after the fall of Roanoke Island, designed "to settle colored people on unoccupied lands . . . and to train them for a free and independent community."

Later, when the war was over and claims were being pressed against the United States by loyal Southerners for damage to their property during the period of hostility, a man named John Wescott, of Manteo, filed a claim in the amount of $1,500 for 3,000 trees destroyed on his property.

Though this was the only attempt at establishment of a full-scale community for the contrabands, efforts were made elsewhere along the Banks to care for them. At one time in 1864, there were almost one hundred contrabands on Hatteras Island, most of them apparently working for the occupation troops.

Farther down the Banks, at Beaufort, as many as 3,245 were under the jurisdiction of the Federal occupation forces, but at that time "less than three hundred colored persons [were receiving] assistance from the Government in Beaufort and vicinity." The remainder were engaged in their usual pursuits, oystering and fishing, and "not less than one hundred men constantly employed in boating, this business being wholly in the hands of the Negroes." The bulk of these were operating small passenger and freight boats between Morehead City and Beaufort, "meeting every train of cars, and beating to and fro in every breeze," though some ran also "to Fort Macon, Shackleford Banks, the Lighthouse, Harker's Island and elsewhere." This was a lucrative business, too, a contemporary observer stating that the average boat took in three dollars a day and that "it may be set down that the freedmen of Beaufort, North Carolina, earn a thousand dollars a week, or fifty thousand dollars a year."

As in the other wars which have come to the Banks, the area soon made the return to normalcy. Because there had been proportionately little slave ownership on the Banks before the war, the Bankers had comparatively little difficulty adjusting to the new order. Some of the former slaves remained in the area, and like the free colored people who had lived there for many years, they soon were living side by side with the white people, fishing the same kinds of nets for the same species of fish in the same places as their white neighbors, accepted as members of the Banks community, not quite on an equal plane, but so close to it that it took a keen observer to tell the difference.

Ushering in the Modern Era

ELSEWHERE in North Carolina and the war-torn South the people who had formed the Confederacy were facing the initial hurdles in that long, lean, and trying period known as Reconstruction, but on the Outer Banks the prospect was brighter, for the federal government was preparing to distribute the first in what was to become a steady flow of vouchers and pay checks. It was almost as if the Bankers were being rewarded for their wartime loyalty with steady jobs in numerous new lighthouses, lifesaving stations, weather stations, and post offices.

The lighthouse jobs came first, for the Outer Banks lights were in miserable shape. As early as 1852 Lieutenant David D. Porter had described Cape Hatteras Lighthouse as "the most important on our coast, and without doubt the WORST light in the world." He added that "the first nine trips I made I never saw Hatteras light at all, though frequently passing in sight of the breakers; and when I did see it, I could not tell it from a steamer's light, excepting that the steamer's lights are much brighter." At the same time Lieutenant H. J. Hartstene had said that the lights at Hatteras and Lookout, "if not improved, had better be dispensed with, as the navigator is apt to run ashore looking for them."

As a result of these and similar complaints, the Cape Hatteras Lighthouse had been elevated to 150 feet * in 1854, and in 1859 two new lighthouses had been built, a 150-foot high structure at Cape Lookout and a smaller one at Bodie Island. During the war, however, the Confederates had destroyed the new Bodie Island light and damaged the others, and though temporary repairs were made at Ocracoke and Hatteras, the Banks warning system was in need of major improvements.

These improvements were begun in 1867 when new iron stairways were installed in the Cape Lookout tower. At the same time a working party was making preliminary arrangements at Cape Hatteras for the construction there of the largest brick lighthouse in the world, and from then until 1875 men worked steadily on the Banks constructing a chain of tall lighthouses designed to provide the most modern navigation aids for the North Carolina coast.

The new Cape Hatteras Lighthouse, with a focal plane of 180 feet, was completed and first lighted on December 16, 1870. Then the scows which had been used for hauling materials to the Cape were moved up the Banks to Oregon Inlet for the construction of a third Bodie Island Lighthouse—this one 150 feet high and located on the north side of the inlet—which was completed on October 1, 1872. The third and final major lighthouse on this stretch of coast, a 150-foot high structure located at Currituck Beach, was completed on December 1, 1875.

Many Bankers had been provided with work on these lighthouse construction jobs; many others were accepted in the lighthouse service as keepers and assistants, for preference was given local residents when the jobs were filled. In addition, merchants on the Banks, at Roanoke Island, and at Beaufort were usually awarded the contracts to provide fuel and other supplies, and it was not long before a steady flow of federal money was filtering through the communities.

Meanwhile, the U.S. Lifesaving Service had expanded its operations to include the North Carolina coast, and in the twelve months preceding December 7, 1874, seven stations had been constructed. These were listed as "Jones's Hill, Caffrey's Inlet, Kitty Hawk Beach, Nag's Head, Bodie's Island, Chicamicomico, and Little Kinnakeet," though the station referred to as "Bodie's Island" was actually located south

---

* Elevations given here are for the focal plane—the distance from ground level to the center of the lantern.

of Oregon Inlet and "Jones's Hill" was later known as Currituck Beach and Whales Head. Several of these original buildings are still standing although most of them were converted into boathouses when larger stations were built in later years.

During the first winter season of lifesaving activity on the Banks, each of the new stations was in charge of a keeper * who received an annual salary of $200, and each crew consisted of six surfmen employed for an average of four months—December, January, February, and March—at a salary of $40.00 per month. The surfmen were required to live at the stations during the active winter season, and as stated by the superintendent, their services were "at the disposal of the Government upon any occasion of shipwreck at other times, for attendance at which they are paid $3. each."

The difficulty in securing competent keepers was pointed up during the 1875-76 season in the report of a special board which examined the personnel of the seven North Carolina stations and three on the adjoining Virginia coast, an area designated as Lifesaving District Number 6.

The Board next visited the sixth district, in which they examined seventy-nine keepers and surfmen, of whom sixty-four were accepted and fifteen were rejected, four of the latter being keepers. Of these four keepers, two were rejected as having no knowledge whatever of the duties required of them, one being a blacksmith and the other a teacher by occupation; the third as lacking experience as a surfman; and the fourth as physically disqualified.

Competent persons were substituted for these as soon as they could be obtained. On account of the inadequate compensation paid to keepers, it was some time, however, before suitable persons could be found to accept the positions. Of the eleven surfmen rejected, five were found to be without experience or skill in the use of boats, four of them being by occupation farmers and one a carpenter. Four of the five belonged to the station, the keeper of which was a teacher, there being but two competent persons in the entire crew. Of the remaining six, three were physically disqualified; one was the son and another the brother of the keepers of the respective

---

* The early keepers were: Jones's Hill, Keeper John G. Gale; Caffrey's Inlet, Keeper W. G. Partridge; Kitty Hawk Beach, Keeper W. D. Tate; Nag's Head, Keeper John W. Evans; Bodie's Island, Keeper Edward Drinkwater; Chicamacomico, Keeper Benjamin S. Pugh; Little Kinnakeet, Keeper Banister Midgett. All of these, with the exception of Tate, were appointed December 4, 1874; Tate was appointed September 30, 1875.

stations to which they were attached; and one was insubordinate. All these were immediately discharged and their places supplied by competent persons.

Although implications can be read into this report that all was not well in the newly-formed Sixth Lifesaving District, the true state of affairs was not revealed until after the examination in the winter of 1876-77. Referring to the condition of the District the previous year, the board reported:

Its demoralization in 1876 is referable to ... the temporary control of its affairs gained by petty local politicians, whose aim was to subordinate the service to their personal ends; their method being to endeavor to pack the stations with their own creatures, without the slightest respect to use or competency. The success of these maneuvers would at once involve the utter ruin of the service; for what stranded crew, clinging to the shrouds of a vessel going to pieces in the breakers, could hope for succor in the hour of their bitter extremity, from life-saving stations recruited from the cross-roads grocery?

There is, however, abundant cause for gratulation, that not in a single instance have these attempts upon the integrity of a noble service ... proceeded from any representative man in our State or national politics. ...

But, considering the criminal mischief and disaster their success would involve, they acquire a deeper baseness from the circumstance of their having been invariably resorted to for no better purpose than to further the election of some local nobody to an office of no higher dignity than that of town constable or pound-keeper.

By the winter of 1876-77, however, this same board reported that the incompetents had been weeded out, the influence of the politicians had been nullified, and the superintendent of the district had been "indefatigable in his efforts to perfect the discipline and efficiency of the stations under his charge, and the district now ranks well with the older ones."

If some of those early Banks' lifesavers lacked experience, it seems to have been compensated for in part by their willingness to risk their own lives in the attempt to save others, as was demonstrated at the wreck of the Italian bark *Nuova Ottavia* at Currituck Beach in early March, 1876. When the vessel struck on the bar in a rough sea, the lifesavers from Jones Hill Station immediately launched their surfboat in the darkness of night in an attempt to rescue the seven stranded seamen—and the entire station crew perished when the surfboat capsized.

Aside from the attempted interference of petty politicians, there were two serious defects in the lifesaving activities along the Banks in those early days of service. The first was that the stations were manned only during the four winter months and were locked up for the rest of the year. If a vessel came ashore in the spring, summer, or fall, there was no certainty at all that it would be sighted, the keeper located, and a lifesaving crew rounded up before it was beaten to pieces in the surf. The second fault was that the seven stations were located from twelve to fifteen miles apart, and though an attempt was made during the active season for the crews to maintain constant beach patrols, it was obvious that the six surfmen assigned to a station could not properly patrol such an area on foot, and horses had not at that time been made available to them.

The loss of 188 lives in two shipwrecks within a thirty-mile area on the North Banks during the winter of 1877-78 was directly attributed to these two causes.

When the *U.S.S. Huron* stranded at Nags Head in the early morning of November 24, 1877, the nearby lifesaving station was deserted, for the season of active service had not yet begun. "The calamity, therefore, occurred and was almost over before, on that desolate coast, the tidings of the disaster had spread beyond a few fishermen," the superintendent of the Lifesaving Service reported later. Ninety-eight lives were lost in the wreck (plus five more in subsequent salvage efforts), and it was thought that if the station had been activated, the wreck would have been discovered at an early hour by the patrol, "and, considering the contiguity of the vessel to the shore, it is probable that every person on board might have been saved."

On the other hand, when the wooden-hull steamer *Metropolis* struck on Currituck Beach four and one-half miles south of Jones Hill Station at approximately 6:30 A.M. on January 31, 1878, more than five hours elapsed before news of the wreck had been sent to the station and the lifesavers had managed to tow their heavy apparatus cart over the soft sand to the wreck scene. Eighty-five lives were lost in the wreck of the *Metropolis*, and the superintendent stated later that "the fundamental cause of the loss of life upon this occasion was the undue distances which . . . separated the stations."

This high loss of life in the wrecks of the *Huron* and *Metropolis* focused attention of the Congress on the need for additional stations on the North Carolina coast, and in an act passed June 18, 1878, several were authorized. By the winter of 1878-79 eleven new stations were in operation—Deal's Island (later named Wash Woods); Old Currituck Inlet (later named Currituck Inlet, and still later, Pennys Hill); Poyners Hill; Paul Gamiels Hill; Kill Devil Hills; Tommy's Hummock (located north of Oregon Inlet and later named Bodie Island); Pea Island; Cedar Hummock (later named Gull Shoal); Big Kinnakeet; Creeds Hill; and Hatteras (later named Durants).

By 1883 most of the remaining voids on this stretch of coast had been filled in with the construction of stations at New Inlet (which was located between Pea Island and Chicamacomico and was later burned), Cape Hatteras, Ocracoke (just west of Hatteras Inlet and later named Hatteras Inlet), and Cape Fear. Still later additional stations were constructed at Ocracoke village, Portsmouth, Core Banks (later named Atlantic), Cape Lookout, Fort Macon, Bogue Inlet, and Oak Island, bringing the North Carolina coast total to twenty-nine, of which all but four were on the Outer Banks.

Arrangements were made, also, for the surfmen to be employed for eight months each year beginning September 1, and in 1883 a seventh surfman was added to the crew. Thereafter, throughout the fall, winter, and spring—and later, on a year-around basis—the lifesavers maintained a constant patrol of the shoreline of the Outer Banks. Small structures, known as half-way houses, were erected between the stations, and these marked the boundaries of each station's patrol area. Thus, at any given time of day or night on Hatteras Island, for example, there would be both a north and south patrol on the beach from each of ten different stations—a total of twenty men walking the beach in that one section of the Banks, on the lookout for vessels in distress. The total loss of more than 650 vessels on the Outer Banks of North Carolina has been verified,* but the vigilance and bravery of

---

* There have been many references, particularly in newspaper and magazine articles, to "documentary evidence" of 2,400 shipwrecks at Cape Hatteras alone. This unfortunate misstatement was originated by a writer of fiction and has been accepted by others without any effort to check the facts.

the lifesavers have kept the loss of life remarkably small. On January 28, 1915, the Lifesaving Service was combined with the Revenue Cutter Service to form the U.S. Coast Guard, and the record of vigilance and bravery continues.

The flow of government pay checks which began with the construction of the lighthouses was greatly increased by the employment of native Bankers in the lifesaving stations, but the government was not yet done. On August 16, 1874, a U.S. Weather Station was established in the lighthouse keeper's quarters at Cape Hatteras, and it has been in continuous service since that time, though for most of the time it has been located in the village of Hatteras. A second Weather Bureau Station was established in the Kitty Hawk Lifesaving Station in 1875 and remained there until its discontinuation in 1904. Other Weather Bureau Stations on the Banks were located at Cape Lookout (1876 to 1904), Portsmouth (1876 to 1885), Beaufort Inlet (1878 to 1886) and Wash Woods (1878 to 1888), and sub-stations have been established in several other Banks communities.

At the close of the Civil War the only post offices in the Banks area were at Portsmouth, Ocracoke, Hatteras, and Knotts Island. Three others were established in 1873—at Manteo, Kinnakeet, and Cape Hatteras—and thereafter new post offices were added every few years, until every little hamlet seemed to have one. In the process the postal authorities managed to do away with a large number of the old community names.

The procedure followed in the selection of a name for a new post office was for the applicant or applicants to submit to the postal authorities one or more names of their choosing. Any of these which duplicated names already in use for North Carolina post offices or those which were considered too long or too hard to spell were discarded; and frequently the authorities in Washington just did not like any of the names submitted, so new ones were arbitrarily selected.

In this manner the community of Chicamacomico became Rodanthe in 1874; the one at Cape Hatteras, long known as The Cape, was changed to Buxton in 1882; Kinnakeet was changed to Avon in 1883; Ashby's Harbor, the location of the Old Dominion docks on the western shores of Roanoke Island, became Skyco in 1892; Whales Head or Currituck Beach became Corolla in 1895; Trent was changed to Frisco in 1898; Clarks to Salvo in 1901; Wash Woods to Deals in

Deals * 1907

Seagull * 1908

Corolla – 1895

Duck * 1909

Kitty Hawk – 1878

* Otila – 1905

* Colington – 1889

Kill Devil Hills – 1938

Nags Head – 1884

* (Griffin) – 1909

Manteo – 1873

* Skyco – 1892

Wanchese – 1886

Rodanthe – 1874

Waves – 1939

Salvo – 1901

Avon (Kinnakeet) – 1873

Buxton (The Cape) – 1873

Frisco – 1898

Hatteras – 1858

Ocracoke – 1840

Portsmouth – 1840

OUTER BANKS
POST OFFICES

WITH ESTABLISHMENT DATES

NOTE — POST OFFICES MARKED
WITH AN ASTERISK HAVE
BEEN DISCONTINUED

*Cape Lookout – 1910

1907; Pennys Hill to Seagull in 1908; Naghead was changed to Griffin in 1915 and then Nags Head in 1916; and South Rodanthe became Waves in 1939. Of the remaining Banks post offices, Kitty Hawk was established in 1878, Wanchese in 1886, and Kill Devil Hills in 1938. A number of others, once active, have since been discontinued. These, with the date of establishment of each, were: Colington, 1889; Otilla, 1905; Deals, 1907; Seagull, 1908; Duck, 1909; and Cape Lookout, 1910. Otilla, Deals, Seagull, and Duck were located on the North Banks.

From an economic standpoint these post offices, weather stations, lighthouses, and lifesaving stations were of great importance, providing a stable economic base which would tide the communities through periods of recession, and they still do.*

The influence and political standing of the keepers or "Captains" of the lifesaving stations were as much an accepted part of Banks life as the steady flow of government money. Many of the early lifesavers—and some of the later ones—were unlettered men, and in many instances their wreck reports doubtless took longer to compose than did the rescues they wrote about. But whether or not they possessed formal education, when problems arose in the community their neighbors most often turned to the keepers for guidance.

When Dan Yeomans of Harkers Island joined the Lifesaving Service and was stationed at Portsmouth in 1899, he said the keeper there was receiving $60.00 a month in salary. He was not only the number one man in the station, but in the community as well. "We looked on him as President," Yeoman said.

The minority political party was not at all pleased with this condition, however, as was indicated in a letter written at Buxton, September 16, 1898, in which A. W. Simpson complained to J. H. Small that Hatteras Island was solidly Republican because of the influence of the Lifesaving Service.

"Before President Cleveland placed the L.S. Service under Civil Service rules every young man in the neighborhood of a station was promised 'The first Vacancy,'" he said. "And when he came to vote he knew he must vote for the Keeper who had promised him the

---

* Of 179 heads of families listed in the 1950 census for Dare County's Kennekeet Township—Avon, Rodanthe, Waves, and Salvo—56 were retired from service, and 37 were on active Coast Guard duty, a total of 93, or well over half of the families, receiving regular federal pay checks from this one branch of service.

place, or lose it." He stated that the Republican majority in the two townships on Hatteras Island was between 150 and 175 votes, but he added that "by the judicious use of proper means this majority can be reduced to less than 75." An indication of his definition of "proper means" is gathered from the further statement that "there are only 4 colored voters in the two townships—And $5. will control them." Simpson, a staunch Democrat in an obviously alien land, complained that "the backbone of the Republican party here are — 'Yeopon-Choppers', 'Mullet-Gillers', and 'Beach-Combers', and it is no wonder they are 'political floaters' " since "A large per cent of them are up 'For Value Received.' "

Simpson's reference to "Yeopon-Choppers" might seem innocuous, but in 1898 it was about as derogatory a term as he could have used.

Yaupon is a bush of the holly family (*Ilex Vomitoria*) which grows in great profusion on the Banks, and from the leaves of which a tea is made. John Lawson said that the native Indians held yaupon "in Veneration, above all the Plants they are acquainted withal" and that it was the only prescription known to them "for Purging and Emeticks." He said they got the full benefit of the yaupon tea "in drinking vast Quantities . . . and vomiting it up again, as clear as they drink it. This is a Custom amongst all those that can procure that Plant, in which manner they take it every other Morning, or oftner."

A few years after Lawson's book appeared, Mark Catesby said that yaupon tea "is as much in use among the white people as among the Indians, at least among those who inhabit the sea-coasts." At the close of the Revolution a visitor to Edenton got his first taste of "Japan" tea and described it as "universally known and beloved in North Carolina." In the census of 1860 a man named Quidley, in Hatteras Township, listed his occupation as "Yappan manuf[acturer]," and as late as 1903 an elderly Negro man named Scarborough operated a "yopon factory" at Frisco, selling much of his product on the mainland.

Despite the long-standing and wide-spread popularity of yaupon tea, a connotation of inferiority came to be associated with yaupon drinkers on the Banks.

At a ball game between Kinnakeet and Hatteras many years back, for example, one Hatteras spectator is said to have composed a simple ditty designed to arouse ire in the breast of the opponent.

"Kinnakeeters, Yaupon Eaters," he shouted, and the chant was immediately taken up. Though there is no record of the outcome of that particular contest, it is certain that these words, even today, are best not uttered in the presence of a resident of Kinnakeet.

These same Bankers who improvised tea from a local bush demonstrated their self-sufficiency in many other ways. Because of the isolation of the Banks, almost all transportation was by small boats, and through the years local builders developed special types of craft particularly suited for use in the broad, shallow sounds.

In the colonial period the residents of coastal North Carolina had made extensive use of vessels made from cypress logs. A canoe was hollowed out of a single large log, and a perriauger, from two logs— or from a single large log cut in half—laid parallel to each other, several feet apart, and joined by a plank decking. The canoes were later designated simply as "dugouts," while the larger perriaugers became known as "kunners." The canoes or dugouts were equipped with oars or paddles, and sometimes with small sails; the perriaugers or kunners—some of them large enough to carry a hundred barrels of tar—usually had a mast and sails, and despite their clumsy appearance, they were fast sailers.

The canoes, the perriaugers, and the small schooners and sloops which were used in the sounds were not designed for all-weather use, however, and shortly after the Civil War, according to Horace Dough of Kill Devil Hills, an East Lake man named Creef designed a boat which was so admirably suited to the needs of the Bankers that it almost replaced the older types.

The basic problems which Creef tried to cope with were the extent of shallow water, which necessitated a shallow draft boat, and the extreme and rapid changes in wind velocity in the sounds, which called for the use of a large amount of sail during the calm periods and of practically none when squalls came up. Creef designed a round-bottom boat with a square stern, a sharply-pointed bow, and a shallow keel. He fitted it with a large sprit mainsail and a jib—not an unusual rig in those days—and then added a topsail which could be raised and lowered independently of the others. In calm weather all three sails would be employed, and the boat proved to be an exceptionally fast sailer; when sudden squalls came up the topsail could be lowered in a few seconds and sometimes even was allowed to fall overboard to be picked up later. To compensate for this extra canvas the boat was designed to carry ballast, usually twenty to forty sandbags weighing sixty pounds each which could be shifted when tacking.

Because Creef's boat was used in the shad fisheries it became known as a "shad boat" or "Pamlico Sound Fisherman." One of its distinctive features was that the frames were made from naturally-curved cypress-knee roots; and in almost all instances the remainder of the boat was made of native juniper or white cedar. The average length of the shad boats was twenty-three to twenty-six feet.

A second type of boat used extensively in the area, particularly in the lower sounds, was an adaptation of the sharpie with a rounded stern. This was called a "Core Sound Sharpie" and later simply a "Core Sounder," and today almost any boat built in that area with a round stern is designated as a "Core Sound Boat."

When motor boats replaced the sailing craft, the shad boats were still used; but gradually the dead-rise skiff, or "V-Bottom" boat, became popular, and shad boats are now seldom seen.

Commercial hunting, already an important source of income in the Currituck Sound area before the Civil War, became even more widespread toward the end of the nineteenth century, and the shad boats were used extensively by the gunners. Much of the hunting was done from sink boxes, located on shoals in the sounds and equipped with canvas extensions which could be raised when the tide rose, or from one-man floating batteries, which were coffin-like boxes surrounded by floating platforms or wings on all sides to break the waves. The shad boats were used to put the rig in place, including flocks of hand-made wooden "idols" or decoys, to transport the gunners to and from shore, and to pick up the game that was shot down.

The most popular gun at first was the muzzle loader, but this was replaced by the double-barrel breech loader and later, about 1908, by the automatic shotgun. There were early instances of the use of a cannon-like contraption with a ten-foot barrel known as a punt gun. The game was usually sold to local buyers who shipped it north, after gutting it and hanging it overnight. About 1874 icing was introduced, and thereafter the birds were generally packed in barrels, sometimes with alternate layers of ducks and ice, at other times with a stovepipe full of ice in the center and the game placed around it.

Prices for wildfowl varied according to the season and the type of fowl. Strangely enough the Canada goose generally brought a much smaller price than certain species of duck, particularly canvasbacks and redheads. Average prices were: canvasbacks and redhead, $1.00 to $4.00 per pair; ruddy ducks, teal, bufflehead, and other small ducks, 25¢ to $2.00 per pair; common ducks or marsh ducks, 25¢ to $1.00 per pair; and Canada geese 25¢ to 50¢ each. According to T. S. Critcher, the record kill in Currituck Sound was made about 1905 by Russell and Van Griggs who killed 892 ruddy ducks in one day. In recounting that experience recently, Russell Griggs said the barrel of his gun got so hot he had to stick it overboard into the water to cool it off.

The Migratory Bird Treaty Act, passed in 1918, made the sale of migratory waterfowl illegal, but by then sports hunting had become very popular, and hunting clubs owned by wealthy Northerners were located up and down the Banks. With the passing of stringent game laws which shortened the season, lowered the bag limit, and outlawed batteries, live decoys, and certain types of guns, sports hunting declined in the 1930's, and today most of it is carried on from brush blinds near the shore.

Still another type of hunting in which a few Bankers engaged profitably for a short time involved the shooting of egrets and terns for the feathers which were sold to millinery firms. The wearing of egret-plume hats was, of course, the height of style at the turn of the century, and in a short time certain species became almost extinct. Through the efforts of the Audubon Society and similar groups, legislation was enacted which outlawed the needless massacre of these beautiful birds, and on the Banks this lucrative business was brought under control with the arrival of special wardens in 1903.

During the first years of this century the Outer Banks seemed to have an unusual appeal for inventors, for in addition to the activities of the Wright brothers at Kitty Hawk and Kill Devil Hills between 1900 and 1903, important experiments were carried on at almost the same time at Hatteras and Roanoke Island in the development of wireless telegraphy, the forerunner of modern radio.

In 1901 Reginald L. Fessenden, former chief chemist on the staff of Thomas A. Edison and a pioneer in the field of wireless telegraphy, began experimenting with the transmission of messages between two fifty-foot towers, one near Cape Hatteras and the other on the north end of Roanoke Island. Though Guglielmo Marconi, the Italian physicist, has been generally credited with the development of wireless telegraphy, Fessenden was engaged on the Banks at approximately the same time in perfecting an entirely different system, which his backers claim was the true basis for radio broadcasting.

A letter from Fessenden to his patent attorney, dated Manteo, April 3, 1902, recounts the success of his activities: "I have more good news for you. You remember I telephoned about a mile in 1900—but thought it would take too much power to telephone across the Atlantic. Well, I can now telephone as far as I can telegraph, which is across the Pacific Ocean if desired. I have sent varying musical notes from Hatteras and received them here with but 3 watts of energy, and they were very loud and plain, i.e., as loud as in an ordinary telephone."

One of the most far-reaching changes on the Outer Banks in the period following the Civil War was the declining importance of the inlets. Ocracoke Inlet had long since shoaled up so badly that few vessels dared to attempt the passage there, and the newer Hatteras Inlet was almost as bad. The problem was pointed up in a report by Major W. S. Stanton of the Army Corps of Engineers, who investigated the desirability of improving Ocracoke Inlet channel in 1893:

One mariner wrote me in July last that on a trip he was then making he had been three weeks trying to get round Hatteras, beating against a southwester, and counted 55 vessels around him likewise baffled. Another writes that he has known vessels detained off the shoals fifteen to twenty days, and cites an instance of a vessel bound to the Pamlico River which abandoned its attempt to round the cape after a persevering effort, sailed back to Hampton Roads, returned south through the Albemarle and Chesapeake Canal and the sounds to the Pamlico River, there received its cargo, and sailed out through [Hatteras] Inlet, passing, as it rounded Cape Hatteras, the very vessels with which it had attempted to double the cape going south, still to the north of it waiting for a favorable wind.

Another instance is given of two vessels arriving at the cape together, bound, the one through Hatteras Inlet, 11 miles south of the cape, and the other to Galveston, Tex. The latter reached Galveston while the former was still waiting to get around Hatteras and through the inlet.

By that time the Army Engineers were responsible for the maintenance of inland water routes, and Major Stanton and his associates concluded that no amount of improvement to Ocracoke Inlet or Hatteras Inlet could solve the problem. The greatest difficulty was not in going through the inlets but in getting around Cape Hatteras. Nevertheless, a project for dredging Wallace's Channel in Ocracoke Inlet was begun in 1895, the year the last commercial vessel is said to have passed through Hatteras Inlet. But the re-emergence of Ocracoke Inlet as a port of entry was destined to be brief, for a long-range plan was being evolved which would circumvent Cape Hatteras by providing canals to the north and south of sufficient depth to accommodate any vessel which could navigate the sounds and rivers.

Already the privately-owned Albemarle and Chesapeake Canal connecting Currituck Sound with Chesapeake Bay was handling more traffic than had ever passed through the inlets, the figures for 1892 * showing that tolls had been collected on 4,061 steamers, 1,817 schooners, 1,150 barges, 62 lighters, 329 sloops, and 298 rafts. In 1891 the government had purchased the old Clubfoot Creek–Harlowe Creek Canal connecting Pamlico Sound with Beaufort, and plans were made for construction of a deeper and straighter and wider canal roughly paralleling the old one, to be known as the Adams Creek Canal. This was completed in 1910, and three years later the government purchased the Albemarle and Chesapeake Canal.

To complete this inland waterway between Chesapeake Bay and Beaufort Inlet, it was decided to abandon the old connecting link through Croatan and Pamlico sounds and build a canal through the swamp wastelands which separated Alligator River and Albemarle Sound, on the north, from Pungo River and the Pamlico, on the south.

With Cape Hatteras successfully circumvented for vessels of up to ten-foot draft, there remained still the problem of providing a harbor of refuge for larger ships in time of storm. Two locations were suggested, one in the bight of Cape Hatteras, the other at Cape Lookout. The advocates of the Cape Lookout location talked of extending the

---

* In that year, according to an article by Samuel Ward Stanton in *Seaboard*, the following steamers were being operated on regular schedules: The Old Dominion Steamboat Company passenger steamer *Newberne* between Norfolk and New Bern, with stops at Skyco on Roanoke Island; the *Albemarle* between Norfolk and Washington; and the *Neuse* between Elizabeth City and New Bern. The Clyde Line freight steamers *George H. Stout* and *Defiance* connected Baltimore, Norfolk, and New Bern, and the *Vesper* ran between Norfolk and Washington. The Rogers Company was operating the *Comet* and *W. B. Rogers* between Norfolk and Currituck Sound points, while more or less regular schedules were maintained between the same places by the side-wheeler *Bonita* and the propellers *Helen Smith* and *Harbinger*. In addition, other steamers were running on regular schedules on and between the Chowan, Roanoke, Alligator, Pamlico, Neuse, and Tar rivers.

railroad from Beaufort to the cape to provide a deep water harbor for loading and unloading ocean-going vessels, and with this incentive, work was begun on a harbor of refuge there. As early as 1888 the Army Engineers had constructed sand fences and jetties at Beaufort Inlet to stabilize the shores, and in 1913 similar work was begun at Cape Lookout. Construction of what was intended to be a 7,000-foot jetty at the hook of the Cape was begun also, but by 1918, when the jetty was 4,800 feet long, the railroad project was abandoned and it was found that use of the new facility as a harbor of refuge was limited, so the work was discontinued.

The construction of the all-weather Intracoastal Waterway from Beaufort Inlet to Chesapeake Bay killed all hopes of again making Ocracoke Inlet or Hatteras Inlet major ports of entry; the establishment of the harbor of refuge at Cape Lookout did away with the potential usefulness of the older inlets for that purpose. Thereafter the work of the United States government engineers in the area was limited to making the inlets navigable for small fishing boats and constructing small harbors and shallow channels leading to the villages.* The days of extensive maritime activity along the Banks were ended.

* The original harbor dredging projects were undertaken in the following years: Manteo Harbor (Shallowbag Bay), 1908-1910; Ocracoke (Silver Lake Harbor, formerly known as Cockle Creek), 1931; Hatteras (Rollinson Channel), 1936; Rodanthe (a harbor built by U.S. Coast Guard), 1936-37; and Avon, 1946. The most extensive modern-day project, involving the deepening of Oregon Inlet and dredging a deep channel from there to Manteo, is being undertaken as this is written. No attempt is being made at permanent stabilization, and even before the work is finished, the dredged-out channels are filling again with sand.

F.S.

Diamond City

THOUGH IT WOULD be difficult to find visual evidences of it
there today, one of the largest communities on the Outer Banks in the
latter part of the last century was Diamond City, which was located
a short distance west of the Cape Lookout Lighthouse, just beyond
The Drain.

People had been living in that vicinity since the early days of Banks
settlement, but the life of Diamond City itself was a short one, with a
strange and unhappy ending. It was not until about 1885 that this
community of several hundred persons acquired a name, yet in less
than twenty years the name was about all that was left of it, for the
people had moved, and when they moved they took Diamond City
with them—except for the name, that is, and the little family graveyards where the houses used to stand.

The written records in the story of Diamond City begin as early as
1723. On September 2 of that year two Carolinians, brothers-in-law
named Enoch Ward and John Shackleford, signed an agreement for
the equal division of some 7,000 acres of Banks land they had acquired
jointly. Their original holdings extended from Beaufort Inlet, around
Cape Lookout, and up the Banks to Drum Inlet, an entire Banks island
some twenty-five miles in length. In the division, Ward agreed to take

the eastern half, the part known as Core Banks; Shackleford took the western half, from Cape Lookout to Beaufort Inlet.

Seven years later a man named Ebenezer Harker purchased Craney Island, containing approximately 2,400 acres and located directly across the sound from Cape Lookout and less than three miles from the Banks John Shackleford had acquired in his division with Enoch Ward. These two pieces of land, Harkers Island and Shackleford Banks, were to figure prominently in the story of Diamond City.

Equally important were the New England whalers, who made an appearance on the coast about that same time (the first permit was issued in 1726) and used Cape Lookout harbor as a base of operations as they attempted to intercept the northbound migration of whales in the early spring. They sometimes spotted the giant creatures from their anchored vessels, launched small boats for the attack, and captured the whales within sight of shore. This was not an especially profitable operation for the large whaling vessels, since the catch was spotty at best, but it set some of the Bankers to thinking. Before many years they were trying it themselves, going to sea after the whales in small pilot boats, specially designed craft which they could launch from the beach.

The extent of those early shore-based whaling operations at Cape Lookout is not known, though there are indications that one or more crews were whaling there almost continuously over a period of more than 150 years. In the 1750's the heirs of John Shackleford sold several tracts of his Banks land, and in the deeds to Joseph Morss and to Edward Fuller in 1757, for example, it was stipulated that the purchasers should have the privilege "to fish and whale it . . . and also to have a landing at the said Point Look Out Bay." At least one person, a man named Davis, had built a permanent house there by the 1760's, and when Captain Lobb of *H.M.S. Viper* made a detailed survey of Cape Lookout in 1764, he showed several buildings just west of the cape and identified them as "Whalers Hutts."

There are frequent references to these shore-based whaling operations in the Cape Lookout area in the century or so preceding the Civil War, but the New England whalers—who had never really made extensive use of the Cape Lookout grounds—concentrated their southern activities on the open sea off Hatteras after the whaler *Edwin and Rienzi*, searching for blackfish in that area in 1837, discovered a new "sperm-whale cruising ground" which became known as the Hatteras Ground.

Since whaling was a seasonal occupation at Cape Lookout limited almost entirely to the months of February, March, and April, the shore-based whalers were engaged also in mullet fishing, and some of them operated porpoise fisheries as well. By 1853, when the original U.S. Coast Survey of Shackleford Banks was made, the whales, mullets, and porpoises had attracted a sizable community. Several buildings were shown on the beach in that vicinity, and a larger settlement was located in an area designated as "Lookout Woods" a mile or so west of the lighthouse.

The New England whalers did not give up entirely until the 1870's, when two of them returned to Cape Lookout. In 1874 and 1875 the *Daniel Webster* cruised for three months out of Cape Lookout harbor without capturing a single whale; then, in August, 1879, the *Seychille* came into the harbor for the same purpose. The story is that the *Seychille* was commanded by a Captain Cook, who went ashore and asked the Bankers when he could expect to find the best weather in that area. He was told that, year in and year out, August probably brought the best weather, and, no doubt pleased that he had picked that very month for his first operations, he began to prepare for a whaling cruise in the vicinity. Before the vessel put to sea, however, a severe storm struck with hurricane-like winds and extreme high tides. The vessel broke her anchor chain and drifted across Wreck Point into the open sea; then the wind shifted and **forced her back** over Wreck Point again, across the open bay, and high up on the beach. She was, one Banker said, "stripped clean by wind and water" and was in no shape thereafter for whaling. For many years afterward the Bankers referred to that storm as Old Cook's Storm.

The *Daniel Webster* is credited with introducing the whaling gun to the shore whalers at Cape Lookout in 1875, and in the years that followed the gun was used extensively. The plan of operation followed by the shore-based whalers was described by A. Howard Clark in 1880, as follows:

When the season arrives for whaling, three crews of six men each, unite to form a camp, and proceed to build a house out of rushes in some desirable location near the shore, for protection against the weather. Their boats, usually three in number, and their implements, are placed in readiness on the beach, and a lookout selected, where one man is stationed, to give the signal if the whales come in sight.

At this season of the year the whales are moving northward, and in their migrations often come within a short distance of the shore, where they are pursued and often captured by the fishermen. As soon as the whale is harpooned the "drug" is thrown over, and when he turns to fight, the fishermen, armed with guns, shoot him with explosive cartridges, and after killing him with their lances, tow him to the shore.

According to Clark "the number of crews varies with the season, it formerly averaging but two or three, of eighteen men each." In 1879, however, four crews were engaged in the general area of Cape Lookout, and they captured five whales, while the number of crews was increased to six in 1880 though only one whale was taken. Generally the yearly catch was "about four whales, averaging 1,800 gallons of oil and 550 pounds of bone each, giving the catch a value of $4,500."

The proceeds from the whaling activities were divided on a share basis, and in a typical crew in 1880 each of the men would have received a single share, each boat one share, each gun two shares, each gunner an extra share, and each steersman an additional one-half share, making a total of between thirty and forty shares for an eighteen-man crew.

By then there was a veritable city in the Lookout Woods west of the cape, and a number of the people were employed in a porpoise processing plant which had been started there by a New Jersey man named Gardiner. The settlement had no name, being referred to simply as "the eastern end"—to differentiate it from the smaller community closer to Beaufort Inlet known as Shackleford Banks, or Mullet Shore, or Wade's Shore, and the settlement near the lighthouse known as Cape Hills—and some of the residents were of the opinion that a definite name should be adopted. There was, however, disagreement as to what the name should be, and the matter was not resolved until it was brought to the attention of Joe Etheridge who was superintendent of the lifesaving stations in the area.

Etheridge was stranded in the community during a severe storm—afterwards they called it the Canadian blizzard—probably in the winter of 1885. Noting that the distinguishing feature of the community was the 150-foot-high Cape Lookout Lighthouse which towered above it to the east and observing that the exterior of the lighthouse was painted in a distinctive diamond design, alternately white and black, he suggested that a logical name would be Diamond City. The suggestion is said to have met with immediate approval, and the name Diamond City was quickly adopted.

As this is written there are people still living in eastern North Carolina who were born at Diamond City and who resided there as children, who watched the menfolk put to sea in their small boats when the whales passed by, and who helped the women tend the fires when the blubber was boiled to extract the oil. They were there when the storms struck that literally frightened Diamond City out of existence; and they rode in the open sail boats across the sound, sitting on top of door openings and window frames, when the houses were moved away. There is something akin to reverence in their voices as they talk of Diamond City and a note of longing for the happy days in the whaling community on the Banks before the storm came. Let them tell the story of Diamond City as they knew it as children in the 1890's; listen to Jimmy Guthrie, and his wife Miss Cary, and her brother Dan Yeomans; and listen, also, to Captain Iredell Rose, Captain Joe Rose, and others who remember when Diamond City was something more than just a name.

Who lived at Diamond City? Well, there was Tom Salter and his wife Jenny Lind. And the widow, Miss Caroline Salter, and her sons John, Tom, and Sam, and daughter Nicey. There was James Johnson, the Yankee soldier who married Sally Ann, and Charley Hancock who kept store, and his wife Aggie, and their children Louie and Louisa. Then there were Willises—why, there were so many Willises it would take half a day just to count them—and the Guthries were as thick as the Willises. There was one family of Nixons, and another of Wades; and two named Styron; and of course the Yeomanses, and the Roses.

How many people lived there? Two hundred; no, three hundred; maybe even as many as five hundred. Diamond City was big, spread over half the island, beginning at The Drain and spreading toward Beaufort Inlet. But Diamond City wasn't all. Maybe a hundred people or more lived at the other end of Shackleford Banks at Wade's Hammock; and four or five families at Kib Guthrie's Lump, and there was the colored man, Sam Winsor, with his family at the place called Sam

Winsor's Lump. You could get some idea of the number of people who had lived there before by the graveyards; little ones, off beside the houses, and one big one—Ben Riles Graveyard, they called it—right in the middle of Diamond City, with maybe as many as 500 graves in it.

There were other stores besides Charley Hancock's; Ambrose Lee Guthrie ran one, and Clifford Hancock another. They were small stores, carrying a little bit of everything, and a man named Johnson ran a boat from Beaufort to bring in supplies and the mail.

The people built a schoolhouse at Diamond City, a big one, though it was only used for a month or two months in the summer, usually in July and August. For a long time the teacher was a man named Tom Arrendel who came over from the mainland. They paid him twenty dollars a month, and at one time there were probably as many as a hundred young folks going to him, maybe even more. Down at Wade's Hammock there was another school, but the big one was at Diamond City.

They used the schoolhouse for services too—Methodist, Baptist, Mormon, Pentecostal—not regularly, though sometimes a preacher would come to stay for a while. Then, usually down at Shackleford's, the Pentecostals held their camp meetings; sometimes they lasted as much as three or four weeks. They met out in the open, "under the cedars" they called it, and people came from all over, not just Pentecostals but others too, as many as two or three thousand for a special day with "grub on the ground." The bigger boats couldn't get in close to shore, and one time they brought over a lot of smaller boats from the mainland and made a bridge out of them, from the shore out to deep water where the big boats had to anchor.

There were some Guthries over at Wade's Hammock, too, but most of the people there were Lewises and Myerses and Moores and Davises. There wasn't a doctor there or at Diamond City either; and when people really had to see a doctor they went over to the mainland, to Beaufort or Straits. Most of the doctoring, though, was done by two midwives at Diamond City, Margaret Ann Willis and Rachael Willis. People lived a long time at Shackleford and Diamond City, longer than they do now it seems like; maybe what they ate had something to do with it, seafood they caught themselves, mostly, and garden crops they raised.

The porpoise factory the New Jersey man started lasted only a few years, but other people were always trying something like it. At one time there was an oyster house at Diamond City, run by a man named Druden; and then a crab-packing house, owned by a big company. The people caught the peelers and sold them to the plant; and when the peelers shed, the soft crabs were packed up and shipped away. Then in 1897 or 1898 some men came down from up the Banks and brought sturgeon nets and tried to work up that business. Their name was Hayman; easy to remember the name, because there was a cold spell that winter, froze up the sound, and afterwards people called it the Joe Hayman Freeze.

That's the way things were remembered—storms, and shipwrecks, and other important things, even whales—by a special name, because of something that happened at just that time. There was the Sheep Storm for instance, in the 1880's, when so many sheep were drowned; and in December, 1902, the Olive Thurlow Storm, when the barkentine *Olive Thurlow* was wrecked below the cape; and just recently, in 1933, the Jimmy Hamilton Storm, the one when Jimmy drowned.

What about the whales? Well, there was the Mayflower Whale, and the Lee Whale, and the Tom Martin Whale, and the John Rose Whale, and the Little Children Whale. That one was named because most of the men were away when the whale was sighted, and a lot of young boys had to take oars in the whaleboats.

The way they did the whaling was like this: the old men were lookouts, and one of them stayed all day on top of Lookout Hill— though the oldtimers said they used to build lookout cabins up in the branches of high trees near the water. The boats were kept on the beach, all the gear in place except for the gun, the gunner keeping care of that, sleeping with it practically, to be ready when the whales showed up.

The boats were about twenty-five feet long, lap-streak pilot boats with high pointed bows and sterns. They didn't carry sails, just four oars, and the steering oar; and some of those crews could get the boats launched and underway so fast you almost wouldn't believe it.

Usually there were four to six boats on the beach abreast of Diamond City, and they all worked together, like a team, because they all shared equally in the profits. There were two whale guns at Diamond City, one was a half-pounder, the other a quarter-pounder, hand weapons both, to fire the harpoon spears. It was exciting enough with the whale guns, but think what it was like before they got the guns and had to hit those whales with a hand spear.

Sometimes they would get in close enough to hit a whale and it would still get away; sometimes they'd get too close and a flipper would strike one of the boats, turn it over, or tear it up. Once they harpooned the whale and killed him, the boats would all hook on and start towing him in to the beach, usually right abreast of Diamond City. They'd wait until high tide and then beach the whale, and when the tide went down, there he'd be, clear out of the water.

But chasing the whale, and spearing him, and getting him up on the beach, was just the beginning. After that the real work started, with practically everybody in the community joining in. They had to work fast, too, for fear of a storm washing the whale away and to keep the blubber from drying out too much, but most of all because of the stink after a few days.

Even before the whale had been beached at high tide, the women and children and men who were left behind would be making the camp, hauling down the kettles, great big ones that would hold sixty gallons, rigging up shelters, bringing the knives and scrapers and other gear. Usually they'd bring down bricks, too, and make big ovens to hold the kettles, building hot fires of driftwood underneath. The men would get up on top of the whale with the big cutting spades and start peeling off the blubber, cutting it into pieces about two feet square. Then other people would cut these into smaller chunks, about the size of your hand, and dump them in the pots. Everybody had a job to do. Some would be in charge of fixing a bite of something to eat or getting fresh water; others gathered up the driftwood and kept the fires going. Then there were the dippers who used big ladles to dip out the oil in the kettles when it was separated from the blubber. Usually they poured it into a special trough, beside the kettles, and it would run down the trough, passing through a sort of strainer made out of reeds, and then into a barrel which had been sunk in a hole in the sand. The barrels usually were old molasses barrels, sometimes as big as a hogshead, and when one was filled the men would lift it out and put another one in the hole at the end of the trough.

Uncle Billy Hancock's job was to cut out the bone in the whale's mouth. He wore a suit of oilskins, fitted tight so there was hardly a piece of him that wasn't covered; then he'd take his axe and go into the whale's mouth. Sometimes he'd disappear inside, and you could hear him cutting away with his axe; then he'd come out again, bringing a piece of mouth bone with him. The ones from the Little Children Whale were seven and a half feet long.*

Usually it took about two weeks to cut up a whale and boil out the oil, with everybody in the community taking some part in the business. Most times the bone and oil were sold over in Beaufort; the last few times they were sold to Guy Potter, who shipped them off to New Bedford. Then it was time to share up, and every man in each of the crews had a full share, with extra ones for the boats and the gear.

What happened to Diamond City? Well, everything went along fine until the late 1890's when a couple of storms came over the beach and flooded some of the gardens and even got into a home or two. Some people then talked about leaving, and several of them went over to Morehead City and bought lots in a place called The Promised Land.

Then, in August of 1899 a real hurricane hit—the worst one the old folks could remember. There was water over everything, with just a few of the bigger sand hills sticking their tops out, and the houses mostly looking like house-boats, surrounded by sea water. It washed over the stones in the graveyards and uncovered the bones of the folks buried there; it killed most of the big trees, and flooded the gardens with salt water and cut the beach down so low in spots that almost every high tide would come over. And it washed a lot of the houses off their foundations, smashed up boats, blew down outhouses, and "mommicked up" just about everything else in Diamond City. Most

---

* Eugene P. Odum (ed.), *A North Carolina Naturalist—H. H. Brimley: Selections from His Writings* (Chapel Hill: The University of North Carolina Press, 1949), p. 104, described whalebone as follows: "The whalebone ... consists of a large series of horny (not bone) plates that grow downwards and outwards from the upper jaw of the animal, their inside thin edges being developed in the form of long, hair-like fibers, the whole series being enclosed by the wall-like lips of the lower jaw when the mouth is closed.

"The Bowhead and Right Whales [the type usually caught in the Cape Lookout area] carry something like 350 to 370 of these laminae on each side of the mouth. This mass of lamina—or plates—constitutes a very perfect strainer. The whale swims slowly through the masses of small crustacea, etc. that constitute its food, lower jaw hanging low. When sufficient food for a swallow has been accumulated, the mouth is closed—the great tongue virtually filling the mouth cavity—the water gushing out between the plates of whalebone, leaving the food inside. It is then, of course, swallowed."

people, when it was over, figured next time a storm like that hit Diamond City none of them would live long enough to tell about it, and some of the older folks began talking about moving away.

The people at Diamond City had built their own homes, or their ancestors had, and many of them had been moved there from other places. Eugene Yeoman, for example, had built a house on Harkers Island about 1870, then tore it down, and moved it to Diamond City board by board, where he set it up again about 1888. Another man had built at Diamond City, moved up the Banks to Guthrie's Hammock, then moved back to Diamond City again, taking his house with him each time he moved. The moving that went on after that August storm in 1899, though, was something else again.

William Henry Guthrie was the first one to leave. He went over to Harkers Island—there were only about thirteen families at Harkers in 1899—and bought sixty acres of land, and early the next spring, 1900, he tore down his house and moved it across the sound. Several neighbors went to William Henry, bought lots out of his sixty acres, and made arrangements to move over with him. After that there was hardly a week went by that some house wasn't torn down at Diamond City, loaded on sailboats, and moved across the sound to Harkers Island. It kept up all through 1900 and 1901, and by 1902 there wasn't a house or a person left at Diamond City, only some old deserted shacks and what was left of the graveyards.

Some of the houses were torn down, board by board, and rebuilt over on Harkers. Others were cut in half, or even moved whole, using a couple of boats joined together by big planks, sort of twin-hulled barges. It only took two or three days to move a house, and thirty or forty men would join in helping; no money changed hands as it would today, for the same people would pitch in together and move your house for you, when your turn came; only the person whose house was being moved was supposed to provide something to eat—a lot of something to eat, too, for thirty or forty hungry men.

A few of the Diamond City people moved to the lots they had bought in The Promised Land, a few others went to Marshallberg, and some moved up the Banks to the more sheltered section at the Cape Hills. Most of the folks on the other end of Shackleford Banks went down to Bogue Banks, to a place called Gillikin, now known as Salter Path, and their children live there still. But two out of three of the families from Diamond City moved to Harkers Island, and by 1902 the population there was several times what it had been before. These were the same people who had lived at Diamond City and the same houses they had lived in there; and when it came to something for them to do, these people who had moved to Harkers Island from Diamond City, why they just naturally kept right on doing what they had done before. They fished for mullet and for porpoise off the beach at Diamond City and, in February and March and April, set up a lookout on top of one of the high sand hills with an old man on the watch for whales. The men would camp there, sometimes for several weeks at a time, nearby where their houses used to be. But the whales seemed to stop coming up the coast past Cape Lookout, and there were several years when none at all were sighted. The last one was killed in 1909.* After that even the fishermen stopped going back to Diamond City, and only the stock remained to graze along the winding paths that once had been the streets of the city; but today even the paths are gone, and over on Harkers Island there are young folk who've heard of Diamond City but can't rightly tell you where or what it was.

* A very interesting account of whaling operations at Cape Lookout has been preserved in Odum (ed.), *A North Carolina Naturalist—H. H. Brimley*, pp. 97-115. He quotes John E. Lewis as saying that a whaler named Absalom Guthrie, who was in one of the boats which took the Mayflower Whale about 1874 after a fight of half a day, kept a record of the whales he helped kill, and the total figure was fifty-two.

The Wright Brothers

HE WAS a young man, thirty-three years old, but prematurely balding, five feet ten and one-quarter inches in height, his normal weight about 140 pounds; but when he stepped ashore at the landing on Kitty Hawk Bay the morning of September 13, 1900, his weight was doubtless under the 140-pound mark, for he had eaten nothing but a small jar of jelly during the preceding two days.

He asked directions to William J. Tate's house, and a young boy, Elijah Baum, led him along one sandy ridge running back from the bay and down another to the Tate place. He had never seen Captain Bill Tate before, nor had Tate seen him, but he doubtless thought then of the letter Captain Bill had written him less than a month earlier. It was because of the letter that he had decided to make this trip to Kitty Hawk. The letter was dated August 18, 1900, and was addressed to Mr. Wilbur Wright, Wright Cycle Company, Dayton, Ohio:

Mr. J. J. Dosher of the Weather Bureau here has asked me to ans. your letter to him, relitive to the fitness of Kitty Hawk as a place to practise or experiment with a flying machine, &c.

In answering I would say that you would find here nearly any type of ground you could wish; you could, for instance, get a strech of sandy land 1 mile by five with a bare hill in center 80 feet high, not a tree or bush anywhere to break the eveness of the wind current. This in my opinion would be a fine place; our winds are always steady, generally from 10 to 20 miles velocity per hour.

You can reach here from Eliz. City, N.C. (35 miles from here) by boat direct or from Manteo 12 miles from here by mail boat every Mon., Wed. & Friday. We have Telegraph communication & daily mails. Climate healthy. You could find good place to pitch tents & get board in private family provided there were not to many in your party; would advise you to come any time from Sept. 15 to Oct. 15. Don't wait untill Nov. The autumn generally gets a little rough by Nov.

If you decide to try your machine here & come I will take pleasure in doing all I can for your convenience & success & pleasure, & I assure you you will find a hospitiable people when you come among us.

Wilbur Wright had come alone on this first trip to Kitty Hawk, and his twenty-nine-year-old brother Orville was scheduled to follow a few days later with most of the baggage and equipment. Acquaintances could have predicted this, for the two brothers, sons of a Bishop of the United Brethren church, seemed almost inseparable. In addition to their family association and companionship, they were business partners as well, owning and operating the Wright Cycle Company in Dayton, selling popular makes of new bicycles, repairing old ones, supplying parts and equipment, even manufacturing their own bicycles in the dull months.

Some people might have called them tinkerers, for they were always experimenting, always building something new just to see if they could build it. In his teens Orville, the younger one, had made a small printing press out of junk, then with his brother's help a larger one, still using junk, and with it he had published a small newspaper in Dayton (weekly at first, then daily) of which his brother Wilbur was the editor. On another occasion Wilbur, having taken a job folding the entire press-run of a weekly church paper, built a machine operated by a foot-treadle which did the job faster. Together they built a wood lathe, then a tandem high-wheel bicycle that only they could ride. Then they created what their biographer, Fred C. Kelly, describes as "doubtless the first pair of 'balloon' tires ever installed on a vehicle," with a special "front fork" and frames to go with it. When Wilbur was only eleven or twelve years old his father had brought the boys a toy helicopter, invented by a Frenchman, which was made of cork, bamboo, and thin paper and was powered with rubber bands. Wilbur, fascinated by the toy, tried to build a larger model, and then another larger still, only to find that the larger he built them the less readily they would fly. Later, Orville became interested enough in kites that he designed and built his own; then he branched out and made kites to be sold to other boys.

Neither of the boys was a high school graduate—Wilbur finished high school, but the family moved before diplomas were given out, and he did not bother to return for his—but both did a lot of reading, especially Wilbur, whose activities were confined for several years as the result of an accident. Both were interested in scientific articles, and they often discussed what they read, checking further points in the family encyclopedia. One of their passing interests was the attempt of man to fly, especially that of Otto Lilienthal, the German who had made extensive glider experiments. They had first read of Lilienthal in 1895 when Wilbur was twenty-eight and Orville was twenty-four. But not until 1899, three years after Lilienthal's death, did they decide to try to learn more about human flight than they could get from the reference books at home or in the Dayton Public Library.

On May 30, 1899, Wilbur wrote to the Smithsonian Institution, requesting copies of any papers the Smithsonian had published on the subject and a list of other reputable works. In the letter he said:

Birds are the most perfectly trained gymnasts in the world and are specially well fitted for their work, and it may be that man will never equal them, but no one who has watched a bird chasing an insect or another bird can doubt that feats are performed which require three or four times the effort required in ordinary flight. I believe that simple flight at least is possible to man and that the experiments and investigations of a large number of independent workers will result in the accumulation of information and knowledge and skill which will finally lead to accomplished flight....

I wish to avail myself of all that is already known and then if possible add my mite to help on the future worker who will attain final success....

He and Orville began adding their mite in a space of just a few weeks. Years later, in 1920, in a deposition regarding patent claims, Orville said: "After reading the pamphlets sent to us by the Smithsonian we became highly enthusiastic with the idea of gliding as a sport. We found that Lilienthal had been killed through his inability to properly balance his machine in the air. Pilcher, an English experimenter, had met with a like fate.

"We found that both of these experimenters had attempted to maintain balance merely by the shifting of the weight of their bodies. . . . We at once set to work to devise a more efficient means of maintaining the equilibrium. . . ."

In less than two months after the original letter had been sent to the Smithsonian, Wilbur and Orville Wright had not only reached the conclusion that the answer to the equilibrium problem was to make the wings flexible so they could be warped in flight, but they had devised a method of building such a control system, had constructed a five-foot kite-like model glider, incorporating their ideas, and had tested it successfully.

They then determined, according to Orville, "to experiment with a man-carrying machine embodying the principle of lateral control used in the kite model already flown. From the tables of Lilienthal we calculated that a machine having an area of a little over 150 square feet would support a man when flown in a wind of 16 miles an hour. We expected to fly the machine as a kite and in this way we thought we would be able to stay in the air for hours at a time, getting in this way a maximum of practice with a minimum of effort. . . ."

That fall Wilbur Wright wrote to the U.S. Weather Bureau requesting information regarding wind velocities at Chicago in the months of August, September, October, and November, and he received in reply not only the specific Chicago information but several charts showing the average wind velocities at all weather stations throughout the country. The bicycle business kept them busy throughout the winter and spring, but in late summer of 1900 they began making plans for experiments with a man-carrying kite. They looked again at the wind velocity charts, found several places that seemed satisfactory, but most of them were in populous areas or too far from home. They decided finally to investigate the possibility of going to Kitty Hawk on the North Carolina coast, and Wilbur wrote a letter to Joseph J. Dosher, who was in charge of the weather bureau station there. Under date of August 16, 1900, Dosher replied: "In reply to yours of the 3rd, I will say the beach here is about one mile wide, clear of trees or high hills and extends for nearly sixty miles same condition. The wind blows mostly from the north and northeast Sept. and October. . . . I am sorry to say that you could not rent a house here, so you will have to bring tents. You could obtain board."

Dosher also gave Wilbur's letter to Bill Tate, former postmaster and county commissioner, and as soon as the Wright brothers received his letter of August 18, they began making definite plans for the trip to Kitty Hawk, gathering materials for their large kite or glider and doing most of the assembling in Dayton before Wilbur's departure.

When Wilbur Wright reached Elizabeth City he learned that the weekly mail boat had left the day before, so he employed a man named Israel Perry, captain of a small schooner, to take him to Kitty Hawk. As they encountered bad weather, the trip took two days, and because of the unsanitary appearance of the galley on Captain Perry's schooner, Wilbur declined the offer of food, and subsisted instead on the small jar of jelly his sister had thoughtfully put in his suitcase.

Upon arrival at Bill Tate's home on the third morning, he was practically famished and ate heartily when Mrs. Tate prepared a big breakfast for him. He boarded with the Tates until Orville arrived on September 28, and the two of them remained there for five more days, borrowing Mrs. Tate's sewing machine to resew some of the cloth covering of the glider. Wilbur had pitched a tent on a high ridge between sound and ocean just south of Kitty Hawk Village and had hauled part of the equipment down there. Five days after Orville arrived they took the last of their gear to the tent and moved in themselves.

Wilbur had already written to his father, Bishop Wright, announcing his arrival at Kitty Hawk, explaining that he was staying with Captain Bill Tate, and describing his house and the village:

His house is a two story frame with unplaned siding, not painted, no plaster on the walls, which are ceiled with pine not varnished. He has no carpets at all, very little furniture, no books or pictures. There may be one or two better houses here but his is much above the average. You will see that there is little wealth and no luxurious living. A few men have saved up a thousand dollars but this is the savings of a long life. Their yearly income is small. I suppose few of them see two hundred dollars a year. They are friendly and neighborly and I think there is rarely any real suffering among them. The ground here is a very fine sand with no admixture of loam that the eye can detect, yet they attempt to raise beans, corn, turnips, &c., on it. Their success is not great but it is a wonder that they can raise anything at all.

This was primitive living for the two young men from the city. Everything was new and different to them, and Orville, especially, wanted the folks back home to know what they were doing and what Kitty Hawk was like. The following excerpts are from a detailed letter he wrote his sister, Katharine Wright, on October 14:

We have been having a fine time. Altogether we have had the machine out three different days, of from 2 to 4 hours each time. Monday night and all day Tuesday we had a terrific wind blowing 36 miles an hour. Wednesday morning the Kitty Hawkers were out early peering around the edge of the woods and out of their upstair windows to see whether our camp was still in existence. We were all right, however, and though wind continued up to 30 miles, got the machine out to give it another trial. The wind was too strong and unsteady for us to attempt an ascent in it, so we just flew it like a kite, running down a number of strings to the ground with which to work the steering aparatus. The machine seemed a rather docile thing, and we taught it to behave fairly well. Chains were hung on it to give it work to do, while we took measurements of the "drift" in pounds.

In the afternoon we took the machine to the hill just south of our camp, formerly known as "Look Out Hill," but now as the "Hill of the Wreck." (I have just stopped a minute to eat a spoonful of condensed milk. No one down here has any regular milk. The poor cows have such a hard time scraping up a living that they don't have any time for making milk. You never saw such poor pitiable looking creatures as the horses, hogs and cows are down here. The only things that thrive and grow fat are the bedbugs, mosquitoes, and wood ticks. This condensed milk comes in a can and is just like the cream of our homemade chocolate creams. It is intended to be dissolved in water, but as we can not down it that way, we just eat it out of the can with a spoon. It makes a pretty good but rather expensive desert that way.)

Well, after erecting a derick from which to swing our rope with which we fly the machine, we sent it up about 20 feet, at which height we attempt to keep it by the manipulation of the strings to the rudder. The greatest difficulty is in keeping it down. It naturally wants to go higher & higher. When it begins to get too high we give it a pretty strong pull on the ducking string, to which it responds by making a terrific dart for the ground. If nothing is broken we start it up again. This is all practice in the control of the machine. When it comes down we just lay it flat on the ground and the pressure of the wind on the upper surface holds it down so tightly that you can hardly raise it again.

After an hour or so of practice in steering, we laid it down on the ground to change some of the adjustments of the ropes, when without a sixteenth of a second's notice, the wind caught under one corner, and quicker than thought, it landed 20 feet away a complete wreck. . . .

We had had a number of interesting experiences with it before, performing some feats which would almost seem an impossibility. We dragged the pieces back to camp and began to consider getting home. The next morning we had "cheered up" some and began to think there was some hope of repairing it. The next three days were spent in repairing, holding the tent down, and hunting; mostly the last, in which occupation we have succeeded in killing two large fish hawks each measuring over five feet from tip to tip, in chasing a lot of chicken hawks till we were pretty well winded, and in scaring several large bald eagles. Will saw a squirrel yesterday, but while he was crawling about over logs an through sand and brushes, trying to get a dead shot on it, it ate up several hickory nuts, licked chops, and departed, goodness knows where.

We did have a dinner of wild fowl the other day, but that was up to Tate's. He invited us up to help dispose of a wild goose which had been killed out of season by one of the neighboring farmers. The people about Kitty Hawk are all "game hogs" and pay little respect to what few game laws they have. But wild goose, whether due to its game flavor or not, tasted pretty good after a fast of several weeks in any kind of flesh except a mess or two of fish.

Kitty Hawk is a fishing village. The people make what little living they have in fishing. They ship tons & tons of fish away every year to Baltimore and other northern cities, yet like might be expected in a fishing village, the only meat they ever eat is fish flesh, and they never have any of that. You can buy fish in Dayton at any time, summer or winter, rain or shine; but you can't here. About the only way to get fish is to go and catch them yourself. It is just like in the north, where our carpenters never have their house completed, nor the painters their houses painted; the fisherman never has any fish.

This is a great country for fishing and hunting. The fish are so thick you see dozens of them whenever you look down into the water. The woods are filled with wild game, they say; even a few "bars" are prowling about the woods not far away. At any time we look out of the tent door we can see an eagle flapping its way over head, buzzards by the dozen—till Will is 'most sick of them—soaring over the hills and bay, hen hawks making a raid on nearby chicken yards, or a fish hawk hovering over the bay looking for a poor little fish "whom he may devour." Looking off the other way to the sea, we find the seagulls skimming the waves, and the little sea chickens hopping about, as on one foot, on the beach, picking up the small animals washed in by the surf.

But the sand! The sand is the greatest thing in Kitty Hawk, and soon will be the only thing. The site of our tent was formerly a fertile valley, cultivated by some ancient Kitty Hawker. Now only a few rotten limbs, the topmost branches of trees that then grew in this valley, protrude from the sand. The sea has washed and the wind blown millions and millions of loads of sand up in heaps along the coast, completely covering houses and forest. Mr. Tate is now tearing down the nearest house to our camp to save it from the sand. . . .

A mockingbird lives in a tree that overhangs our tent, and sings to us the whole day long. He is very tame, and perches on the highest bough of the tree (which however is only about ten feet high) and calls us up every morning. I think he crows up especially early after every big storm to see whether we are still here; we often think of him in the night, when the wind is shaking the top and sides of the tent till they sound like thunder, and wonder how he is faring and whether his nest can stand the storm. The mockingbird is the most common about here. The redbird, brown thrasher, wren, sparrow, and dozens of birds which I do not know by name, are thick in the woods nearest our camp.

The sunsets here are the prettiest I have ever seen. The clouds light up in all colors, in the background, with deep blue clouds of various shapes fringed with gold before. The moon rises in much the same style, and lights up this pile of sand almost like day. I read my watch at all hours of the night on moonless nights without the aid of any other light than that of the stars shining on the canvas of the tent.

I suspect you sometimes wonder what we eat, and how we get it. After I got down we decided to camp. There is no store in Kitty Hawk; that is, not anything that you would call a store. Our pantry in its most depleted state would be a mammoth affair compared with our Kitty Hawk stores. Our camp alone exhausts the output of all the henneries within a mile. . . .

We need no introduction in Kitty Hawk. Every place we go we are called Mr. Wright. Our fame has spread far and wide up and down the beach. Will has even rescued the name of Israel Perry, a former Kitty Hawker, from oblivion, and it now [is] one of the most frequently spoken names about the place. . . .

I believed I started in to tell what we eat. Well, part of the time we eat hot biscuits and eggs and tomatoes; part of the time eggs, and part tomatoes. Just now we are out of gasoline and coffee. Therefore no hot drink or bread or crackers. The order sent off Tuesday has been delayed by the winds. Will is 'most starved. But he kept crying that when we were rolling in luxuries, such as butter, bacon, corn bread and coffee. I think he will survive. It is now suppertime. I must scratch around and see what I can get together....

During their stay at the Kitty Hawk tent-camp in 1900 the brothers made numerous notes concerning their experiments and life on the Outer Banks. Here are some made by Wilbur:

"Hawks are better soarers than buzzards but more often resort to flapping because they wish greater speed."

"A damp day is unfavorable for soaring unless there is a high wind."

"No bird soars in a calm."

"Birds cannot soar to leeward of a descending slope unless high in the air."

The brothers remained at Kitty Hawk until the latter part of October. On the eighteenth Orville again wrote to his sister:

When one of these 45-mile nor'easters strikes us, you can depend on it, there is little sleep in our camp for the night. Expect another tonight. We have just passed through one which took up two or three wagonloads of sand from the N.E. end of our tent and piled it up eight inches deep on the flying machine, which we had anchored about fifty feet southwest. The wind shaking the roof and sides of the tent sounds exactly like thunder. When we crawl out of the tent to fix things outside the sand fairly blinds us. It blows across the ground in clouds. We certainly can't complain of the place. We came down here for wind and sand, and we have got them.

We spent half the morning yesterday in getting the machine out of the sand. When we finally did get it free, we took it up the hill, and made a number of experiments in a twenty-five-mile wind. We have not been on the thing since the first time we had it out, but merely experiment with the machine alone, sometimes loaded with seventy five pounds of chains. We tried it with tail in front, behind, and every other way. When we got through, Will was so mixed up he couldn't even theorize. It has been with considerable effort that I have succeeded in keeping him in the flying business at all. He likes to chase buzzards, thinking they are eagles, and chicken hawks, much better. . . .

If the wind is strong enough and comes from the North East, we will probably go down to the Kill Devil Hills tomorrow, where we will try gliding on the machine. . . .

It is now after eight and "time to be abed." A cold nor'easter is blowing tonight, and I have seen warmer places than it is in this tent. We each of us have two blankets, but I 'most freeze every night. The wind blows in on my head and I pull the blankets up over my head, when my feet freeze, and I reverse the process. I keep this up all night and in the morning am hardly able to tell "where I'm at" in the bed clothes. . . . Will start Tuesday for home.

They left their glider at Kitty Hawk, planning to return again the next fall. During the winter, spring, and early summer of 1901 they built a second glider, larger than the 1900 model and incorporating many improvements. One serious mistake they had made in selecting Kitty Hawk for their experiments was in accepting the monthly wind velocity figures from the Weather Bureau charts as the actual speed of the ordinary winds, whereas they were in reality only averages. Thus, during their 1900 visit, the wind would blow forty-five miles per hour one day and five miles per hour the next, and there were many days when they could not experiment. In 1901 they decided to go to Kitty Hawk in the summer instead of the fall, arrived there about the tenth of July, and proceeded to set up a more permanent camp about four miles below their old one just north of the Kill Devil Hills. They constructed a building sixteen feet wide and twenty-five feet long, taking only three days to do the job; drove a well point, which they lost in the sand, and then another; and then began putting their new glider in shape for their experiments.

The Wrights were joined at their Kill Devil Hills base in the summer of 1901 by several other aviation enthusiasts, and they made extensive tests with their new glider, many of them with a man on board. The longest such flight, 335 feet, was thought to have been a world's record. For part of their stay they were plagued by mosquitoes, and on July 28 Orville wrote his sister:

This was the beginning of the most miserable existence I had ever passed through. The agonies of typhoid fever with its attending starvation are as nothing in comparison. But there was no escape. The sand and grass and trees and hills and everything was fairly covered with them. They chewed us clear through our underwear and "socks." Lumps began swelling up all over my body like hen's eggs. We attempted to escape by going to bed, which we did at a little after six. . . . We put our cots out under the awnings and wrapped up in our blankets with only our noses protruding from the folds, thus exposing the least possible surface to attack. Alas! Here nature's complicity in the conspiracy against us became evident. The wind, which until now had been blowing over twenty miles an hour, dropped off entirely. Our blankets then became unbearable. The perspiration would roll off of us in torrents. We would partly uncover and the mosquitoes would swoop down upon us in vast multitudes. We would make a few desperate and vain slaps, and again retire behind our blankets. Misery! Misery!

That particular crop of mosquitoes soon died out, however, and for the remainder of their six-week visit to Kill Devil Hills they were able to concentrate on the glider experiments.

Back in Dayton that winter they studied the notes they had taken and frequently stayed up late at night discussing minute points. Fred C. Kelly, who spent many similar evenings with Orville after Wilbur died, described these early discussions in his *Miracle at Kitty Hawk* in these words: "Their arguments were sometimes so persuasive that each would convert the other; Orville would come to Wilbur's point of view, and Wilbur to Orville's, and they would still be as far apart as ever. . . . It was in these discussions that they invented the airplane!"

Even before this time Wilbur Wright had been carrying on an extensive correspondence with Octave Chanute, a pioneer in aviation experimentation, and Chanute had visited the Kill Devil Hills camp that summer. In the fall Chanute offered to assist the Wright brothers financially, to which Wilbur replied, on October 24, 1901:

We very much feel the generosity and kindly spirit which has prompted your offers of financial assistance in our experiments. For the present we would prefer not to accept it for the reason that if we did not feel that the time spent in this work was a dead loss in a financial sense, we would be unable to resist the temptation to devote more time than our business will stand. After a number of years struggle we have at last reached a point where we feel justified in expanding our business and upon our efforts of the next five or ten years will depend what it shall become. Practically all of the expense of our aeronautical experiments lies in the time consumed, and we do not wish to increase the temptation to neglect our regular business for it.

So the Wright brothers continued to concentrate on the bicycle business, reserving for slack business periods and evenings the secondary matter of attempting to solve the problem of human flight. At Kitty Hawk that summer their glider had not behaved as their calculations based on the existing tables on air pressure on curved surfaces had led them to expect, and they began to wonder if the tables might not be wrong. They constructed a wind tunnel, generating the necessary wind with a one-cylinder gasoline motor they had made earlier, and built a number of miniature wings, testing them singly and in pairs, and sometimes with as many as three in different positions. As a result of these experiments they not only were convinced that the wind tables used as the basis for all earlier aeronautical experiments were seriously in error, but they acquired what no one ever had before —knowledge of air pressures on curved surfaces to enable them to build wings of the right design for a machine that could fly. And they set about immediately building a new and improved glider.

The Wright brothers returned to Kill Devil Hills in the fall of 1902, assembled their new and larger glider—a wing span of thirty-two feet, opposed to twenty-two feet for the 1901 model—and constructed living quarters adjacent to their workshop. They made more than 1,000 gliding flights during the approximately two months they remained there, some of the glides more than 600 feet.

On October 23, 1902, Orville wrote to his sister Katharine from the camp at Kill Devil Hills:

The past five days have been the most satisfactory for gliding that we have had. In two days we made over 250 glides, or more than we had made all together up to the time Lorin left.* We have gained considerable proficiency in the handling of the machine now, so that we are able to take it out in any kind of weather. Day before yesterday we had a wind of 16 meters per second or about 30 miles per hour, and glided in it without any trouble. That was the highest wind a gliding machine was ever in, so that we now hold all the records! The largest machine . . . the longest time in the air, the smallest angle of descent, and the highest wind!!!

* Their brother Lorin had visited them for a while in camp.

At this point, just three and one-half years after the two young men had decided to make a thorough study of the problems of flight, they had, in addition to breaking all the gliding records, compiled the first accurate charts on wind resistance; had built the first wind tunnel in which different types of wings were actually tested; had discovered, devised, and invented a number of improvements in flying machine construction; and had built by far the most efficient glider in existence. The time had come to turn their attention to a motor-driven flying machine.

With modifications resulting from their continued experimentation and practice at the Kill Devil Hills, they anticipated little difficulty in building the flying machine, since it would be simply an adaptation of their gliders. The two remaining problems, therefore, were in securing a motor light enough to be mounted on the machine, yet powerful enough to do the job required of it, and in building a propeller or propellers (they usually called them screws) which would push the machine through the air. They hoped to buy a suitable gasoline engine from one of the automobile manufacturers and had been led to believe that they could get the screw information they needed in a short time from the technical studies of shipbuilding engineers. They were wrong on both counts.

All efforts to buy a gasoline motor to meet their specifications—it had to weigh less than 200 pounds and generate at least eight horse-power—ended in failure, and it became necessary for them to design, in their spare time, the kind of motor they needed. This was constructed in their shop with the assistance of a mechanic, Charlie Taylor, who worked for them. In a letter dated February 28, 1903, to George Spratt, who had assisted in some of the experiments at Kill Devil Hills, Wilbur wrote: "We recently built a four-cylinder gasoline engine with 4" piston and 4" stroke, to see how powerful it would be, and what it would weigh. At 670 revolutions per min. it developed 8¼ horsepower, brake test. By speeding it up to 1,000 rev. we will easily get eleven horsepower and possibly a little more at still higher speed, though the increase is not in exact proportion to the increase in number of revolutions. The weight including the 30-pound flywheel is 140 lbs."

Turning their attention then to the screws or propellers, they found that practically nothing was known about the theory of the operation of boat screws. They discovered that the designers could not predict in advance how much push the screws would give and frequently had to install larger, and then still larger, screws in ships after they were launched. Obviously this could not work with a flying machine, since they would have to know in advance exactly what the screw would produce. Once again they were forced to turn their attention to finding out more than any other individual had ever known about a basic matter of science—utilizing only their own reasoning power, ability to experiment, and scrap materials at hand. They spent long hours at night arguing minute points and, during the winter and spring of 1903, probably devoted more time to the propeller problem than to any other they had faced. After being convinced that they had the answers, the brothers designed and built twin propellers to be mounted on the rear of their machine.

There were other problems, of course, such as figuring out how to connect the chains which ran from the motor to the propellers, for example, and locating the engine so that the machine would be properly balanced. (They finally put the engine on the lower wing, slightly to the right of center, and counterbalanced it by placing the operator in a corresponding position, slightly to the left of center.)

They returned to Kitty Hawk and Kill Devil Hills for the fourth time, in late September, 1903, and spent the first few days repairing their buildings and making additions. The 1902 glider had been left in the workshop and they did some more practice gliding with it. The 1902 machine had been equipped with two runners, roughly like sled runners, on which it landed. The runners on the engine-powered machine were extended further to the front, and a special launching mechanism was constructed. This consisted simply of a small cradle or cart with two wheels, one behind the other, which was designed to roll on a long monorail made of 2 x 4's. The flying machine rested on top of the cradle, and when it started forward it was necessary for someone to run along beside, holding to one wing as a balance, until speed was attained. When the machine took to the air, the cradle would fall off the rail. On November 23, 1903, Wilbur wrote to his family from Kitty Hawk: "Our track for starting the machine (total cost about $4) amused Mr. Chanute considerably, as Langley is said to have spent nearly $50,000 on his starting device, which failed in the end to give a proper start he claims. At least this is the reason he gives for the failure last month. We have only tried ours with the little machine, so far, but it seems to work well." *

Throughout the fall at Kill Devil Hills in 1903 there was one disappointment after another for the Wright brothers. A propeller shaft broke loose and had to be sent back to Dayton to be strengthened; sprockets kept coming loose, and methods had to be devised for holding them in place; bad weather set in, snow and rain and heavy winds; and in late November, ready at last for the final test, one of the new propeller shafts split, and Orville rushed back to Dayton himself this time to repair it.

Orville returned to Kill Devil Hills on December 11, 1903, the shafts were installed that evening, and the following morning they were ready for the test but the wind was too light. Not until December 14 were conditions satisfactory, though even then the wind was not so strong as they had hoped it would be. Nonetheless they hoisted a signal that afternoon, previously arranged, to notify the crew of the nearby Kill Devil Hills Lifesaving Station that they were ready to attempt the flight, and when members of the lifesaving crew arrived the monorail was laid on the slope of Kill Devil Hill. The brothers tossed a coin, and Wilbur won the right to attempt the first flight, but the machine had hardly cleared the end of the monorail when it stalled, slipped sideways, and dug into the side of the hill, landing considerably below the point of take-off after a flight of 3½ seconds. This was far below the standards for their ordinary glides, but the test convinced both brothers that they had solved the problem of human flight. In a letter to his father and sister written the night of the December 14 trial, Wilbur said: "The machinery all worked in entirely satisfactory manner, and seems reliable. The power is ample, and but for a trifling error due to lack of experience with this machine and this method of starting, the machine would undoubtedly have flown beautifully. There is now no question of final success."

---

* The reference was to the flying machine, then being tested with much fanfare on the Potomac, which had been built by Samuel P. Langley, secretary of the Smithsonian Institution. "Langley's folly" failed to fly.

Orville Wright picks up the story in his diary:

Tuesday, December 15, 1903

Spent day in making repairs to front rudder and rudder frame. Wind 5 to 6 meters.

Wednesday, December 16, 1903

Wind of 6 to 7 meters blowing from west and northwest in morning. We completed repairs by noon and got the machine out on the tracks in front of the building ready for a trial from the level. The wind was gradually dying and by the time we were ready was blowing only about 4 to 5 meters per sec. After waiting several hours to see whether it would breeze up again we took the machine in.

Thursday, December 17, 1903

When we got up a wind of between 20 and 25 miles was blowing from the north. We got the machine out early and put out the signal for the men at the station. Before we were quite ready, John T. Daniels, W. S. Dough, A. D. Etheridge, W. C. Brinkley of Manteo, and Johnny Moore of Nags Head arrived. After running the engine and propellers a few minutes to get them in working order, I got on the machine at 10:35 for the first trial. The wind, according to our anemometers at this time, was blowing a little over 20 miles (corrected) 27 miles according to the Government anemometer at Kitty Hawk. On slipping the rope the machine started off increasing in speed to probably 7 or 8 miles. The machine lifted from the truck just as it was entering on the fourth rail. Mr. Daniels took a picture just as it left the tracks. I found the control of the front rudder quite difficult on account of its being balanced too near the center and thus had a tendency to turn itself when started so that the rudder was turned too far on one side and then too far on the other. As a result the machine would rise suddenly to about 10 ft. and then as suddenly, on turning the rudder, dart for the ground. A sudden dart when out about 100 feet from the end of the tracks ended the flight.

In these matter-of-fact, unemotional words, Orville Wright had described the first successful flight by man in a heavier-than-air machine—a flight which had lasted about twelve seconds and covered approximately 100 feet over the ground. The fact that they had set their camera in just the right position to catch the flight, and had carefully instructed lifesaver Daniels on how and when to snap the shutter, indicates that the Wright brothers were fully aware of the significance of their activities that morning. But there was no wild celebration, no joyous shouting or embracing one the other, nor did Wilbur run beside the flying machine shouting "Eureka" as was reported the next day in a Norfolk newspaper.

Instead, they carried the machine back to the starting point, set it down on the monorail, and prepared for another flight. During the next hour and a half the brothers flew three more times, Wilbur at the controls for the second flight, Orville again for the third, and Wilbur for the fourth. The last flight lasted fifty-seven seconds and covered 852 feet over the ground. When the machine had been carried back to the camp and the men were standing around calmly discussing the events of the preceding two hours, a sudden gust of wind lifted one wing, and the craft rolled over and over. By the time they were able to reach the machine and hold it down, the legs which supported the engine were broken off, the chain guides bent, and nearly all of the rear ends of the ribs, and of one spar, were broken.

At any other time they might have gone to work again, repairing the damage, making ready for further experiments. But they had accomplished what they had set out to do, and more, and they were anxious to get home. That afternoon Orville went over to the Kitty Hawk Weather Station and sent the following wire to Bishop Wright:

KITTY HAWK, DECEMBER 17, 1903
SUCCESS FOUR FLIGHTS THURSDAY MORNING ALL AGAINST TWENTY-ONE MILE WIND STARTED FROM LEVEL WITH ENGINE POWER ALONE AVERAGE SPEED THROUGH AIR THIRTY-ONE MILES LONGEST 57 SECONDS INFORM PRESS HOME CHRISTMAS.

Thus the two young bicycle builders from Dayton, possessed of the desire to find out things for themselves, had succeeded where many of the world's greatest scientists had failed. Through their efforts the age of human flight had begun.

A Living from the Sea

ONE OF THE most common misconceptions about the Outer Banks is the belief that commercial fishing has been the primary occupation and source of income in the area since the days of earliest settlement.

Certainly, even in colonial times, a large number of the Bankers fished, both in the sounds and from the sea beach. But it was primarily a part-time activity, engaged in by the stockmen, pilots, boatmen, and other Banks residents to supply their own needs for food.

Even as late as 1850, the first time the Banks census was sufficiently detailed to show the occupation of the residents in the various communities, there were 48 boatmen and mariners and 22 pilots at Portsmouth, to only 4 fishermen; while at Ocracoke there were 18 seamen, 35 pilots, and only 5 fishermen. Only on Hatteras Island, of all Banks areas, was commercial fishing the primary occupation in 1850. Even with the census figures available, it is difficult to get a true picture of Banks occupations, for the man who listed himself as a fisherman might have been devoting an equal portion of his time to stock raising and hauling freight in his boat, while the boatman might have owned a net and done some fishing too.

The one certain thing is that full realization came to most Bankers at the time of the Civil War that the seafood in the nearby waters represented a vast source of potential income, with the result that the three-quarters of a century or so between then and World War II might best be described as the great era of commercial fishing on the Banks. Even then the term "fishing" would be misleading, for the Bankers caught and sold practically everything they could find in the water, from whales and porpoises to turtles, oysters, and even seaweed.

Some of the most successful fisheries were carried on exclusively from the ocean beach; others were limited to the channels in the sounds or to the shallow reefs, flats, and marshes. Some species, once plentiful, are now rarely found; others have just recently become marketable. A distinguishing feature of the fishing activity in the area is that it has been listed almost without exception in the classification of shore and boat fisheries, as compared with the more common vessel fisheries in other states—in this case a fishing vessel being designated as a craft of five or more net tons.

One of the factors which retarded the development of commercial fisheries along the Banks before the advent of power boats, highways, or refrigeration was the near impossibility of delivering seafoods to the consumer while they were still fresh. Consequently, the earliest fisheries were engaged in catching those types of fish which could be salted or smoked, or from which valuable oils could be extracted.

It was only natural, therefore, that the first commercial fisheries up the rivers and sounds should have concentrated on such fish as alewives (herring) and shad, which could be smoked or salted without losing their flavor. By the same token, the demand for whale oil and bone and for porpoise oil made those fisheries profitable on the coast; while probably the first really extensive fishery on the Outer Banks proper resulted from the widespread popularity, both in North Carolina and elsewhere, of salted mullet.

Writing from the Beaufort area in 1871, H. C. Yarrow had the following to say about mullet: "This species is the most abundant of the locality, and affords sustenance and employment to thousands of persons on the coast of North Carolina. From the month of May, when small sized individuals appear, fishing continues during the entire summer . . . and frequently until November. . . . The numbers taken are simply enormous, sometimes as many as 500 barrels being secured at a single haul. It was estimated by competent observers that not less than 12,000 barrels of mullet were captured on the coast of North Carolina Friday, September 22, 1871."

In 1880 R. Edward Earll made a thorough investigation of the mullet fisheries in North Carolina and found that the majority of the mullet fishermen were farmers from the mainland. "When the fishing season arrives," he said, "they leave their homes and proceed in gangs of four to thirty men to the seashore under the leadership of a 'captain,' who controls their movements. . . . On reaching the shore they at once build rude huts or cabins, in which they eat and sleep until the close of the season."

Photographs of the huts used by the early mullet fishermen have been preserved, together with detailed descriptions of their construction. From a distance they looked like nothing more than hollow haystacks, but on closer examination they proved to be substantially built. In 1908, for example, Collier Cobb said one of the huts on Shackleford Banks had been in use for at least twelve years.

In constructing one of the huts a framework of heavy poles was first made, the butts imbedded in the sand, the tops bent over and tied to a ridge pole. "These answer the purpose of studding," Earll said in 1880, "each being notched at the point where the eaves should come, that they may be easily bent inward to the ridge-pole to support the roof." The framework was completed by tying "laths" or small sticks to the studding in horizontal rows a foot and a half to two feet apart. Earll's description follows:

A ditch is then dug along the outside of the frame, into which the base of a thick layer of rushes, is placed. Other long sticks, called "liggers", are now placed on the outside of the rushes, directly opposite the laths, the two being sewed or fastened together by means of threads of beargrass, in order that the rushes may be held in position. When the bottom tier has been fastened another row of rushes is placed higher up, overlapping the first like shingles on a roof. . . . The same process is continued until the ridge-pole is reached and the entire structure has been inclosed. The layers of rushes are sufficiently thick to shed water and to break the force of the wind, though for better protection against cold the fishermen frequently "bank" their houses with sand. The only openings in the house are a small hole at the rear gable, to allow the smoke from the camp fire to escape, and a square aperture 2 or 3 feet in height at the front, which serves as a door. Two tiers of berths are now put up on either side of the shanty, and each fisherman gathers grass or leaves, out of which he makes his bed.

Mullet fishing was carried on extensively both in the ocean and in the sound, and sometimes a single crew would work both areas. Regardless of where the camp was located, however, a lookout was posted continuously, either on top of a large sand hill or on a specially constructed lookout tower. Earll described such a tower as "simply a tripod composed of two medium-sized and one large pole, the last-named having pegs inserted by means of which the man climbs to the crow's-nest in the crotch."

Sometimes when the mullet were swimming deep, their presence could be detected only by a dark mass in the ocean, and it took an experienced lookout to spot them. Most often, however, the presence of a school moving along the coast was made known by the ripple on the water as they swam close to the surface; and on occasion, even, they could be seen jumping and thrashing on the surface. During the fall the schools were so large that one observer said "the noise of their splashing resembles distant thunder."

When the lookout saw a school he left his post, "walking down the beach toward the camp, keeping directly opposite to the fish, and indicating their movements to the other members of the crew by a peculiar motion of his arms." Finally, at the proper signal from the lookout, the fishermen would launch their boat through the surf, and "shoot" their seine in front of the approaching school of fish. The boat used on the sea beach was usually the so-called pilot-skiff, with four men on the oars, a fifth man steering and directing the crew. In 1880 the operation was described as follows:

One end of the net is connected with the shore by means of a rope, and as the fish approach this end is drawn rapidly to land by men on shore to prevent them from passing. Even if not quite in, the fish are readily turned back by a rapid movement of the line. The boat at this time brings the other end of the net to the shore and the movement of the fish in this direction is thus shut off. When they find themselves surrounded, the mullet usually sink and make a circuit of the bottom for an opening through which to make their escape. When a large school is inclosed the pressure of the fish against the seine often lifts it from the bottom, and many pass under the lead-line; but failing to get out at the bottom, they rise to the surface and begin to jump over the cork-line with a rapidity that is truly surprising. Frequently a large part of the fish escape in this way, the air being at times completely filled with mullet. When the water is calm, boats are placed behind the seine to catch the "jumpers," these often being completely filled in a few moments. As soon as shoal-water has been reached, some of the fishermen wade out to hold up the back of the seine and thus keep the fish from escaping. They are obliged to turn their backs to the fish that pelt against them in such numbers as to make their position anything but a pleasant one. In some instances a second seine is hauled behind the first to secure the runaways. The method of using a second seine, or of placing boats behind the first to intercept the escaping fish, is called "backing" the seine; and men frequently agree to assist in the regular work of cleaning and salting for the privilege of keeping such fish as they may take in this way while the water is still too deep to permit the men to wade out and hold up the cork lines.

The larger nets used for fishing from the beach were 12 to 18 feet deep and from 900 to 1200 feet long. In the 1880's the average net cost between $150 and $200, and it required 15 to 20 men to properly handle it.

Smaller nets, of several different types, were used in the sounds. Probably the most common was a type of gill net known as a sweep net, usually from 200 to 300 feet long and 4 to 6 feet deep, with a mesh varying from 2¼ to 4 inches. Earll described the small sweep-net operation in 1880 as follows: "Two men usually own a net in common, going out together in a small boat on their fishing trips. As soon as a school has been surrounded by the net, the fishermen proceed to the inside of the circle and, by pounding on the gunwale, splashing the water with oars, or, when shoal enough, jumping overboard and running about within the circle, drive the mullet into the meshes. If left to themselves, many of the fish would see the net and avoid it, but in their effort to escape from the noise and splashing they soon become entangled in the twine. When all have been gilled, the net is hauled into the boat and the fish are secured."

Sometimes several sweep-net crews would join forces, and Allen H. Taylor of Sealevel, now in his eighties, recently described the procedure followed by the joint crew with which he fished as a boy and young man in Core Sound and Pamlico Sound.

Since the members of the Taylor crew lived in the down-east

section of Carteret County on the north shore of Core Sound, the men operated as a mobile unit, setting up temporary camps on various islands in the sound, frequently having nothing more than the sails of their boats for shelter. They fished mostly at night, employing four small boats and four sweep nets, and would cruise the mullet grounds in formation, with two of the boats in the center as lookouts and the other two on the flanks. They would try to locate the schools of mullet by listening for the sound of the jumping fish.

"When the first net was close to the school," Taylor says, "the lead man would sing out to set nets, and the other boats would circle the school, each setting its own net, until a great circle was formed around the school, the men beating on the sides of the boats to drive the fish into the nets. The circle was then made smaller by drawing in the nets, and sometimes one or two of the nets would be used to form a separate pocket within the circle as the others were drawn together. When all of the fish were gilled the nets were drawn into the boats, the fish removed, and if conditions were right the search for another school would be begun."

Back at the temporary camp in the daytime, all hands would pitch in on the job of cleaning and salting the catch. Rough tables were set up, and a man would stand in front of these for hours, a knife in his right hand, picking up the fish in his left—"one slit down the belly, take out the guts, then one or two scores on the thick side and maybe another on the thin side if it was a big fish"—and when the fish was gutted and scored it was thrown into a porous basket beside the splitter. When one of the baskets was filled it was taken down to the water where the gutted fish were washed, and finally the clean fish were salted, care being taken that salt got into the scores before being packed in barrels.

Later, if the mullet catch was taken into Beaufort to be sold, the fish were removed from the barrel, since the blood would have mixed with the salt to form a dark brine. They were then resalted and repacked. Some of the larger crews took their mullet to the fish house while still fresh, and the gutting, cleaning, and salting were done there.

In addition to the seines and the sweep nets, some mullet were caught in the sounds in the 1880's and 1890's with small dragnets. In the 1870's several pound nets—stationary nets laid out in various funnel arrangements and strung between heavy stakes across passages in the sound—were set in Core Sound, "but not being properly arranged they took but few fish, and were soon taken up."

One of the early difficulties in marketing salted mullet in North Carolina was that "all kinds and sizes of barrels were formerly used indiscriminately, but the quantity of fish contained in them varied so much that no uniform standard of price could be adopted, and much hard feeling arose between the fishermen and the merchants." To solve this problem the state legislature passed a law in 1879 "requiring that mullet should be put up in barrels having a stave 25 inches in length and a head 13 inches in diameter," and these were found to hold approximately 100 pounds of salted fish.

The financial arrangement—or lay—of the men in a mullet crew was similar to that employed in other fisheries from that day until this, with shares allotted for each fisherman, boat, and net. In addition, some of the larger holders of sound-front property claimed ownership of the adjacent mullet grounds as well, and for many years the beach owner participated in the lay. A typical lay on Core Banks in 1879 was described as follows: "The seine receives from six to ten shares; the boat takes one; the beach three to ten, according to its relative importance as compared to other shores in the vicinity; one share is given to the man who supplies the camp with wood; and the remainder is divided among the members of the crew, including the captain. . . . During the season of 1879, which lasted from the middle of August to the 1st of November, the catch for the different seines averaged about 300 barrels each, a share thus consisting of 10 barrels."

The actual cash value of a barrel of salted mullet in the 1880's fluctuated between $2.75 and $3.50 per barrel, but few mullet were sold for cash. Almost all of the catch was disposed of in eastern North Carolina, a large part of it through a peculiar arrangement between the mullet fishermen and the owners of small schooners, by which the boatmen were hired to peddle the fish.

As soon as the fishing season was over the mullet were loaded upon these vessels, in charge of the captain, who was to exchange them for corn with the farmers living along the banks of the navigable streams tributary to the Carolina sounds. The captain was at liberty to make the exchange upon any basis that he might think proper, but as he was given a percentage—usually one-fifth of the corn received—for his services, he was apt to drive the best possible bargain. Five bushels of shelled corn for one barrel of mullet was considered a fair exchange, though the price varied somewhat from year to year.

Having secured his cargo of fish, he usually set sail for some small town on one of the larger rivers, where he remained until all of the mullet were sold. The arrival of a "mullet-trader" soon becomes known among the residents of any locality, and the farmers of the region at once load their wagons with corn and start for the landing to secure their fish.

The mullet fishery was one of the first employed on the Banks and for many years was the most important in the Beaufort vicinity. In the records of commercial fisheries in this state, which have been kept regularly since 1887, the mullet catch has remained fairly constant, averaging between 5 and 10 per cent of the total catch of edible fish and approximately the same percentage of the total value of the catch.

For many years herrings provided the largest quantity of North Carolina food fish, constituting almost 60 per cent of the total in 1887 and almost 50 per cent as late as 1918. This fishery was carried on primarily in the Albemarle Sound region, but because the herring was a cheap fish the total value of the annual catch was usually no more than that of the mullet.

The big money catch, throughout the 1880's and 1890's, and even until comparatively recently, was shad, and after shad fishing was extended to Pamlico Sound in 1873 many of the commercial fishermen in the Roanoke Island area concentrated on it exclusively. In 1887, when the shad fisheries produced just over 15 per cent of the total catch of food fish in North Carolina, the receipts were almost 40 per cent of the total. The listed price for shad during the 1880's and 1890's was usually well over 5¢ a pound, while mullet averaged about 3½¢, and herring was less than 1¢.

Shad is an anadromous fish, a fish which must spawn in fresh water, and in the spring the shad enter Pamlico Sound through the inlets, passing from there into the rivers, or more often, through Croatan Sound to the spawning grounds in and near the Albemarle. The early shad fisheries in the sounds were almost exclusively operated with pound nets, and these became so extensive that the state geologist reported they "served as almost complete barriers to the passage of the fish." One result of this was a 1905 law "maintaining an open channel, free from nets of all kinds, from the inlets to the spawning grounds."

Later laws shortened the season and governed the size of the mesh of the nets, and sizable hatcheries were established in an attempt to increase the number of shad.* But the decline continued, some attributing it to stream pollution, others to overfishing, and still others to "the violation of the laws that have been passed to regulate fishing."

In addition to mullet, the primary food fish caught from the ocean beaches along the Banks are: gray trout or northern weakfish, once known in this area as squeteague, which has ranked consistently among the leading food fishes caught in North Carolina since the latter part of the last century; bluefish; spot or chub; salmon trout, also known as speckled trout, spotted trout, and southern weakfish; and king whiting or sea mullet. Less extensive catches were made from the beach of blackfish or sea bass, butter fish, and Spanish mackerel. There was a brief period when sturgeon were caught in ocean nets, and in 1907 it was stated that "the sturgeon is by far the most valuable fish, individually considered, inhabiting the waters of North Carolina," since a single fish at that time could bring as high as $80. However, after a few years of extensive fishing in the early part of this century the sturgeon supply diminished rapidly.

In recent years croakers or hard heads, and rock or striped bass, have ranked with or ahead of shad both in the quantity of fish caught in the sounds and in the value of the annual catch, while the catch of flounder in the vicinity of the inlets and in the outside sea lanes has also shown a decided increase.

Some of the most interesting fisheries along the Banks and in the sounds have never figured prominently in the over-all statistics. For a number of years the catch of large mouth black bass by commercial fishermen accounted for something like 2 or 3 per cent of the total value of food fishes, but in the early 1920's commercial fishing for this species was discontinued, and it is now fished exclusively by sportsmen.

Carp, introduced to this country from Europe in 1877 and to North

* A leading North Carolina ichthyologist informs the writer that the failure of the hatcheries to produce the desired result could be attributed to the fact that the shad were released while virtually in an embryonic stage and "too young and weak to escape their natural enemies." During the depression special pools were authorized at the Edenton hatchery, in which it was planned to retain the young shad until they reached a size of two inches; but the pools were built with relief funds, utilizing hand labor, and were not deep enough for the purpose.

Carolina two years later, "soon became widely distributed and abundant," but because it was considered to have an inferior taste and flavor, it has never figured prominently in the fisheries of the area and is taken in only a few localities. There is a similar abundance of eels in certain parts of the sounds, and a corresponding lack of interest in catching them. In 1907 H. M. Smith had this to say about the eel fisheries in North Carolina: "About 1897 a religious band, called the 'Arkites,' went to Beaufort from Virginia in a houseboat or ark, taking with them eel pots; they began to fish for eels, marketing their catch in Newbern, but the business never met with much success. . . . At one time a religious sect, known as the 'Sanctified,' made a business of catching eels in the lake [Mattamuskeet] and shipping them north.

"Eels have a very delicate, well-flavored flesh which is white when cooked, and rank high as food fishes, although many people refuse to eat them on account of their supposed snakish affinities."

In recent years a few eels have been taken in the vicinity of Colington Island and the village of Duck. These are caught in eel pots and are kept alive until mid-December, when special tank trucks come down from the Northern cities to pick up the catch, which is delivered alive to the cities in time for the holidays.

The uncertainties of eel fishing were aptly summed up a couple of years back in a conversation with a young Colington boy who was just completing his first season of eeling.

"What kind of bait do you use in the eel pots?" he was asked.

"Crabs."

"How do you catch the crabs?"

"In crab pots."

"What do you bait the crab pots with?"

"Eels."

"How are you making out?"

"Just about even, I guess. It takes all the crabs I can get to catch the eels, and all the eels I can get to catch the crabs."

In addition to the mullet, shad, gray trout, rock, eels, and other species already mentioned, the term "commercial fisheries" as used in North Carolina applies as well to oysters, shrimp, whales, porpoise, clams, scallops, and crabs. And at one time it applied, also, to turtles and diamondback terrapins.

In the 1880's Frederick W. True gave the following description of the method of capturing loggerhead turtles, which averaged about fifty pounds each, in the inlets through the Banks:

The capture of loggerheads in this vicinity was formerly effected by means of spears or "gauges." The turtles were struck by the fishermen with these implements while swimming in the water. They were frequently very badly wounded, however, and often injured to such a degree that they were unfit for shipment or sale. To avoid this difficulty Mr. Joshua Lewis, of Morehead City, conceived the idea of diving upon the turtles while in the water, and securing them with his hands. When starting out in search of them he ties the painter of his boat to his leg; then rowing along leisurely until one is seen, he approaches it and dives upon it from the boat. Seizing the anterior edge of the carapace with one hand, and the posterior edge with the other, he turns the head of the turtle upward, when the animal immediately rises to the surface, bringing the fisherman with it. If the water is deep he steers the turtle toward a shoaler spot, keeping hold of it with one hand; and with the other pulling the boat after him. When a suitable spot is reached he seizes the animal and throws it into the boat. Usually there is no difficulty in bringing turtles to the surface and directing them toward shallow water, but occasionally a very large one is encountered, which is strong and unmanageable. In such case the fisherman is forced to let go his hold and return to the surface, allowing the turtle to escape.

The method of capturing turtles by diving is employed at present by many of the fishermen in this locality, and the greater portion of those taken are captured in this way. Good swimmers do not hesitate to dive for a turtle when seen, however great may be the depth of the water.

The going price for fifty-pound loggerhead turtles at that time was about fifty cents each; the price of smaller green turtles, which were caught in the same way, was about fifteen cents.

Diamondback terrapin, on the other hand, at one time commanded a price considerably higher per pound than that of any of the other products of the fisheries, for gourmets have long considered diamondback terrapin soup (made from the head, and from the meat attached to the shells) and diamondback terrapin stew (made from the rest of the terrapin) as unexcelled delicacies.

The primary breeding ground of diamondback terrapin is the brackish water marshland which covers so much of the sound side of the Banks and the adjoining islands, and they rarely exceed a size of

6½ inches (measured the length of the under shell). At one time, before their economic value in the Northern markets was realized, there were great numbers of diamondbacks in this area. Though a few were caught and eaten locally, for the most part they were a nuisance, frequently getting entangled in fishermen's nets. The story was told in 1902 that they were at one time so numerous in the Stumpy Point area that it was "sometimes necessary to lose a haul of fish because the quantity of terrapins unavoidably taken when hauling a net near the marshes prevented the drawing in of the net."

Since the terrapin hibernate during the winter, most of those taken for home use in the early days were caught in spring, summer, or fall. But in 1845 "Mr. William Midgett, of Roanoke Island, invented a 'terrapin drag,' which he used in obtaining a supply for himself during the winter, when the animals lie dormant, buried in the mud." This drag resembled an oyster dredge, and proved so successful that several of Midgett's neighbors copied the idea. One of these, Captain John B. Etheridge, keeper of the Bodie Island Lighthouse, used a dredge with such good results in February of 1849 that he soon caught 2,150 diamondbacks, considerably more than he could make use of. So Captain Etheridge took the catch to Norfolk, where he promptly sold it for $400; and "returning immediately he captured 1,900 more terrapins, and sold them in Baltimore for $350. The news of his success spread rapidly, and many men went into the business and prosecuted it with such vigor that the terrapins were shortly almost exterminated."

In addition to dredging, the diamondbacks were also caught with dip nets along marshy shores, by digging in mud banks while they were hibernating, and even by using dogs to track them in the summer. When they became scarce the price steadily increased, so that at one time the six-inch females, known as "counts," brought $30 to $36 per dozen, and there were recorded sales of seven-inch counts as high as $120 per dozen. After the Civil War several attempts were made to cultivate the terrapins in specially made pounds. The most extensive operations of this kind were carried on in the 1870's and 1880's in a four-acre pound on Roanoke Island and just before World War I at Beaufort. Both efforts failed, however, and the terrapin fishery has never regained its early prominence, though present-day residents of the North Banks can remember selling diamondbacks to a man named Grandy Beasley at Kitty Hawk just before World War I for as high as a dollar each for the counts.

Oysters, on the other hand, have always been a leading product of the fisheries in the area, maintaining a steady average of 5 to 20 per cent of the total value of the over-all catch in North Carolina. Extensive Indian shell mounds or kitchen middens throughout the area attest to the popularity of oysters among the native population before the white men came, and even in recorded times most of the sounds were covered with natural oyster beds, which at first were gathered by hand and then tonged by the residents.

Allen Taylor of Sealevel says that in the 1880's he was a member of a four-man oyster crew operating from the schooner *J. J. Taylor*. Portsmouth was the hub of the oystering activity at that time, and in the great freeze of 1895 more than a dozen oyster schooners were caught in the sound in that vicinity, the crews marooned until the ice became sufficiently thick to support their weight for the walk to shore. The *J. J. Taylor* crewmen did their oystering from small skiffs, transferring the catch to the schooner when a skiff was full. When the *Taylor* was loaded two of the men would take her up one of the rivers to peddle the oysters, and it was not unusual to dispose of the entire load in a single community. Sometimes part of the load was wholesaled to wagoners, who for years had carried on a fairly extensive business by retailing the catch from village to village and house to house.

In more recent times the extent and value of the Pamlico Sound oyster fishery has been influenced by oystering activities in Chesapeake Bay, a situation which has applied as well to eeling, crabbing, and certain types of fishing. For when the Northern markets could be supplied with all they needed from Chesapeake Bay, the dealers did not bother to come as far south as North Carolina to make purchases. (As late as 1955 the eel catch at Colington and Duck was not sold because of a bumper catch that year in the Chesapeake area.)

There were a few efforts to control or limit oystering activities in the sounds before 1880. At this time Ernest Ingersoll reported that some of the fishermen in the Pamlico Sound area, during the summer season "when the weather becomes warm and there is no other employment for their boats," rake up poor quality oysters "and carry them to the farmers up the rivers to be sold and used as manure, for which from 3 to 5 cents a bushel is paid."

By 1885 a decided decrease in the numbers of oysters in the natural beds was noted, and Lieutenant Francis Winslow of the U.S. Navy was detailed to make a thorough study of the situation. His resulting report, published in 1886, contained more than 150 pages. "In this State," he reported, "the oyster industry is yet in its infancy. The population is too sparse and the present demand too slight to have caused any continuous fishery or even any general knowledge of the positions or areas of the natural beds." He found, nonetheless, that the beds were "threatened with complete destruction in the future" if action was not taken to further control the fishery and to institute an extensive program of oyster propagation.

One result of this was the employment of Winslow to transplant oysters from the more extensive beds to other areas where the supply had become depleted. However, according to Stacy Howard, the Ocracokers claimed that he was digging up their natural beds under the guise of this propagation program and was selling the oysters to dealers instead of transplanting them. They asked him to stop dredging in their section, and when he refused and reportedly kept individual Ocracoke oystermen away from the beds by armed force, practically every able-bodied man in the community took down his gun, boarded small boats, and headed up the sound shore to where Winslow's crew was dredging. The approach of a formidable armada of Ocracoke boats filled with armed men was too much for Winslow, and he hoisted anchor and departed from that part of the sound.

By that time many areas had been set aside as private oyster beds. To do this it was necessary only to file an application for a private bed, accompanied by a description, with the local clerk of court. The great difficulty was that the descriptions were seldom accurate, and there was much controversy over the oystering rights. A law had been passed by the state legislature in 1882 prohibiting the use of oyster drags or dredges, so that oysters could be legally gathered only with hand tongs. All indications are that most of the local oystermen respected this law, but in 1890 the Chesapeake beds had been depopulated to such an extent that many of the Chesapeake oystermen came down to Pamlico Sound both to secure oysters for sale and for breeding, and they paid no attention at all to the laws prohibiting the use of dredges.

Allen Taylor has told the writer that some of the Chesapeake oystermen loaded their catch on large barges which could carry as many as 3,000 bushels. The seriousness of this situation was pointed up in a letter, written January 5, 1891, by Sam C. Whitehurst, agent for the Old Dominion Steamboat Company at Skyco on Roanoke Island, to Colonel Harry Skinner in Raleigh:

Dear Colonel:—This will be handed you by Hon. Geo. C. Daniels, Representative from this county. Though differing from us politically, yet he is a personal friend of mine, and any assistance given him will be deemed an especial favor.

The people here are poor and depend entirely upon the waters for support, in the way of fishing and oystering. But the Virginia men are down here and have taken entire possession of all the oyster grounds; their boats are much larger than those here, and when these are at work the Virginians will run down upon them and tear them up; and when they try to retaliate it is useless, for they are armed to their teeth with Winchester rifles and some have 36 lb. guns. Unless something is done to stop their dredging, these people will be in a starving condition in twelve months, for it will be useless for the fishermen to put in any shad nets, for these Virginians pay no attention whatever to their nets; they run their boats through them and tear them up, and the consequence will be these nets will be all cut to pieces, and no fish caught, and when there are no fish caught there will be no bread.

What I have stated I know to be facts, and any assistance rendered will be greatly appreciated by all the citizens of Dare County, as well as myself.

The same year forty residents of Mount Pleasant in Hyde County petitioned the Governor "to supress the illegal dredging which is now being carried on by Maryland vessels to an extent which threatens our very existence." The petition stated that "There are now about one hundred and fifty sail of Maryland dredge-boats at work in the waters of Pamlico Sound. We are helpless in the presence of these armed dredge-boats, without the intervention of your Excellency in our behalf."

These appeals resulted in the passing of laws which stopped the invasion by the Chesapeake oystermen, but subsequent legislation made legal the use of oyster drags or dredges, and a decline in oyster production resulted. Later, the state instituted a rather extensive program of oyster cultivation and millions of bushels have been planted in Pamlico Sound, though without appreciably beneficial results.

Four other types of shellfish—clams, scallops, crabs, and shrimp—have at one time or another figured prominently in the fisheries along the coast. Clams have been taken regularly since the 1890's, mostly at the mouths of inlets, and have averaged about one-third the annual value of the oyster production. Scallops were taken fairly extensively over a period of ten years or so following World War I, but the fishery declined rapidly thereafter. Both crabs and shrimp, on the other hand, have grown steadily in their popularity as choice foods and occupy positions of importance in the fisheries; however, lack of control and lack of normal conservation practices threaten the early extinction of shrimp in the North Carolina sounds.

There is a close parallel between the development of the shrimp industry and the blue crab industry in the Banks area. Two separate reports, both made in the 1880's, point up this similarity. Of blue crabs, Richard Rathbun wrote:

Blue crabs are very abundant on this coast, where they often receive the name of channel crabs, but they are not much in demand as food... About Beaufort and Morehead City, the fishermen take them in immense numbers in their drag-nets while fishing for sea-trout, mullet, and other fish, and consider them a great annoyance, as it is difficult to remove them from the nets. They kill nearly all that are captured in this way by a blow from a stick carried along for the purpose, and then throw them away, or use them as manure. A few are kept for food, but none are sold, beyond an occasional barrel-full, mostly soft-shelled, which are sent to some of the larger inland towns. A few soft crabs are also sent to northern markets, but most of the crabs sold in this vicinity are gathered by negro children, who take them on the ebb tide in the little pools of water left on the shore. The price is from 15 to 20 cents per dozen. The fishery for this crab promises to become of great importance when a ready market for the catch has been established.

On the subject of shrimp, R. Edward Earll wrote:

There is no shrimp trade anywhere within the district comprising Pamlico, Albemarle, Roanoke, and Croatan Sounds, although shrimp are very abundant in many localities, and enterprise alone is required to develop an important industry. The fishermen often catch the shrimp in their ordinary nets, along with fish, but find no sale for them at home, and their means of shipping them fresh to outside markets are imperfect. ... The New Berne fishermen often secure from 30 to 40 bushels at a haul of their fish-nets, and have frequently offered them for sale to the market dealers at the low price of 50 cents per bushel, which has almost always been refused. The fishermen eat very few themselves and throw the bulk of their catch away.

In the years that followed there was a slow but steady increase in the catch and sale of soft-shell blue crabs, but both hard crabs and shrimp continued to be an annoyance good for little more than manure until well into this century. Both finally began to assume an important status in the fisheries during the depression of the 1930's, and in 1939 shrimp had become the most important product of the food fisheries of the state, with crabs not too far behind. Probably the peak period for shrimp production came just following World War II, when practically everybody who owned a boat large enough to pull a trawl dropped whatever else he was doing, rigged up for shrimp, and converged on the shrimping grounds. In the process millions of small fish were caught in the shrimp nets and killed; and it was not long, also, before it became more and more difficult for the shrimpers to make profitable hauls. As this is written the shrimp seem to have been pretty well cleaned out of the sounds, and anybody interested in buying a shrimping boat and outfit can have his choice of a dozen or more, in this immediate area, at bargain prices.

The crabbers, on the other hand, are doing as well now as ever, though the fact that the crabbing here is an adjunct of the Chesapeake operation—with most of the processing plants being located in Virginia and Maryland—still makes it an uncertain occupation for the individual crabber.

In crabbing, as in many other types of fishing, the methods employed today are essentially the same as those devised centuries ago. In 1782 Samuel Kelly described crabbing in coastal Carolina as follows: "The way to catch them is to get into the boat alongside with a line to reach the bottom and to which any animal substance may be fastened. After lying at the bottom a few minutes, it is drawn up softly and you will find the crabs fast to the bait, which they will hold fast to the water's edge. Then, having a cabbage net extended on a small hoop, you place this gently beneath the crabs and secure them, for they always quit their hold on being lifted out of the water."

Throughout the summer it is still a common sight along the Banks to see people leaning over the side of a boat or the edge of a dock, a crab line in one hand and a dip net in the other, catching crabs in this exact same manner. Even the commercial crabbers employ the same basic principle, except that they do their crabbing in the open sounds from power boats, and their lines are hundreds of feet long with bait attached every two feet or so. They set a trot line in the early morning, then run down the length of it, letting the line pass over a roller attached to the side of the boat, dipping up the crabs as they release the bait. Beef entrails once were used as bait, then tripe, and in more recent years bull-nose.

One of the most interesting fisheries on the Banks, long since abandoned, was the porpoise fishery, and possibly the first instance of porpoise being taken commercially in the area was at Ocracoke Inlet in 1797 when the proprietors of Shell Castle established a porpoise fishery. From about 1810 until the Civil War, "from one to three crews followed it quite regularly," but because it required an outlay of about $400 for nets and boats to get started again after the war, it was not until the early 1880's that porpoise fishing was resumed.

Howard Clark described, in 1880, the pre-Civil War porpoise fishery on the Banks, stating that the average rig consisted of four seines, each one 200 yards in length and loaded in separate boats. When the porpoise were sighted the four boats would move out from the shore, the seines would be "shot" so that they formed a continuous semicircle, the ends of the seines being lashed together once they were in the water. Very heavy twine with a mesh of almost a foot was used for the porpoise nets, and while the net was being hauled toward shore one or two men would remain in each boat "to pound on his boat, or 'jab' the bottom with an oar to keep the porpoise from escaping; but when the ends reached the shore and the porpoise securely penned, the net was dropped and a smaller net, made of heavy rope, was used to drag them upon the shore."

Clark also had this to say about the problems of porpoise seining: "Though the porpoise seldom tried to break through the net they often jumped over the cork line, and it is said that if one jumped it was difficult to keep the rest from following, and that they would often jump 4 to 6 feet out of the water.

"An average catch in former years was from four to five hundred porpoises to the season, requiring from five to six for a barrel of oil. The crews usually numbered from fifteen to eighteen men, and the season lasted from the latter part of December to the 1st of April, some fishing as late as the 15th of April."

In the 1880's a "porpoise factory" was established near Hatteras village by a Colonel Wainwright, and at least two crews were engaged in catching porpoise from the beach in the Hatteras area. John W. Rolinson, in charge of one crew, kept a rather detailed diary which showed the extent of his catches from 1885 to 1891. In the winter of 1885-86, from November 21 to the following May 21, his crew caught a total of 1,295 porpoises, including 171 in November and December, 165 in January, 210 in February, 205 in March, 282 in April, and 262 in May. In most months only five or six days were smooth enough for porpoising, and of course the catch varied considerably, the high being 142 caught on April 23. During this same six-month period another crew, under Tom Fulcher, fishing opposite Trent caught a total of 754.

Another porpoise factory was opened in the area by a man named Zimmerman in 1887, and James M. Stow headed a crew fishing for him, though their catches were far below those of the Rolinson outfit. The largest single-day catch recorded by Rolinson was 170, taken at one set on November 1, 1886; but that was an exceptional month, and his crew was able to fish eight days of the first fifteen, the smallest catch being 31 and the total for the period between the first and fifteenth of the month being 618, probably the record for Banks porpoise fishing.

In 1896 T. K. Bruner reported that "the porpoise industry and fishery which it supports are of less extent than formerly, owing to the diminished inducements offered to the fishermen by the low prices received for the raw products. In 1890 only two firms were engaged in handling the porpoises, in preparing their hides, and in trying out their oil. The number of porpoises killed was 1,747, for which the fishermen received $4,398. The resulting manufactured products were valued at $10,350."

Actually, in terms of total pounds caught annually, the menhaden fishery has been the most productive in North Carolina for something like seventy-five years. Menhaden, also called fat-back, bug-fish, and yellow-tail, is not generally considered a food fish, though at one time a considerable business was carried on in shipping salted menhaden to the West Indies for human consumption, and there have been several efforts to can the small ones as substitutes for sardines (the latest such effort was during World War II). Basically, however, the value of the menhaden has been in its use as a fertilizer, in the manufacture of meal for animal food, and in the extraction of the oil which is used extensively today in paint.

Menhaden is a school fish found in quantity along the Banks, and at one time large catches were made in the sounds. In fact, the menhaden fishery in North Carolina had its beginning in the sounds, and in reviewing the history of menhaden in this state William A. Ellison, Jr., of the University of North Carolina Institute of Fisheries Research, stated that the early menhaden fishery "was limited almost entirely to the sound waters, Core and Pamlico sounds and a part of Bogue Sound being the principal fishing grounds, with the exception of one fishery that was established on the Cape Fear River."

Ellison stated that the first menhaden processing plant in North Carolina, a small one, was established on Harkers Island in 1865; a second and much larger one was built by the Excelsior Oil and Guano Company at Portsmouth in 1866; and a third was started by the Church brothers of Rhode Island at Oregon Inlet in 1870. The Portsmouth operation lasted for only three years and was abandoned at a reported loss of $75,000; the Oregon Inlet plant, in which a steamer had at first been used for fishing, lasted only two years; and the small Harkers Island plant, holding on a little longer than the others, operated until 1873 when the equipment was moved to Cape Lookout, but the plant never resumed operations there.

The basic reasons for the failure of these operations—and for still another, established on Roanoke Island by Captain I. Kain in 1879— were said to have been a deficiency in the oil yield from the menhaden in the sound and the difficulty in entering Oregon Inlet and Ocracoke Inlet with the sea catch. Consequently, when the menhaden industry was re-established on a firmer footing at a later date, the sounds were bypassed. Today Morehead City is the center of the menhaden industry on this coast, though long-net fishermen frequently catch large quantities in Pamlico Sound and are forced to throw them overboard because there is no local market for them.

Sharks have been caught by sports fishermen along the Outer Banks for centuries, and there have been sporadic efforts to fish for them commercially. F. C. Salisbury, Carteret County historian, has kindly provided the following information on shark factories in the Beaufort area:

In 1920 the Ocean Leather Company formed by northern interests built a plant some three miles west of Morehead City along Bogue Sound where sharks were skinned and the livers refined. Fins were also prepared for the Chop Suey trade. This firm operated several large boats, using gill nets some 300 yards in length, 15 feet deep, and with a 20-inch mesh, which were hauled each day. Operations were discontinued after about five years and the firm moved its plant to the west coast.

Cecil Nelson operated a small plant, using two boats, beginning in 1936 and continuing until war conditions prevented carrying on the business. In one season, from April to June, Nelson brought in 3,500 sharks, all over 6 feet long. Besides the skins and liver, the jaw bones were saved for ornaments, and the teeth sold for one cent each. Nelson maintained a small factory over on Crab Point, but shipped the skins, liver oils and fins (which brought the highest price of any part of the shark) to northern markets, where the tanning of the hides was done. What was left of the shark after he was through with it either went overboard or farmers would get the remains and bury them for fertilizer.

Salisbury adds the following: "Nelson says the only good shark is a dead shark."

The efforts of the Bankers to extract a living from the sea have gone beyond the fisheries. As early as the Revolutionary War special ponds were built at Beaufort for the purpose of evaporating the sea water and extracting the salt. During the Civil War a rather extensive salt works was set up at Morehead City, and a smaller one was started on the North Banks near the Virginia line. There is little doubt that a number of the Bankers procured their own salt supplies in times of shortage by boiling sea water.

So far as is known, of all the Bankers, only the residents of Kinnakeet managed to come up with a profitable business in harvesting the seaweed which washes ashore on the fringes of the sounds. This unusual industry was begun about 1912 by C. T. Williams II who still lives in the community. According to him it started strictly by chance when a neighbor, walking along the docks in Norfolk, happened to see a number of bales of a type of seaweed known as eel grass. Since eel grass grew in great profusion in Pamlico Sound and in the spring would break loose from the bottom and float ashore in vast rafts a hundred feet or so across, Williams' neighbor copied down the name and address on the bales. On his return he told Williams what he had seen and gave him the name and address—C. T. Winchester, Baltimore, Maryland.

Williams immediately wrote to C. T. Winchester in Baltimore, asking what the baled eel grass was used for, what Winchester paid for it, and whether he could use additional sources of supply. The reply to this letter set in motion an operation which at its peak involved thirty or forty residents of Kinnakeet. Eel grass, the Baltimore buyer said, was used as packing in the manufacture of mattresses and stuffed furniture, and it was also used for putting the final polish on fine wooden furniture. Further, the demand far exceeded the supply, and Winchester was willing to pay a good price for any that Williams could provide.

At one time Williams harvested the entire sound shoreline from Little Kinnakeet to Buxton. In the spring and summer, when the rafts of eel grass drifted ashore, he and a small crew would wade out into the shallow water, pick up the eel grass that had floated in with pitchforks, and spread it two to four inches thick on the dry ground along the shore. A day or so later they would turn the grass so the other side would be exposed to the sun and air for curing purposes, and it was sometimes necessary to repeat this turning process several times.

Under normal conditions it required a week or so of exposure to the sun and air for the grass to be sufficiently cured for baling. In the beginning the baling was done on the shore, though at a later date warehouses were built, and the grass was sometimes carried back to the warehouses to be baled. Most of the balers, similar to old hay balers, were made locally. The usual procedure was to throw the cured grass on top of slats laid in the bottom of the baler until a fairly high pile was accumulated; then a boy hired for the purpose would jump up and down on the pile of grass until it was tightly packed, more grass would be added, and the boy would continue his jumping until the baler was filled. Finally, more slats were put over the top, and baling wire was clamped around to make the bale. The finished bales ran from 100 to 125 pounds in weight and were about the size of a bale of hay.

As soon as a sufficient number of bales were ready they were shipped on small freight boats to Elizabeth City or Norfolk, and then transported by larger boat or railroad freight car to the final destination. For several years Williams sold an average of between 100 and 200 tons of eel grass a year, receiving between $15 and $30 a ton for it at the destination. In addition to the Winchester Company, he sold eel grass to firms in Norfolk, Portsmouth, High Point, New York, and as far west as Chicago.

Though Williams started the business on the Banks, other residents of Kinnakeet engaged in it at one time or another. These included F. L. Scarborough, Tom Gray, and D. F. Meekins, each of whom employed as many as ten people in the peak season, which extended from late spring until early fall. At one time, also, some people from Norfolk started up a business at Frisco and built an extensive warehouse, but because of the scarcity of eel grass there they soon sold out to Williams. There were also limited operations for a while at Wanchese on Roanoke Island.

In addition to the monetary return, there was yet another advantage to the citizens of the area in the eel grass harvesting business, for when eel grass was allowed to accumulate along the shore it would rot in a short time, giving off a chemical which sometimes caused outside house paint to turn black. Williams thinks this was investigated by a chemical company and that some kind of dye was extracted later from the eel grass.

Though attempts were made to revive the business following World War I, and Williams operated until about 1925, the price was low at the outset. When finally the price began to rise, a blight struck the eel grass all along the Atlantic coast, and it almost completely disappeared from the area.

Some twenty years after the Kinnakeet eel grass industry ceased operating, a plant was established at Beaufort for processing other types of seaweed found in the sounds. The function of this plant was to extract from the seaweed a gelatin-forming substance known as agar which is used as "roughage" in certain medicinal preparations; as a thickener and stabilizer in foods such as icings, pie fillings, salad dressings, jellies, and canned meats; in dental molds; and in lubricants. Unfortunately, however, the supply of agar-producing seaweeds in the North Carolina sounds was not constant enough to permit year-around operation of a plant, and it was necessary to import seaweed from Florida during the poor seasons. As a result the Beaufort factory was sold three times between 1945 and 1948, and the plant has been closed down since 1951.

If some of the old-timers could come back today to join in the fishing, most of the nets and other equipment would be familiar to them, as would the methods employed. The boats in use today are generally the same kinds the old-timers developed especially for the shallow sounds, though the sails are gone and marine or second-hand automobile engines put in their place; and the nets they once tied by hand are now purchased factory-tied.

The old appeal remains, too, and is as compelling as it ever was: the freedom which comes from being your own boss, working out of doors, spending much of your time on the water in your own boat— just you, the boat, the wind, and the sky, and the waves slapping against the hull as you head into the sound and watch the sun inch over the horizon. Or you may be fishing from the beach, rowing your dory out through the surf, trailing your net along behind; then waiting back on shore until time to pull it in, as often in the night as in the daytime; and always thinking that maybe this is the time the net will be so full you just can handle it, all top-grade fish, bringing twelve or fifteen cents a pound instead of two or three or four.

It seldom works that way, of course, because the very same spirit of independence among the fishermen which is a chief attraction has at the same time served as a deterrent to any workable sort of organization among them. They sell their catches to the buyers for whatever they are offered, and almost invariably when the price is high there are few fish, and when the fish are plentiful the price is low.

The fishermen not only do not establish the price for their catch, they seldom know who does. The price may be set by the local buyer, the wholesale dealer in Norfolk, the operator of a retail market on Fulton Street in New York, or the housewives in Baltimore who are buying Wednesday morning's catch on Thursday afternoon for Friday's fish dinner. Not only are there no unions or organization among the Banks fishermen, there is none of the paternal interest of the type shown by the federal government toward the farmers and stockmen—no parity, no stockpiles of surplus, no guaranteed prices—just the fishermen and the fish, one catching, the other being caught.

Most of the successful commercial fishermen on the Banks today are Jacks of a dozen trades. They have to be carpenters to construct the little buildings in which the net is stored; they must be engineers to design the docks on which the buildings so often stand; they must be mechanics to keep their power boats running, to design and build the beach-buggy trucks they need for hauling their equipment down to the sea. Many build their own boats and houses, are electricians and plumbers and masons, raise garden crops on the side, take out hunting parties in the winter season, are sports-fishing guides in the slack of summer.

Those who try to fish throughout the year—and most of the successful ones do—find it necessary to own several different kinds of nets and half a dozen boats. Chances are they fish at times from the ocean beach, at times in the sound, and at other times way out in the shipping lanes opposite some inlet. Though there are weeks when they may get two or three times as much pay as the average wage earner, there are many other times when they do not even make expenses, for commercial fishing along the Banks is a gamble from start to finish, and only the persistent ones manage to make a go of it.

To get a better idea of what this year-around operation entails, come along for a close-up look at a typical Dare County crew. There are three men in this one, though many crews have four. The owner of the rig—the captain, really, though nobody calls him that—started out many years ago with a small net and a second-hand boat, and he has been improving and adding equipment until now the boats are all in good condition, the nets all fairly new. His equipment, at this point, is worth something like $15,000, and since good equipment is an essential to successful fishing, the other men are as anxious as he to provide a sufficient share of all proceeds to make certain that aging equipment can be replaced when necessary. Thus a share basis has been worked out among the three men in which expenses for groceries, gasoline, and oil are deducted from the week's proceeds. The balance is divided into equal shares, of which two go to the rig and one share to each man. Other crews may work out a different division, particularly when each member of the crew owns some part of the rig.

Since this crew fishes every month of the year there is no time of beginning, so we will join them in March when the spring run of anadromous fish begins.

This is long-net fishing time, and our long-net crew (called drag-netters, or haul-netters elsewhere) fishes the upper sounds, between Point Harbor and the south end of Roanoke Island, hoping to intercept the early run of rock or possibly even of shad. Their net is approximately 1,500 yards long and 5 to 5½ feet deep, heavily tarred, with cork floats attached to a cord along the top and lead weights on another cord along the bottom to make it stay upright in the water. They leave the dock long before daybreak, riding in the 35-foot cabin boat which is their home afloat and towing behind it two smaller open boats, each with its own motor, a 25-footer on which the net is loaded and a slightly larger one to carry the fish.

Reaching the fishing grounds they anchor the cabin boat and run the net boat in a great circle, playing out the net as the circle is made, so that the net is fully set by the time they return to the spot in which the cabin boat and fish boat are anchored.

Now the three men begin the long and strenuous job of hauling in almost a mile of heavily-tarred net, pulling on one end and piling it back in the net boat as they make the circle smaller and smaller. Finally all of the net has been hauled in except the bunt, a piece deeper than the rest and about fifteen yards long, in which all of the fish are impounded. One man with a large dip net starts dipping the fish out of the bunt, throwing them over his shoulder into the fish boat, until the bunt is empty—and if they are lucky, the boat is nearly filled.

At this time of year in Croatan Sound, they are fishing for rock, and like most other fish the larger rock bring a premium price. There are two grades of rock: pan rock, over twelve inches in length but under a pound in weight, on which the price usually runs between 5¢ and 12¢ a pound; and medium rock, over a pound in weight, with a usual price of 12¢ to 20¢ a pound. In years past this is where some of the great catches of shad have been made, bringing as high as 40¢ to 45¢ a pound; more often the big catch is herring, averaging only a cent or so a pound.

This long-net operation continues through March and into April. Then, in late April or early May, the spring run of rock, shad, and herring ended, the crew moves its base of operations to the ocean beach. Their net this time is a 300-yard seine, 14 feet deep, with a 3-inch mesh. Their equipment consists of a large dory with an inboard motor and auxiliary oars and a four-wheel-drive jeep pick-up truck. They sleep at night—when they can arrange to get in some sleep at night—in a little one-room shack they have built on the beach. Usually the net is set in the late afternoon or early evening, the shore end anchored to a long line which extends through the breakers and up on the beach. The inside end of the net itself is just beyond the breakers, the 300-yards of seine in a crescent out beyond.

If there are a lot of sharks in the area, or great quantities of seaweed or similar "junk," they sometimes haul in the net within a couple of hours to keep it from being torn to pieces; if conditions are right, they leave it out all night and haul it in early the next morning. The dory is used in setting the net, one man playing the net out behind as the dory heads out to sea; the jeep truck is used to haul in the net, pulling a line attached to the outer end until all 300-yards of net have been pulled in through the breakers. The last few yards up onto the beach the net must be pulled by hand. In place of a four-wheel-drive jeep, many beach seine crews use old cars equipped with extra-large tires—with only about fourteen pounds of air in them so they will spread out flat on the sand—and most often with the back of the car cut out to make a truck bed. These old beach-buggies, as they are usually called, are used for hauling net to the beach, for transporting the dory, and for removing the fish. In addition, when it comes time to haul in the net, the rear end is jacked up, and one of the rear wheels is used as a sort of winch to haul in the line holding the net.

All members of the crew participate in picking fish out of the net and sorting them, each kind in a different box. They are then delivered to the buyer where they are weighed. As a rule the catch at this time of the year will include mullet, gray trout, and butterfish. The beach seine fishing continues through the spring, usually into early July, and sometimes when the weather has been bad, the crew will be lucky to make a set on the average of once every other day.

In early July the crew moves again, this time down to Rodanthe, Kinnakeet, or Hatteras, long-netting in the shallow eastern edge of Pamlico Sound, operating with ten or a dozen other long-net crews in the area between Oregon Inlet and Hatteras Inlet. They have equipped the windows and door of the cabin boat with screens and sleep there at night, leaving the harbor at 4:00 or 4:30 A.M. and returning with their catch in mid-afternoon. The buyer weighs their catch at the dock, and trucks pick it up, heading north immediately to cross Oregon Inlet before the ferries stop running for the night; so the fish caught during the day in Pamlico Sound are delivered that night to the dealer in Norfolk, Portsmouth, or Elizabeth City.

The long-net operation continues here until the middle of October or so, with five days of fishing each week, then the week end at home with the family. The catch, mostly, is spot and croakers, and sometimes there are blues, gray trout, and pig fish.

By mid-October the fall run is well started along the sea beach, and the crew moves again back to the beach shack, back to the dory, the jeep, and 300-yard beach seine. They fish from the beach during the latter part of October and all of November, usually catching spot as the money fish, with some mullet, bluefish, and other species on occasion.

When fishing from the sea beach ends in early December, some crews break up for the winter, take it easy, mend net, repair their boats, and maybe do some work around the house. But in this particular crew only one man drops out, the other two switching to still other kinds of fishing during the winter season when the long net and beach seine are laid up.

In December the two of them move down to Oregon Inlet in their 38-foot flounder trawler, anchor at the inlet each night, and go out to sea with their trawl net each day the water is calm enough. They trawl for flounders twelve to fifteen miles offshore, right in the shipping lanes, running out early in the morning, fishing most of the day, and returning to the inlet in the evening. The fish buyers bring their trucks down to the landing at the inlet, mount big scales on the tail gates, weigh the flounders right there, and pay cash for them; sometimes the price is as little as 4¢ to 5¢ a pound when there is a big run or as high as 25¢ a pound when flounders are scarce.

Flounder trawling requires special equipment—the 38- to 45-foot trawlers and the trawl nets—but the operation lasts only a few weeks, and usually before Christmas the two-man crew has suspended operations to spend the holiday at home.

These two men are full-time fishermen, however, and shortly after New Year's they are at it again, this time fishing in Currituck Sound for perch with a 400-yard drag seine and a small skiff in which they have mounted a small air-cooled engine. They live on the cabin boat in the sound and drag their net in a small circle out from the shore, making several hauls in the course of a day and taking their catch across the sound to a buyer at Poplar Branch. Frequently they fish six days a week during January and February, returning home only for Saturday night and Sunday. Sometimes, in addition to perch, they get carp and other fish. The price they get for perch, probably because few people fish for them in the area, is generally higher than the price of the fish they get in their long net or beach seine.

Sometime in February they drag their little seine for the last time, load it on the skiff, and head back home in the cabin boat. Then the third man joins them again, and for a few days or weeks they work on their rig, sometimes replacing a whole section or just putting on new corks or sinkers; they may install a new motor in one of the boats, build a new bottom for another, or paint the whole fleet, because March is almost here, and soon the spring run of rock and shad will begin; and when it does, these three men want to be right out there in Croatan Sound again, setting their long net where they think the fish will be.

This is not a typical operation, because no two crews fish the same times with the same rigs in the same places. Some turn to shrimping at certain times of the year and some to oystering; and in the lower sounds, especially, there is a lot more mulleting than in the area just described. Some of the long-netters are wary of beach seining because you are lucky to be able to fish half the time, and sharks, seaweed, or a sudden storm can wipe out your entire investment in a single night. But those who have been at it the longest and have made the most money have long since learned that the only way you can catch fish is to have your net overboard when they come along.

The decline in commercial fishing in the Banks area is partly attributable to the rising cost of boats, nets, and other equipment without a commensurate rise in the wholesale price of fish. The great increase in the tourist business along much of the Banks, with attendant demands for employment in the construction trades and with increased opportunities for small businesses, has lured away large numbers of fishermen. Most of the fishermen will tell you, however, that the big reason is the scarcity of fish, the virtual disappearance of "big money fish" such as shad and the absence of the great runs of other species. The fishermen blame this on the shrimpers, claiming they destroy millions of baby fish or fingerlings each season, and on the pollution of the streams and rivers which flow into the sounds. Ichthyologists seem to agree, on the other hand, that the fishermen themselves must shoulder an equal portion of the blame, stating that the sounds and rivers have been overfished, that conservation and propagation laws have not been strictly observed, and that the long-netters have themselves destroyed millions of small fish. Certainly, whenever there is a poor season for commercial fishing, some of the fishermen usually appeal to state authorities to relax regulations or to extend the season on a specific type of fish into the spawning period.

So the lot of the commercial fisherman, whether through his own fault or as the result of the actions of others, becomes harder and harder as the years pass, and as this is written there are only a handful of full-time fishermen in an area which once supported thousands. But there always remains the chance that a crew will make a fabulous haul —$1,000 worth of spot from the beach in a single night or up to $4,000 from a long-net haul of rock, croakers, or shad—and a certain number stick with it. These are the real fishermen, unwilling to sacrifice their independence or to remain for long away from their boats and the water. With proper development of related facilities, with some sort of organization among the fishermen to insure a decent price for the fish they catch, with the establishment of processing plants for canning crab meat and freezing shrimp and food fish, and with continued thought and consideration for the propagation and protection of declining species, commercial fishing could again become an important phase of the Banks economy.

New Life for the Banks

O N THE EVE of the Great Depression the fortunes of the Bankers had reached a new low. Because no effort had been made to improve the strain of beef cattle, stock raising was relegated to minor importance. Shipwrecks were becoming a rarity, and a decrease in the lifesaving operations was in prospect. More stringent hunting laws and a growing shortage of wildfowl were causing dissatisfaction among the non-resident owners of the large gunning clubs. Maritime traffic through the Banks inlets was confined largely to small fishing vessels, and the steamboat lines no longer operated on the sounds.

There was no shipbuilding on the Banks, no commercial outlet for yaupon; no more shore whaling; no porpoise seining from the beach. Commercial gunning was outlawed, the diamondback terrapin was practically extinct, and a blight was destroying the eel grass. Even the commercial fishermen were beginning to have difficulties.

Further, from Currituck to Beaufort Inlet, erosion had become such a problem that much of the Banks was swept clean by storm-driven waters whenever a hurricane passed over. Diamond City had disappeared. Portsmouth was fast becoming a ghost town. Little Kinnakeet existed in name only. In the other communities the older folks stayed on, but many of the young men and women were leaving the Banks to seek a livelihood elsewhere.

During prohibition a single new industry appeared—bootlegging—and East Lake, on the mainland opposite Roanoke Island, was called by some the "corn likker" capital of the nation. But the bootleggers seldom paid taxes, and taxes were needed to finance the growing cost of local government—the cost of the six-month school term made mandatory by the North Carolina General Assembly, of the county's greatly increased pauper rolls, of constructing and maintaining the secondary roads.

When Wash F. Baum of Manteo took office on December 2, 1924, as chairman of the Board of Commissioners for Dare County, the situation was acute. Dare, formed in 1870 from parts of the counties of Currituck, Hyde, and Tyrrell, included all of the Banks from Hatteras Inlet north to Caffeys Inlet, plus Colington, Roanoke Island, and a big chunk of the sparsely populated mainland. Because four out of every five Bankers lived in Dare, what happened there was the key to the future of the Banks.

"Dare County just couldn't remain a county for long, the way things were going," says Wash Baum. "We had to do something or get out. We were cut off from everything—from the rest of the state, and the rest of the country; why the different parts of Dare County were even cut off from each other. The only way to get to Hatteras, or Kitty Hawk, or the mainland was by boat.

"Some men from up in Jersey came to Dare County about that time and started buying up land on the beach. One of them stayed at my place when he was in Manteo, and all he talked about was our beaches. Said he'd been all over the country and they were the finest beaches he'd seen anywhere. Kept telling me Dare County had a wonderful future, if only we could get road and bridge connections so people could come down here. That's when I began trying to figure out some way to get those roads and bridges."

Wash Baum did more than think about roads and bridges; he started building them. A canal was dug, at county expense, west of Manteo to Croatan Sound, so the Dare mainlanders would have a decent harbor for their boats when they came to the county seat, and a roadbed was thrown up beside it. Another was dug on the west side of the sound at Manns Harbor, with a road from the canal to the village proper.

The Metropolitan Life Insurance Company had acquired the old Dare Lumber Company holdings, consisting of more than 150,000 acres of timber and swamp land on the mainland, and arrangements were made for the construction of a road through the Metropolitan property from Stumpy Point in Dare County to Englehard in Hyde. (Dare built its part of the road in 1926 with $40,000 borrowed from Metropolitan at 5 per cent interest, and paid off both the $40,000 and the interest by raising the taxes on Metropolitan's land.)

Meanwhile, Wash Baum was still trying to formulate a plan for getting the roads and bridges which would open up the Dare County beaches. He found an enthusiastic ally in Harry C. Lawrence, a Minnesota dipper-dredge contractor who had built the road through the Metropolitan property and the landings at Manns Harbor and Manteo. But when they approached state highway officials in the capital at Raleigh they got a cold reception.

"One of the highway engineers told us we might as well return to Dare County and forget it," Lawrence remembers. "He said it would be fifty years or more before there'd ever be bridges across Roanoke Sound and Currituck Sound, and a road along the beach at Kitty Hawk and Nags Head."

They did return to Dare County, but Wash Baum refused to forget it, for a definite plan of action had taken shape in his mind.

"Since the state wouldn't help us, then I figured we had to get the job started ourselves," he said. "But I felt sure if we got the first link built—the bridge across Roanoke Sound—then sooner or later the state would have to come in and help out on the road up the beach and a second bridge across Currituck Sound. So Harry Lawrence and I went all over Roanoke Sound, taking soundings from a skiff, and we picked out the best place for a bridge." *

Baum's plan involved expenditures far beyond the means of a nearly bankrupt county such as Dare, and consequently it could be financed

---

* The location they selected was essentially the same as the site proposed for Hamilton Fulton's Roanoke Sound dike more than a hundred years earlier. At that point a chain of small islands extended into the sound from the beach for almost a mile, which meant that a causeway could be constructed that far and the bridge itself would be slightly less than a mile in length.

only by the issuance of long-term county bonds which had to be authorized by the North Carolina General Assembly.

"We wanted to be able to sell up to $300,000 in bonds," he said. "I was sure a lot of people wouldn't like it, so I waited until I was re-elected. Then I went down to Wanchese to talk it over with Mathias D. Hayman, our representative to the General Assembly. He finally agreed to go along with me, and I went right back and told Lawrence to start digging the causeway on the Roanoke Island end. When people asked what we were doing, we told them what a big help it would be to have a canal and good boat harbor there. We didn't say anything about a bridge."

The news was bound to leak out, however, and when it did it brought forth the very reaction Baum had anticipated. That day one of the leading businessmen in Manteo came up to him.

"Wash," he said. "What in hell are you trying to do, ruin us?"

The comment was typical, for feeling was high throughout the county. Many merchants felt sure what little business remained would leave them the day the bridge opened, that they would all go broke in short order trying to pay off the indebtedness.

Most people thought of the bridge simply as a means for Roanoke Islanders to get to the beach and beach people to get to the island. Few felt there was any great potential value in the miles of undeveloped beach land.

"I have to admit that I couldn't see what was going to happen on the beach," says R. Bruce Etheridge, astute Dare political leader who was first elected to represent the county in the General Assembly in 1903 and was back there again as late as 1957. "Wash Baum put that bridge across there and a lot of people thought he was crazy, but the results have proven him out." The immediate results, however, were not so clear.

The causeway on the beach side was built by Harry C. Lawrence who also designed and supervised construction of the bridge. The contractor for the bridge was the W. J. Jones Construction Company of Elizabeth City. More than $20,000 was saved by using an old twelve-foot-wide railroad draw span abandoned by the Dare Lumber Company at Mill Tail Creek on the mainland. The final cost of the bridge, draw span, and causeways was approximately $140,000, and by early

1928 the new installation was in general use—with a toll charge of one dollar per car.

The trouble at that point was that the bridge did not seem to go anywhere. On the Roanoke Island end the dirt causeway was connected with the only hard-surfaced road in the Banks area, built by the state in 1924 between Manteo and Wanchese; but on the beach side it terminated in sand tracks leading off in all directions, and it took an experienced sand driver to get from there to wherever he was going without getting stuck. A lot of people still thought Wash Baum had ruined Dare County.

Almost as soon as the Roanoke Sound bridge was finished, however, a group of Elizabeth City businessmen, led by Carl Blades, formed the Wright Memorial Bridge Company, bought some seven miles of beach land north of Kitty Hawk, and made arrangements to build a second toll bridge, this one across Currituck Sound between Point Harbor and Martins Point. This Wright Memorial Bridge across Currituck Sound—nearly three miles long—was completed late in 1930. By that time even the officials in Raleigh could see that the state of North Carolina had an obligation to take part in opening up the Dare County beaches, and construction was started on a eighteen-mile sand-asphalt highway connecting the two toll bridges.

In 1931, only four years after Wash Baum had pushed forward with his plans for the Roanoke Sound bridge, the state highway through Kitty Hawk and Nags Head beaches was completed, and it was possible to drive from Point Harbor on the Currituck mainland to Manteo or Wanchese over modern bridges and highways.

At the same time other improvements had come which made the outlook much brighter. In 1927 crusading editor W. O. Saunders of the Elizabeth City *Independent* had advocated the construction of a national monument to the Wright brothers at Kill Devil Hill. Congressman Lindsay Warren secured passage of a bill authorizing such a monument, and the owners of Kill Devil Hill and the adjoining property—a group of New Jersey residents—had donated the necessary land without cost and, when more was needed, had purchased it from the owners and donated that too. On the twenty-fifth anniversary of the first flight the cornerstone for the Wright Memorial was laid, then the hill itself was stabilized, and by early 1931 actual construction of the Wright Memorial was in progress.

Further, Captain Tom Baum of Kitty Hawk, who formerly had run ferries from Point Harbor to Kitty Hawk and from Point Harbor to Roanoke Island, was by that time operating regular ferry schedules across Croatan Sound from Roanoke Island to Manns Harbor, while Captain Toby Tillett of Wanchese was providing similar service across Oregon Inlet.

With the new roads, bridges, and ferries, Dare County and much of the more heavily populated part of the Banks was no longer cut off from the outside world; the owners of property in the Nags Head and Kitty Hawk areas were subdividing acreage tracts into lots and there was an attendant increase in the taxable valuation of the beach property; and much outside interest was being manifest in the aviation shrine under construction at Kill Devil Hill.

But paralleling these progressive developments, even outweighing them, were other problems for the Bankers, for the nation-wide depression had come and unemployment had reached an all time high on the Banks. In addition, many areas, particularly on the lower Banks, had eroded so badly that they were now only bald beach, and at Cape Hatteras the shore had cut in so severely that the lighthouse was threatened by the sea.

At the height of these bad times there came a heartening note, in the Elizabeth City *Independent* for July 21, 1933, under the headline: "A COASTAL PARK FOR NORTH CAROLINA." In this and subsequent articles by adopted Banker Frank Stick, the details of a proposal for a vast rehabilitation program for the Outer Banks were unfolded. The first step would be the reclamation of the areas which had been denuded of vegetation, an organized erosion control and sand fixation project designed to reclaim the bald beaches and rebuild the eroded dunes, which would at the same time provide work and income to help the residents of eastern North Carolina survive the depression. This would be followed by the establishment of a national seashore park to preserve most of the Banks from Oregon Inlet to Cape Lookout in its natural state. Finally, a modern coastal highway would be constructed from Nags Head to Beaufort to enable outsiders to visit the reclaimed Banks in this national seashore park.

Whereas the initial reaction to Wash Baum's plan for a Roanoke Sound bridge had been skeptical at best, the response to this suggested program for Banks rehabilitation was immediately favorable. The need for some such drastic action was dramatically pointed up only a month after the original proposal had been made when a severe hurricane struck the Outer Banks. This was followed by a second hurricane of even greater intensity in September. When the waters subsided it was found that the new highway through the Nags Head and Kitty Hawk beaches was extensively damaged; New Inlet had reopened, once again isolating Hatteras Island; hundreds of Banks houses were damaged or destroyed; and long lines of the remaining protective dunes were washed away.

Soon after this second hurricane a group of prominent North Carolinians visited the Outer Banks to pass judgment on Frank Stick's park and rehabilitation proposal.

Frank Page, former chairman of the North Carolina Highway Commission, said, "I consider that this general program of coast development means the preservation of Eastern North Carolina for the future." State Forester J. S. Holmes was confident that "this beach section can be made one of the finest timber producing areas in the country." State Geologist H. J. Bryson said, "There is no question but that reforestation along this beach would stop the erosion to a large degree." And H. D. Panton of the North Carolina State Highway Department expressed the opinion that the construction of an Outer Banks highway "will be one of the easiest jobs of this whole program, because it will come after everything else has been planned."

Leading citizens of the Banks were equally enthusiastic, and former Dare County representative R. Bruce Etheridge, then serving as Director of the North Carolina Department of Conservation and Development, set in motion the mechanics whereby the plan could become a reality, and arranged and presided over numerous conferences with state and federal officials. In Washington, meanwhile, Congressman Lindsay Warren, whose district included most of the Banks, succeeded in transmitting his personal enthusiasm to high officials of the federal executive branch.

The program was expanded to include the restoration of the "Cittie of Ralegh" on Roanoke Island, improvements at the Wright Memorial, which had been taken over in the spring of 1933 by the National Park Service, and mosquito control work all along the Banks. On November 21, 1933, just four months after the publication in the *Independent* of the original proposal, assurance was given by the federal Civil

Works Administration that funds in excess of a million dollars would be made available for various phases of the project.

By the following April, a camp for transient laborers had been established at Nags Head, sand fences were being constructed,* and grasses were being planted on the bald beaches. By June the restoration of the "Cittie of Ralegh" was underway, with the work being done by local labor. In June, 1935, some 999 acres, including Cape Point and the lands surrounding the Cape Hatteras Lighthouse, were donated by J. S. Phipps, J. H. Phipps, Winston Guest, and Bradley Martin, all non-resident club owners, as a nucleus for the proposed park. That same spring the North Carolina General Assembly enacted legislation which prohibited stock from running at large on the Banks areas of Dare County from Currituck to Hatteras Inlet. Efforts to enact similar laws governing the free ranges on Ocracoke Island in Hyde County and on Portsmouth, Core Banks, Cape Lookout, and Shackleford Banks in Carteret County were unsuccessful, and since it was practically impossible to carry on a program of grass planting and dune building where cattle and horses were running at large, the erosion control work was for the most part limited to the Dare County Banks.

Meanwhile, the state of North Carolina had purchased the Roanoke Sound and Currituck Sound bridges, and by the time the restored "Cittie of Ralegh" was completed Saunders suggested that a pageant be held at the Fort Raleigh site commemorating the 350th anniversary of the birth of Virginia Dare and the lost colony. Pulitzer prize winning North Carolina playwright Paul Green agreed to write the script, and when he was through he had more than a pageant, for he had devised a new theatrical technique—a full-length play to be presented out of doors, combining elements of pageantry with historic setting, action, music, and the dance, which he called "a symphonic drama." A natural amphitheatre, overlooking the water front at Fort Raleigh and seating more than 3,000 people, was constructed, and though it was necessary to import the choir and leading actors, Green's *The Lost Colony* proved so successful during the 1937 season

* Where those first low, zig-zag sand fences were erected on a flat beach in the vicinity of the Nags Head Coast Guard Station, there is today a line of stabilized dunes, covered with beach grass and sea oats, averaging 150 feet in width and 15 in height.

that it was repeated the next summer and the next, and except for the war years the drama has been presented throughout the months of July and August ever since.

Even as arrangements were being made for the initial presentation of *The Lost Colony* at Fort Raleigh, the plan for establishing of a national seashore park on the Outer Banks was taking shape. The National Park Service had joined in the rehabilitation work, and, after conducting a thorough survey of available oceanfront areas on all parts of the Atlantic coast, announced in 1937 that it was recommending the establishment of the Cape Hatteras National Seashore Recreational Area on the Outer Banks. A bill establishing the Cape Hatteras Seashore was introduced by Congressman Warren, July 13, 1937, and enacted into law. Subsequently the North Carolina General Assembly, at the instigation of Senator D. Bradford Fearing of Manteo, created "the North Carolina Cape Hatteras Seashore Commission," which was "authorized, empowered and directed to acquire title in the name of the State of North Carolina" for the needed land.

For several years thereafter, while the CCC boys and transient laborers under National Park Service direction continued their erosion control work along the Banks, the Cape Hatteras Seashore Commission sought donations of land for the proposed park. The success of the land acquisition program was largely due to the work of D. Victor Meekins of Manteo, publisher of *The Coastland Times*, who has hammered away editorially for more than twenty years on the thesis that tourism is the salvation for what he calls "The Sir Walter Raleigh Coastland."

In a report dated July, 1940, A. C. Stratton and James R. Hollowell of the National Park Service summarized the erosion control work:

Southward from the Virginia State Line extending to Hatteras Inlet a great barrier dune has been built for the protection of the Banks from the ocean. In some places it is as much as twenty-five feet high with a base of nearly three hundred feet. . . . In addition to this a barrier dune was built up on the shoreline of Ocracoke Island for about half of the distance of the island. . . . In all, one hundred and fifteen miles of barrier dune has been constructed. Over six hundred miles of fencing was used. . . . A total of 141,841,821 square feet of grassing has been planted . . . 2,552,359 seedlings and shrubs were set out.

Late that year plans were made for the National Park Service to assume jurisdiction over the Fort Raleigh site on Roanoke Island, and by the summer of 1941 new hotels and tourist cottages at Nags Head and Kitty Hawk Beach were doing a big business, lot sales showed a marked increase, attendance at *The Lost Colony* and visitation to the Park Service facilities at Fort Raleigh and the Wright Memorial were at an all-time high. In addition, the first national seashore recreational area had been authorized for the Banks, and considerable land, including Cape Hatteras itself, had been donated for that purpose; and for the first time large areas of Hatteras Island were sufficiently stabilized to make the construction of a hard-surfaced road feasible. Suddenly people on the Banks began to realize that they had not only weathered the depression but that an entirely new life was in prospect for them.

That was 1941, and in December the Japanese attacked Pearl Harbor. The sand-fixation program was discontinued, and no effort was made to maintain the new protective dunes. *The Lost Colony* was suspended for the duration of the war, travel was sharply curtailed, and the beach areas were blacked out as Nazi submarine packs took a terrific toll of shipping off the Banks. So great was the exodus of able bodied Bankers to the armed forces that more than a hundred Dare County Midgetts enlisted in the services between 1941 and 1945.

Even before the war ended, oil companies came to the Banks, began buying up mineral rights, and made plans to drive test wells. People who had enthusiastically supported the Cape Hatteras Seashore park program in time of depression when it meant jobs and income now as bitterly opposed it in the face of the prospect of oil royalties, and they even succeeded in securing passage of a North Carolina law prohibiting further donation of Banks land for park purposes.

The beach development envisioned by Wash Baum when he planned the Roanoke Sound bridge in 1927 had been held up first by depression, then by war. But V-E Day was almost like a long awaited go-ahead signal, and even before the defeat of Japan in 1945, the boom began on the North Banks. By the summer of 1946 and the resumption of *The Lost Colony*, new hotels, motels, restaurants, stores, and cottages were open for business at Nags Head, Kill Devil Hills, and Kitty Hawk, and many more were being planned. Land prices rose steadily, new real estate developments were opened, and tourists poured across the Currituck Sound and Roanoke Sound bridges in throngs.

The oil companies had drilled their test wells—some of the deepest ever drilled, it was claimed—then had given up their leases and moved out. On Hatteras Island the North Carolina highway department had begun construction of a road from Hatteras village through the Frisco woods to Buxton and on to Avon, and tourist facilities had begun to appear along this new Hatteras highway.

Most people assumed by then that the Cape Hatteras Seashore Recreational Area project was dead, and when Representative Dewey Hayman of Dare County put through a bill in the North Carolina General Assembly reactivating the Cape Hatteras Seashore Commission and the National Park Service announced that it still hoped to go ahead with the project, the cries of dismay raised by some of the Banks property owners could be heard as far away as Raleigh and Washington, D.C.

Then, in June of 1952, when the furor had subsided and the prospects for a national park on the Banks were truly dim, an anonymous donor offered to give $618,000 for the purchase of park lands if North Carolina would match the figure. Four days later the North Carolina Council of State appropriated $618,000 for the purpose, and it was announced that the private donation had been made by the Old Dominion Foundation and the Avalon Foundation, both created by the children of the late Andrew W. Mellon. It had been almost twenty years since the original suggestion for a national park on the Outer Banks, but at last it was assured.

Since then the hard-surfaced highway has been completed from Nags Head to Ocracoke village, with state-owned ferries carrying traffic across both Oregon Inlet and Hatteras Inlet, and large sums have been expended by the federal government to repair the dunes and restore the vegetation, not only in the Cape Hatteras Seashore area, but on the North Banks as well. The growth of Hatteras and Ocracoke Island and the beach areas of Nags Head and Kitty Hawk as summer resorts has been something to behold. Dare County's Atlantic Township, for example, which includes Kill Devil Hills, Kitty Hawk, and the new resort area of Southern Shores, valued on the tax books at a little over $100,000 in 1926, had increased to more than $6,250,000 in 1957. A former commercial fisherman there is now running a general store, another is in the construction business, a third is a plumbing contractor; a former game warden operates his own drive-in restaurant; a retired Coast Guardsman owns a cottage court, another runs a filling station, and a number of others get seasonal work on house construction jobs to supplement their retirement pay.

This change from the declining economy of the early 1920's, which was largely dependent on commercial fishing, maritime traffic, and the Coast Guard, to the rising economy of the 1950's, which is based on tourism, has been gradual but overwhelming. On the North Banks the construction of bridges and roads, the elimination of the open stock range with the attendant sand fixation and erosion control projects, and the establishment of the various National Park Service facilities have made this change possible. On Ocracoke Island, still isolated until North Carolina provided the new road and free ferries in 1957, the change is just now taking place. But on the lower Banks, at Portsmouth, Core Banks, Cape Lookout, and Shackleford Banks, where stock continued to graze on an open range through World War II and afterwards with no effort made to control erosion, where there was no one like Wash Baum to push through the construction of roads and bridges, and where there still is no connection with the mainland, the long stretches of bald beach remain, devoid of vegetation and flooded by every storm tide—but the people have long since departed.

The Banks
Today

THE OUTER BANKS today is an area of marked contrast. On the one hand are the highly developed resort beaches and extensive National Park Service facilities accessible by modern roads and toll-free bridges and ferries; on the other are the barren, isolated stretches of bald beach and the deserted or nearly deserted communities of earlier times.

Today the visitor can approach the Banks from the north across the rebuilt Currituck Sound Bridge or from the south and west across the new Croatan Sound Bridge, first opened to traffic in the spring of 1957. He can drive his automobile down the Banks from the village of Duck above Kitty Hawk, through Southern Shores, Kitty Hawk Beach, Kill Devil Hills, Nags Head, and Bodie Island Beach to the Oregon Inlet ferry; then on to Pea Island, Rodanthe, Waves, Salvo, Avon, Cape Hatteras, Buxton, Frisco, and Hatteras village; and finally, across Hatteras Inlet by ferry to the new Ocracoke Island highway which terminates at the village of Ocracoke. In the process he can take side trips on hard-surfaced roads to Kitty Hawk village, the Wright Memorial, Colington Island, the old Nags Head soundside resort, and he can cross the new Roanoke Sound Bridge to Fort Raleigh, Manteo, and Wanchese on Roanoke Island.

Above Duck, along Currituck Banks to the Virginia state line and beyond, there are no roads, only the treacherous sand ruts or the wash at low tide, and this area should be avoided by the neophyte sand driver. Below Ocracoke, access is by boat only, and few tourists ever see Ocracoke Inlet, Portsmouth, Core Banks, Drum Inlet, Cape Look-out, and Shackleford Banks.

The following pages contain descriptions of each of the Banks communities and other major points of interest. To simplify reference the arrangement is geographical, from north to south, with descriptions of the nearby islands at the end. Salient historical facts and other pertinent notes are included, making each section a capsule history of the locality. The chapter is designed, also, to serve as a handy tour guide for visitors making their first trip to the Outer Banks.

CURRITUCK BANKS

THE NAME Currituck Banks, or North Banks of Currituck, was applied for many years to the area from old Currituck Inlet and the Virginia line southward to Bodie Island. Included were the older communities at Wash Woods, Pennys Hill, Currituck Beach, Poyners Hill, Caffeys Inlet, Jeanguite, Kitty Hawk, Rowsypock, Colington, and Nags Head, and the more recent Seagull, Deals, Corolla, Duck, Southern Shores, and Kill Devil Hills.

Originally the name Currituck referred to one of the four early precincts of North Carolina, and then it became the name of a county, a sound, two inlets, a port, and the Banks. It is of Indian derivation and was spelled at least two dozen different ways—including Caratut, Carahtuck, Curahuk, Caratock, Corrituck, Caratuk, Curretucke, and Currytuck—before being standardized as Currituck.

On the 1657 map by Nicholas Comberford, the area was shown as an island and was named Lucke Island, and in the charter to the Lords Proprietors in 1663, the beginning point of Carolina was at "the north end of the island called Lucke Island." During the early colonial period it was bounded on the north by old Currituck Inlet and on the south by Roanoke Inlet. Later, other inlets, including New Currituck, Crow, and Caffeys, cut through the Banks to make it a series of islands, but today all of those inlets are closed and it is part of a long peninsula extending from Cape Henry to Oregon Inlet.

The original boundary between Virginia and North Carolina was fixed at old Currituck Inlet, and when the boundary line was finally surveyed in 1728, a cedar stake was driven in the sand 200 yards north of the inlet to mark the point. The survey party found the inlet so badly shoaled up that it was impossible for any vessels to pass through, but they reported that another inlet had opened several miles to the south providing a ten-foot channel. This was called New Inlet or New Currituck Inlet, though after the old inlet had been entirely obliterated, people finally got around to calling the new one Currituck Inlet.*

When this second Currituck Inlet closed in 1828, all water communication between the ocean and Currituck Sound was blocked off with rapid, and in some respects disastrous, results. Several years later Edmund Ruffin reported that within twenty-four months the Currituck Sound water had changed from salt to fresh, "the oysters and other sea shell-fish all died; the water grasses were entirely changed in kinds" and "the mosquitoes were more numerous than ever known." In 1897 G. R. Weiland reported in *The American Journal of Science* that this was "one of the most important geological changes which has taken place along the Atlantic coast in recent times" and that "upwards of one hundred square miles" of shallow salt and brackish water was converted to fresh water. One result of this change which figured on the credit side was that great quantities of ducks were attracted to Currituck Sound by the new type of vegetation.

Among the earliest residents of Currituck Banks were some nefarious characters, and there were oft-repeated charges that numerous runaway slaves and criminals were hiding out there. William Byrd described two of the residents in 1728:

On the South Shore, not far from the Inlet, dwelt a Marooner, that Modestly call'd himself a Hermit, tho' he forfeited that Name by Suffering a wanton Female to cohabit with Him.

His Habitation was a Bower, cover'd with Bark after the Indian Fashion, which in that mild Situation protected him pretty well from the Weather. Like the Ravens, he neither plow'd nor sow'd, but subsisted chiefly upon Oysters, which his Handmaid made a Shift to gather from the Adjacent

---

* There were two other inlets in this same area. Musketo Inlet, shown on the Ogilby map of 1671, was located south of old Currituck Inlet. Crow Inlet, south of New Currituck Inlet, was open for a few years just before 1800.

Rocks. Sometimes, too, for the Change of Dyet, he sent her to drive up the Neighbour's Cows, to moisten their Mouths with a little Milk. But as for raiment, he depended mostly upon his Length of Beard, and She upon her Length of Hair, part of which she brought decently forward, and the rest dangled behind quite down to her Rump.

Currituck Banks was a favorite hunting grounds for the Poteskeet Indians who lived on the mainland above Powells Point, but the Bankers tried to prevent them from hunting on the lands which they were converting to a stock range. After some of the Bankers not only refused to let the Indians hunt on their land but threatened to break their guns if they did not go home, the Indians took their case to the North Carolina Council, and on March 10, 1715, the Council ordered that the Poteskeets should "henceforward have Liberty to hunt on any of the said Banks land" without being disturbed. This writer has found more than two dozen arrowheads and numerous potsherds in a small, now barren, area near Duck, further attesting to the presence of these and other Indians in the past.

During the early colonial period, vessels going through Currituck Inlet were required to register with the collector for "Port Currituck," but with no established spot for the collector's office, the law was not strictly adhered to. During the Revolutionary War the North Bankers were subjected to repeated attacks by British privateers, and for a while an independent defensive company was stationed near Currituck Inlet, with Dennis Dauge as Captain, John Jarvis, First Lieutenant, Legrand Whitehall, Second Lieutenant, and Butler Cowall, Ensign. After this company was withdrawn, the Bankers had to protect their stock and their other belongings as best they could, and some sought draft deferment on the grounds that what they were doing at home on the Banks was of more importance to the war effort than anything they could do in service. Samuel Jarvis, prominent representative of the people of Currituck, dubbed the North Banks "Currituck Liberty Plains" during this period of British attacks.

Today the North Banks from the Virginia line southward to Caffeys Inlet is in Currituck County, below that, in Dare County. For a number of years there has been agitation for the construction of a hard-surfaced road from the North Carolina state highway at Duck northward to Virginia Beach, and at one time both Virginia and

North Carolina authorized private interests to build a toll road between those two points. This project failed, and except for a graded sand road between Duck and Caffeys Inlet, there are no roads on the northern Banks, though with the rapid growth of the adjoining resort areas and the prospect of a bridge-tunnel across Chesapeake Bay, it seems probable that a North Banks highway will materialize in the comparatively near future. Recently the Virginia Electric and Power Company has extended its power lines as far north as Corolla.

WASH WOODS AND DEALS

MOTORISTS DRIVING along the wash south of the Virginia line on Currituck Banks today can tell at a glance why this area is known as Wash Woods, for old tree stumps are still there, at times hundreds of them exposed at low tide, the waves washing over them when the tide is in.

Approximately twenty families were living at Wash Woods in the 1850's, and Edmund Ruffin said they gained their living in part by cultivating small patches of Indian corn and sweet potatoes. The federal government established a Lifesaving Station there in 1878 named Deal's Island, but this was later changed to Wash Woods. That same year a U.S. Weather Bureau Station was located there also, but it was discontinued in 1888.

When a post office was established at Wash Woods, January 22, 1907, with Sarah A. Dasher as postmaster, it was given the name of Deals, but the post office was discontinued September 29, 1917.

PENNYS HILL AND SEAGULL

THE LARGE sand hill bearing the name Pennys Hill, originally located just north of New Currituck Inlet, has been a prominent landmark since the early days of North Banks settlement. The movement of this dune toward the southwest is reported to have had some effect on the closing of the inlet in 1828.

A Lifesaving Station, originally called Old Currituck Inlet, was established there in 1878. The name was later changed to Currituck Inlet and still later to Pennys Hill, and when the succeeding Pennys Hill Coast Guard Station was decommissioned following World

War II, the buildings were sold to private individuals and moved to Corolla.

The Seagull Post Office was established at Pennys Hill May 2, 1908, with Boyd O'Neal as postmaster, but it was discontinued on October 31, 1924. There are a few houses there now.

COROLLA AND CURRITUCK BEACH

FOR A NUMBER of years this was the largest community on the Banks between Kitty Hawk and Virginia and was known as Currituck Beach. Since World War II the population has declined sharply and less than a dozen families live there now, though a number of the older houses are still standing.

The large sand hills which dominate the scenery, both north and south, are Whales Head Hill and Jones Hill. A Lifesaving Station, one of the seven original stations on the Banks, was built there in 1874 and was named Jones Hill, though this was later changed to Whales Head and finally to Currituck Beach.

The Currituck Beach Lighthouse, the last major lighthouse constructed on the Outer Banks, was begun June 19, 1874, and was first lighted December 1, 1875. An impressive red brick structure 150 feet high to the center of the lantern, it was built at a cost of $178,000 on a tract of land purchased from Edmund C. Lindsey.

Several gun clubs have been located at Corolla, and one of the early ones was called The Lighthouse Club. Probably the most expensive and most pretentious clubhouse ever built on the Banks was the nearby Whales Head Club built in the 1920's and still standing.

When a post office was established at Currituck Beach on March 6, 1895, with Emma V. Parker as postmaster, it was given the name Corolla, and it is the only Banks post office north of Kitty Hawk still in operation.

POYNERS HILL

THIS WAS once a small soundside community and the scene of the wreck of the steamer *Metropolis*, January 31, 1878, with the loss of eighty-five lives. A Lifesaving Station was established here soon after the loss of the *Metropolis*, and during World War II a temporary

Coast Guard base was located here. The temporary buildings were sold and moved to Corolla when the station was decommissioned.

CAFFEYS INLET

IN 1788 A MAN named George Caffee bought a hundred acres of Banks land north of the present village of Duck and added forty more acres in 1792. But Caffee soon saw his holdings considerably reduced when a small inlet cut through his property.*

This inlet was known as Caffee's Inlet at the time—and also as Providence Inlet—and remained open for only a comparatively short period, though it has threatened to open again on several occasions.

A Lifesaving Station, one of the first on the Banks, was located here in 1874, and the Coast Guard Station which replaced it is still in use.

DUCK

THIS IS a small fishing community located on the sound side between Caffeys Inlet and Martins Point. The name is of comparatively recent origin as the Duck Post Office was established on June 29, 1909, with Lloyd A. Toler as postmaster. The post office was discontinued several years ago, and the community is now served with rural free delivery from Kitty Hawk.

A U.S. Navy bombing range is located just north of Duck and travel through the range area in automobile, boat, or airplane is partially restricted.

Duck is located at the northern end of the Outer Banks highway which extends as far south as Ocracoke village.

MARTINS POINT AND SOUTHERN SHORES

ALMOST EVERYONE who has written on the subject of Sir Walter Raleigh's attempts at colonization seems to have expressed an opinion

* Anyone planning to buy property adjoining an Outer Banks inlet would do well to purchase on the north side rather than on the south. The movement of the inlets, especially above Cape Hatteras, is always to the south, with the land invariably building up to the north. The property owner on the south side is out of luck; the property owner on the north side, providing his deed calls for the inlet as a boundary and contains full riparian rights, stands to gain several acres every year.

Wright Memorial Bridge
Duck
Kitty Hawk
Kill Devil Hills
Croatan Sound Bridge
Nags Head
Roanoke Sound Bridge
Alligator River Ferry (Free)
Oregon Inlet Ferry (Free)
Rodanthe
Waves
Salvo
Avon
Buxton
Cape Hatteras
Hatteras
Hatteras Inlet Ferry (Free)
Ocracoke
Ocracoke Inlet
Cape Lookout

THE OUTER BANKS
ROADS, BRIDGES and
FERRIES, 1958

as to the location of the inlet through which the explorers Amadas and Barlowe first entered the Banks in July of 1584 and the spot on the south side of that inlet where they first landed to take possession of the new land for Queen Elizabeth.

These opinions vary considerably, placing the location anywhere from modern Virginia to Core Banks. This writer is convinced that the entrance was made through what is shown as Trinety Harbor on the John White map entitled "The Arrival of the Englishmen in Virginia" and that Trinety Harbor was located approximately at the mouth of the present-day Martins Point Creek, or Jeanguite Creek, at the northern end of Southern Shores.

This area was one of the first to be settled extensively on the North Banks, and numerous early deeds in the Currituck County Courthouse bear descriptions beginning at "Jean Guite Creek," "Jeangite Creek," or "Jane Gute Creek." The name "Martins Pint" appears first in a deed dated 1786.

In the 1850's Edmund Ruffin described the area as follows: "The sand-reef is penetrated by Guinguy's creek, running nearly parallel with the ocean-beach and about a mile distant, and which makes a secure and deep harbor for sea vessels."

All of what is now Martins Point and Southern Shores, plus considerable land adjoining, was owned then by a man named Hodges Gallop who cultivated a portion of Martins Point, producing crops of vegetables and as much as 2,500 bushels of corn in the sandy soil. Gallop is the subject of numerous local legends. At one time a preacher, he was a hard man on family and slaves, and it is said he was buried standing up in order that he might keep an eye on his property.

Ruffin found a large growth of loblolly pine east of the creek and was informed that "live oaks, large enough for ship timber had been formerly cut down here, for that use." East of the pine forest was the sand beach covered with large dead cedars. In recent years, since the removal of stock from this part of the Banks, the red cedars have again taken root and literally cover what was formerly a bare sand beach. The virgin pine forest extending from the mouth of the creek to Kitty Hawk was systematically cut over early in the twentieth century—a network of tram railway tracks being laid for the purpose—but a forest of large pines has once again grown up there.

Apparently there was once a large sand hill in this area known as

Paul Gamiels Hill, and in 1870 when plans were being made to improve the lighthouses on the Outer Banks, it was tentatively decided to build one midway between Cape Henry and Cape Hatteras. The Paul Gamiels Hill site was selected. An appropriation of $60,000 for this purpose was made on July 15, 1870, but even at that time consideration was being given to the construction of two lighthouses, instead of one, on this stretch of coast; and that year the Paul Gamiels Hill site was abandoned and plans were made to build the new Bodie Island and Currituck Beach lighthouses in its place. The Paul Gamiels Hill Lifesaving Station was built in the winter of 1878-79, and the Coast Guard station which succeeded it was active until after World War II.

In 1947 an oceanside development, known as Southern Shores, was begun in the area, and this community now contains more than 150 modern houses.

KITTY HAWK

THE MOST popular theory concerning the origin of the name Kitty Hawk is that it derives from the local Indians' reference to the time for hunting geese as "killy honker" or "killy honk." Through the years it is said to have changed from "Killy Honk," to "Killy Hawk," and finally to "Kitty Hawk."

Another story is that it derives from the large number of mosquito hawks frequently found in the area. This became "Skeeter Hawk" and then "Kitty Hawk." Strangely enough there seems to be no local legend concerning an even more plausible possibility, for "kitty" was a name once applied to a type of wren, and a "kitty hawk" would then have been a hawk which preyed on wrens.

The probability that the name stems from an actual Indian place name, however, is attested by the appearance on maps as early as 1738 of the name "Chickehauk." But regardless of its origin, by the time the area was fairly well populated in the middle and late 1700's, the residents were spelling the name much as it is today, there being frequent references in old deeds to "Kittyhuk," "Kitty hark," "Kitty-hawk," and "Kitty Hawk."

The early residents of Kitty Hawk included Mathias Tolar or Towler, a builder and merchant; Edmund Beacham, shoemaker; James

Gamewell, "Minister of the Gosple"; and others who usually classed themselves as "mariners" or "planters," including John and Phillip Northern, Jesse Pateridge, Thomas Best, Joseph Perry, William Dunstan, Daniel Haman, John Gallop, Thomas Hill, John Luark, and Hanny Wright, all of whom lived in the area before 1790.

Kitty Hawk consists of a series of ridges and swamps, most of them running north and south, and by the time of the Revolution these and other prominent landmarks had been given descriptive names, such as Bull Ridge Marsh, Snake Run, Duck Pond Ridge, Seeder Hamock Ridge, Mingoes Gut, Mill Point, Yopon Hill, Panters Creek, and Shellbank. The name Shellbank, which was applied to a great mound of oyster shells at the mouth of Kitty Hawk Bay, was the only name appearing in this area on a number of the old maps.

One of the few early Banks wills which has been located was that of Richard Etheridge of "Currituck Banks and Bay of Kitty Hawk," who died in 1750, leaving to his son Adam, "the plantation whereon I now live, commonly known by the name of the Whale House."

One of the seven original Lifesaving Stations on the Outer Banks was constructed on the beach opposite Kitty Hawk in 1874, and a U.S. Weather Bureau Station was located there from 1875 to 1904. The first Kitty Hawk Post Office was established on November 11, 1878, with Sophia D. Tate as postmaster, but she was succeeded the following November by Joseph M. Baum. In the seventy-seven years between then and 1955 only four other postmasters saw service, two of them Tates and the other two Baums. A second post office, serving the western section of the community adjacent to Albemarle Sound, was established on September 20, 1905, with Francis H. Perry as postmaster. This post office, known as Otila, was discontinued in 1914.

The village of Kitty Hawk, with a fairly static population of about 300 people, is known throughout the world because of the successful flights in a heavier-than-air machine at nearby Kill Devil Hills by Orville and Wilbur Wright in 1903. A stone marker, erected by the citizens of the community, marks the location of the house where Wilbur Wright first stayed on his initial trip to the village.

With the completion of access roads and bridges in the early 1930's, an extensive summer resort began to grow on the ocean front opposite

Kitty Hawk village, and this area, known as Kitty Hawk Beach, now contains more houses than the village itself.

In 1924 the residents of the Kitty Hawk school district voted a special $7,000 bond issue for a new building which served as both grammar school and high school until the high school was consolidated with Manteo in 1956. At this time the citizens voted a second bond issue, this one for $200,000, for a new grammar school located in the wooded section of Southern Shores adjacent to the old Duck road.

Many of the permanent residents of Kitty Hawk are retired Coast Guardsmen.

COLINGTON

COLINGTON ISLAND was the first land in the Province of Carolina—and thus the first in the southern third of what is now the United States—granted to an individual by the Lords Proprietors.

There had been earlier purchases from the Indians for land north of Albemarle Sound, and even some grants from the Governor of Virginia, but these were superseded by the charter issued the Proprietors under the date of March 20, 1663, and by a subsequent document of August 12, 1663, which voided all earlier charters.

The original Colington grant was dated September 8, 1663, and under it Sir John Colleton, one of the Proprietors, was given title to "the island heretofore called Carlyle now Colleton Island, lyeing near the mouth of Chowane now Albemarle river [and now Albemarle Sound] contayneing in lenkth 5 or 6 myles, in bredth about 2 or 3 myles."

Colleton had big plans for his new island and soon made arrangements with Captain John Whittie to proceed to Carolina to establish a plantation there. Whittie arrived late in 1664 and entered at old Roanoke Inlet. He set out beacons to mark the channel, and then he went on to Colington where land was cleared and what was undoubtedly the first Banks settlement was founded.

Colleton soon took in three partners in the Colington plantation development, one of whom, Peter Carteret, was sent to Colington to take active charge, arriving there in the spring of 1665.*

---

* Peter Carteret was the nephew of Sir George Carteret, one of the Lords Proprietors. The other partners, both Proprietors, were Sir William Berkeley and William, Lord Craven. Peter Carteret served as Governor of Carolina from 1670 to 1673.

The four partners secured a grant for Powells Point (now Point Harbor) just north of Colington, land was cleared there and corn planted, and a "hogg house of 80 foot long & 20 broad with nessesarie partitions" was built. At the suggestion of Colleton, Powells Point was used for raising hogs and Colington Island for cattle and horses. A profitable side business was started in extracting oil from whales which washed ashore on the beach, and even before Carteret arrived, Captain Whittie had "Shipped one hundred nynty five Barrels of Whale Oyle for London," realizing almost 250 pounds on the sale.

Grapes were planted with the idea of developing a winery, and an attempt was made to grow tobacco between the rows of grape arbors, but on August 27, 1667, a "great storme or reather haricane" destroyed the corn and tobacco crops, blew down the eighty-foot-long hog house on Powells Point, and severely damaged other buildings.

The operation was dogged with ill luck from that point on. There was a drought in the spring and early summer of 1668, a deluge of rainfall in early August, another hurricane on August 18, 1669, and still a third on August 6, 1670.

Following the apparent failure of this project in the 1670's, little is known of the development of Colington for a number of years, though a house is shown there on the James Lancaster map of 1679, and there are indications that Seth Sothel, who served as governor from 1682 to 1689, may have acquired the Colington cattle. By 1750, however, the entire island was owned by Thomas Pendleton of Pasquotank County, who died that year and left the island to his three daughters. Probably about that time a meandering creek which ran about halfway through the island was extended (apparently by slave labor) from Kitty Hawk Bay on the north to Roanoke Sound on the south, dividing the island in half. This combination creek and canal was known as "The Dividing Creek," and by 1769 the two islands thus formed were known as "Great Colenton" and "Little Colenton."

An extensive community grew up on the south and west sides of Great Colington (or Big Colington, as it is now known) and a post office was established on the south side at Shingle Landing on June 14, 1889, with Ezekiel Midgett as postmaster.

By the end of the nineteenth century, however, many of the people had moved to the northern side of the island where deeper channels were available for their boats, and as this is written this writer and his

family are the only residents of the entire south and west shore of Big
Colington. For many years cattle ran loose on the island, while the
primary source of income for the Colingtonians was commercial fishing. With the removal of the cattle and the decline in fishing, a number
of people moved away, the post office was discontinued, the Colington
school was consolidated with Kitty Hawk (which in turn has since
been consolidated with Manteo), and more and more Colingtonians
are now seeking a living from the construction trades.

The topography, particularly on Big Colington, is unusual in that it
consists of high, steep, and irregular hills, covered with thick growths
of longleaf and loblolly pine, holly, dogwood and live oak. These
thickly-forested hills, separated by valleys and swamps, were at one
time wind-blown sand dunes.

Today Little Colington is joined to the Banks by a bridge and to Big
Colington by another, and a two-and-one-half-mile hard-surfaced state
road meanders almost the length of both islands.

KILL DEVIL HILLS

THROUGH THE YEARS there has been much controversy as to whether
this name should be spelled "Kill Devil Hill" or "Kill Devil Hills."
Actually both are correct, for they refer to different things. "Kill
Devil Hill" or "Big Kill Devil Hill" is the largest sand hill in the area,
now grassed over, on which the Wright Memorial has been erected.
"Kill Devil Hills" is the name given to the surrounding community,
the Coast Guard Station, and the post office. In times past there was
yet a third name, "The Kill Devil Hills," which referred to a group of
sand hills of which "Kill Devil Hill" was the largest.

There are a number of different legends and stories dealing with
the origin of the name, with no clear-cut evidence to substantiate one
rather than another.

In 1728 William Byrd of Virginia, a caustic critic of Carolinians,
wrote that "Most of the Rum they get in this Country comes from
New England, and is so bad and unwholesome, that it is not im-
properly call'd 'Kill-Devil,'" and there is a story that a ship loaded
with this "Kill-Devil Rum" was wrecked opposite the sand hills, thus
accounting for the name.

More interesting but less plausible is the story that bales and boxes from a vessel wrecked long ago were piled on the beach opposite the hills with men detailed to guard the salvaged cargo during the hours of darkness. The first night the guards dozed and awoke to find several boxes missing. The next night the guard was doubled, but even as the men kept a close watch they saw a large bale detach itself from the rest and move off across the sand, apparently under its own power. The horrified guards, convinced that this was the work of the Devil, refused to have anything further to do with the job, but an old Banker, sometimes called Devil Ike, came forth the next day and volunteered to stand watch.

That night, as before, a box suddenly began moving off across the beach, and Devil Ike, armed with a gun, quickly ran after it. Catching up with the moving box he discovered that a line was attached, and on the other end was a beach pony led by one of his neighbors. Devil Ike quickly cut the line, fired a single shot in the air, and frightened his neighbor away. He then returned to the pile of salvaged cargo and told the others gathered there that there would be no more trouble, for he had killed the Devil.

Yet another story, which is strictly legend, concerns a Banker who made a bargain with the Devil whereby, in exchange for a bag of gold, the Devil would take possession of his soul. Arrangements were made to make the trade on top of the highest sand hill at midnight, and when the two approached each other at the time appointed for the rendez- vous, the Banker called out to the Devil, telling him to throw the bag of gold ahead of him and come forward to claim his reward. This the Devil did, but as he stepped forward he suddenly fell into a deep pit— which the Banker had dug beforehand—and was immediately covered with sand. Thus, again, the name "Kill Devil Hill."

The opinion has been advanced, also, that the name derives from the kildee or kildeer, a small shore bird once common in the area, and that the hills nearby became known as the "Kildeer hills" and eventually as the "Kill Devil Hills." And there is the reminder that in the colonial period the word "kill" was sometimes used in place names to designate a stream, creek, or channel and that "devil" had reference to "a moving sand spout." At the same time "kill-devil" was the name of "an arti- ficial bait, made to spin in the water like a wounded fish."

Finally, in 1851, the editor of the Norfolk *American Beacon* had the following to say about the origin of the name: "In the vicinity of Nag's

Head, very conspicuous when sailing down the sound, there is a range of sand hills called Kill Devil Hills, not because his satonic majesty was there disposed of . . . but because sailors say, it is enough to kill the devil to navigate that part of the sound."

Apparently the first appearance of the name in writing was the designation "Killdevil Hills" which appeared on the Price and Strother map in 1808, and by the time the Lewis map was published in 1814, it appeared in its present form as "Kill Devil Hills."

When the United States government constructed a Lifesaving Station nearby in 1878, it was given the name "Kill Devil Hills" as was the post office, established there on January 17, 1938, with Irene L. Twiford as postmaster. Finally, when the area was incorporated in 1953, it was named "The Town of Kill Devil Hills."

The western shore of Kill Devil Hills, between the Wright Memorial and Colington Island, was settled before the Revolution, and it seems probable that more people were living there in the middle of the eighteenth century than in the middle of the twentieth. At the time of the early settlement the area bore the Indian name of Rowspock or Rosepock, a name which appears in varied spellings on numerous old deeds and other documents—probably the first being a grant to John Wade in 1712 for 480 acres of land at Roesepock—and is still remembered by a few of the older residents.

There are recurrent stories, locally, that an inlet existed at Kill Devil Hills during colonial times and that the oldtimers could remember when the remnant of this inlet formed such a pronounced cove on the ocean side that seagoing vessels could be anchored there in safety. Some say Kitty Hawk Bay formed the western end of the inlet, and certainly there are indications that an inlet was located there at some time in the past; others claim the Fresh Ponds, two miles to the south and about a mile from the ocean, are all that is left of the old inlet but that their grandparents could remember when the Fresh Ponds were connected with Roanoke Sound by a creek known as "The Run."

A careful examination of all available maps fails to show even an indication of such an inlet during recorded time, and further, the Fresh Ponds seem to have existed in something approximating their present state when the first settlers arrived. A grant to William Johnson, dated December 19, 1716, for example, calls for 480 acres "on ye E side of ye great fresh pond"; a deed from Philip Burgis to Charles Thomas, May 16, 1737, was for "50 acres on the Northern Banks joyning the Great Fresh Pond beginning at or near the Run side." This was also referred to sometimes as the "Great Fish Pond."

By the 1840's, when George Higby Throop wrote his *Nag's Head, or Two Months among the "Bankers,"* an exciting part of the summer vacationer's life at Nags Head was a day-long picnic to the Fresh Ponds, and Throop devotes a full chapter to a description of such an outing. It is frequently said, incidentally, that the largest of these ponds, almost a mile long, is bottomless; certainly it is considerably deeper than the nearby sounds, but anyone who takes the trouble to do a little sounding can find bottom wherever he wants.

Kill Devil Hills is best known, of course, as the scene of the first successful flight by the Wright brothers in 1903, and of their glider experiments in 1900, 1901, and 1902. Big Kill Devil Hill and neighboring West Hill were stabilized in the late 1920's, using a combination of crotalaria from Puerto Rico, marram grass from Australia, and native wiregrass, yaupon, and other vegetation after the hill had been covered with woods mold from nearby Colington and Kitty Hawk. The monument on top of the 91-foot-high hill, erected in 1931 and 1932 at a cost of $285,000, was constructed of Mt. Airy granite under the direction of the U.S. Army Engineers. The monument is sunk thirty-five feet into the hill and rises sixty-one feet above it. Originally designed as a lighthouse, it was not used for that purpose after it was discovered that mariners confused it with existing lighthouses, but it is now lighted with flood-lights each evening until midnight. Taken over by the National Park Service, June 10, 1933, it was designated "Kill Devil Hills Monument National Memorial." Now the "Wright Brothers National Memorial," the 314-acre Park Service reservation includes the reconstructed Wright hangar and workshop and other visitor facilities near the exact site of the first flight on level ground north of the hill.

Like Kitty Hawk Beach and Southern Shores to the north, and Nags Head to the south, Kill Devil Hills is now primarily a resort community with several hotels, motor courts, and a number of private cottages. The most extensive development has been in an area north of the Wright Memorial, Avalon Beach, once known as Moore's Shore.

NAGS HEAD

SINCE THE 1830's Nags Head has been noted throughout eastern North Carolina as a summer resort, and the name is still applied by many North Carolinians to all of the Dare Beaches resort area, including Kitty Hawk and Kill Devil Hills—a usage not kindly taken to by the Kitty Hawkers and Kill Devilites. The original resort was on the sound side and remained there until the state highway was built along the oceanfront in the early 1930's; at this time several hotels and the post office were moved across the beach from the sound to the ocean.

Several large wooden hotels were built on the sound side in the nineteenth century, and of these one was covered over by moving sand and another burned. At one time just before the Civil War a dock extended almost half a mile into Roanoke Sound. This was connected with the hotel and in turn with the bathing area on the seaside by a railroad, on which vacationers were transported in mule-drawn cars, which later gave way to a "trolley car" towed at one time by a blind horse or by oxen.

A permanent community of Banks residents, mostly fishermen, was located just north of the soundside resort in the Nags Head woods, but in recent years this has been deserted.

One of the features which has attracted vacationers to Nags Head for so many years is the large sand dunes, always referred to locally as "hills" or "ridges," which are likened by some to the barkhans or marching dunes of North Africa. These include Run Hill, the Round-About Hills, Scraggly Oak Hill, Graveyard Hill, and Jockeys Ridge, all north of Nags Head, and Engagement Hill, Pin Hill, and the Seven Sisters to the south. Of these Jockeys Ridge is the largest, tallest, and most imposing, and on a calm day in the summer it is not uncommon to see hundreds of people, their shoes in hand, climbing to the summit. One of the earliest references to Jockeys Ridge was in a 1753 grant to John Campbell in which it was referred to as "Jockey's Hill."

The artist-writer for *Harper's New Monthly Magazine*, who visited Nags Head and described the place in an article dated May, 1860, seems to have been the first to put down in writing the now popular story concerning the naming of Nags Head. "Nag's Head derives its name, according to the prevalent etymology," he said, "from an old device employed to lure vessels to destruction. A Banks pony was driven up and down the beach at night, with a lantern tied around his neck. The up-and-down motion resembling that of a vessel, the unsuspecting tar would steer for it."

The *Harper's* correspondent qualified this by adding that the Banker's "kindness and hospitality to wrecked seamen is unfailing and unlimited," and about the only thing that comes close to substantiating the story was a report in 1700 that when *H.M.S. Hady* was driven ashore between Roanoke and Currituck inlets a few years before, "the Inhabitants robed her and got some of her guns ashore and shot into her sides and disabled her from getting off." *

Though the lantern story persists, there are other explanations for the name which seem to date back even further. Leigh Winslow of Hertford in Perquimans County, whose ancestors have been coming to Nags Head since the early days of the settlement, says the name was bestowed by an Englishman named Leigh who moved to Perquimans County in the early part of the nineteenth century, joined his neighbors in visits to the Jockeys Ridge area and found a striking resemblance between the sand hills and a place called Nag's Head on the coast of England.

Edward R. Outlaw, Jr., in his interesting recollections published under the title *In Old Nags Head*, reports that he secured from the British Information Service a list of three different places there with the name of Nags Head, including a hamlet, a promontory, and a hill.

On the other hand, in 1850 George Higby Throop wrote: "If I may credit half of what I hear of Nag's Head in the olden times . . . the headland then bore some resemblance, in the sea-approach, to the head of a horse, and thence its name."

Further confusing the matter was the following story, published by the editor of the *American Beacon* of Norfolk, August 25, 1851:

---

* *Harper's Monthly* for March, 1874 (p. 467), reported that Congress had passed a law in 1825 deeming it a felony "if any person or persons shall hold out or show any false light or lights, or extinguish any true light, with the intention to bring any ship or vessel, boat or raft, being or sailing upon the sea, into danger or distress or shipwreck." The article also reported that "it is said that evil-minded persons on the Bahamas and elsewhere used systematically to hang out false lights to lure ships off their course and onto reefs, and that their rude method for imitating a revolving or flash light was to tie a lantern to a horse's tail and walk the animal around in a circle.

Until my recent visit I had heard from many persons that the name Nag's Head was bestowed on these hills by some old mariner, from a fancied resemblance to the head of a horse. . . . But, sir, the reason for the name of Nag's Head is a better reason than the one above suggested. Many years ago there stood on the hills alluded to a large live oak tree, whose branches were twisted and knarled by the winds, and whose position was long disputed by the ocean and storm. It was the practice of the horses and cattle, large numbers of which are still raised in this vicinity, to assemble under this oak, both for shelter and to rub themselves against its trunks and branches. On one occasion a horse caught his head between the crooked limbs of the tree, and absolutely hung himself—His body remained a long time suspended but for many years after it had fallen away by the action of time, his head was kept secure among the branches, and hence the name of Nag's Head was given to the hills.

In all this confusion and contradiction concerning the name, one thing is certain—the name "Nags head" was in use at least as early as 1738, for in that year it was shown on the James Wimble map in its present location.

When asked about local history, one of the first stories most Nags Headers tell is that of Theodosia Burr Alston, daughter of former vice-president Aaron Burr and wife of Governor John Alston of South Carolina, who was killed there early in 1813. Theodosia is known to have left Georgetown, South Carolina, December 30, 1812, enroute to New York in the former pilot boat and privateer, *Patriot*. The vessel failed to reach New York, and Burr and Alston found no further trace of Theodosia, but on two different occasions between then and 1850 reputed former pirates "confessed" that they had participated in the capture of the *Patriot* and in the murder of all hands.

In 1869 a summer vacationist at Nags Head was given a small oil portrait of a young lady, which was said to have been removed from an abandoned vessel which was wrecked at Nags Head during the War of 1812. The portrait was later identified as that of Theodosia Burr.

Calvin H. Wiley, author of the 1849 novel *Roanoke: or, Where is Utopia?* (reprinted later as *Adventures of Old Dan Tucker and his son Walter: a tale of North Carolina*) used the Nags Head woods area as a setting for the first part of his story, and he may have been the first person to describe the Bankers as "Arabs" and the Banks as "Arabia," a fairly common usage for a number of years.

The Nags Head Lifesaving Station, located approximately a mile south of the resort on the oceanfront, was one of the seven original stations built on the Outer Banks in 1874. Three years later, on November 24, 1877, the U.S. man-of-war steamer *Huron* came ashore just north of Jockeys Ridge with the resultant loss of 103 lives—one of the worst shipwrecks in the history of the coast.

The first post office serving the community was established, June 27, 1884, with John A. Hollowell as postmaster. The post office name at that time was "Nags Head," but it was changed to "Naghead," November 15, 1893. A second post office in the area, this one named "Griffin," was established on June 26, 1909, and on April 27, 1915, the "Naghead" Post Office was discontinued and all mail was handled through the Griffin Post Office. This caused considerable confusion and many complaints, however, and on May 15, 1915, the name of the Griffin Post Office was changed to "Naghead." Finally, March 6, 1916, the name was changed again to "Nags Head," and in 1934 the post office was moved from the sound to the oceanside.

Nags Head was incorporated in 1923, but because of inactivity the incorporation was allowed to lapse. Today, unincorporated, it continues as a popular and prosperous oceanside summer resort with a number of hotels and other tourist facilities.

ROANOKE INLET

WHEN THE permanent settlement of North Carolina began in the early 1660's practically all of the oceangoing vessels serving the colony entered through Roanoke Inlet, and for more than fifty years this cut below Nags Head was by far the most important on the Banks. As early as 1665 Captain John Whittie had reported that the inlet channel was between eleven and fifteen feet deep, but by 1736 Governor Burrington said it had shoaled up so badly that it was barely six and one-half feet in depth and only the smallest vessels could enter. After that the shoaling continued and by 1783 nothing remained but a shallow overflow area between ocean and sound not more than a foot deep.*

* For all practical purposes Roanoke Inlet was then closed. But because the trickle of water continued for a number of years, permitting skiffs and similar small craft to pass through, there has been considerable disagreement as to the actual date of

Roanoke Inlet was of inestimable value to the economy of the Albemarle Sound area and the far flung valleys of the Roanoke and Chowan rivers, for it provided them with a direct outlet to the sea. Beginning about 1787 and continuing to the modern era there was steady pressure to reopen Roanoke Inlet, and especially between 1820 and 1850 hardly a year passed that some group or other did not present a petition or memorial on the subject to the North Carolina General Assembly or the United States Congress.

Consequently, at least eight separate detailed surveys were made by competent engineers to determine the feasibility of reopening the inlet; dozens of reports and suggestions were submitted by men prominent in public life; two different companies were formed to undertake the construction of toll canals or toll inlets there; on two other occasions residents of North Carolina were reported to have started digging the inlet on their own; and finally the United States government appropriated $50,000, moved a dredge to Nags Head, and began digging a canal from sound to ocean. Yet today the average person can see no visual trace of Roanoke Inlet, and people living right where the old channel was located are not now aware of its ever having existed.

The initial effort to provide this navigable passage through the Banks was the establishment of "The Raleigh Company" by the North Caroline Legislature in 1787-89 for the purpose of digging a twenty-yard-wide inlet, to be known as "Raleigh Canal," from Roanoke Sound to the ocean. This project failed, and the real drive for reopening the inlet did not begin until about 1815 when Archibald D. Murphey came forward with his comprehensive plan for internal improvements in North Carolina.

In the summer of 1816 a Captain Clarke began a preliminary survey, but his work was never completed. Then, in 1820, Hamilton Fulton, a prominent English engineer employed by the Board of Internal Improvement at a salary almost double that of the governor of North Carolina, made a thorough study and survey and reported that the project was feasible. He was convinced, however, that it would be necessary to erect stone embankments across both Roanoke and Croatan sounds, in order to divert the flow of water from Albemarle

---

closing. Gary S. Dunbar has studied this closely and has found references to its closing entirely as early as 1795 or as late as 1819, though he prefers the date 1811.

Sound through the new inlet, and that ten-foot-thick stone facings would have to line the sides of the man-made inlet. Fulton estimated that the project would cost approximately $2,333,000, and for the next twenty-five years everybody seemed to think Roanoke Inlet should be reopened, but nobody could figure out how to finance it.

In 1821 the North Carolina Legislature authorized a second toll-canal company, this one to be called "The Roanoke Inlet Company," but again the results were negative. Detailed surveys were made by Captain Hartman Bache, U.S. Topographical Engineers, in 1828-29; civil engineer Walter Gwynn, 1840; Captain C. Graham, U.S. Topographical Engineers, 1843; Lieutenant W. B. Franklin, U.S. Topographical Engineers, 1852; and Lieutenant D. P. Woodbury, U.S. Army Engineers, 1853. Almost all were in agreement that the Fulton plan would accomplish the purpose, but in the interest of economy Bache had suggested the possibility of installing a tide lock, while Gwynn had questioned whether the embankments across the sounds could not be made of wooden cribs filled with sand and mud. (At the same time a man named Cadwallader Jones had advocated building a canal through Roanoke Island and a viaduct across Roanoke Sound to provide a flow of water from Croatan Sound through the proposed inlet.)

When Lieutenant Woodbury made his survey in 1853, however, he became convinced that the inlet could be reopened by digging a canal through the Banks 150 yards wide and 6 feet deep and by running "piers of masonry" out into the ocean at either side of the cut, half a mile on the north, a quarter of a mile on the south.

Congress made available $50,000 for the dredging phase of the project, but by 1857, when Lieutenant Colonel W. Turnbull inspected the project, he found that drifting sand was "filling in the trench as fast as it was excavated by the dredging-machine." The end of the project came on August 15, 1857, when the sand-bound dredge was sold.

Despite this failure and the existence of newly-opened Oregon Inlet nearby, the pressure continued. In 1870 Colonel J. H. Simpson of the U.S. Army Engineers made yet another survey and concluded that "it would be an unwarrantable waste of the public money to apply it to any such object." As late as 1923 a number of residents of the Albemarle Sound area appeared before the North Carolina Fisheries Commission Board to urge the cutting of an inlet "At Nagshead or Kitty

Hawk," and the 1925 General Assembly passed a law calling for an investigation of the feasibility of placing a dam across Roanoke Sound to open an inlet.

With the construction of a highway through the Nags Head beach area the inlet project at last died.

At one time when it was being used by seagoing vessels, Roanoke Inlet was reported to have been approximately one and one-half miles below the present Nags Head resort, but by the time it closed it had moved south at least a mile and was located in the general vicinity of the Roanoke Sound bridge.

BODIE ISLAND

ONE OF THE most common family names on the Outer Banks is Midgett (or Midget, Midyet, Midgette) and apparently the first North Carolinian with that name was Mathew Midgett, who lived near Alligator River in 1712 and in the 1720's was granted Bodie Island.

At that time variously known as Bodys Island, Bodies Island, Body Island, Micher Island, and Cow Island, it was nine and one-half miles long, extending from Roanoke Inlet on the north to Dugg Creek or Inlet on the south, and it contained an estimated 1900 acres.

Mathew Midgett lived on Bodie Island for a few years and died in 1734, leaving four sons to carry on the family name, an assignment which they and their successors have fulfilled admirably.

Another indication of the origin of the name Bodie Island appeared in Lawson's *History of Carolina*, written about 1700. Referring to the scarcity of English "coneys" (rabbits), he said: "I was told of several that were upon *Bodies* Island by *Ronoak*, which came from that Ship of *Bodies*, but I never saw any."

The area immediately south of Bodie Island has been especially susceptible to the opening and closing of inlets, and at least six different inlets have been located at one time or another between the present Bodie Island Lighthouse and Rodanthe. Consequently the size, shape, and even the location of Bodie Island has changed several times, and when Oregon Inlet opened in the hurricane of September 7, 1846, part of the original island remained south of the new inlet.

Three different lighthouses have been built at Bodie Island and have borne that name. The first, located south of Oregon Inlet, was constructed in 1847 and 1848 at a cost of $12,000 and was 56½ feet high and had a range of twelve nautical miles. In less than ten years, however, the lighthouse was in such poor condition that it could no longer be operated, and in 1857 an appropriation of $25,000 was made for rebuilding the lighthouse and fitting it with an improved lens. The new lighthouse, also located south of Oregon Inlet, was completed and first lighted July 1, 1859.

During the Civil War the Confederate forces destroyed this second Bodie Island Lighthouse, and work was begun in November, 1871, on the structure which remains in service to this day. Because Oregon Inlet was gradually moving southward and by 1871 was within 500 yards of the site of the old tower, the new lighthouse was built north of the inlet. The site was bought from John B. Etheridge for $150, and when the 150-foot-high structure was completed and lighted October 1, 1872, it had cost $140,000. Soon after it was lighted the keeper reported that "a flock of wild geese flew against the lantern breaking three panes of glass and considerably damaging the lens apparatus." When repairs were made a wire screen was placed around the lantern to protect it.

The name "Bodie's Island" was given to one of the first Lifesaving Stations built on the coast in 1874, but that original station was actually located south of Oregon Inlet. When a second station was constructed north of the inlet in 1878 it was named "Tommy's Hummock," but later the original "Bodie's Island" station was changed to "Oregon Inlet," and "Tommy's Hummock" became "Bodie Island."

Several large gun clubs have been located in the Bodie Island area, including the Bodie Island Club which was adjacent to the lighthouse; Goosewing and Lone Cedar clubs, near Old Roanoke Inlet; and Duck Island and Off Island clubs, in the sound west of the lighthouse.

When the Cape Hatteras National Seashore Recreational Area was established in 1953, most of Bodie Island was included. The original Tommy's Hummock Lifesaving Station has been converted into a residence for Park Service personnel, the newer Bodie Island Coast Guard Station is being used as park headquarters, and the old keeper's quarters at the lighthouse has become a natural history museum. A day-use area, called Coquina Beach, has been constructed by the Park Service on the oceanfront south of the former Coast Guard Station.

Oregon Inlet

RECENTLY the theory has been advanced that certain areas of the Outer Banks are "inlet prone" and that when new inlets form it is invariably in these areas. One such locality cited, by Gary S. Dunbar in his *Geographical History of the Carolina Banks*, is in the vicinity of Oregon Inlet, and certainly there have been enough inlet changes there to give some credence to the claim.

The John White maps of 1585 showed two inlets near there, the first named Port Fernando and also referred to as Hatarask, Hatoras, or Hatorasck, the second known as Port Lane. When the area was permanently settled, inlets continued to open and close between the present Bodie Island and Rodanthe, and some of those shown on maps or mentioned in written accounts were Gun, Gunt, or Gant Inlet, Chick, Chickinacommock or Chicamacomico Inlet, and Dugg Inlet.

In 1845 there were two inlets there, Loggerhead Inlet just north of the village of Rodanthe, and New Inlet at the south end of Pea Island. Then, on September 7, 1846, a hurricane struck the Banks and water piled over the beach from the sound, forming what was later to become Oregon Inlet. C. O. Boutelle, assistant superintendent of the U.S. Coast Survey, who was running a base line on Bodie Island that fall, wrote the following account of the opening:

On the morning of the September gale the sound waters were all piled up to the southwest, from the effects of the heavy northeast blow of the previous days. The weather was clear, nearly calm, until about 11 A.M., when a sudden squall came from the southwest, and the waters came upon the beach with such fury that Mr. Midgett, within three quarters of a mile of his house when the storm began, was unable to reach it until four in the afternoon. He sat upon his horse, on a small sand knoll, for five hours, and witnessed the destruction of his property, and (as he then supposed) of his family also, without the power to move a foot to their rescue, and, for two hours, expecting every moment to be swept to sea himself.

The force of the water coming in so suddenly, and having a head of two to three feet, broke through the small portion of sea beach which had formed since the March gale, and created the inlets. They were insignificant at first—not more than 20 feet wide—and the northern one much the deepest and widest. In the westerly winds which prevailed in

September, the current from the sound gradually widened them; and, in the October gale, they became about as wide as they are now. The northern one has since been gradually filling, and is now a mere hole at low water ... [but the southern one] between high water marks, measured on the line, is 202 yards [wide, and] between low water marks, 107 yards.

Subsequent reports by Coast Survey engineers contained predictions that the new inlet would soon close up, but it enlarged instead and within a few years was one of the primary inlets on the Banks. The inlet was named for the first vessel to pass through—said to have been the side-wheeler *Oregon*, owned by William H. Willard.

During the early part of the Civil War, the Confederates built a small fort on the south side of the inlet which they named Fort Oregon. The fort was abandoned by the Confederates soon after Federal forces captured Hatteras Inlet in 1861, and at approximately the same time the Confederates destroyed the Bodie Island Lighthouse (second of that name and located south of Oregon Inlet). In 1874 a Lifesaving Station was constructed south of the inlet also and was named "Bodie's Island," but the name was later changed to "Oregon Inlet" and the Coast Guard Station bearing that name is still active.

Since it opened in 1846, Oregon Inlet has moved steadily to the south as the result of the littoral current—the south shore being cut away and the north shore building up— so that the original sites of the Confederate fort, the early Bodie Island lighthouses, and the 1874 Lifesaving Station have washed away, and the inlet is now located where some of them once stood.

Efforts to improve the navigation of Oregon Inlet have always been half-hearted, but as this is written the federal government is spending nearly half a million dollars in dredging. There has been no provision for permanent stabilization, however, and already part of the dredged area has filled in again.

Oregon Inlet has been used primarily by small fishing vessels, and at one time a menhaden processing plant was located nearby. In recent years a rather extensive marina has been developed on the north side of the inlet, to provide docking facilities for the numerous sports fishing boats attracted there by the annual runs of channel bass and bluefish and for the offshore fishing in the Gulf Stream.

In 1924 Captain Jack Nelson of Colington Island inaugurated ferry service across Oregon Inlet, towing a small barge behind his fishing boat, and when Nelson quit a couple of months later Captain Toby Tillett of Wanchese began providing the same sort of service. Tillett stuck it out for more than twenty-five years, acquiring larger and better ferries, and finally sold out to the North Carolina Highway Department in the early 1950's. Using converted Navy landing craft, sometimes shuttling back and forth on half-hour schedules, the Highway Department has been unable to satisfactorily handle the ever increasing traffic attracted to the Cape Hatteras Seashore, and the construction of a bridge across the inlet seems inevitable.

THE CAPE HATTERAS NATIONAL SEASHORE

THIS FIRST national seashore recreational area includes the southern part of Bodie Island, and all of Hatteras and Ocracoke islands except the immediate village areas. Even in the vicinity of the villages, however, a 500-foot strip along the ocean beach is included in the park facility, so that an unbroken stretch of oceanfrontage more than seventy miles in length has been retained in its natural state.

Originally proposed in 1933 and authorized in 1937, the park was not established until 1953 and was dedicated on April 24, 1958. Temporary headquarters has been established in the old Bodie Island Coast Guard Station, and the Bodie Island section of the park is being developed as a day-use area, with bathing and picnic facilities at Coquina Beach (coquina is a shellfish of the conch family), a visitor's center and natural history museum in the old keeper's quarters at the Bodie Island Lighthouse, and a marina near the ferry landing on the north side of Oregon Inlet.

On Hatteras Island a museum of the sea has been established in the keeper's quarters at the Cape Hatteras Lighthouse; another visitor's center, emphasizing the activities of the Lifesaving Service and Coast Guard, is planned for the old Chicamacomico Coast Guard Station; camping facilities are provided just west of Cape Point at Hatteras; and roadside parking areas and restrooms are located or are being built at various other points. Through arrangement with the Coast Guard, the Cape Hatteras Lighthouse is open to visitors on a regular schedule, and in cooperation with the North Carolina Highway Department new access roads have been constructed to the lighthouse and Cape Point, and others are contemplated.

Still another visitor's center is located on Ocracoke Island, park rangers are stationed permanently in each locality, an extensive program of erosion control is now in progress, and a program for providing access trails and information signs at the scenes of important shipwrecks and other points of interest is in progress.

The Cape Hatteras Seashore was established with the intent of retaining most of the area in its natural state. Village areas excluded from the park are of sufficient size to permit future expansion, and commercial facilities including restaurants, filling stations, hotels, motor courts, rental cottages and stores are located in the villages. Surf fishing is permitted practically the length of the park, and limited hunting is authorized by permit in certain soundside areas.

PEA ISLAND

IN 1837 Congress appropriated $5,000 for construction of a lighthouse "on Pea Island, near New Inlet," but when Captain Charles W. Skinner inspected the site for the Navy Board, he found it unsatisfactory and recommended another location several miles up the Banks on Bodie Island, where the lighthouse was finally built ten years later.

This seems to have been the first printed use of the name Pea Island, but it must have been applied much earlier than that, for by 1837 it was not an island at all, since the inlet which had once separated it from Bodie Island had long since closed.

The name is said to derive from the wild peas which grow there in great profusion, and this may have had something to do with making it a favorite spot for hunting geese, ducks, and brant. For a number of years the Pea Island Gunning Club was located there, but just before World War II the Pea Island National Wildfowl Refuge was established, and today it is a principal winter resting ground for the rare greater snow geese, as well as Canada geese and several types of ducks.

The Pea Island Lifesaving Station, built in 1878, was commanded by "Captain" Richard Etheridge, a Negro, and for a number of years it was the only all-Negro lifeboat station in the Coast Guard. The station was decommissioned following World War II, and the buildings are now used in conjunction with the Wildfowl Refuge.

NEW INLET

IT SEEMS to be the practice along the North Carolina coast, when an inlet cuts through the Banks, to refer to it as "The New Inlet" until a newer one appears; and on several occasions the name "New Inlet" has stuck.

Such was the case with the "here-again gone-again" inlet between Pea Island and Chicamacomico Banks. The name New Inlet at this point first appeared on a map in 1738, but during the colonial period it was unstable and of little importance. The schooner *Fanny* stranded on the north point of the inlet in 1789 with the loss of all hands, and in 1836 the large passenger steam-packet *William Gibbons* was lost there. By the time Oregon Inlet opened in 1846, New Inlet was in the process of closing, but it remained more or less open until 1922. The following year serious consideration was given by North Carolina authorities to artificially reopening the inlet, and this in fact was attempted in 1925, but in a short time it shoaled up and closed again.

New Inlet opened in the fall hurricanes of 1933 with two small but separate channels, and narrow wooden bridges were constructed across both to permit the passage of automobiles. Soon after the bridges were put in use, however, the inlet closed again, and though parts of the bridges still stand, traffic now moves along the newer hard-surfaced highway to the east.

Almost invariably when a severe storm hits the Banks, water passes through the old channels, flooding the state highway and usually causing some washouts. Recently the National Park Service and North Carolina Highway Commission have constructed extensive sand fences and have planted grasses on the dunes formed behind the fences, with the hope of stabilizing the beach in the vicinity of the old inlet bottom.

A Lifesaving Station was constructed on the south side of New Inlet about 1882, but a few years later it burned and was never replaced.

CHICAMACOMICO

THIS IS A designation applied in the days of early settlement to what is now the entire northern section of Hatteras Island, as well as to an inlet which was then located in the vicinity of Pea Island and to the shoal formation now referred to as Wimble Shoals.

Undoubtedly it derives from an Indian name, and the early settlers seem to have had a difficult time deciding just how to spell it, for at least fourteen different spellings have been found on maps and in written records between 1730 and 1799. Among the earliest were "Chickony-Commock," "Chichinnacomoc," "Chickinocommock," and "Chickinocommuck." Later it appeared as "Chick," "Chickama-comick," and "Chickamicomico" before becoming Chicamacomico in more recent times.

All this confusion could have been averted if the first permanent settlers had retained the same name the Raleigh colonists used, for they called this area Hatorask—a designation which was applied later to the section farther south.

A number of people had settled on Chicamacomico Banks well before the outbreak of the Revolutionary War. In 1744, when commissioners set out to survey the line which separated the so-called Granville Grant from the rest of North Carolina, they began at "a cedar stake set upon the sea side . . . being six miles and a half to the southward of Chickmacomack inlet," and then they ran a line westward across the Banks, passing "twenty-five feet to the southward of the house wherein Thomas Wallis Liveth" before striking Pamlico Sound. In 1764 a commodity inspection point was located "At Chico-nocomick, at Thomas Paine's Landing."

Soon after Federal troops captured Hatteras Inlet in 1861 a regiment was dispatched to Chicamacomico, where an outpost called "Live Oak Camp" was established. Even before the camp was completed, the Confederates attacked this position, chasing the Federal troops southward to Cape Hatteras, while most of the residents of Chicamacomico, having cast their lot with the Federals, fled ahead of the attacking force. The next day, however, Federal reinforcements arrived and the Confederates fled back up the Banks again, embarking on boats at

Chicamacomico for their base at Roanoke Island. This engagement was referred to as "The Chicamacomico Races."

In 1874, when the federal government constructed the first seven Lifesaving Stations on the Outer Banks, one was located at Chicamacomico, and crews from that station accomplished numerous noteworthy rescues between then and the decommissioning of the station in June, 1954, including that of crewmen from the burning British tanker *Mirlo* during World War I. The original Chicamacomico station, long since replaced by a more modern building, was used for a boat house for many years, and is still standing. Both buildings are now maintained by the National Park Service.

When a post office was established at Chicamacomico on November 6, 1874, with Edward Pain, Jr., as postmaster, it was designated as Rodanthe. By that time three well-defined communities were located there, and all three acquired distinct names, the southernmost being known as Clarks or Clarksville and the other two as South Rodanthe and North Rodanthe. However, when a post office was established at Clarks, January 26, 1901, with Kenneth R. Pugh as postmaster, it was named Salvo, and when one was established at South Rodanthe on March 27, 1939, with Anna E. Midgett as postmaster, it was named Waves, and the three communities at Chicamacomico are now known as Rodanthe, Waves, and Salvo.

The most eastern point on the Banks is at Chicamacomico, and the theory has been advanced by David B. Quinn that the coast once jutted out here to include the present submerged Wimble Shoals, thus forming a pronounced cape.

For many years at Rodanthe the Chicamacomico people have been observing "Old Christmas" on the night of January 5, and this annual festivity, featuring the appearance of "Old Buck," attracts more and more outsiders. It is thought to be a carry-over from Epiphany which is celebrated on January 6.

In 1936 and 1937 the Coast Guard built a channel and harbor on the sound side at Rodanthe. A camp for CCC boys engaged in erosion control work was located there at that time.

GULL SHOAL

As EARLY AS 1794 the name "Gull Shore" was applied to an area approximately five miles south of Chicamacomico, and later the name became Gull Shoal and referred to a small island just back of the Banks in the sound.

When a Lifesaving Station was built on the beach in that vicinity in 1878-79, it was given the name Cedar Hummock, but this was later changed to Gull Shoal.

A number of noteworthy rescues were carried out from this station and from the Coast Guard Station which succeeded it. Probably the most famous of these was the feat of Rasmus Midgett in rescuing ten people from the wrecked barkentine *Priscilla* without assistance, August 18, 1899. The original Cedar Hummock Lifesaving Station and Gull Shoal Coast Guard Station buildings have been torn down since the decommissioning of the station following World War II.

KINNAKEET AND AVON

IN THE EARLY DAYS of Banks settlement, Kinnakeet Banks was an area extending from Cape Hatteras woods north to Chicamacomico. The primary community was Kinnakeet, now Avon, though later there were two smaller communities a couple of miles to the north, Scarborotown (Scabbertown) and Little Kinnakeet.

Beginning about 1820 large quantities of live oak and cedar were cut on Kinnakeet and Chicamacomico Banks, and the timbers used in many of the famous clipper ships were said to have come from there. This denuding of the beach, however, caused "blow-out" areas, and small sand dunes began to appear near the ocean. As these grew in size they moved across the Banks, forming a veritable sand wave, covering the living forests in its path and uncovering graveyards as it passed on toward the sound. When a correspondent for *Scribner's Magazine* visited Kinnakeet in 1890 to get a first hand look at "The Sand Wave of Hatteras," he found that it had travelled "through the thickest part of the grove one hundred feet in five months, and the Sound but half a mile away." Today trees are found only in the community and at other isolated spots on the sound side.

Kinnakeet was noted for the small schooners built there, and in the period following the Civil War, it was the base for a large fleet of these vessels, many of them used in oystering. Today Little Kinnakeet and Scarborotown are deserted, and most of the residents of Avon are either retired from the Coast Guard and Lifesaving Service or gain a livelihood from commercial fishing.

One of the earliest landowners in the area was William Reed, who secured a grant for 480 acres in 1711 "beginning at a Spainish oak at Keneckid Inlet." This is the only reference this writer has been able to find to an inlet of that name, though there are several places above Avon where the Banks are less than half a mile wide and where the North Carolina Highway Department has had difficulty preventing wash-outs in the highway during storms. South of Avon, nearer Buxton, there is a low, narrow area known as "The Haulover," and an inlet was shown near there on the White maps of 1585. It was given the name Chacandepeco on the Velasco map about 1611.

On December 4, 1873, the Kinnakeet Post Office was established with Damon G. Meekins as postmaster. The name was changed to Avon, March 22, 1883.

The southernmost of the seven original Lifesaving Stations constructed on the Banks in 1874 was located at Little Kinnakeet and bore that name. A second station was constructed approximately a mile south of the main village in 1878-79 and was named Big Kinnakeet station. Later when this was replaced by a more modern structure, the new site was approximately two miles south of Avon. Both stations have been decommissioned, Little Kinnakeet being used by the Park Service, and Big Kinnakeet in private ownership.

A landmark at Avon—and at several other communities along the Banks a few years back—was the freight houses built on stilts out in the sound. Here the larger freight boats would pick up the freshly caught fish and deliver freight consigned to the village, the local people transporting it from there to the village in small boats. When the U.S. Army Engineers dug a channel and harbor at Avon in 1946 it became possible for the larger boats to land at the village, and the need for the freight houses on stilts was gone.

Two of the more extensive gunning clubs on the Banks, the Kinnakeet and Buxton clubs, were built between Avon and Buxton in the 1930's, and though the buildings are gone—both were practically demolished in the 1944 hurricane—the dikes and ditches for the old ponds are still in evidence.

CAPE HATTERAS

THIS IS THE focal point of the famous Graveyard of the Atlantic, with its dreaded Diamond Shoals stretching seaward to touch the Gulf Stream. Known locally as Cape Point, it has gradually moved southward, its formation ever changing.

The Outer Banks highway passes through the village of Buxton just above Cape Hatteras, but a hard-surfaced road leads to the lighthouse and Cape Point, a favorite spot for surf fishermen. Ample parking areas and camping grounds have been provided nearby.

The name, originally spelled Hatorask, was applied by the Raleigh colonists to part of the Banks in the vicinity of Chicamacomico, and the cape itself was called Cape St. John by the early Spanish explorers.

A Lifesaving Station was constructed near Cape Point in the early 1880's, and crews from the Cape Hatteras station have effected many daring rescues from ships lost on Diamond Shoals. The old building is now being used as a Loran station, and the newer Coast Guard Station is still in service.

A U.S. Navy installation—its mission clouded in secrecy—has been built just north of the lighthouse. The old keeper's quarters at the lighthouse has been converted into a Park Service museum of the sea.

CAPE HATTERAS LIGHTHOUSE

THE FIRST lighthouse at Cape Hatteras was authorized by the United States Congress on May 13, 1794. It was an octagonal stone structure ninety feet high, resting on a stone foundation sunk thirteen feet below the water table, and was topped with a ten-foot-high oil lantern covered by a five-foot-nine-inch dome or roof. (Thus the total height of the structure was nearly 120 feet, of which more than a hundred feet were above the ground level.) The tower was mounted by wooden stairs—eight pairs, in all—and a two-story house, with cellar, was provided for the keeper. When the lighthouse was completed about 1802, oil was stored in a twenty-by-twelve-foot vault which contained nine cedar cisterns, each with a capacity of 200 gallons.

In 1806 William Tatham described it as "a handsome plain edifice, well calculated for the purpose; and an excellent piece of masonry." However, he felt that "its being composed of two kinds of stone renders its party colour an architectural Eye Sore," and he suggested that the white part should be painted the same color as the red stone. Tatham found that cracks had appeared in the structure and concluded it was the result of the lighthouse being "too ponderous for the nature of the foundation." He learned, also, that the gallery around the lantern was so narrow that it frequently caused "the breaking of glass, by the attendant himself, when keeping back from the excessive heat of the lamp in discharging his duty."

In 1852 the newly-formed Lighthouse Board published a report on the condition and effectiveness of the structure, which included observations by a number of sea captains who passed Cape Hatteras regularly. They were unanimous in their criticism of the lighthouse, the feeling being summed up by Captain C. R. Mumford who said it was "a disgrace to our country." After that Congress appropriated $15,000 for fitting it with a new lens and lantern and for elevating the structure to 150 feet, and this extensive work of alteration was completed in 1854.

Early in the Civil War the lens and lantern were destroyed—both sides blamed the other, but the Confederates seem to have been the guilty party—but by 1862 a temporary light had been installed, and in 1863 this was replaced by the most modern illuminating apparatus yet made. After the war, however, concern was expressed over the fact that the old wooden stairs constituted a fire hazard; but when it was learned that it would cost $20,000 just to install new iron stairs, Congress decided to stop trying to patch up the old lighthouse and to build a new one instead.

The new lighthouse the engineers designed for Cape Hatteras was to be 180 feet high and of brick construction—"The most imposing and substantial brick lighthouse on this continent, if not in the world." The first working party arrived at the Cape in November, 1868, and by late the next year buildings to house the workmen, a blacksmith shop, and wharves had been built, and a tram railway had been laid "from the wharf to the light-house, upon which to transport materials."

The site for this new structure was located 600 feet northeast of the old one, and to secure a proper foundation the engineers dug a large hole below the water level—keeping it clear of water by enclosing it in a coffer dam—and then laid a foundation which consisted of "two thicknesses of yellow pine timber, each 6 by 12 inches, laid cross ways, close together, and immediately upon the sand." This placed "the timber-work well below low-water level," and when inspected approximately sixty-five years later, the timbers were as sound as when they had been laid in place. A second foundation, composed of large blocks of granite arranged in an octagonal formation, was laid upon the timbers, then a course of granite and brick, and finally the circular brick lighthouse. The focal plane of the light (the center of the lantern) was 180 feet above ground and 184 feet above sea level. The total height of the structure, according to the National Park Service, is 208 feet from top to bottom, and 268 steps must be climbed to reach the lantern.

This new Cape Hatteras Lighthouse was first illuminated on December 16, 1870, and shortly afterwards the old tower—rendered useless—was blown up and destroyed, though the original foundation can still be seen.

The new tower was struck by lightning in 1879 and cracks appeared in the masonry, but a metal rod was installed, connecting the iron work of the tower with the earth, and there has been no further trouble on that score.

The shoreline in the vicinity of Cape Hatteras is forever changing. A survey of the old lighthouse site made in 1854 showed that the ocean was more than half a mile to the east and a mile and one-half to the south and that most of this was of comparatively new formation. By the time the new structure was begun, the beach to the east had begun to erode, and in the 1930's the high-water line was back where it had been years before—almost at the base of the new lighthouse. Efforts to control this erosion by installing bulkheads were fruitless, so in 1935 a skeleton steel structure was erected back up in the Buxton woods and the famous Cape Hatteras Lighthouse was abandoned.

Attempts at erosion control continued, however, and CCC crews built numerous sand fences on the beach in front of the lighthouse and planted grass on the dunes they formed. They then put in more fences, built more dunes, planted more grass. When finally the structure was considered safe, and partly as the result of a one-man campaign waged by Ben Dixon MacNeill, the lighthouse was reactivated.

Today the tall brick lighthouse, painted in a distinctive black and white spiral design, is equipped with "a 36-inch duplex rotating beacon, with one 1,000 watt lamp in each beacon." These produce 250,000 candlepower, and the light is normally visible in clear weather for about 20 miles, though it has been observed at sea from a distance of 51 miles and, from an altitude of 1,000 feet, from a distance of 115 miles.

DIAMOND SHOALS

FOR CENTURIES mariners have dreaded the passage around Cape Hatteras and many of them, and their ships, have been lost on the shoals spreading out in a southeasterly direction from Cape Point. On numerous occasions writers have referred to those shoals as treacherous and shifting; and so they are to the unacquainted seamen. But for more than 150 years Outer Banks pilots have known that the shoals off Cape Hatteras were not a continuous mass, but rather a series of three distinct shoals with channels between them, through which vessels could pass with safety in calm weather.

As early as September 24, 1806, for example, William Tatham wrote: "After dinner we examined the situation of the lighthouse, and saw 27 sail of vessels pass the inner slough together, supposed to be about five miles from the land."

A comparison of charts and directions for pilots since the end of the Revolution shows that the general arrangement of the shoals and channels has undergone little change and that the shifting for which they are so famous has occurred within the individual shoals.

Today the entire series is designated as Diamond Shoals (by a ruling of the U.S. Board on Geographic Names, March, 1949), the innermost is Hatteras Shoals, the middle section is Inner Diamond Shoal, and the outer section is Outer Diamond Shoal.*

Names have been given, also, to the channels which pass between these shoals, and in 1949 the U.S. Board on Geographic Names desig-

* In 1881, however, the one closest to the point was called The Spit, the middle one was Diamond Shoal, and the one furthest from land was designated Outer Shoals. In 1795 the name Cape Hatteras Shoals was used for the whole group, and the innermost one was called "the Diamond Shoal, from its figure." Even earlier, in 1792, it was reported that Outer Diamond Shoal "was formerly of vast extent, and called the Full-moon-shoal."

nated the one between Hatteras Shoals and Inner Diamond Shoal as "Hatteras Slough," and the one between Inner Diamond Shoal and Outer Diamond Shoal is called "Diamond Slough."

The treacherous nature of the shoals stems not so much from their extent—for the shoals off Cape Fear are longer and larger, and those off Cape Lookout are almost as extensive—as from their location, since they mark the junction of the warm Gulf Stream waters flowing up from the south and the cold arctic waters coming down the coast from the north. It is this collision between the moving water masses which maintains the shoals and which causes the constant turbulence which has given them their reputation.

Because of the danger to shipping there have been a number of efforts to mark the shoals with lights or other warning devices. As early as 1822 an appropriation was made for buoys to be placed on the shoals, and in June of 1824 a 320-ton lightship was stationed there. It remained on duty on and off until August of 1827 when the vessel was driven ashore by hurricane winds. There was no light on the station for a number of years, but in 1851 an appropriation of $8,000 was made for a floating bell beacon, though it was reported that it disappeared less than four months after being put in place. Other efforts were made to place buoys on the shoals but were not successful, and in 1889 Congress authorized the construction of a lighthouse on the outer tip of the shoals.

Details of the proposed Diamond Shoals Lighthouse were released by the Lighthouse Board in 1890. It was to be "150 feet high from low water mark to the focal plane of the structure," with a "solid and massive" base to withstand the impact of the waves and protected by a "riprap packing, composed of granite blocks weighing not less than 2 tons" each. The foundation, consisting of "an iron caisson filled solidly with cement concrete" and fifty-four feet in diameter at the bottom, was to be sunk a hundred feet below the bed of the shoals.

The first floor of the lighthouse itself was to be at least thirty feet above high water mark and large enough to house three boats, thirty tons of coal, six cords of wood, and 8,000 gallons of fresh water. There was to be a second floor for machinery, a third floor for storage of oil, fourth and fifth floors for bedrooms, sixth floor for a kitchen, seventh floor for a sitting room, and an eighth floor for a service room, with the main gallery above that.

A contract for $485,000 was awarded to Anderson and Barr of New Jersey, the first section of the caisson was assembled at Norfolk, Virginia, and in July, 1891, it was towed into place on the shoals. But soon after it was lowered onto the sands, the caisson began to settle unevenly, and within a few weeks a severe storm struck the area, scattering the service vessels and destroying part of the caisson.

After that experience it was decided to build an entirely different type of structure on Diamond Shoals, a skeleton tower mounted on heavy iron piles, and though bids were asked for, Congress decided almost at the last moment to provide a lightship instead of a lighthouse for Diamond Shoals. That second Diamond Shoals Lightship was placed on station in 1897, but it was driven ashore at Creeds Hill in the hurricane of August, 1899.

There was still another effort to build a lighthouse on Diamond Shoals, this one by private individuals in 1904, but it was unsuccessful. Except for brief periods the Shoals have been guarded since then by lightships. Diamond Shoals Lightship Number 71 was sunk by a German submarine August 6, 1918, after warning allied shipping of the presence of the U-boat, and it was replaced by a larger vessel.

People visiting the Cape Hatteras area for the first time should drive to the end of the pavement below the lighthouse and walk out on Cape Point for a first-hand look at the clashing waters over Diamond Shoals.

BUXTON

JUST WEST of the Cape Hatteras Lighthouse is the beginning of a high, heavily-wooded area which extends for eight miles or so toward Hatteras and is known variously as the Cape Hatteras Woods, Hatteras Woods, or Buxton Woods. This is one of the most thickly populated sections of the Banks, but because of the heavy forest growth, the extent of the occupation is not at first apparent to the visitor.

Before the recent construction of a hard-surfaced highway, the woods were crisscrossed with sandy trails leading to isolated dwellings set back in the forest. A trip through these woods, with the twin tracks of the road usually following the tops of the long, meandering pine-covered ridges, was formerly a pleasant, even sublime, experience, especially after half a day of tortuous beach driving on the trip down the Banks from Oregon Inlet. But when highway forces moved in to build their modern road, sawyers and bulldozers cut a wide swath through the forest, making it straight where before it had been meandering, level where it had been pleasantly rolling. Today the visitor driving along the woods' road misses much of the natural beauty that is still there, for it is away from the modern highway swath, down the narrow, pine-needle covered trails that still crisscross the woods.

When a post office was established in the eastern end of these woods, December 29, 1873, with Pharaoh Scarborough as postmaster, it was called The Cape. The name was changed to Buxton, March 6, 1882.

Because of the close proximity to the Gulf Stream semitropical vegetation thrives in Buxton Woods, and a number of orange and grapefruit trees have reached maturity and bear fruit annually. This is the location of the Hatteras Island Health Center, the consolidated Hatteras Island High School, and the new Cape Hatteras Weather Station.

Since the completion of the Outer Banks highway and the establishment of the Cape Hatteras National Seashore, a number of motels, restaurants, and other facilities for the tourist have been constructed at Buxton, particularly east of the woods and near the lighthouse. Quite a few Buxton residents own beach buggies, either stripped-down jeeps or older cars equipped with oversized tires, special racks for fishing rods, and boxes for carrying gear, picnic lunches, and the fish which are caught from the surf.

FRISCO

ORIGINALLY known as Trent, this is a small community at the western edge of the Cape Hatteras Woods between Buxton and Hatteras village.

In 1795 Jonathan Price referred to "three large and remarkable sand hills, called Stowe's Hills" in this vicinity. Later the dominant landmark was a large sand hill known as "Creed's Hill," located south of the village near the sea beach—possibly the same as the earlier "Stowe's Hills." A Lifesaving Station was established on the beach in 1878-79 and was named Creeds Hill, but the Coast Guard Station which succeeded it has been deactivated and the building is now in private hands.

During the Civil War small fortifications were constructed at Trent by the Federal occupation forces, but no fighting took place there.

The Frisco Post Office was established on January 31, 1898, with Thomas Wallace as the first postmaster. It is thought the change from Trent was dictated by the postal authorities because of the similarity to the earlier established Trenton Post Office on the mainland and that the name San Francisco was suggested but was shortened to Frisco.

HATTERAS VILLAGE

WITH A CAPE, a lighthouse, a village, and an inlet all named Hatteras and spread over some twenty miles of the Banks, visitors tend to become confused—but when Bankers use the word Hatteras, they invariably refer to Hatteras village.

This is one of the largest communities on the Banks and was the first one north of Ocracoke to secure a post office. This was established on July 15, 1858, with Robert Styron as postmaster. The post office was discontinued between August 9, 1869, and November 9, 1871, and again between April 27 and May 23, 1877, but it has been in use continuously since then.

During the Civil War, after Federal forces captured the nearby forts Hatteras and Clark, the community was overrun with Federal soldiers. A large encampment known as Fort Wool was constructed just east of the village, and windmills, old boats, and abandoned shacks were used as pickets and outposts by the soldiers.

A Hatteras Lifesaving Station was constructed opposite the village in 1878-79, but because of confusion with the stations at Cape Hatteras and Hatteras Inlet, the name was later changed to Durants.

The Hatteras Weather Station, originally set up in the lighthouse keeper's quarters at the Cape, August 16, 1874, was transferred to Hatteras Lifesaving Station, December 1, 1880, and to a private residence in Hatteras village, October 1, 1883. The weather station was moved to a new building in 1902 and remained in the village until 1956-57, when it was relocated near Cape Hatteras.

In September, 1923, U.S. Army airmen, under command of Brigadier General Billy Mitchell, taking off from an improvised air strip southeast of the village, sank the obsolete U.S. Navy battleships *Virginia* and *New Jersey* anchored near Diamond Shoals. The success of this experiment established Mitchell's claim that aerial bombing was essential in modern warfare.

The property of the former Gooseville Gun Club, west of the village and a famous area for channel bass fishing, is now part of the Cape Hatteras Seashore. After the Hatteras Inlet Coast Guard Station was destroyed by storms and erosion in 1955, arrangements were made for the Coast Guard to use the old Gooseville Club buildings on a temporary basis.

The Hatteras Island highway, which originally terminated at Hatteras village, is being extended closer to the inlet, and the Hatteras Inlet ferry docks are to be moved from the village to a new slip at the end of the highway. Rollinson Channel, which connects Hatteras village with the deeper channels in Pamlico Sound, was dredged out by the Army Engineers in 1936, and in 1956 extensive improvements were made both to the channel and to the harbor on the sound side of the village.

HATTERAS INLET

Two DIFFERENT inlets have borne this name since the first settlers arrived on the Banks.

The first was shown on all of the early maps as being approximately midway between Ocracoke village and the location of the present inlet, and what is known locally as Shingle Creek may well be the remnant of this original Hatteras Inlet. There is a persistent story that it started closing when a British ship grounded there and was abandoned in the 1730's. At any rate by 1755 it was reported "often closed up" and in 1764 was said to be "completely closed."

For a number of years after that, Ocracoke and Hatteras were joined, and people could travel by land from one to the other. Redding R. Quidley, an Ocracoke pilot, lived at Hatteras and walked to and from work. Later Quidley described the opening of the second—and present-day—Hatteras Inlet to a man named W. L. Welch.

"Hatteras Inlet was cut out," he stated, "by a heavy gale, a violent storm on the 7th of Sept., at night, 1846." * He said he and his brother

* This was the same hurricane which opened Oregon Inlet the following day.

had worked "cutting wood and chopping yopon, where now, I have no doubt there is three or four fathoms of water; the growth was live oak principally, did not grow tall, but large trunks and spreading limbs. I had an old uncle lived about where the inlet is, who had a fine fig orchard, and many peach trees on his lot, with fine potato patch and garden."

He said there were several other families living in the immediate area where the inlet cut through, and "to their great surprise, in the morning they saw the sea and sound connected together, and the live oaks washing up by the roots and tumbling into the ocean."

Quidley piloted the first vessel through the new inlet to Pamlico Sound, the schooner *Asher C. Havens*, on February 5, 1847. He also piloted the first outbound vessel, a small steamer, and from then until the Civil War, the traffic through the new Hatteras Inlet steadily increased.

Soon after the outbreak of the Civil War, the Confederates constructed two forts east of the inlet, naming the larger one Fort Hatteras and the smaller one, closer to the village, Fort Clark. These were attacked by a strong Federal naval force on August 28, 1861, and were surrendered to an army landing party the following morning. The sites of the two forts are now bare beach, flooded by every tide.

The large Federal fleet which attacked Roanoke Island in February of 1862 entered the sounds through Hatteras Inlet, which by then was more suited for navigation than the older Ocracoke Inlet. Because of the decline of coastal shipping soon after the war, however, it has been used primarily by small craft in recent years, and in fact the oldtimers in the area say the last commercial vessel passed through Hatteras Inlet about 1895.

The Lifesaving Station located on the Ocracoke Island side of the inlet was named Ocracoke at the outset, but this was later changed to "Hatteras Inlet." The Coast Guard Station which succeeded it was threatened by erosion in recent years, and in a storm in 1955 a new channel cut through west of the inlet, and the Coast Guard buildings disappeared.

After World War II, Frazier Peele of Hatteras began providing ferry service across the inlet, using a small wooden ferry capable of carrying four automobiles. Peele sold out to the state of North Carolina in 1957, and regular schedules are now maintained with a larger ferry.

OCRACOKE

SINCE COLONIAL days this name has been applied variously to an inlet, an island, and a village on the Outer Banks, though the spelling has undergone some drastic changes.

On his map in 1585 John White spelled it "Wokokon," to designate the inlet, the name probably deriving from that of the nearby tribe of "Woccon" Indians. In 1657 Nicholas Comberford showed the island as "Wococock," and in 1665 surveyor T. Woodward referred to an "Inlett at Wococock or Wococon." Thereafter the letter "W" was usually dropped, and the name was spelled more than two dozen different ways before it became standardized. The earlier spellings included "Oakacock," "Oacock," "Ocock," and "Okok." Before the Revolution one of the most common ways of spelling the name was "Occacock" or "Ocacock," and later this became "Okercock," "Ocre-cock," and "Ocracock" before the present-day spelling was adopted.

OCRACOKE ISLAND

THE OPENING and closing of inlets has made dramatic changes in the geography of Ocracoke Island; so much so, in fact, that for a time Ocracoke, as an island, ceased to exist.

When the Raleigh colonists visited the island in the 1580's, and thereafter until the middle of the eighteenth century, Ocracoke Island was approximately eight miles long, bounded on the west by Ocracoke Inlet and on the east by what was known as Hatteras Inlet. In the 1730's, however, the inlet marking the eastern boundary began to close, and until 1846 there was no Hatteras Inlet, and consequently no Ocracoke Island. Ocracoke was simply a peninsula attached to Cape Hatteras.

In the hurricane of September 7, 1846, a new inlet was cut through the Banks just west of Hatteras village and several miles closer to Cape Hatteras than the site of the former Hatteras Inlet. This was promptly named Hatteras Inlet (a smaller cut, closer to Ocracoke was named Wells Creek, but it was not open for long) and once again Ocracoke was an island, though this time it was half again as long as it had been in colonial times. This series of events seems to have eluded most of the historians, probably because the new inlet was given the same name as the old, though the two were several miles apart.

Contemporary government officials apparently were equally confused by these changes in geography, for in 1770 it was discovered that the part of Cape Hatteras Banks originally known as Ocracoke Island was "not included in any County within this Province; by which Means the Inhabitants thereof are not liable to pay Taxes, or perform any Public Duties whatsoever." This was quickly rectified by attaching the area to Carteret County, and in 1845—the year before it became an island again—it was annexed to Hyde County, to which it still belongs.

In 1719 the original "Ocacock" Island, containing 2,110 acres, was granted to John Lovick. Later it was acquired by Richard Sanderson, who at the time of his death in 1733 bequeathed to his son, Richard Sanderson, "ye Island of Ocreecock w'th all the Stock of Horses, Cattle, Sheep & hoggs, thereunto belonging." This livestock attracted the attention of French and Spanish privateers in their raids on shipping at Ocracoke Inlet, and they frequently came ashore to steal fresh beef and mutton, the Spaniards actually setting up a tent camp on the western end of the island while stocking up on fresh meat in 1741.

A large Spanish vessel, carrying specie and cargo valued at more than a million pieces of eight, was forced into Ocracoke Inlet for repairs in 1750-after encountering a terrific storm at sea. The vessel was beached nearby, and for some time there was a constant furor as the residents of Ocracoke, the Spaniards, officials of the colony, and opportunists attracted to the scene all tried to lay claim to the valuable cargo.

Numerous ships have been wrecked on Ocracoke, including the steam-packet *Home* in 1837 with the loss of ninety lives, the steamer *Ariosto* in 1899 with the loss of twenty-one lives, and the six-masted schooner *George W. Wells* in 1913.

The first Lifesaving Station on the island and bearing that name was located near Hatteras Inlet. When a second station was built at Ocracoke village, however, the name of the first was changed to "Hatteras Inlet" and the second one was called "Ocracoke."

A feature of Ocracoke Island for many years was the annual roundup or "penning" of the Banks ponies. In recent years this has been held on July 4, but the number of wild ponies has decreased sharply and those used by the mounted Ocracoke Boy Scout troop now constitute the bulk of the herd.

In 1953 all of Ocracoke Island except the land in the immediate vicinity of Ocracoke village became a part of the Cape Hatteras National Seashore, and in 1957 a hard-surfaced highway was constructed from the village to a point near Hatteras Inlet. It is now possible to drive the ordinary car to Ocracoke village, crossing Hatteras Inlet on the state operated ferry.

OCRACOKE VILLAGE

IN 1715 the North Carolina Assembly passed "An Act for Settling and Maintaining Pilots at Roanoke & Ocacock Inlett." The pilots who were attracted to Ocracoke as the result of this and subsequent such acts were responsible for establishing one of the first communities on the Outer Banks near the western end of Ocracoke Island. But because Ocracoke Island was privately owned, these first Ocracokers were squatters, and in 1760 a bill was passed to set aside fifty acres for their use. This was amended in 1766 to provide for the government to purchase twenty acres to lease to the pilots for their temporary homes.

It is probable, though by no means certain, that this early community of temporary shacks was located at a place called Cockle Creek, about three miles east of the inlet; for by the 1770's a permanent community was beginning to grow up there, and for a number of years it was identified as "Pilot Town." Cockle Creek is the modern Silver Lake; Pilot Town is the present-day Ocracoke village.

Ocracokers take questionable pride in pointing out to visitors the deep channel between the village and Ocracoke Inlet known as Teaches Hole and in stating that this was where the pirate Blackbeard, or Edward Teach, was killed in 1718.

One of the earliest written descriptions of Ocracokers was set down in 1783 by Francisco de Miranda. He said: "All the people ... seemed very robust and fat to me.... The people of that country attribute their fleshiness to their food which consists entirely of fish, oysters, and some few vegetables which they grow in the small gardens they cultivate not far from their houses." Twelve years later Jonathan

Price wrote a description of the village area which indicates there has been comparatively little change in the ensuing century and a half. "Its length," he said, "is three miles, and its breadth two and one half. Small live oak and cedar grow abundantly over it, and it contains several swamps and rich marshes, which might be cultivated to great advantage."

The first school on Ocracoke was built about 1808, and the first Outer Banks post office was established there, August 21, 1840, with William H. Howard as postmaster. A clam factory was located in the village in 1877, and at one time was said to have employed as many as fifty people. A second was built on Windmill Point in 1898. For the most part the residents of Ocracoke have been engaged in seafaring pursuits, first as pilots, then as "boatmen," fishermen, and government lifesavers or Coast Guardsmen.

In comparatively recent times there have been three important developments affecting the community. The first was the dredging out of Cockle Creek and construction of Silver Lake Harbor in 1931. The second was the establishment of the Cape Hatteras National Seashore in 1953. The third was the construction of the Ocracoke Island highway in 1957.

The dredging of Silver Lake Harbor made it possible for fairly large vessels to come into dock in the village proper. Since then a sizable fishing industry has been developed, an ice house and electric light plant have been constructed, and during World War II, a Navy Section Base was located there (1942-44), though this later became an Amphibious Training Base (1944-45) and still later a Combat Information Center (1945). The establishment of the Cape Hatteras Seashore and the construction of the highway came in a period when fishing and shrimping was on the decline, and it promises to make the tourist business an important source of income for the villagers.

Largely through the efforts of such people as Stanley S. Wahab, a native Ocracoker who was successful in business in Baltimore and returned home to put his money into tourist facilities, fishing boats, the ice plant, and similar improvements, and Mr. and Mrs. Theodore Rondthaler, experienced teachers who came to Ocracoke to teach school and have taken an active part in many community projects, Ocracoke is today a modern and nearly self-sufficient community, yet retaining much of its earlier charm.

There is still an underlying social distinction between the "Creekers" who live in one part of the community and the "Pointers" in the other; but when it comes to such things as raising money for the PTA, sponsoring the mounted Boy Scout troop, or participating in other civic projects, everyone seems to pitch in and help.

As is the case in many of the Banks communities, the basic source of water supply is rain water, caught in cisterns. As this is written the Outer Banks highway dead-ends at Ocracoke village, but the All-Seashore Highway Association has been very active in attempting to secure an outlet to the south, and there is serious talk of inaugurating ferry service between Ocracoke and nearby Cedar Island, the eastern terminus of U.S. Highway 70.

OCRACOKE LIGHTHOUSE

THE FIRST lighthouse at Ocracoke was authorized by an act of the North Carolina General Assembly in 1789, and the following September 13 a one-acre site on the island was deeded to North Carolina by William Williams, John Williams, Joseph Williams, William Howard, Jr., and Henry Gerrish. In November of that year, however, Governor Martin informed the General Assembly that North Carolina could not go ahead with the project because lighthouse construction was an obligation which had been assumed by the federal government, and as a result the Assembly passed a law ceding the land to the United States.

Nothing was done about the one-acre site on Ocracoke Island, in fact nothing at all was done, until May 13, 1794, when Congress authorized construction of a lighthouse on Shell Castle Island just inside the entrance to Ocracoke Inlet.

Details of the Shell Castle Lighthouse were contained in an invitation for bids published in the *N.C. Gazette* for May 23, 1795. It was to be a pyramidal-shaped wooden tower, 54½ feet high, covered with shingles, and set on a ten-foot-deep submerged stone foundation. The tower was to be capped with a six-foot enclosure for the lantern and a three-foot dome. The dwelling was to be 20 x 50 feet with a cellar, and an oil vault, 10 x 12 feet, was included also. The low bidder was H. Dearborn, who was also awarded the contract to build the larger Cape Hatteras Lighthouse at the same time. A lot on Shell Castle

Island, 70 x 140 feet in size, was sold to the government for the light-house, November 9, 1797, by John Gray Blount and John Wallace.

The Shell Castle Lighthouse was completed in 1798, but it was found that "in the process of time the channel leading in and out of Ocracoke left the light-house the distance of a mile so as to render it altogether useless." On May 15, 1820, an appropriation of $14,000 was made for a light vessel to replace the Shell Castle Lighthouse. The light vessel was placed in service at the inlet but did not prove satisfactory either, and on May 7, 1822, Congress authorized an expenditure of $20,000 for construction of a lighthouse on Ocracoke Island to replace the light vessel.

The Ocracoke Lighthouse and a one-story three-bedroom keeper's dwelling with gabled roof were constructed by Noah Porter of Massachusetts in 1823 at a cost of $11,359.35. This is the lighthouse still in service at Ocracoke and the oldest lighthouse structure on the North Carolina coast. In 1862 the lens was removed, but it was refitted and put back in service in 1863. In 1897 the roof of the dwelling was removed and a second story was added. The lighthouse, measured from the ground to the center of the light, is sixty-five feet high.

OCRACOKE INLET

THE VESSELS carrying the first colonists to Roanoke Island in 1585 made their initial landing at Ocracoke Inlet, where the flagship grounded on a shoal. The vessels remained there for more than three weeks while Sir Richard Grenville and Ralph Lane explored the sounds and mainland to the west. On subsequent voyages, the vessels frequently landed at Ocracoke Inlet before moving up the coast to Roanoke Island and Fort Raleigh.

Later Ocracoke Inlet became the primary point of entry for vessels bound to the comparatively populous northern part of North Carolina, resulting in the establishment of the largest communities on the Banks at nearby Ocracoke and Portsmouth. It was not uncommon, during the latter part of the eighteenth century and the first half of the nineteenth, to see thirty to forty vessels waiting inside the inlet to pass out to sea.

The pirate Blackbeard was killed there in 1718 in an engagement with two sloops of the British Navy, sent out under the auspices of the Governor of Virginia and commanded by Lieutenant Robert Maynard.

During the Revolutionary War, British vessels frequently raided shipping in the inlet. Before regular defending forces were sent there, the Ocracoke pilots captured several of these armed vessels; later a militia company and a large row galley were stationed at the inlet to guard American shipping, and supplies destined for Washington's army at Valley Forge were brought in through Ocracoke Inlet at that time.

About 1790 John Gray Blount and John Wallace set up extensive wharves, warehouses, a tavern, and other facilities on a dry shoal known as Shell Castle just inside the inlet, and this became an important trading center where seagoing vessels could unload their cargo without having to cross the shallow swash between the inlet and Pamlico Sound. A lighthouse was built on Shell Castle by the federal government at the same time, but when the channel which passed by Shell Castle began to close up, both the Blount-Wallace facilities and the lighthouse were abandoned.

Plans were made also for a fort on Beacon Island near Shell Castle, and for a number of years the area around Ocracoke Inlet was known as Beacon Island Roads. The Beacon Island Fort, or Fort Ocracoke or Fort Morgan, as it was called during the Civil War, was abandoned by the Confederates when Federal forces captured Hatteras Inlet in 1861. Soon afterwards, the Federals sank several stone-laden schooners in Ocracoke Inlet and effectively blocked off the channel during the remainder of the war. By that time, however, the newer Hatteras Inlet had already replaced Ocracoke Inlet as the main point of entry through the Banks.

Efforts to improve the navigation of Ocracoke Inlet date back to the 1820's when the U.S. Engineers began an extensive dredging project. This was finally abandoned in 1835 after it was learned that the dredged channels were filling in as fast as they were dug, and a jetty was damaged seriously by a hurricane before it could be finished. In 1895 the channel was effectively opened by dredging, but by then the switch to railroads and other land transportation kept it from regaining its former status. Still another dredging project, authorized in 1954, is now being undertaken.

PORTSMOUTH

PORTSMOUTH, authorized by the Colonial Assembly in 1753, was the first and for many years the largest town on the Outer Banks. Unlike Ocracoke, Hatteras, and the other communities further north which simply grew from single houses to community size as people moved in, Portsmouth was planned from the start. In fact it was a town, with a name, before there was any evidence on the ground to show for it.

In 1753 the main channel at Ocracoke Inlet was on the south side, nearer Core Banks than Ocracoke Island, and though it was possible for large vessels to enter the inlet and pass through the channel to "commodiously ride at anchor in the harbor adjoining Core Banks," that was about as far as the big ones could go. Beyond this harbor was the swash—sometimes called swath, or swatch—a shoal area at the junction of inlet and sound, over which only small craft could pass. For this reason, as it was explained at the time, "the merchants and other traders are obliged to employ small vessels, in lightening others of greater burden over the swatch, which is not only very expensive, but also very dangerous."

Since most of the vessels bound to and from northern Carolina were forced to use Ocracoke Inlet, something had to be done to provide wharves, warehouses, and other facilities near the harbor where cargo could be stored and transshipped. It was for this reason that Portsmouth was authorized by the Assembly in 1753.

The land selected for the new town had been granted to Richard Lovat in 1738, deeded by him to Thomas Nelson in 1739, and by 1753 it was owned by a man named John Kersey who had been hailed before the vice admiralty court in his younger years for the purchase of some illegal rum from the master of the sloop *Kathrine* at Ocracoke. Kersey was to receive the proceeds from the sale of Portsmouth building sites, but the work of laying out the town into half-acre lots with convenient streets, and finding purchasers, was delegated to a commission of five leading citizens of the inland communities.

Those early purchasers of Portsmouth town lots, who paid twenty shillings each and were required to build "a good substantial habitable framed or brick house or good substantial warehouse, of not less dimensions than twenty feet in length and sixteen feet wide" within eighteen months, included John Tolson, who bought the first lot February 12, 1756, John Tweton, William Martiner Denham, Joseph Tweton, Charles McNair, Valentine Wade, John Campbell, and James Bun.

As early as 1748 the Assembly had authorized the construction of a fort to guard Ocracoke Inlet, but when Governor Dobbs arrived there May 9, 1755, he found that nothing had been done. Dobbs immediately made plans for construction at Portsmouth of a "fascine battery on pilings" and a barracks building for forty men. This fort, named Fort Granville, was sufficiently near completion in 1758 to be garrisoned, and a force under Captain Charles McNair was stationed there. By 1764, however, the garrison was discharged, and the barracks and other buildings were ordered sold.

Meanwhile, Portsmouth continued to grow. In 1764 it was listed as an official commodity inspection point, and in 1766 when Minister Alex Stewart visited the town he baptized twenty-seven children from the nearby Banks. On the Mouzon map of 1775, a road—the only road on the Banks—was shown extending from Portsmouth to Core Banks, and by 1800 Portsmouth included not only the original fifty acres of John Kersey, but all of the land between Ocracoke Inlet and Drum Inlet, and the population was listed as 246.

There was an "Academy" on the map of Coles and Price in 1806, and by 1810 the population had risen to 387. Three years later the British captured the town and stole large quantities of cattle and sheep, and though the Wallace-Blount installation at Shell Castle ceased to operate not long after the end of the War of 1812, Portsmouth town continued to prosper as more and more vessels used the inlet.

Figures compiled in 1836-37 showed that in excess of 1,400 vessels had passed through Ocracoke Inlet in a twelve-month period. Because many of the seamen on these vessels were sick, or were placed in quarantine, it became necessary in 1846 for the federal government to construct a marine hospital at Portsmouth. By that time there was a post office on Portsmouth—established September 25, 1840, with Samuel W. Chadwick as postmaster—but 1846 was the year Hatteras Inlet and Oregon Inlet opened, and it marked the turning point in Portsmouth's fortune.

After the Civil War, when almost all traffic through the Banks had switched from Ocracoke Inlet to Hatteras Inlet, there were attempts to provide an industry for Portsmouth, the most extensive being the construction of the Excelsior Oil and Guano Company menhaden processing plant there in 1866, but all such attempts resulted in failure.

A U.S. Weather Bureau Station was located at Portsmouth from 1876 to 1885, and a Lifesaving Station was established there also. With the decline of maritime traffic through the inlet and the failure to establish new industry, the population declined rapidly from the high point of 505 which had been reached in 1850. A hundred years later only fourteen people remained, and an enterprising real-estate man had bought up practically all of the unoccupied houses, offering them in 1950 to the prospective buyer in bargain basement fashion, $495 and take your choice. Today there are many more houses on Portsmouth than people.

DRUM INLET

THIS IS A small inlet which divides what is sometimes called Portsmouth Banks or Portsmouth Island from the rest of Core Banks. It is located approximately twenty miles west of Ocracoke Inlet and was opened in the early 1930's by storm tides. In 1938 Congress authorized the Army Corps of Engineers to dredge out the Drum Inlet channel (200 feet wide) to a depth of twelve feet, and though more than $50,000 was expended on this project, the controlling depth in 1957 was listed as less than a foot and a half.

One of the difficulties in maintaining a channel through Drum Inlet is that most of the Banks area between there and Portsmouth is so low that the water flows over it during storms instead of being funneled through the inlets. Shrimpers and commercial fishermen use the inlet when navigable and are attempting to get Congress to approve another major dredging project. A number of sports fishing camps are located near the inlet.

This is not the first inlet in that particular area, for the old maps show at least six different ones, with as many as four open at one time; nor is it the first with that name, for there was a Drum Inlet west of the present location in the early colonial period.*

---

* The earlier inlets, most of them closer to Portsmouth than to Cape Lookout, included Normans Inlet, Hunting Quarter Inlet, Cedar Inlet, Cedar Island Inlet, and

CORE BANKS

IN 1713 a man named John Porter secured a grant for 7,000 acres of Banks land, extending from old Drum Inlet to old Topsail Inlet (now Beaufort Inlet) and including Cape Lookout. This was soon acquired by John Shackleford and Enoch Ward who divided the property in 1723—Shackleford taking Cape Lookout and the western part, Ward taking the eastern part. Though the name Core Banks was sometimes applied to all of this area, the original Shackleford property in time became known as Shackleford Banks, and in today's usage Core Banks is the area between Drum Inlet and Cape Lookout.

The name Core Banks—and Core Sound, which separates it from the mainland—derives from the Coree Indians who once lived on the mainland and hunted on the Banks.

Among the earliest residents of Core Banks, particularly in the section near Cape Lookout, were whalers who operated from camps on the beach. Old names such as Whale Creek, Whalers Camp, Middle Whales Camp, and Whalers Camp Point, of course, stem from this. Among other early place names, most of them forgotten for many years, were Briery Hills, Three Hats Creek, Thompsons Hammock, The High Hills, Pettartory Hill, Horse Pen Creek, and Jacks Place.

The name of Core Banks Lifesaving Station, one of the last established on the North Carolina coast, was later changed to Atlantic. Located near the present Drum Inlet, the Coast Guard Station there was decommissioned in 1957.

CAPE LOOKOUT

EARLY MAP MAKERS had difficulty differentiating between Cape Lookout and Cape Fear, with the result that Cape Lookout was shown on the De Bry engraving of White's 1585 map as "Promontorium Tremendum" and on the Velasco map of about 1611 as "Cape Feare,"

Porters Inlet, though in some instances the names seem to have been interchangeable. For a number of years before the Civil War all of the old inlets were filled up. Whalebone Inlet opened just west of Portsmouth in the 1860's, though it never amounted to much and closed in the early 1900's. A small cut between Drum Inlet and Portsmouth, periodically open and closed, cut through at about the same time as Drum Inlet and is sometimes called Swash Inlet.

but by the time the first permanent settlers were entering Carolina, the name "Cape Look Out" was well established.

In the colonial period, the cape was more of a hook than it is now, and the bight or bay thus formed was considered one of the finest harbors on the Atlantic coast. It was used by Spanish privateers in the 1740's as a hiding place, and when Governor Dobbs visited the cape in 1755, he described it as "the best, altho small, of any harbour from Boston to Georgia" and tried to interest the home government in building a fort there.

At that time the Bankers living in the vicinity of the cape were engaged primarily in whaling, sighting the schools of whales from the higher hills and then going after them in small rowboats. In addition, New England whaling vessels for a number of years used Cape Lookout Bight as a base of operations between Christmas and April.

During the Revolution a group of French volunteers, with some slight assistance from the government of North Carolina, constructed a fort back of the cape. It was later named Fort Hancock and was garrisoned for approximately two years, but no trace of it remains today.

The first lighthouse at Cape Lookout was authorized by Congress, March 26, 1804, and the following February, Joseph Fulford and Elijah Pigott deeded a four-acre site to the government for a lighthouse "on the west side of Cape Hills." When William Tatham inspected the cape two years later, his instructions were to find a suitable location for the lighthouse. He determined that the highest elevation, Blinds Hill, located about a mile from the cape, was 60 feet above sea level and that there were several other hills nearly as high, including Fulfords Hill, 47 feet; Old Well Hill, 30 feet; Canada's Hill and Lattitude Hill, 40 feet; Lazy Hill, 30 feet; and the Cape Hills, 25 feet. Tatham concluded that these high hills would block the view of the light, and he recommended that a wooden structure 140 feet high should be placed on top of Blinds Hill, giving an elevation of 200 feet to the light. These recommendations were not followed, and in the intervening years the large hills have practically disappeared.

The exact date for the completion of that first Cape Lookout Lighthouse is not known, though it seems to have been put in service sometime in 1812. At a later date, keeper William Fulford said: "The light-house is built with two towers; the inside one is brick—the outside one is a wooden framed building, boarded and shingled, and painted in red and white stripes horizontally."

In 1852 the Cape Lookout Lighthouse tower was listed as being ninety-three feet high. There was a recommendation that year that the height be increased to 150 feet to make it more effective, but because drifting sand was threatening the base of the structure it was decided in 1857 to build a new tower, and this second Cape Lookout Lighthouse, 150 feet high and still in use, was first lighted on November 1, 1859.

In 1861 the new tower was slightly damaged and the lens ruined by a Confederate raiding force, but it was refitted and the light re-exhibited in 1863. Again in 1865, however, a group of Confederate raiders dynamited the structure, destroying the lower part of the stairs, and the following year Congress appropriated $20,000 for replacing the damaged wooden stairs with iron ones. The original lighthouse was damaged by the raiding force also, though it was reported in 1868 that "the old tower at this place is old and dilapidated, but answers very well as a day mark for passing vessels." Today all that remains of the old lighthouse is a pile of rubble, though the 1859 tower, its exterior painted in a distinctive black and white diamond design, seems in as good shape as ever.

In the 1880's a Lifesaving Station was constructed on the cape, and this and the Coast Guard Station which replaced it have been in active service ever since, the crews making a number of daring rescues from vessels wrecked on Lookout Shoals which stretch out for approximately ten miles into the Atlantic. The spray tossed up over these shoals by breaking waves frequently obscured the lighthouse, and as an additional aid to mariners a steel hull lightship, 112 feet long and of 465 gross tons, was placed there in 1904.

A U.S. Weather Bureau Station was located at Cape Lookout from April, 1876, to 1904, and a Cape Lookout Post Office saw brief service also. It was established on April 6, 1910, with Amy Clifton as postmaster and was discontinued June 10, 1911.

Lookout Bight, the harbor formed behind the hook of Cape Lookout, is small but deep, the controlling depth in the bight reported by the U.S. Army Engineers as thirty feet. Beginning in 1912 there was an effort to turn this into a harbor of refuge for ocean-going ships in time of storm, and at the same time, by connecting Cape Lookout with the railroad at Beaufort, it was hoped to make it a major seaport. The engineers began constructing sand fences on the cape in 1913, and in 1914 construction was started on a 7,050-foot rubble stone breakwater to protect the bight. The work was stopped at the outbreak of World War I, at the time the breakwater was 4,800 feet long, and because plans to extend the railroad had not materialized and the use of the bight as a harbor of refuge was below expectations, the project was discontinued. Today, after an expenditure of more than $1,250,000, the breakwater is visible only at extreme low water.

On several different occasions a small inlet, known as "Cape Inlet," or "The Drain," has opened just west of the lighthouse, and in 1937 approval was given for dredging this to a depth of seven feet. The project was finally completed in 1956 after an expenditure of $88,328. It is still open, though in 1957 the controlling depth was only four and a half feet.

SHACKLEFORD BANKS AND DIAMOND CITY

SHACKLEFORD BANKS, acquired by John Shackleford when he and Enoch Ward divided their 7,000-acre tract of Banks land in 1723, extends now from The Drain, or Barden Inlet, on the east to Beaufort Inlet on the west.

Once heavily forested, it was partly cut over more than a hundred years ago to provide live oak and cedar timbers for the construction of ships in Beaufort boatyards, and in the hurricane of August, 1899, and successive storms it has been practically denuded.

In the latter part of the nineteenth century there were two well defined communities on Shackleford Banks, Wade's Hammock near Beaufort Inlet and Diamond City near Cape Lookout, the latter named for the diamond pattern on the nearby lighthouse. Diamond City was a community of approximately 500 people, most of whom were whalers, and when the August hurricane of 1899 flooded their homes they decided to move. Within a three-year period all of the residents had left Diamond City, taking their houses with them.

At the present time there are no permanent residents on Shackleford Banks, though there is talk of converting it into either a summer resort or a park. Until very recently it was used extensively for grazing horses, cattle, and sheep, and the open grazing undoubtedly has had a lot to do with the destruction of the vegetation which had previously protected Shackleford Banks from the storms.

BEAUFORT INLET

THIS MARKS the south and west boundary of the area most often thought of as the Outer Banks, though Bogue Banks extends on beyond, and in fact there are small sand banks or islands between the mainland and the sea for most of the length of the lower Carolina coast.

Variously known as Topsail Inlet, Core Sound Inlet, Old Topsail Inlet, and Port Beaufort Inlet, it has been much more stable than any of the inlets on the northern Banks. It was open and deep when the first permanent settlers arrived, and though it was made an official port in 1722 and the town of Beaufort was established nearby in 1723, it proved impossible for vessels entering Beaufort Inlet to reach the more populous areas along the upper sounds and rivers. Consequently it did not become an important factor in North Carolina commerce until the railroad to nearby Morehead City was completed in 1858.

Governor Burrington claimed in 1731 that vessels drawing twenty feet of water could enter Beaufort Inlet, and the depth of the channel seems to have remained between fifteen and twenty feet until jurisdiction was turned over to the Army Engineers in 1880. At that time the controlling depth was a little over fifteen feet, but "the harbor entrance was rapidly deteriorating; its width, measured from Fort Macon Point to Shackleford Point, having increased 500 feet between the years 1864 and 1880." In the next twelve months the width increased 900 feet more, and the engineers built jetties into the inlet on both sides and stabilized the shore with sand fences. In the ensuing years five jetties were constructed on Shackleford Point and six on Fort Macon Point, and by 1889 it was reported that the erosion had been halted and the jetties were being covered with sand. This was so successful, in fact, that when the jetties were uncovered during a series of hurricanes in the mid-1950's, most people in the area were mystified as to where they had come from.

The controlling depth of the inlet and channel when surveyed in 1957 was thirty feet, and this depth extended to the North Carolina

Ports Authority terminal in Morehead City, thus allowing large ocean-going vessels to dock there.

Blackbeard the pirate purposely wrecked his flagship, *Queen Anne's Revenge*, at Beaufort Inlet in 1718, and he marooned some of his pirate crewmen nearby while he sailed off for Ocracoke in a small sloop, *Adventure*, with most of the booty and a few picked crewmen. During the 1740's Spanish privateers frequently attacked the inlet and in 1747 actually captured the town, and similar attacks were made by British vessels during the Revolution.

A fort, named Fort Dobbs, was constructed on the Bogue Banks side of the inlet in 1756, a second one named Fort Hampton was built in almost the same location in 1808, and a third one named Fort Macon was erected there in 1834. Fort Macon, captured by Federal forces after a bitter battle in 1862, is preserved as a North Carolina State Park and is accessible by modern bridge and highway from Morehead City.

A Lifesaving Station, later a Coast Guard Station, was located near Fort Macon and is still active. A U.S. Weather Bureau Station also was located at the inlet from 1878 to 1886.

NEARBY ISLANDS

THREE ISLANDS just back of the Banks have been closely linked to them throughout their history. These are Knotts Island, which is located at the northern end of Currituck Sound; Roanoke Island, opposite Nags Head; and Harkers Island, across from Cape Lookout.

KNOTTS ISLAND

BECAUSE of its proximity to the early Virginia settlements Knotts Island was inhabited by white settlers before most of the Banks. The early residents included George Booth, William Hardin, and John Simpson, and the island was originally known both as "Knots Island" and "Mackeys Island," though today Knotts Island and Mackey Island are considered separate.

When the boundary line between North Carolina and Virginia was surveyed in 1728, the lower part of Knotts Island was placed in North

Carolina and the upper part in Virginia, a situation which continues to this day with the result that the residents of lower Knotts Island, in order to drive to their county seat at Currituck, must pass into Virginia enroute.

Many of the early residents of Knotts Island were seafaring men whose boats operated out of Currituck Inlet, and a tavern, located on the south end of the island and catering to the Currituck Inlet traffic, at one time was said to have been a hangout for thieves and pirates.

A post office, the first in the Banks area, was established on Knotts Island, January 5, 1833, with William Smith as postmaster, but it was discontinued August 3, 1835. The post office was re-established, January 30, 1856, discontinued on December 11, 1866, re-established again September 1, 1868, discontinued on March 23, 1870, and finally re-established, April 27, 1874.

ROANOKE ISLAND

ROANOKE ISLAND, best known as the site of the early attempts at English colonization in America under the direction of Sir Walter Raleigh between 1584 and 1590, was inhabited by the Roanoke Indians when the Raleigh colonists were there. But in 1654 Francis Yeardley of Virginia arranged with "the great emperor of Rhoanoke" for the Indians to move inland and turn the coastal area over to the Virginians.

In 1676 the Lords Proprietors ordered their representatives in Carolina to build the "chiefe towne" of the colony on Roanoke Island because of its proximity to Roanoke Inlet, which was used at that time by practically all vessels entering Carolina. Nothing was done about this, however, and subsequent efforts to establish a town—near the present location of the town of Manteo—failed in 1716 and again in 1723. The name "Town of Carteret" was adopted during the latter attempt, and at that time it was planned to make Carteret the county seat of Currituck County. The prime mover in both of these efforts was a man named Richard Sanderson who owned considerable property on Roanoke Island and the Banks. The body of water now known as Roanoke Sound was then called Sanderson's Channel.

Long before these unsuccessful attempts to create a town on Roanoke Island, however, all of the island was claimed and a large portion of it settled. In 1669 the entire island was owned by Governor Samuel Stephens, who raised livestock there. Stephens died in 1670, willing it to his widow, who later married Sir William Berkeley—Governor of Virginia and one of the Lords Proprietors of Carolina—and in 1676 Berkeley and his wife sold the island for 100 pounds to Joshua Lamb, a New England merchant. Lamb, a shrewd businessman, sold half of the island the next year to Nicholas Paige, a Boston merchant, for 150 pounds, thus realizing a profit of 50 pounds on his investment while still retaining a half interest in the property.

Lamb sold a quarter interest in the island to a man named George Pardage or Patridge, while Paige left his half interest to Mrs. Martha Hobbs in 1703. In 1719 Mrs. Hobbs and her husband, Nathaniel Oliver, sold the half interest to Oliver Noyes for 240 pounds. As late as 1729, Lamb's heirs and George Patridge each claimed a quarter interest, and the Noyes heirs claimed one half, but controversy had already arisen as to the validity of their claims, and from that point on it is difficult to trace land ownership on Roanoke Island. Long before the Revolution, however, the principal landowners included people named Baum, Daniels, Mann, and Meekins, as is the case to this day.

Roanoke Island was raided by the Mattamuskeet Indians in 1713, and about twenty people were killed or carried away.

During the Civil War an important battle was fought on the island, and with the capture of the extensive fortifications which had been erected by the Confederates, both on the northwestern shore of the island and on the causeway about a mile and a half below the present town of Manteo, the Federal forces gained control of eastern North Carolina. Immediately following the fall of Roanoke Island, thousands of freed slaves or contrabands flocked to the Federal banner, and a contraband community was laid out on the northern end of the island. Here the freed slaves built more than 500 houses, though they were dispossessed at the end of the war.

Roanoke Island is connected with Nags Head Beach by a modern bridge over Roanoke Sound and with the mainland by another bridge over Croatan Sound. A hard-surfaced road, the original part constructed in 1924, extends from north to south, with shorter connecting roads at the various communities.

Fort Raleigh, on the northeast side of the island, is the scene of the

Raleigh colonization attempts. In the 1930's a project to reconstruct some of the buildings in the "Cittie of Ralegh" was undertaken, and in 1937 Paul Green's symphonic drama *The Lost Colony* was presented in a natural amphitheatre at Fort Raleigh for the first time. The National Park Service assumed jurisdiction over the site in 1941, and it became the Fort Raleigh National Historic Site. Extensive excavations under the direction of Park Service archeologists made possible the reconstruction of the original fort built by Ralph Lane in 1585, and a museum now houses many items of interest connected with the so-called lost colony.

On the northwestern side of the island, below the approach to the new Croatan Sound bridge, is the scene of the experiments in wireless telegraphy conducted in 1901 and 1902 by Reginald L. Fessenden, and further south along the western shore, near the site of the Civil War forts, is the Dare County Airport, built during World War II as an auxiliary Naval Air Station.

"Mother Vineyard," on the eastern shore of the island between Fort Raleigh and Manteo, is thought to be both the oldest and largest scuppernong grape vine in existence. The late Dr. William C. Etheridge, who made a detailed study of the origin of the "Mother Vineyard," reported that it was "big and old" when Abraham Baum was a boy about 1750. There is a possibility, as pointed out by David B. Quinn, that the actual settlement of the so-called lost colonists—as differentiated from their fort—was located in the general vicinity of the "Mother Vineyard." Though a residential development is growing up along the shore in this area, a visit to "Mother Vineyard" is still an interesting part of the tourist's trip to Roanoke Island.

In 1870, when Dare County was formed from parts of Currituck, Hyde, and Tyrrell, there still were no regular towns on Roanoke Island. A fairly extensive settlement on the southern part of the island was known as "the lower end," and another community to the north was known as "the upper end." However, a site for the county seat of the new county was selected in the middle of the island on the eastern shore facing Shallowbag Bay. The new commissioners first met there April 4, 1870, two weeks later picked out a "site for the court house," and accepted a donation of one acre of land for the purpose from John Wescott. On June 7, 1870, they "ordered that a temporary building be erected at Shallow Bag Bay for the use of the county." This was replaced by a wooden courthouse in 1873, at which time the area was still referred to as "Shallow Bag Bay" or "the upper end."

As happened in so many other communities on the Banks the name of this county seat, Manteo, was applied first not to the town but to the post office which was established there, October 24, 1873, with Martha J. Etheridge as postmaster.

A brick courthouse was constructed at Manteo in 1904, and extensive additions were completed in 1957. At one time, when the steamer *Trenton* was making daily runs from Manteo to Elizabeth City, there were rather extensive and well-kept docks along Manteo's waterfront. But many of the wooden structures in that area burned in an early morning fire on September 11, 1939, and with a decline in the use of boats, few of the docks were rebuilt.

The economy of Manteo was given a big boost by the influx of tourists visiting Fort Raleigh and *The Lost Colony*, and in addition to being the county seat, Manteo is the trading center of Dare County.

Even as Manteo was acquiring a post office and a name, the people living on "the lower end" were growing tired of that particular designation for their community. Most of the people living there were engaged in commercial fishing, and a good many of the fishing rigs were owned or financed by a man named Ezekiel R. Daniels. When a post office was established there on June 14, 1886, Ezekiel R. Daniels was the postmaster—in the seventy-one years of its operation only four people have served as postmaster there—and the name "Wanchese" was adopted.

Bill Sharpe points out in his interesting *New Geography of North Carolina* that Daniels not only financed many of the fishing rigs but bought the fish catch and provided groceries and other supplies, on credit through his store, so that "it is a legend that many a Wancheser was born, reared, worked and died with a full and prosperous career without ever having more than a few cents in his possession."

The dependence of the Wanchese economy on periodic and uncertain catches of fish—and the attendant necessity of many of the fishermen to buy their food and other supplies on long-term credit, paying up their bills when they make a good catch—remains to this day. In order to attract this important credit business, Wanchese merchants have long since disregarded the widespread modern merchandising

practices. They charge the full price for cash purchases but give a
10 per cent reduction at the time of payment on credit accounts.

Manteo and Wanchese, of course, were named for two of the
Indians encountered by the Raleigh colonists and taken back to England by them. When a third Roanoke Island Post Office was established, September 1, 1892, at Ashby's Harbor on the west side of the
island with Mollie H. Midgett as postmaster, a third Indian name,
Skyco, was adopted. Skyco was the Roanoke Island terminal for the
steamers of the Old Dominion Steamship Company, but the steamship
business declined and the Skyco Post Office was discontinued, January 13, 1913.

HARKERS ISLAND

ORIGINALLY known as Crany Island or Crane Island, it was first
granted to Thomas Sparrow, who sold it to Thomas Pollock, who
in turn willed it to his son George Pollock in 1722. At that time it was
listed as containing 2,400 acres, and in 1730 George Pollock sold the
island to Ebenezer Harker for 400 pounds. Three years later Harker
got back most of his investment when he sold a half interest to John
Stevens for 300 pounds.

Harker continued to live on his part of the island, and in time
it became known as "Harker's Island." The population was practically
doubled between 1899 and 1903 when most of the residents of
Diamond City on nearby Shackleford Banks, frightened by the effect
of the August hurricane of 1899, moved their houses across the sound
to Harkers. Many of the present residents are fishermen and boat
builders, and the Core Sound Boats turned out on Harkers Island
are widely known for their excellence.

References and Bibliographical Notes

IN ORDER to locate factual written material concerning the Outer Banks it has been necessary to go far afield, for practically none of it has been preserved by the Bankers. No one in the area seems to have bothered keeping old maps, business records, or correspondence. No early Banks diary has come to light. Few old books have been preserved, and genealogical records are surprisingly sketchy. There is, further, a dearth of stories handed down to the present generation by earlier Bankers, and even the personal recollections of many of the old folks living today are so garbled that it is necessary to double check them carefully.

When the researcher leaves the Banks and starts searching for material in libraries, archives and similar depositories, there are other difficulties which soon become apparent. Though there has been a tremendous amount of material printed on the subject of the Banks, it is widely scattered and hard to find; and it is seldom listed in any library card catalogue or index under a heading which would help the Banks researcher.

A large proportion of the detailed Banks material which I have located deals with problems of navigation and could not be used in this book. On the other hand, there is a scarcity of data which would shed light on the way the earlier Bankers lived—on their dress, food, recreation, religion, and habitations.

A basic source of material for this book has been government records. There are reports, both printed and in manuscript, of such federal agencies as the Coast and Geodetic Survey, Lifesaving Service, Lighthouse Board, Corps of Engineers, Weather Bureau, Census Bureau, and Post Office Department, and their predecessors. Official records of the state of North Carolina have been equally productive, and few if any other states can boast of printed compilations of their early records as extensive as the *Colonial Records of North Carolina*, Vols. 1-10 (Raleigh, 1886-90) edited by W. L. Saunders, and *State Records of North Carolina*, Vols. 11-26 (Winston, Goldsboro, Charlotte, 1895-1905) edited by Walter Clark, with the accompanying *Index to the Colonial and State Records of North Carolina*, Vols. 27-30 (Goldsboro, Charlotte, Raleigh, 1909-14) edited by Stephen B. Weeks. Most of the state laws and legislative journals are available in printed form, and together with the series of printed public documents they pick up where the Saunders and Clark works end; and in turn they are succeeded by the more recent biennial reports and other publications of individual state agencies. There are, in addition, numerous manuscript records, many of which are preserved in the State Department of Archives and History in Raleigh, while the original land grants in the office of the Secretary of State have produced information on the early ownership of Banks land not otherwise available. Finally, the deed books and other records in the county courthouses, particularly Carteret and Currituck, contain considerable information on Banks history.

In addition to the federal, state, and county records, the numerous newspapers published in eastern North Carolina and preserved by the American Antiquarian Society in Worcester, Massachusetts, and in depositories within the state of North Carolina have been most productive.

Because such a large number of documents, periodicals, books, pamphlets, maps, and manuscript records were consulted in piecing together this history of the Outer Banks, more space than is available would be required to cite each specific reference. On the other hand, I do not feel that the lay reader would be interested, or the more serious student appreciably assisted, if I listed all sources alphabetically without some critical analysis of their comparative worth. For this reason I shall simply outline, chapter by chapter in narrative form, the sources which have proven most productive in preparing this book.

For the student interested in finding specific citations on many phases of Banks history, I can recommend Gary S. Dunbar, *Geographical History of the Carolina Banks*, Technical Report No. 8, Pt. A, Coastal Studies Institute (Baton Rouge, 1956), which has been made available in mimeographed form to a select list of libraries, including the Louis R. Wilson Library of the University of North Carolina in Chapel Hill.

SAND, SOUNDS, AND INLETS

A LARGE PART of the material in this first chapter is based on personal observation by the author, particularly as relates to the effect of hurricanes and the destruction of stabilizing vegetation by blowing sand.

Some of the more technical matters have been clarified as the result of conversations and correspondence with the following: James P. Morgan and George M. Markey of the Coastal Studies Institute, Louisiana State University, on the geological formation of the Outer Banks; Sam D. Broadhurst, geologist, North Carolina Department of Conservation and Development, on the source of fresh water; and Robert E. Fish, Assistant District Engineer, U.S. Geological Survey, and B. C. Snow, Chief Engineer, North Carolina Division of Water Resources, on the flow of water in rivers, sounds, and inlets.

An attempt has been made to study all known maps showing Outer Banks inlet changes, and W. P. Cumming of Davidson College has unselfishly made available his fine collection of pre-Revolutionary maps for this purpose and has offered many useful suggestions. Other information has been received from the Beach Erosion Board and Corps of Engineers, U.S. Army; the U.S. Coast and Geodetic Survey; and U.S. Weather Bureau.

EXPLORATION

CONSIDERABLE guidance in the preparation of the early part of this chapter was given by Hugh T. Lefler of the University of North Carolina, whose *North Carolina History Told by Contemporaries* (Chapel Hill, 1934, 1948, 1957) contains part of the Verrazzano account, and W. P. Cumming of Davidson College, whose recently published *Southeast in Early Maps* (Princeton, 1958) is an invaluable reference tool. Actually, Verrazzano wrote three different letters concerning his explorations, and the most readily available reference for the letter describing the landing on the Banks is probably Alfred Brittain, *The History of North America*, Vol. 1 (Philadelphia, 1903). Other material on the Ayllón and Verrazzano voyages is found in

Narrative and Critical History of America (New York, 1884-89) edited by Justin Winsor.

Until recently it was necessary to consult a variety of sources in order to piece together the story of Sir Walter Raleigh's attempts at colonization. The basic accounts of Barlowe, Lane, Hariot, and White, as well as other contemporary reports, were published in Richard Hakluyt, *The Principal Navigations, Voyages, Traffiques, and Discoveries of the English Nation* (London, 1589), of which several reprints have been issued. In addition, the Hariot report, under the title *A Briefe and True Report of the New Found Land of Virginia*, was published separately in London in 1588 and has been reprinted. Most of the more recent literature on the subject has been concerned primarily with speculation as to the fate of the lost colony and is too extensive to list here. In 1955, however, the Hakluyt Society published a two-volume set which includes not only all of the material on the subject in Hakluyt but considerable new information, most of it located in archives in England and Spain. This is *The Roanoke Voyages*, 2 Vols. (London, 1955) by David B. Quinn, and I can highly recommend it as the definitive work on the subject.

Fort Raleigh is now a National Historic Site, and unpublished reports of Park Service historians Charles W. Porter and Frederick Tilberg and archeologist J. C. Harrington have been particularly helpful.

PERMANENT SETTLEMENT

THE BASIC source for a study of activities on the Banks during the colonial period is the *Colonial Records of North Carolina* (Raleigh, 1886-90) edited by W. L. Saunders and the *State Records of North Carolina* (Winston, Goldsboro, Charlotte, 1895-1905) edited by Walter Clark. Unfortunately, in the more than 2,000 pages of index, there is no listing under "Outer Banks," and the references under "Bankers" and related headings are all too brief. Consequently it was necessary to go through the books systematically, page by page and word by word, an assignment which took months of time and reams of paper.

A thorough study was made also of the manuscript "North Carolina

Vice-Admiralty Papers," 4 Vols., in State Department of Archives and History, Raleigh; of colonial newspapers published in eastern North Carolina; of original land grants in the office of the Secretary of State, Raleigh; and of all pre-Revolutionary deeds and similar records in the Carteret County and Currituck County courthouses.

For the section on pirates, the chief sources are Captain Charles Johnson, *A General History of the Pirates* (London, 1724), which has often been reprinted, and the previously cited *Colonial Records*. Some additional information on Blackbeard is found in the books of Philip Gosse, particularly his *The Pirate's Who's Who* (London, 1924); in Shirley Carter Hughson, *Carolina Pirates and Colonial Commerce, 1670-1740* (Baltimore, 1894); and in an article by Arthur L. Cooke, in the *Virginia Magazine of History and Biography* (July, 1953) entitled "British Newspaper Accounts of Blackbeard's Death."

Reference has been made also to J. Bryan Grimes, *Abstract of North Carolina Wills* (Raleigh, 1910) and *North Carolina Wills and Inventories* (Raleigh, 1912); the *North Carolina Historical and Genealogical Register*, a periodical edited and published by J. R. B. Hathaway at Edenton from 1900 to 1903; and John Lawson, *The History of Carolina* (London, 1718).

The material on the first Banks settlement on Colington comes from the Chatham Papers in the North Carolina Department of Archives and History, while some of that dealing with Roanoke Island is from the Hayes Collection, Edenton, of which a microfilm copy is in the Southern Historical Collection, Louis R. Wilson Library of the University of North Carolina in Chapel Hill.

THE REVOLUTION

WITH MINOR exceptions the materials in this chapter came from the *Colonial Records of North Carolina*, the *State Records of North Carolina*, and contemporary newspapers.

STATEHOOD

MUCH OF THE material in the early part of this chapter has come from the deed books in the Carteret and Currituck courthouses, from the *State Records of North Carolina*, and from contemporary newspapers, particularly the *North Carolina Gazette* of New Bern and *The State Gazette of North Carolina* published at Edenton.

A basic source for a study of the Shell Castle operations is the writings of Alice Barnwell Keith, though her unpublished doctoral thesis, "Three North Carolina Blount Brothers in Business and Politics, 1783-1812" (University of North Carolina, 1940) seems to contain more on the subject than her published works. Dr. Keith has kindly clarified several points for the author. Additional material on Shell Castle has been found in such varied sources as Carteret County deeds, *The True Republican and Newbern Weekly Advertiser*, and on an old pitcher in the Hall of History in Raleigh.

A summary of the activities of Otway Burns is in Walter Francis Burns, *Captain Otway Burns, Patriot, Privateer and Legislator* (New York, 1905). The letter from Mrs. Thomas Blount to Mrs. Madison concerning the British attack on Portsmouth is in the Dorothy Payne Todd Madison Papers in the University of Virginia Library. Probably the most extensive published account of the British attack is in volume two of Samuel A'Court Ashe's *History of North Carolina*.

The bulk of the lighthouse information in this chapter comes from a file headed "Selected Records of North Carolina coast lighthouses," in Record Group 26, National Archives; and from three printed documents which antiquarian bookseller Samuel Ward kindly located for my library. These are: *Laws of the United States relating to the establishment, support, and management of the light-houses, light-vessels, monuments, beacons, spindles, buoys, and public piers of the United States, from August 7, 1789 to March 3, 1855* (Washington, G.P.O., 1855); *Report of the Officers Constituting the Light-House Board, convened under instructions from the Secretary of the Treasury, to inquire into the condition of the light-house establishment of the United States, under the Act of March 3, 1851*, 32d Cong., 1st Sess., Sen. Ex. Doc. No. 28 (Washington, 1852); and *Compilation of Public Documents and Extracts from Reports and Papers Relating to Light-Houses, light-vessels, and illuminating apparatus, and to beacons, buoys, and fog signals, 1789 to 1871* (Washington, G.P.O., 1871).

With regard to the attempts to reopen Roanoke Inlet at Nags Head, various publications of the state and federal governments once again tell the story. In my personal library there are nearly two dozen of these printed memorials, reports, resolutions, and laws, and I have located at least that many more in public depositories. Much of the pertinent material is reprinted in two of these, *Report of the Secretary of War, with one from the Engineer Department, on the practicability of an Outlet from Albemarle Sound to the Ocean, &c.* (with map), 20th Cong., 2d Sess., Sen. Doc. No. 106 (Washington, 1829); and the report of Colonel J. H. Simpson in *Report of the Secretary of War,* Vol. 2, Appendix Q-14 (Washington, 1871). The Murphey and Fulton material is found in the numerous reports of the North Carolina Board of Internal Improvement, and much of it is reprinted in William Henry Hoyt, *The Papers of Archibald D. Murphey,* 2 Vols. (Raleigh, 1914).

Three eye-witness reports on conditions on the Banks during this period have been located. The most valuable is the manuscript report of William Tatham entitled *Original Report of William Tatham on the survey of the coast of North Carolina from Cape Fear to Cape Hatteras 1806.* The original of this for some reason has been retained in the library of the Coast and Geodetic Survey instead of being turned over to the National Archives, and I was fortunate enough to secure a microfilm copy. A typescript has also been made and distributed to several libraries, but this contains numerous errors. The interesting and much more extensive observations of Edmund Ruffin are in his *Agricultural, Geological, and Descriptive Sketches of Lower North Carolina, and the similar Adjacent Lands* (Raleigh, 1861).

Other important sources for material in this chapter include Jonathan Price, *A Description of Occacock Inlet* (New Bern, 1795), which was reprinted in *The North Carolina Historical Review* (October, 1926); the various articles in the Norfolk, Virginia, newspapers concerning early efforts to provide steamboat transportation in the sounds, as compiled by John C. Emmerson, Jr., in his *The Steamboat Comes to Norfolk Harbor* (Portsmouth, Va., 1949); Gary S. Dunbar's abstracts of United States Census Records; the annual reports of the U.S. Coast Survey which include the first detailed maps of the Banks; certain later annual reports of the U.S. Army Chief of Engineers, which contain reviews of earlier efforts to improve navigation in the Banks areas; and other maps, including those of William Tatham and Coles and Price made during the course of their coastal survey in 1806.

WATERING PLACES

ADVERTISEMENTS, news reports, editorials, shipping lists, and social notes from a number of contemporary newspapers from Norfolk, Elizabeth City, Edenton, and elsewhere have produced a large part of the material on the early life at Nags Head. George Higby Throop, *Nag's Head, or Two Months among the "Bankers": A Story of Sea-Shore life and manners* (Philadelphia, 1850), provides much detailed description of the resort. This work is represented as fiction, but in the many instances where it is possible to check Throop's statements, he is found to be quite accurate.

Burton Alva Konkle, *John Motley Morehead and the Development of North Carolina, 1796-1866* (Philadelphia, 1922), has much detail on the development of Morehead City, including quotations from numerous contemporary newspapers.

The brief description of the lower Banks in the letter from Jacob Henry to Thomas Henderson, dated Beaufort, December 16, 1810, is in the Thomas Henderson Letter Book, 1810-11, in the State Department of Archives and History, and it was reprinted in the October, 1929, issue of *The North Carolina Historical Review*.

STORMS AND SHIPWRECKS

FEW INCIDENTS in the Banks history have been as widely publicized as the loss of the steamboat *Home*. Probably the most detailed accounts are found in Captain Carleton White, *Narrative of the Loss of the Steam-Packet Home* (New York, 1837); in S. A. Howland, *Steamboat Disasters and railroad accidents in the United States* (Worcester, 1840); and Charles Ellms, *The Tragedy of the Seas* (Philadelphia, 1848). Two articles by D. H. Redfearn, *Florida Law Journal*, Vol. IX, No. 5 (May, 1935) and Vol. XXIII, No. 9 (Nov., 1949), contain considerable information on the Croom case. Numerous contemporary newspapers have been referred to also. The best account of the *Charleston* episode is in the previously cited Howland book. For basic information on Racer's Storm, as well as other hurricanes, Ivan Ray Tannehill, *Hurricanes, Their Nature and History* (Princeton, 1950), is a convenient reference tool.

The Civil War

As MIGHT be expected there is a wealth of material on the Outer Banks operations during the Civil War. The more important general printed sources include: Vol. 1 of *Battles and Leaders of the Civil War*, 4 Vols. (New York, 1887) edited by Robert Underwood Johnson and Clarence Clough Buel; Vols. 3 and 4 of *The Rebellion Record*, 12 Vols. (New York, 1862-71) edited by Frank Moore; parts one and three of *Report of the Joint Committee on the Conduct of the War*, 3 Vols., 37th Cong., 3d Sess., Sen. Ex. Doc. No. 1152 (Washington, 1863); and Vols. 1 and 5 of *Histories of the Several Regiments and Battalions from North Carolina in the Great War of 1861-'65*, 5 Vols. (Goldsboro, 1901) edited by Walter Clark.

Good accounts, from the Confederate viewpoint, are in J. Thomas Scharf, *History of the Confederate States Navy* (New York, 1887); William Harwar Parker, *Recollections of a Naval Officer* (New York, 1885); John F. Wise, *The End of an Era* (Boston and New York, 1899); and in D. H. Hill, Jr., *North Carolina*, Vol. 4 of *Confederate Military History* (Atlanta, 1899).

Among the better Federal accounts are: W. P. Derby, *Bearing Arms in the Twenty-Seventh Massachusetts Regiment* (Boston, 1883); Ben Perley Poore, *The Life and Public Services of Ambrose E. Burnside* (Providence, R.I., 1882); Thomas H. Parker, *History of the 51st Regiment of Pennsylvania Volunteers* (Philadelphia, 1869); Charles F. Walcott, *History of the Twenty-First Regiment Massachusetts Volunteers in the War for the Preservation of the Union* (Boston, 1882); and B. Estvan, *War Pictures from the South* (New York, 1863).

Probably the most detailed account of the "Chicamacomico Races" is in E. A. Duyckinck, *Natural History of the War for the Union*, 3 Vols. (New York, n.d.), while Charles F. Johnson, *The Long Roll* (East Aurora, N.Y., 1911), contains by all odds the largest and most interesting group of wartime sketches at Hatteras and Roanoke Island to come to my attention.

Finally, in searching for Civil War material in Washington, I was fortunate to be able to see the recently declassified maps and plans in

Record Group 77 at the National Archives and to obtain photostatic copies of those bearing on the Outer Banks area.

THE FEDERAL OCCUPATION

HERE I have relied heavily on newspapers, particularly the *New York Times*, for material on the "loyal residents of Hatteras Island" and on the rump government formed there. E. A. Duyckinck's *Natural History of the War for the Union*, 3 Vols. (New York, n.d.) contains a very interesting summary of these activities also, and substantiation of much of the printed material has come in numerous interviews with present-day Banks residents.

The primary sources for details on the Roanoke Island contraband camp are Vincent Colyer, *Report of the Services Rendered by the Freed People to the U.S. Army, in North Carolina, in the spring of 1862, after the Battle of Newbern* (n.p., n.d.); the Reverend Horace James, *Annual Report of the Superintendent of Negro Affairs in North Carolina, 1864* (Boston, 1865); and the *Reports of Assistant Commissioners of Freedmen*, 39th Cong., 2d Sess., Sen. Ex. Doc. No. 6 (Washington, 1866). Other information has come from some of the Civil War unit histories, U.S. Census records, and U.S. Coast Survey charts; and interviews with numerous residents of Roanoke Island and the Banks have supplied many details.

USHERING IN THE MODERN ERA

IN THIS chapter I have depended heavily on official records of various federal agencies, including the U.S. Lifesaving Service; U.S. Lighthouse Board; Commissioner of Lighthouses; Chief of Engineers, U.S. Army; U.S. Coast Survey; U.S. Weather Bureau; U.S. Census Bureau; and U.S. Post Office Department. The printed annual reports of the Lifesaving Service, Commissioner of Lighthouses, Chief of Engineers, and the Coast Survey have produced much information. Most of the material on the Post Office Department and Census Bureau has come from manuscript records in the National Archives, as has additional material on lighthouses and the Lifesaving Service. The bulk of the weather station information has come from Leslie Smith, Director,

National Weather Records Center, Asheville, N.C., and from the printed local climatological summaries.

Much background has been provided in interviews with a number of residents of the area over a period of several years, though special mention should be made of Horace Dough, Superintendent of the Wright Brothers National Memorial, who furnished information concerning the development and use of the shad boat.

Special thanks are due Helen M. Fessenden, author of *Fessenden, Builder of Tomorrow* (New York, 1940); and to the publishing firm of Coward-McCann for permission to reprint part of a letter from Reginald L. Fessenden to his patent attorney; and to the Duke University Library for permission to reprint part of the letter from A. W. Simpson to John Humphrey Small.

Some of the quotations on the use of yaupon by the Indians are from John Lawson, *The History of Carolina* (London, 1718). For the person interested in studying the subject of yaupon more fully, I recommend H. H. Brimley, "Yaupon Factory," *The State* (Dec. 17, 1955). An interesting summary of Currituck Sound hunting is found in T. S. Critcher, "An Investigation of the Waterfowl Resources of Currituck Sound" (unpublished master's thesis, North Carolina State College, 1949). Samuel Ward Stanton's article on early steamboating, "In North Carolina Waters," published in *Seaboard* (May, 1892), is found also in the Steamboat Historical Society of America's Reprint Series, No. 4, under the title of *Steam Navigation on the Carolina Sounds and the Chesapeake in 1892* (Salem, Mass., 1947).

DIAMOND CITY

FORMER RESIDENTS of Diamond City really wrote this chapter—at least they talked about the old times, while all I did was ask questions and take down what was told me. Some additional information has come from sources cited in the text, from Carteret County Deed Books and early Carteret deeds preserved in the North Carolina State Archives in Raleigh, and from maps of the Cape Lookout area, particularly the manuscript map in the Coast and Geodetic Survey in Washington designated T-416, and from George Brown Goode (ed.), *The Fisheries and Fishery Industries of the United States* (Washington, G.P.O., 1887).

THE WRIGHT BROTHERS

THE EXTENSIVE Wright Papers were turned over to the Library of Congress in 1949 under terms which prohibited their being consulted or reproduced, except in special instances, until 1960. Therefore, it was necessary for me to study these papers in the two excellent compilations which have been published, first in Fred C. Kelly, *Miracle at Kitty Hawk* (New York, 1951), and then in the more extensive Marvin W. McFarland, *The Papers of Wilbur and Orville Wright*, 2 Vols. (New York, 1953). Later I was able to secure photostatic copies of those letters from which I have used quotations in this chapter.

I am particularly indebted to Mr. Kelly, Mr. McFarland, and Harold S. Miller, co-executor of the Orville Wright Estate, for their advice and cooperation and, in the case of Mr. Miller, for permission to reprint certain of the Wright Papers. In addition I have found Fred C. Kelly, *The Wright Brothers* (New York, 1943), and Orville Wright, *How We Invented the Airplane*, edited by Fred C. Kelly (New York, 1953), particularly useful in supplying details on certain scientific matters pertaining to the experiments of the Wrights.

A LIVING FROM THE SEA

OBVIOUSLY, much of the material in this chapter has come from personal observation and from interviews with residents of the Banks area, particularly fishermen. I am especially indebted to Allen Taylor of Sealevel for information on mullet fishing and oystering early in this century; to Henry Beasley of Colington for material on diamondback terrapins; to C. T. Williams II of Avon and Curtis Gray of Kitty Hawk for the eel grass story; to F. C. Salisbury of Morehead City for his notes on the shark fishery; and to Donald Dough of Colington and Kill Devil Hills and Colon Perry of Kitty Hawk for details on long netting.

A valuable source of printed material is George Brown Goode (ed.), *The Fisheries and Fishery Industries of the United States* (Washington, G.P.O., 1887), which is composed of five parts and several volumes. Detailed information on Banks fishing is included in several sections of this work, most notably in R. Edward Earll, "The

Mullet Fishery"; Frederick W. True, "The Turtle and Terrapin Fisheries"; Ernest Ingersoll, "The Oyster Industry"; Richard Rathbun, "The Crab, Lobster, Crayfish, Rock Lobster, Shrimp, and Prawn Fisheries"; and A. Howard Clark, "The Porpoise Fishery of New England and North Carolina."

Acknowledgement is given also to Harden F. Taylor and associates for permission to use references and specific quotations from their *Survey of Marine Fisheries of North Carolina* (Chapel Hill, 1951). Of particular interest in this volume are the chapters by Alphonse F. Chestnut, "The Oyster and Other Mollusks in North Carolina"; John C. Pearson, "The Blue Crab in North Carolina"; William A. Ellison, Jr., "The Menhaden"; and Harold J. Humm, "The Seaweed Resources of North Carolina."

Two bulletins of the North Carolina Geological Survey by R. E. Coker, *The Cultivation of the Diamond Back Terrapin*, Bull. No. 14 (Raleigh, 1906) and *Experiments in Oyster Culture in Pamlico Sound, North Carolina*, Bull. 15 (Raleigh, 1907), contain much detailed information, as do Lieutenant Francis Winslow, *Report on the Waters of North Carolina with reference to their possibilities for oyster culture* (Raleigh, 1886) and *North Carolina and its Resources*, State Board of Agriculture (Winston, 1896).

New Life for the Banks

Much of the material in this chapter is based on personal observation over a period of nearly thirty years and is substantiated by research in the files of the Elizabeth City *Independent*, the *Elizabeth City Daily Advance*, and other periodicals; in examination of the Minute Books of the Dare County Board of Commissioners, and other county records; various publications and records of the National Park Service; pertinent reports and laws of the North Carolina General Assembly and the Cape Hatteras National Seashore Commission; and acts of Congress concerned with the National Park Service facilities on the Banks.

Special thanks for substantiating certain information, and providing specific details, are due W. F. Baum, R. B. Etheridge, M. L. Daniels, L. L. Swain, and H. C. Lawrence.

THE BANKS TODAY

IN COMPILING the material for this chapter, I have referred to as many as a dozen sources in a single page, and since capsule histories of more than forty geographical points on the Banks are included, I will make no effort to list the basic sources of each. As was the case in the earlier chapters, I have drawn heavily on maps showing the Outer Banks, including the fine collection in the State Department of Archives and History in Raleigh; on courthouse records in Currituck, Carteret, and Dare counties; on the *Colonial Records of North Carolina* and the *State Records of North Carolina;* on material in the National Archives relating to post offices; on government documents on the subject of lighthouses, activities of the Corps of Engineers, and the Lifesaving Service; and on the records of the U.S. Bureau of the Census. All of these, and many privately printed works, as well as manuscript material, have been cited specifically in the foregoing chapter references.

In Gary S. Dunbar, *Geographical History of the Outer Banks* (Baton Rouge, 1956), the author presents basic material on a number of Banks communities. For additional information see Bill Sharpe, *A New Geography of North Carolina,* 2 Vols. (Raleigh, 1954 and 1958) (Vol. 1, including Carteret and Dare Counties, and Vol. 2, including Ocracoke).

Frequently where I have referred to sources in this chapter which had not been cited previously, the source has been mentioned in the text.

Index

350